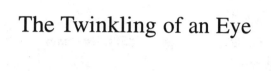

The Twinkling of an Eye

ALSO BY BRIAN ALDISS

The Twinkling of an Eye

Or, My Life as an Englishman

Brian Aldiss

St. Martin's Press

New York

Some names have been changed to protect the innocent and the guilty.

Library of Congress Cataloging-in-Publication Data

Aldiss, Brian Wilson, 1925-
    The Twinkling of an eye, or, My life as an Englishman / by Brian Aldiss.
        p.   cm.
    Originally published: London : Little, Brown, and Co., 1998.
    Includes index.
    ISBN 0-312-19346-7
    1. Aldiss, Brian Wilson, 1925- . 2. Authors, English—20th century—
Biography. 3. Science fiction—Authorship. I. Title. II. Title: Twinkling of
an eye. III. Title: My life as an Englishman.
PR6051.L3Z478 1999
823'.914—dc21
[B]
                                                                98-51197
                                                                    CIP

First published in Great Britain by Little, Brown and Company
First U.S. Edtion : April 1999

10 9 8 7 6 5 4 3 2 1

If we apply to authors themselves for an account of their state, it will appear very little to deserve envy; for they have in all ages been addicted to complaint ... Few have left their names to posterity, without some appeal to future candour from the perverseness and malice of their own times. I have, nevertheless, been often inclined to doubt, whether the authors, however querulous, are in reality more miserable than their fellow mortals.

Samuel Johnson:
The Adventurer, No. 138

Contents

Book Three: Ascent

It was on 15 November, 1990, in the gloom of winter, as I sat in the car with my wife, a tape of old Jugoslav folk music playing, that I beheld the town where I was born, much changed, and decided to begin the toils that would result in my creature, my book.

The story of my life – to me so individual, yet objectively so commonplace! Myself now subject to decay, I have witnessed the decay of countries, empires, and ideologies; to counterbalance which, I have enjoyed the growth of my own family and survived to see the continuation of my line . . .

Book One

Necessitations

I

The Voyage

Our anchor has been plucked out of the sand and gravel of Old England. I shall have no connection with my native soil for three, or it may be four or five years. I own that even with the prospect of interesting and advantageous employment before me it is a solemn thought.

William Golding
Rites of Passage

'Where the hell are they taking us?' It was a good question. No one could answer. The troop train wound its slow way northwards through England. The troops, crowded close in every compartment, sct up a clatter as they divested themselves of their FSMOs (Field Service Marching Orders), their rifles, their steel helmets, their kitbags. Then silence fell. Some men read whatever was to hand. Some stared moodily out of the window. In the manner of troops everywhere, most men, when not being ordered about, slept. They had been up before the July dawn and parading by sunrise.

Nobody knew where they were going – 'not even the driver,' said one cynic. 'The driver has sealed orders, regarding his destination, labelled NOT TO BE OPENED TILL ARRIVAL.'

The young soldiers, Scottish, Irish, English and Welsh, were dressed in drab khaki uniform. Although they had been trained not to feel – in the manner of soldiers through the ages – the high spirits of youth showed through: the wakeful ones smoked and joked. Nevertheless, knowledge that they were going abroad to fight induced a certain seriousness. When the round of jokes had died and the stubs of their Players and Woodbines had been stamped out, they seized on the opportunity to put their booted feet up. It would be a long journey.

Reveille had sounded in Britannia Barracks at four thirty. By the time it was light, platoons of newly trained soldiers were marching down to Norwich Thorpe Station. The ring of their steel-tipped boots echoed in empty streets. They piled into the waiting train, goaded on like cattle by their sergeants.

When the train pulled out of the station, wartime security ensured that it was for a rendezvous unknown. Also unknown to the men, impervious even to their imaginations, was how the operation in which they were involved was mirrored by another more sinister operation, taking place even then on the mainland of Europe. In the dawn light of many European cities, cattle trucks standing in railway sidings were being filled with Jews, men, women and children. Shrouded in secrecy, German cattle trains were pulling out towards destinations with names then unknown to the outside world, Auschwitz, Belsen, Treblinka, Sobibor.

Some time during that long English day, the troop train drew into Lime Street station in Liverpool. More troops were crammed aboard. The train continued its sluggish journey northwards, crossing into Scotland. Towards the end of the afternoon, it wound through the poor suburbs and peeling tenements of Glasgow, crawled at walking pace as if exhausted by its journey.

Here citizens turned out to wave and cheer and toss buns and ciggies to the troops. Improvised banners hung from slum windows, saying GOOD LUCK LADS and similar encouragements. Women waved Union Jacks. Bright of eye, the troops jostled at the train windows, waving back. No one on that train would ever forget those warm Scottish hearts.

At Greenock docks, security gates opened, to close behind the train. The train halted with a whistle of expiring steam. With a great bustle and kicking of everything in sight, the men about to leave Britain de-trained. Sergeants gave their traditional cries of 'Get fell in!' The troops stood in ranks, rifle on one shoulder, kitbag on the other, now isolated from civilian life.

An entire period of their lives had come to an end. A more challenging one was about to begin.

Towering above the parade, moored to the quayside in the quiet waters of the Clyde, was the troopship *Otranto*, 21,500 tons. Prior to the war, the *Otranto* had belonged to Canadian Pacific Steamships, when it was accustomed to making the journey between Vancouver and Hong Kong. Seagulls screamed about its funnels. Orders were shouted. Loaded down with kit, the men climbed the gangplank, forced by its steepness to cling to a worn wooden rail. One by one, they stepped into the open maw of the ship, to be dispersed among its many decks.

So alien was this experience to most men that some were immediately seasick, although the ship lay without motion at its moorings.

Among the thousands forced to climb that gangplank was a lad not then nineteen. He entered the threadbare floating world with some excitement, being at that period of life where everything is novel, and what is novel is welcome. He was in misapprehension about many things; but many of those things, such as his emotional nature, he was able to set to one side under the greater urgencies of war. With energy and resource, he set about finding himself the best possible position on his allotted mess deck, in the depths of the ship.

He also pursued a line of conduct developed long before at school, that of making light of circumstances by joking with his fellows.

When he left home at the end of his embarkation leave, this young man promised his mother, Dot, that he would write home regularly. This promise he kept over the next four years.

Owing to Dot's dedication, the letter I wrote home after boarding the *Otranto*, complete with its inked illustration, was preserved. It shows me in ebullient mood.

Now as I write it's nearly sunset, with the sun flaming over the waters. Although we have moved away from the port, we're anchored in sight of land – our land . . . I'm writing on a raft on the Boat Deck and a chap with a ukelele is leading community singing. (They're just singing 'Lili Marlene': 'Orders came for sailing Somewhere over there . . .')

I don't actually know how I feel. It's difficult to describe. Everything has a dreamlike quality, we don't quite believe it . . . But I'm trying to record all I see, and store everything that happens in my imagination. It's certainly going to be interesting!

A new life's ahead but, boy oh boy, we're ready for it. Please try and don't worry. As yet I'm enjoying myself – and it's broadening my mind . . .

Some phrases in the letter, such as 'broadening the mind', were family catch phrases, jokes.

Wartime security decreed that we should never reveal where we

were. Troop movements could provide useful information to the
enemy. In everything – as in family life – there was secrecy. And
England was a kind of family in those years. A companion poster
to the ones saying 'Careless Talk Costs Lives' admonished more
gently: 'Be Like Dad – Keep Mum'.

The *Otranto* had been christened *The Empress of Canada* at its
launching in 1922. Came the war and its feminine name had been
ripped from it. Refitting on a large scale had taken place. It had
been painted a North Atlantic grey from stem to stern. Just as
those climbing up its gangplank had suffered the severest haircut
of their lives, so the old ship had been shorn of its luxury trimmings.
Except, that is, in the officers' quarters.

Under cover of dark, the troopship slipped away down the Clyde,
past the Isle of Arran and the pendulous Mull of Kintyre, round the
sleeping north coast of Northern Ireland, to where the shallows of
the continental shelf gave way to deeper waters – still the haunt of
Germany's U-boats at that period.

Dawn came. Ships, naval and merchant, were gathering, and spent
the day manoeuvering into formation. Towards sunset we began
to move. The cold grey ships slid into the cold night. Possibly
twenty-eight ships all told, forming the last of the big wartime
convoys. The strong heartbeat of the *Otranto*'s engines was never
to leave us over the weeks to come.

No smoking allowed on deck. The glow of a cigarette could be
seen seven miles away.

Only the captain knew our destination. North America? The
Middle East? Not, with luck, *not* India! India meant Burma. Our
progress southwards consisted of a series of long zigzags, to west,
to east: a manoeuvre against an enemy who still patrolled Atlantic
waters. Yet by July 1944, the tides of war were turning in the Allies'
favour. No more was the Mediterranean Mussolini's mare nostrum.
Malta had survived more bombs than fell on London, Rommel had
been defeated in North Africa. Our convoy was to be the first one
not forced to sail by the longest route, travelling round the Cape
of Good Hope, calling in at Durban for shore leave.

We sailed into the Mediterranean, through the narrow mouth
guarded by the Rock of Gibraltar. Part of our destroyer escort left us,
turning back into the prison-hued Atlantic. Suddenly, the sea was
blue, sea birds cried, the great rock sang to port. Northern Europe
had sunk below the horizon. My sails filled with excitement. The
world looked wonderful, basking in balmy air. At sunset, a great

warm breath was exhaled from the African coast, the very aroma of all that was exotic: perfume, camel dung, armpits of Oued-Nails, apricots, limes, other unknown fruits, frangipani, and the entrails of Arab towns.

Five thousand men were packed aboard the *Otranto*. On each deck, men, crowded like slaves on the Middle Passage, ate their food at mess tables, lived and slept there. So cramped were our quarters that half the men slept overhead in hammocks, while below them slept the other half, flat on the deck on palliasses.

The *Otranto* had five or possibly six decks above the water line: Sun Deck, Promenade Deck, Boat Deck, where the officers were quartered, A Deck, B Deck and C Deck. The detachment I was with was down on H Deck, the lowest deck in the ship, Damnation Deck, Doolally Deck, Dead Duck Deck, five decks below the water line, carved out of the very keel. To escape to the Boat Deck, the highest deck on which Other Ranks were allowed, entailed a long climb upward, through other crowded decks. Had a torpedo struck us, no one of H Deck would have stood a hope in hell of survival. We knew it.

But underlying the crowded discomfort of the ship, and the tedium of life aboard, went excitement at a first encounter with a hitherto inaccessible world, danger, and the quest for a drinkable mug of tea.

As soon as we were in warmer waters, I slept up on deck. It was permitted, yet few men took advantage of it. Over the rail lived the unceasing sea, heaving as if in the throes of giving birth, often phosphorescent with great sheets of wavering life, murmuring to itself in a green marine dream.

Our only enemies were the matelots. The sailors, hating soldiers, cleansed the decks at dawn every morning and hosed any sleepers with icy jets of sea water. We woke early to avoid them, both sides cursing the other. To return to H Deck was like trying to breathe stale sponge cake.

Of all the troops aboard ship, I seemed almost alone in enjoying the voyage. In the warrens of the ship, looped about with grey pipes of every bore, coiling along the bulkheads or snaking overhead, it was easy to imagine we were on a giant spaceship, heading for unknown planets. It was an enthralling fantasy.

So, in a sense, we were. We passed Malta and Pantelleria. Our first harbour was Port Said, at the head of the Suez Canal.

We passed slowly through the canal, pursued on either side by twin humps of wake. Heaving to in the Great Bitter Lake, we waited while a troopship passed us, heading north, homeward bound for England. Those aboard called mockingly across to us, 'Get your knees brown!' We moved at snail's pace into the Red Sea and a zone of intense heat, where mirages trembled on either desolate bank.

Improvised shower cubicles spurted salt water while we assaulted our bodies with salt-water soap. Emergency urinals – little more than raised troughs – had been clamped on to the Boat Deck. To their notice, NOTHING TO BE THROWN DOWN THESE LATRINES, a wag had prefixed the words IT IS.

By this time, we knew there could be but one destination for us. Burma.

We disembarked on Bombay docks in September 1944. Looking back at the grey walls of the ship, I realised that it had become a kind of womb after thirty days afloat; in the end, we had grown so dependent upon it that we were reluctant to leave.

'Bags of bull, lads!'

Ever obedient to the sergeant, our platoon got fell in and marched to Bombay's *Arabian Nights*-cum-Keble-College railway station.

At the cavernous station we had an hour's wait for our train. An hour to look, to stare, even to speak! The brightness of everything, the nervous energy of the stringy brown men, selling and begging. Here a thousand worlds seemed to be contained, with fascinations inexhaustible.

Our train slunk into its designated platform and we climbed aboard, humping our kit. A whistle blew. We had three hundred miles to go, to Mhow, in Central Provinces.

I described it in a letter home.

We travelled third class on the train. What coaches! – Wooden, ramshackle, a square box for a compartment, ten feet by ten feet, and the seats made for a race that slept on nails. No window glass, no spitting allowed. Eight bells sound, the natives scream, the train gives a compulsive jerk forward . . .

Night swooped down. We smeared anti-mosquito cream on hands and face, and rolled down our sleeves. The winged wildlife of the place soared in and cavorted round the light. From the darkness came hoarse croaks of bullfrogs and the high-speed Morse of crickets.

A considerable portion of the native population sleeps on the stations. They burn herbs which smell strange and musky – whether pleasant or foul you can't quite decide.

We fell asleep uncomfortably, one way or another. When I awoke it was dawn and the sun, donning rouge and roses, climbed back to heaven. Allah be praised! We wiped the mozzy ointment off.

The train clattered through rocky ravines, tree-covered land, wide plains. Strange trees, tropical birds. Parrots and monkeys we saw in the wilder parts. Round the villages cluster padi fields, maize, and what-have-you. The beasts of burden are humpbacked cows, oxen, and sturdy black water buffalo, which wallow in mud holes when they get the chance.

The further we travelled into the interior, the greyer grew the rags and clothing of the people, and the fouler and more frequent became the beggars. We saw old vultures, hawks, and lizards a foot long. Goats roamed the stations. All these attractions palled as we became dirtier, hungrier, and more tired.

It poured with rain, steady beating rain, a reminder that the monsoon was not yet over. We put up the shutters. Night fell, and still it rained.

It rained when we reached Mhow station. Hauling our kit – kitbags, mosquito nets, blankets, big packs, respirators, rifles – we crossed the station to where lorries awaited us. We bumped over to the cantonment . . .

The rain stopped and the night smelt good. In the dim lighting our quarters seemed like a palace: paved floors, lofty ceilings, white paint. By morning light it looks more like a barn!

It's all very fascinating. Tomorrow I hope to look over the village, which seems quite large. We shall spend a month here.

In short, everything's fine, mighty fine.

The train journey to Mhow was the first of many journeys, since the train was such a feature of Indian travel at the time. However long, however arduous the journeys, the spectacle of India itself mitigated the tedium.

Mhow, the village, is best remembered in its picture-postcard aspect, when strident day suddenly marries velvet night and the flying foxes, waking in the tall acacias, take flight for distant fig trees. Summer lightning flickers all round, flirting with the horizon, nervy, noiseless. Then kerosene lamps on stalls lick their yellow tongues, making the bazaars enigmatic. Weird music crackles from radios, and a whole new mystery envelops the world.

In Mhow was a Signals training centre, designed to toughen us up after the voyage, in preparation for more arduous times in Burma. Oh, the wriggling and conniving, the malingering, which went on among men who wished to avoid action in Burma at all costs – including, presumably, a cost to their self-esteem. You see clever soldiers who have found a rock to cling to – barnacles with a job in the quartermaster's stores or service as an orderly in the hospital. Others, perhaps, become *base wallahs* and *box wallahs* in New Delhi, to serve out a safe and boring war, until it is time to return home with a Long Service medal and nothing to report. Anything, rather than be involved with the shooting war further east. My own attitude was that the dice should be allowed to fall where they would. This time was an awakening for me, as no doubt for many others. Such personal matters were never discussed. But I had left behind, not only England, but an inadequate earlier self, as the times demanded.

Much in the Army was startling, not least the chorus of complaint that rose on every side about everything. Many older men had been wrenched from jobs or marriage. They resented a violent disruption to their lives; whereas for me the East *was* life, life at last.

For me, novelty overrode any discomfort. The pre-dawn runs, the petty restrictions, the training, the shouting, caused me little pain: I had survived ten years in boarding schools under rather worse conditions. For this at least the public-school system could take credit: it accustomed one to hardship and injustice.

The war for many provided a kind of release from personal problems. The question bothering humanity, or an intellectual fraction of it, at least since the days of the ancient Greeks, was summarised by H. G. Wells in the touching title of one of his books, *What Are We to Do with Our Lives?* This dilemma was resolved, or at least shelved, by hostilities. Family conundrums were of no moment when one was issued with a Sten gun.

It is this kind of effect that makes war so popular.

Japanese military operations had been widely successful in the Far East. Events unravelled rapidly after the bombing of Pearl Harbor on 7 December 1941.

Hong Kong fell on Christmas Day. On 15 February 1942, the supposedly impregnable base of Singapore fell to a Japanese army. Thirty thousand Japanese confronted 85,000 British and Commonwealth troops. Shortly before the end, General Perceval, in command of the Singapore garrison, sent a message to Churchill in England: 'Have 30,000 rounds of ammunition. What shall we do with it?' Churchill cabled back: 'How about firing it at the enemy?' The suggestion was not carried out. Perceval surrendered, delivering the Commonwealth troops to a bitter imprisonment. A black day for the British Empire.

Two Japanese divisions had already advanced into Burma. Mandalay was taken in May of that year. Disaster and disillusion followed.

The Japanese became regarded as invincible, while their cruelty to the Chinese and other races who fell under their control was such that they were regarded almost as a sub-species of the human race. Their ability to live and fight in dense jungle caused the British to regard them as superhuman.

Clearly, the war in Europe was to be preferred as a theatre in which to fight. Death rates for prisoners captured by German and Italian armies amounted only to some four per cent, whereas under the Japanese the rate was twenty-seven per cent – higher still on the notorious Death Railway.

At this distance in time, it's hard to recall the particular hells conjured up by the very name Burma. Our attitude towards the Japanese was compounded of a toxic mix of reality and racism.

In 1941 and 1942, Japanese advances in seven months were more spectacular than any of Adolf Hitler's blitzkriegs. The wolves came down by boat, plane and bicycle. Their fleets crossed over 3,000 sea miles, their armies engulfed much of China, Hong Kong, the Philippines, Indochina, the Netherlands East Indies, multitudes of Pacific islands, Malaya, Singapore, and Burma, advancing westwards until they stood at the very gates of India. They struck to the south, deeply enough to launch air raids on Darwin in northern Australia. They were a fever virus on the body of the East. Wherever they went, Japanese armies behaved with punishing ruthlessness.

These were the facts we chewed over in Mhow as we handed in respirators lugged all the way from Norwich. We drew jungle green battledress and handed in the absurd KD – khaki drill – and topis with which we had been issued in England. We exchanged gaiters for puttees. Puttees protected ankles and lower legs from venomous things which could be hiding in long grass.

Two Japanese divisions entered Burma in January of 1942. With them went the Burma National Army, led by a man who knew the ground, Aung San, a courageous Burmese destined to fight on both sides in the war, and to father an even more courageous daughter, Aung San Suu Kyi. These divisions captured Rangoon and advanced northwards on Mandalay, which fell in May. It was another in a long line of British disasters. The British and Indians retreated from Mandalay by car, cart and foot. Only one road led out of the trap. They had to travel westwards on the long trail leading to Dimapur, and the railway line to Calcutta.

British counter-offensives along the Burmese coast and in the Arakan, under horrific conditions, met with little success. They served merely to reinforce the picture of a fiendish enemy who could not be beaten. The Japanese would call from the jungle in the dark, like parrots from a thicket, 'Hello, Johnny! Hello, Johnny! Who fuckee your missus?' To fire blindly at the taunting voices was to give your position away.

The struggle for Burma, a country larger than France, is a record of disillusion and heroism on both sides. The main protagonists, Britain and Japan (and the USA, as far as it entered the picture) were far distant from the scene of action. This factor contributed enormously to local difficulties. It explains too why very few war photographers were present to place the struggle on visual record.

Disease – malaria, dysentery and various fevers – accounted for as many men as did Japanese bullets and bayonets. Supplying the British XIVth Army was a very low priority where Churchill was concerned. That army felt itself neglected and abandoned to rot in miserable circumstances. It called itself, in a mood of romantic despair, the 'Forgotten Army'. The label has stuck, and not without reason.

It was the insignia of that army I stitched on to my jungle greens in Mhow, before our detachment was shipped towards the leafy fighting terrain in Burma.

Not for the first time, my life was about to begin anew. But change, uncertainty, had been a feature of life in the years leading up to the outbreak of war with Germany.

II

The West Country

Stop and think sometime about the roller coaster I'm on. Some
day on Titan, it will be revealed to you just how ruthlessly
I've been used, and by whom, and to what disgustingly paltry ends.

Kurt Vonnegut
The Sirens of Titan

S ummer – time of innocence, time of wickedness.
    In the summer of AD 1938, the Boxbaum family came to live
next to the Aldiss family. They came in the night, time of secrets,
husband and wife and two children. The houses in Bernard Road,
Gorleston on Sea, were terraced. Short paths led straight from the
gate, across the front gardens to the front door. My parents went
out to greet the Boxbaums, who were exhausted and disoriented.
Dot took them a standard English panacea, a pot of tea.

The Boxbaums, driven by Nazi tyranny, had arrived safely in
England.

Frau Boxbaum was slight and raven-haired. She arrived in Gorleston
speaking no English. The boy was about eight, tow-haired. His sister
was probably ten or eleven, a pretty girl, dark-haired with eyes of
Aegean blue. They were the first foreign children we had met.
Playing with us, they mastered English very quickly; we were
impressed, it had taken us years to learn the language.

Mother lent Frau Boxbaum cutlery and plates and various neces-
saries. The family had escaped with very few possessions. The behaviour of my parents – and of other people in the road – was exemplary.
Carpets, rugs, an armchair, curtains, other necessities, arrived at
Frau Boxbaum's door. Bill, if not anti-Semitic, had talked freely of

'Jew boys', subscribing to the mild (*mild*?) British anti-Semitism of the time. That was all put away for this special case. The curtain had been lifted on what was happening in Germany.

Frau Boxbaum had brought some photograph albums with her. We looked at pictures of smiling family groups as she turned the pages, trying out her few words of English. Her foreignness held the scent of a wider social sphere than ours, comfortable and yet doomed. These vistas excited Betty and me, already impatient with a knowledge of our provincialism. Other horizons, other costumes, other rooms.

They had lived well, in a large mansion somewhere outside Hamburg. Flowers on side-tables, salon paintings on walls. Plenty of servants, extensive grounds, cream-coloured automobiles with chauffeurs, family picnics in the countryside.

Not unlike the Boxbaums, our family too had come down in the world, from prosperity in East Dereham to a cramped little terraced house called Number Eleven. We felt ashamed for the Boxbaums, descended from luxury to a little hutch in Bernard Road.

Herr Boxbaum was an elegant man who spoke faultless English. Once he had seen his family settled safely in England, out of Himmler's clutches, he determined to return to Germany, to salve some of their worldly goods 'before things got too bad'. He kissed his wife and children goodbye and sailed for Hamburg.

His wife waited for him to return. He never did. The Gestapo caught him. I assume he died in a concentration camp.

The failure of Herr Boxbaum to return from Germany was a watershed, not only for his unfortunate little family. Bill no longer said there would be a war if Winston Churchill did not stop annoying Hitler; instead he warned us that war was coming. And for that event he made sensible preparations.

In that hot summer of 1938, I walked into town and back to buy my favourite magazine, *Modern Boy*. Nobody was about. The streets were deserted. The air was heavy, windows were open. Every radio in every house was tuned to the Test Match. It was England's innings. Len Hutton was notching up remarkable scores against Australia.

Modern Boy had rearmament stamps to collect, battleships, tanks, heavy guns. I was excited; Mother said, 'That's nothing to look forward to.' Neville Chamberlin was preparing to fly to Munich to discuss the fate of Czechoslovakia. In the house next to us, on the other side to the Boxbaums, Mrs Newton – devoted to her afternoon bottle of gin – threw open her bedroom window and screamed. 'Help! Help! The Spaniards are coming!'

A correct statement in essence. Only the nationality was mistaken.

Perhaps in every childhood there comes a defining moment when, by some trick of behaviour, one is made aware for the first time of one's own character, and that one has a personal idiolect of beliefs. And possibly that moment of insight – which remains always in memory – is a herald of one's adult nature.

As a small boy of three or four, I was taken by my parents to a tall narrow stone house in Wisbech, on the Wash. There, among a muddle of armchairs, lived a number of distant cousins on my mother's side of the family.

Permitted to run out into the garden, I saw among a clump of irises the perfect webs of the chubby-backed garden spider (*araneus diadematus*). I had admired this pretty spider, and its industry, in my grandmother's garden in Peterborough. The intricate construction of the web was a task I had watched with respectful attention.

A passing butterfly, a cabbage white, flew into one of the webs. As its struggles began, a small girl in a white frock rushed from the house. Seeing the plight of the butterfly, she screamed at me to save it from the nasty spider.

Although I was keen to please the girl, I could not but see the matter from the spider's point of view; in hesitating, I allowed her to rush out from her corner and seize upon the butterfly. The girl was distressed, and ran back into the house in tears, saying how horrid I was. Well, I too felt it was gruesome; but the butterfly's agonies were brief and the spider had as much right to live as anyone.

Heaving themselves up from their armchairs, emerging from the house, angry distant cousins gained proximity. I was seriously scolded and ushered indoors – unfit to stay in their nice garden.

Upset though I was – and feeling a degree of guilt – I *knew* the grown-ups were wrong. The sundry shortcomings of nature, like the way in which we all ate each other or perished, were givens with which one had to live. In the circumstances, observation made more sense than interference. Unfortunately, this has become rather a lifetime principle.

Dot and I watched Bill as he rubbed black Cherry Blossom boot polish into his sideburns, which grey had already invaded. Preparing a lie about his age, he walked down to the recruiting office in Gorleston and volunteered for the RAF. He could still fly. He was lean and fit, forty-eight pretending to be forty-two. The recruiting officer turned him down. Bill was a brave man, and was shaken by this rejection.

His thoughts then turned to our safety. We could see the North Sea from our attic window. When war came, we would be shelled or bombed – or, of course, invaded. Bill decided therefore that we should move to the other end of the country.

In the school holidays of summer 1939, Betty and I walked barefoot from the house down to the beaches and promenades, to spend our whole sunny day there as usual, on the sand, in the sea, chatting to shopkeeprs, sailing a clockwork speedboat in the yacht pool, or watching the Punch and Judy show (every scene of which we had by heart).

The front at Gorleston provided a spectacle of which we never tired. It was safe and peaceful. Somewhere across the sea, the tyrannies of Nazi Germany and the more firmly entrenched regime of Stalin's Soviet Union were busy at their gruesome tasks of enslaving and killing whole populations.

But the British Empire was safe, the colour bar securely in place in its colonies. Tea was still served at four, while the Yankee dollar was worth only two half-crowns.

Betty and I were happy in Gorleston. When I fell ill and was confined to bed, I wrote and illustrated a long verse drama set in Victorian times. The story moved freely from a stage play into real life and back. Where I got the idea from I do not know; now it is a commonplace of deconstructionists – a word unknown in the thirties. It was my first sustained piece of writing. Its subject was the question of appearances: something was happening but – wait! – it was merely being acted!

From the local Woolworth – then still 'The 3d and 6d Stores' – Betty and I bought issues of *McGlennan's Song Book*. In triple columns, it published the words of the latest popular songs. Betty and I sat in bed together, singing songs made famous by Hutch, Dorothy Carless, Gracie Fields and others: if not melodiously, enthusiastically.

Being mere children, Betty and I were not privy to Bill's plans. One day, we were hauled in from the beach and told we were going on holiday to the West Country, to Devon.

The Bernard Road house was closed up, our beloved cat Tiny was left in a neighbour's care. We then undertook a trek across the south of England, arriving eventually at Witheridge, in the middle of Devon. Norfolk born and bred, we were impressed by, or perhaps a little contemptuous of, the hills and valleys; we had grown to prefer a flat world. In Witheridge we stayed on Thorn's farm, where the young farmer's wife fed us enormous breakfasts and evening meals. My fourteenth birthday occurred on the farm; my parents gave me a watch.

The sights, sounds and smells of the farm absorbed all our attention. In Witheridge, they had never heard of Hitler. Bill had his gun, went out shooting rabbits, was a countryman again, trying to forget his recent disasters in East Dereham.

The time of childhood was not entirely over. Whatever my new watch said, hours and days were still dawdling by. On the farm we had for company other creatures who did not live in the brisk adult time flow: the calves, young sheep, kittens and the Thorns' two dogs. We measured out our days in Wellington boots. It was a timeless time – less than a month away from the declaration of war.

We left the farm and drove to a place called Pinhoe, on the outskirts of Exeter, where Father bought a caravan. We had to live in it for two days on the sales area by a busy road until Bill's cheque was cleared by the local bank.

Towing the caravan, we drove to Cornwall, sleeping overnight – sensation – in a farmer's field. Next day, we arrived at Widemouth Bay, to the west of Bude. Betty and I had yet to realise that that caravan was actually our home.

Widemouth was a beautiful wild place, not far from Tintagel, legendary home of King Arthur. Sheep had grazed the grass short to the very edge of the cliffs. Contained in the bowl of pasture was a small whitewashed cottage which served as the only shop for miles; it sold milk, bread, and – more importantly as far as Betty and I were concerned – Lyons' fruit pies, 4d. Just beyond the shop was a sheer drop of cliff to the rocks below, all vastly different from the tame seasides of the Norfolk coast. We climbed the rocks, ventured into deep pools, caught small fish, watched the waters of the Atlantic wallop into barnacled fissures in the cliff face. Whatever I did, my small sister followed faithfully.

Close by the whitewashed cottage, one other caravan stood. From our caravan window we enjoyed a panorama of the Atlantic. How quiet was the Atlantic in those brassy August days! And I ventured at last to pluck up courage and ask Bill, 'Will I go back to Framlingham?'

He answered casually, as if everything had long been settled in his mind. 'We'll find you a school near here.'

Oh, the joy of it! The relief!

War had presented me with an escape from a fate I feared more than anything else. I firmly believed that Framlingham College spelt spiritual death for me. Every day of my three years there was spent in dread.

To give an instance of the teaching, which was Gradgrindian in temperament: our French lessons were devoted to learning irregular verbs, we were not taught to speak French, or to enjoy the beauties of French literature; long lists of irregular verbs offered better opportunity for chastisement. Days were spent moving from classroom to classroom, carting books about, learning how to escape punishment.

Hardly surprisingly, by reflex we punished each other. Carrying those books about, we always put our Bibles on top of the pile. One boy allowed a Latin textbook to lie on top of his Bible. We beat him up.

And the foul hours of night. Arriving within those walls at the age of eleven, I was unaware of sex, except as a sort of game we had innocently played. Sex had been unknown at St Peter's Court, my preparatory school. That first week in the junior dormitory at Framlingham, the head boy of the dormitory crept into my bed. I was overwhelmed with disgust and shame at his advances, and I feebly pushed him away.

From then on, this sneering bully was always about, always leering at me. Salt in the wound was that his first name was the same as mine. I hated his stupid face, his staring eyes, his winks and jeers, and would have killed him if I could. But he was twice my weight.

That first loathing of homosexual acts remained with me. Rather worse, it left me with a distaste for the flesh for some years.

Perhaps my story-telling in that dorm, at which I became so successful, protected me from further insults of the kind.

So Betty and I played light-heartedly in the rock pools, while time and tide dawdled. It did not bother us that we knew no one else in the world. The sun dazzled on the water, the little crabs scuttled at the bottom of our rubber buckets. We cared as greatly for the events in Europe – the Panzers, the sabres, the fruitless cavalry charges, the Stukas – as did the crabs.

Noon on 3 September. The summer had crumbled away, along with peace. Britain and France declared war on Nazi Germany, only twenty-one years after the last war had run its course. Dot was preparing lunch in our new caravan. Bill and I stood with our neighbour, outside his caravan, where his large wife was frying up. Neville Chamberlain's voice mingled with the gurgle of sausages wallowing in their fat.

I see it all as if it were a photograph. The world has faded to sepia, along with much else. I described the scene in my novel *Forgotten Life*. Fiction is often the best medium for such drama, when momentous and meagre clash.

At that solemn time, with Britain plunging ill prepared into war, I went about in a state of sin, secretly rejoicing, *I don't have to go back to bloody Framlingham! May all those bastards there rot! Thank you, God, thank you, Hitler!*

That night, we blacked out the tiny square window in the caravan roof, some with fury, others with shrieks of laughter which served to ripen the adult anger.

We woke on the 4th and went running out across the green while breakfast was prepared. There was the wonderful view, the sea, the cliffs, the white cottage. Sheep grazed by the wheels of our car. Wartime!

We were to all intents and purposes homeless. Bill drove into Bude, to return with a key. A bungalow stood empty on the cliffs just above Widemouth. We went to look it over with a builder. Bill was agreeing to rent it by the month, Dot was chirping with pleasure.

Betty danced in the empty rooms. Bill shouted, 'Come here! Behave!' Sunlight poured through the front windows. The bungalow was unfurnished, as neat as new, and bereft of everything except a copy of *Fantasy*, lying alone on a window seat.

On the cover of that 1939 issue, *Fantasy: A Magazine of Thrilling Science Fiction*, was an imaginative painting of fire engines drawn up in the centre of London, in Piccadilly, fighting off giant caterpillars with jets of plaster of Paris. In a year's time, the brigades would be dealing with another kind of invasion from the sky.

We moved into the bungalow behind Widemouth cliffs. A few sticks of furniture were bought in Bude. Autumn held its breath: days remained calm and brassy. Looking out of the window at the Atlantic as the sun went down, Bill would say over the frugal supper table, 'It's been a lovely day.' His aggrieved tone comes back to me. *'It's been a lovely day.'* On the horizon, black against the sinking sun, our first convoys – those convoys in which I would one day find myself – were setting out for foreign waters. The weather remained too calm for war to be real.

As that ominous season advanced towards winter, the bungalow crouching near the cliffs became more isolated. Over Bill fell a mood of hopelessness. The whitewashed store on the bay closed its shutters. Cars ceased to run along the coast road. Betty and I wandered about the strange wild place, among the gorse, imitating the shrieks of the seagulls overhead, much as Wordsworth's boy 'blew mimic hootings to the silent owls, That they might answer him'.

The wet Cornish season closed in. Rain pelted down, rushing to get to the centre of the earth. And when the rain abated, the Atlantic became angry, dashing with such force against the rock below the cliffs that spindrift cracked smartly against our window panes, gust after gust.

Before I was installed in a second public school, Bill and I made what I regarded as an epic journey. Setting out at four in the morning in our Rover, he and I, we drove all the way to Gorleston. It was dark when we started out from Widemouth. Roads had no cats' eyes in those days. Our headlights were dimmed to meet blackout regulations. We arrived at the house in Bernard Road at about midday.

The Boxbaums had gone from next door. Their house, like others in the road, was closed up. A forsaken dog wandered loose in the street; Dennis Wheatley's alarming novel *Black August* came to mind, like a vision of the near-future fulfilled. I still wonder what happened to the Boxbaums, in particular to that girl with the blue Aegean eyes. No doubt the Jewish community took care of them.

Bill packed everything into crates, in preparation for a removal firm to come and the house to be sold up for next to nothing. Nobody wanted to live on the east coast now. I helped him – or perhaps hindered, because he told me to take a walk and look at the sea. I made my way down to the front, where Betty and I had spent our most halcyon days.

In the few weeks of our absence a great change had overcome the town. The bandstand was locked, 'for the duration', as the saying went. Everything looked forlorn, with a more-than-mid-winter desertion about it. The lovely stretches of sand were empty. The shops we knew were almost all shut down; some had boarded up their windows with improvised shutters. Barbed wire was being unrolled along the promenade.

Bill and I started back to Cornwall before nightfall with Dot's canary in its cage on the back seat. The canary sang all the way home. Retrieved from the neighbour, Tiny also accompanied us.

Two events on the journey remain in mind, my tongue-tied awe at being alone with my father at close quarters, and our stop for a cup of tea and cake in Oxford – my first sight of that venerable city. I was excited, and not only at the prospect of tea. The waitresses in the St Giles Café were so slow in coming to serve us that Bill, never a patient man, walked out after a minute or two. I perforce followed.

That was the last I saw of Oxford for ten years.

When I was sent to my new school on the fringes of Exmoor, Bill set about finding work. His nest egg from Dereham looked less generous now. He and Dot drove a long way in search of a viable property. He had always been good at property deals, but the war made values uncertain. A newsagent's shop in Chard, Somerset attracted him. There was something in Wincanton. Mother liked the idea of a tearoom. Or perhaps a shop in Exeter?

Exeter had many beautiful old features. Some narrow streets were medieval, resembling the Shambles in York. A particularly interesting book shop stood beside the cathedral. Life continued there as normal; how else? Except that some public buildings were fortified by walls of sandbags.

At first, I hated West Buckland. The grounds on which the school stands were donated by a local landowner, the Second Earl Fortescue, in the 1850s. The Fortescue family still live near by and maintain their friendly connection with the school. WBS consists of a series of stone buildings, not unlike a prison in appearance (in the manner of most public schools), well suited to the rather bare landscape in which it was planted. The quads were of an amazing draughtiness, as the wind howled in from the Atlantic, past Morte Point, bouncing over Fullabrook and Whitefield Downs, clowning its way across the Seven Sisters, to arrive in time for morning parade outside the headmaster's offices.

WBS was heroically uncomfortable. In those early months of the war, everything in the country was in confusion. The school shared in that confusion. Compelled to take on extra boys, many of them evacuated from London, it scarcely knew how to house them. I found myself deposited in an emergency form room with an emergency name, Lower IV A. The room, with its raked desks, had been a chemistry lecture room. The desks were open; nothing could be stowed away in them. Nor were there such luxuries as common rooms. After class, you stayed in the classroom. There was no privacy. The blackout added to the gloom. All around, the winds and rains of Exmoor prowled and hammered at the buildings.

I was completely uprooted. The distance between East Dereham and West Buckland was too great.

I wrote to Bill to say that I wished to be taken away. Answer came from my mother that I would have to stick things out. There was nowhere else to go. My sister, meanwhile, had been sent to a school in Bideford. That did not suit her. She also begged to be rescued. Probably she begged more vehemently than I. She was rescued.

But things sorted themselves out. I was also in the throes of puberty – a rather delayed puberty, it seemed. In the baths after rugger, hulking great dayboys sported clumps of pubic bush, sticking out dismally like Norwegian beards.

A few bubbles foamed from my pipeline, then, at last, the real thing, that phlegm-like substance which makes babies. Puberty is a time of anxiety for boys: will they ever, preferably next week, possess massive dongs like the dayboys, together with thickets of hair like the furze on Hardy's Egdon Heath? Then, low and behold, the miracle happens! There it is, the new weapon, in the pink, sniffing inquisitively at the randy world . . . And many kinds of interesting childish thought are doomed: instead you start wondering how you can get hold of a girl, get a hand down her blouse and up her skirt – particularly up her skirt – and feel her all over, to check on the legends you are hearing from all sides.

It must have been about that time I recited, 'Hush, hush, whisper who dares. Christopher Robin is counting his hairs.'

So there it was. Constant erections to set against the draughty dormitories, the meagre meals, the parades, the clanging of the school bell. Ask not for what the bell tolls: it tolls for your erection.

I grew to love West Buckland. Perhaps it was in my second term, the term when, even on bleak Exmoor, winter yields to spring. The lanes round about East and West Buckland burst forth in primroses, primroses trailing as far as Shallowford, about which Henry Williamson wrote, the hedges fill with birds' nests, and the nests with eggs. Soon, rugger will give way to cricket.

At Framlingham, we were incarcerated within the grounds, as in a high-security prison. At Buckland, we could get exeats which allowed us to wander the countryside on Sundays. You dressed in your rugger kit, collected some rough-and-ready sandwiches from the kitchens, and off you went in twos or threes. Wild Exmoor! How free it seemed, how strange! Once, Bowler and I saw a stag up on the hills. Shallow streams, ideal for damming, meandered about. And there were pits, corries more correctly, full of pure spring water, paved with pebbles six feet down. We actually took dips in them.

They were freezing. We splashed and shouted in agony. Coming out, we pulled on shirt and shorts and ran about howling to restore circulation, yelling and laughing at our own madness.

Beatings at WBS were euphemistically known as 'dabbing'. The custom was to make no sound while the beating was in progress.

I grew to relish the Spartan aspect of WBS and the grittiness of playing rugger in the teeming rain. But wartime WBS lacked the contrasts needed to fill the bleak hours after prep: magnificent productions of opera and plays, films with talks by travellers, scientific demonstrations to excite intellectual curiosity, rich things. Our form was not alone in enjoying education, in seeking to acquire knowledge. Knowledge is to civilisation what DNA is to inheritance.

The nurture side of school life needed improvement; shutting boys up in teenage monasteries was not the answer. WBS went coeducational some years ago, under Michael Downward, an enlightened headmaster. As one token of his enlightenment, Michael recently made me Vice-president of the school.

Bill settled on a property near Barnstaple, a corner shop up for sale. I felt sadness for my father, and disgrace for myself. What a comedown from H. H. Aldiss's shop in Dereham! The Barnstaple shop was a small general store. It sold groceries, cigarettes and newspapers, and housed a sub-post office in one corner.

Bill applied himself to this new trade with dedication. He opened the shop out, incorporating a small storeroom into the design. When rationing began, a coupon had to be exacted for every tin of baked beans, every quarter-pound of sugar. All coupons had to be cut from ration books. Accounting had to be done every weekend. Dot ran the post office. Both of them worked day and night, with no time for their children. We lived in tiny rooms behind and over the shop.

The straggling village of Bickington proved friendly. The post office counter gave Mother an ideal conversation post. Her character changed; she became open and genial. The fears and suspicions of Dereham were things of the past. In no time, she was elected Chairman of the local Women's Institute, and was a popular success. The tradesmen ate out of her hand. Throughout the war, we never lacked for food. Sometimes fresh salmon, poached from a local river, was on the menu.

Cockney evacuees came down from London. The Women's Institute proved equal to the task, and welcomed them with a reception – tea and music. Among the evacuees was a splendid strapping blond woman, a Mrs McKechnie – plainly a whore, loud and rude, but that traditional thing, a whore with a heart of gold – with whom Dot became friendly.

When the first wartime Christmas came round, I asked Bill if we were going to go to church, as previously we had always done in East Dereham.

He regarded me almost with scorn. 'No,' he explained.

It was impossible to make new friends in school holidays. One was there for so short a time. Penny North and I had a pale affection for each other. Betty and I played together, two strange children who got in the way of Bill's shop activities. We dressed up and made stinks with my chemistry set, yet never managed quite to blow anything up. When she was ill, I made her a book of stories and drawings, *The Stock-Pot Book*.

One advantage of the cramped house was that you could climb out of my bedroom window on to a narrow ledge, then to another ledge, and from that get down to the ground. At night, I could escape by that route and walk about the blacked-out village.

More interestingly, I could climb out of a rear window, work my way across a rooftop, and get to a skylight in the roof of a defunct bakery. Levering with a screwdriver, I managed to break the catch of the skylight, and so swarm through into the deserted rooms below.

Here I often stood, wondering, wondering. A certain dark-haired evacuee girl had caught my attention. I talked to her over the back wall and offered to show her my precious secret hideaway, but she would not take the bait, or show me her precious secret hideaway.

The bakery was rat-infested. The rats could get through into Bill's store by the side of the shop and run along a beam at the far end. This store, freezing in winter, had a corrugated-iron roof. Bill developed a hobby. He would stand with his .22 in the kitchen doorway at one end of the store and shoot rats down at the other end, as they ran along the beam, like clay pipes in a shooting gallery at a fair.

Bill had retained his rifles through all our removals. As France fell in 1940, Italy, the Fascist Italy of Mussolini, entered the war against us. Everyone expected that Hitler's next move would be to invade England. Bill handed me one of his guns.

'We may have to defend the street. You never know,' he said. 'Keep it clean.'

The gun was mine. Later, I almost killed my father with it.

At school, we all joined the OTC, the Officers Training Corps, and wore uniform. I became a good shot. When we weren't playing rugger or running round the countryside, we went on military exercises through the local farms. The romps were enjoyable, even in pouring rain, when we wore stiff gas capes. One learnt useful things in the OTC, how to read a compass, how to read a map, how to sneak into an out-of-bounds pub for a pint of cider.

The war was going depressingly badly. After the fall of France, Britain stood alone against the horrible black machine devouring the continent. Bill built an air-raid shelter outside the back door. Dot bought a wind-up gramophone to cheer us up when air raids were in progress.

Once, when a raid was on, we trooped down to the shelter and sat there for an hour or two by candlelight. The shelter proved to be rather damp. After that, Bill used the place as a bacon store, while Betty and I took over the gramophone, on which to play, among other favourites, 'The Ferryboat Serenade', 'Elmer's Tune', 'Green Eyes', 'The Hut-Sut Song' and 'The Memory of a Rose'.

We lay awake at nights, listening to Dornier engines, like an ischaemic event in the lower cerebellum, as Goering's *Luftwaffe* flew overhead. The Dorniers came in squadrons, passing very slowly, throb-throb-throb . . . The distinctive noise rolled down our chimneys. Listening, you felt as an animal feels, hiding when hunters are near.

One night at midnight, Bill roused me from my bed and we walked up the village to climb Belmont Hill, from whence there was a good view of the surrounding country.

A glow lit the whole sky to the south.

'Exeter's getting it,' Bill said.

Later, we drove to Exeter to witness the extent of the damage. Most of the city had gone. Rubble had been cleared away by then. Nothing remained. Nothing, except the cathedral, which stood alone on an unearthly flat plain. Here and there, as we drove, we passed an occasional lamp standard which remained upright. No living person was to be seen; those unburied had decamped to adjoining villages. The Germans had wiped the city off the map. In this surreal landscape, Air Marshal Hermann Goering had done Salvador Dali's work.

The English, so tolerant, so enduring, so brave, during World War II, became a lesser race after the war. Exeter was rebuilt as an anonymous town, without that sense of style its old black-and-white buildings had conveyed. Little memory was retained of what it had once been. The Germans, Poles, French rebuilt their cities according to old plans and photographs, effecting smart restorations and canny improvements. British town planners held no such reverence for what had been, as they plugged the standard chain stores into the city centres. The English made no great protest at what was happening.

The blackout lent an enchantment to banal village streets. On more than one occasion, we climbed Belmont Hill to watch the *Luftwaffe* at their work of destruction.

Far distant, as if an angry planet were about to rise, a fan-shaped light would grow on the horizon. We stood silent on the hill to witness the raid on Plymouth. Even the burning of distant Swansea was visible. Hundreds of civilians died, and with them fabrics and traditions of an earlier age.

After witnessing the air raids we would walk back down the hill, and huddle in the little kitchen behind the shop while Dot made us cups of tea. By the time we were in bed, we would hear the Dorniers returning to Germany. Throb-throb-throb, down the chimney again.

On Belmont Hill stood a small public school, run by a regimental sergeant-major posing as headmaster. The dramatist John Osborne, four years my junior, was incarcerated there as a boy. He used frequently to come down to our shop to buy a packet of Player's 'Weights', whereupon he became friendly with Dot. Growing sick of the sergeant-major, Osborne dotted him a punch in the eye, for which he was expelled.

One great advantage of the blackout was the darkness everywhere, allowing the stars and Milky Way to shine clearly. With my little *Stars at a Glance* in hand, I used to stand on top of our air-raid shelter and watch the constellations. How peaceful were those regions of fire – so different from Exeter burning. Surely in the marvellous beauty of the night sky lay some hope for humanity, war or no war.

Since then, I have stood in the Dandenong Hills in Australia and looked up at a different sky. All the familiar populations of the northern hemisphere have gone. It is as if one stood on a different planet. Even the night sky seen from Mars would appear less alien: the Plough, Cassiopeia, and other constellations would look much the same from Olympus Mons as seen from our air-raid shelter. The distance between Earth and Mars is so short, if insuperable as yet.

At West Buckland, things settled down. The headmaster, Sammy Howells, was a master of sarcasm. He wore pince-nez and had a ginger moustache. The lapels of his suit were permanently discoloured by a W. D. & H. O. Wills' product, Gold Flake cigarettes. Ciggies must have served him as dummy and mistress, and fumigated the perpetual pong of small boys from his nostrils.

To give the devil his due, he ran a tight ship in stormy times. Sammy was a brilliant teacher of English and in particular of English grammar. With his withering tongue, practised at dissecting the language, he could take any unfortunate boy apart. I relished those lessons, much as I feared Sammy. He took a particular dislike to me, calling me 'The Comedian'. Sammy liked to be the one making the jokes.

It was noticeable that when he picked on one boy in the class, everyone else laughed fawningly, protecting themselves from the line of fire. They also professed to like him, for the same reason. I really hated Sammy. The old bastard died just before my first book was published. The smokes got him in the end. His lungs went. Poor Sammy Howells – a good headmaster, a brilliant teacher, a dedicated man, a shit.

One thing stands for ever to Sammy Howells' credit. Whenever Winston Churchill was due to address the nation, Sammy had us all assemble in the Memorial Hall to listen to his speech. Listen we did to that great master of oratory, during those testing years the inspiration of our country.

Obtaining masters to teach was a wartime problem. Most of them had been called up into the Forces. Sammy engaged two conscientious objectors. One was a mathematics teacher, a Mr Coupland, immediately nicknamed, with cruel perception, Chicken Coupland. Coupland knew much maths but could not convey it. Despite furious beatings, liberally dispersed, he could not make us learn. I regret it; I never entered the world of maths, on which most sciences depend.

Mr Foster was a strange man, a refugee from somewhere. We tended to make fun of him. He was known as Mitabout Foreskin, a Bowler christening. Then he took us for a German lesson, and sang 'Roselein' to us in a beautiful tenor voice. From then on we were much more respectful.

'Crasher' Fay taught us German and English in the upper forms. Most lessons were enjoyable. It was the boredom after class, the lack of privacy, the noise that got to you. All well exemplified in Lindsay Anderson's film of public school life, *If . . .*

The truth was that the hardships of wartime Buckland, together with the rigours of the climate – over eighty inches of rain a year, compared with East Dereham's twenty-eight – formed a common bond between masters and staff. Once a term, a barber and his assistant would drive out from Barnstaple on rationed petrol and cut the hair of every boy in the school, working steadily all day, class by class. We went in to the torture chamber maned like lions, to emerge as criminals, scarred here and there by the hasty razor. Of course we laughed, unaware that similar shavings were taking place in Auschwitz and Buchenwald.

Some masters, some boys could not stand the rugged conditions. A brief visitant among the masters was an eccentric S. P. B. Mais, then quite a famous name, a popular broadcaster and writer. I knew his name from the pages of *Modern Boy*, for which he wrote spy stories. He walked about the school complaining, swaddled in sweaters, swathed in scarves. He taught maths in English lessons, algebra in geography, and anything in anything else. I was to meet him later in life. He left Buckland after one or two terms to write a grouchy little book about the place – a book banned by Sammy but adored by Sammy's prisoners.

Certainly the place was remarkably cold and wet. Spartan was its ethos. After lights out in our house dormitory, the blacked-out windows had to be opened, the ones to the north, the ones to the south. Mid-ocean gales blew through the rafters, wafting Atlantic chill with them. Plumbing was rudimentary. Each of us had an enamel bowl, filled overnight with cold water. Many a winter's morning we broke the ice before we could wash. I'm convinced this hardship was good for us, at least for those who survived.

Then came summer. We did not at that time appreciate the beauty of North Devon. But there were long evenings spent out on the playing fields, rehearsing cricket strokes, feeling both the sound and the motion of bat striking ball; or simply playing catch with friends, the leather pill flying high in the air as the shadows of the trees along the drive lengthened. We could also swim in the school pool, but the rule of nudity was never to my taste, concerned as I was with privacy and secrecy.

Once my parents had enlisted me in Buckland, they never visited the school again, although it was only eleven miles from the shop. At the end of term I might cadge a lift in a van to Barnstaple or else walk with others three miles down the valley to Filleigh station, there to catch a Barnstaple train. (Filleigh station has long since been closed.) From Barnstaple, one caught a bus up Sticklepath Hill to Bickington, where it stopped almost opposite our shop.

On one occasion, I returned from school, went upstairs, flung myself on an ottoman, and lay there reading in peace. The relief after the racket of school was considerable. Dot came upstairs from the shop, annoyed because I was so unsociable. I used to stay awake at nights, reading into the small hours.

Having exhausted all the astronomy books in the school library, I turned more eagerly to science fiction magazines, which in those days regarded astronomy as the queen of the sciences. In the fifties they were to become propagandists for space travel. Curious to think that today much SF finds its place less among the stars than inside computers, in games and thought-sequences that recycle old ideas in new form. Not, in fact, outward but inward.

SF magazines introduced me to the name of Friedrich Nietzsche. I went to the Barnstaple Atheneum and applied for membership. The old men were curious to find a fifteen-year-old in their midst. Sitting in a large leather chair, I read *Thus Spake Zarathustra*. There I came across that conception of the *Übermensch* which was enjoying such popularity across the Channel in Berlin.

Nietzsche's ideas filled me with indifference, even when I encountered them, diversified, diluted, in the writings of such SF authors as Ayn Rand and Robert A. Heinlein, whose books enjoyed wide popularity. I marked myself down as the eternal underdog. This canine trail led upwards later, from underdog to *Steppenwolf*.

As for the *Übermensch*, they were part of the fantasies with which I, like many others, scared myself. To relieve the tedium of the bus ride from Bickington to Barnstaple, I would play the British spy travelling on a German bus. The innocent conductor, working his way along the aisle to sell us tickets, was the Gestapo *Überleutnant*, checking papers and passports. He would find me out. I would be captured and shot, and my body flung into the Rhine.

This drama so took hold of me that on one occasion I jumped from a moving bus as it crossed the Taw bridge, to go sprawling in the road. The conductor watched grinning from the back of his bus, but luckily did not fire at me.

At the Atheneum I became acquainted with the writings of a local Barnstaple author, W. N. P. Barbellion, author of *The Journal of a Disappointed Man*. The misanthropic *Journal* was more to my taste than *Zarathustra*. Barbellion is splendid on himself and on the War – even if in his case it was the Great War. He writes, 'They tell me that if the Germans won it would put back the clock of civilization for a century. But what is a meagre hundred years? Consider the date of the first Egyptian dynasty! We are now only in AD 1915 – surely we

could afford to chuck away a century or two? Why not evacuate the
whole globe and give the ball to the Boche to play with – just as
an experiment to see what they can make of it. After all there is
no desperate hurry. Have we a train to catch?'

How could Barbellion foresee that within about twenty-five years
after he wrote, the Boche were indeed intent on experimenting with
the globe – and making a hell of it (aided and abetted by their allies
the Japanese)? Did I but know it in AD 1942, they had already put
the clock back by many centuries.

As for Barbellion on himself – to read him was to see myself in
his sickly mirror.

'I am so steeped in myself – in my moods, vapours, idiosyncrasies,
so self-sodden, that I am unable to stand clear of the data, to marshall
and classify the multitude of facts and thence draw the deduction
what manner of man I am. I should like to know – if only as a matter
of curiosity. So what in God's name am I? A fool, of course, to start
with – but the rest of the diagnosis?

'One feature is my incredible levity about serious matters. Nothing matters, provided the tongue is not furred.'

The adventures of Barbellion's psyche led me to that epicentre of
adolescent turbulence, *The Journals of Marie Bashkirtseff*. I came
across the book in two tall volumes, translated by Mathilde Blind – a
name in its way as exciting as Bashkirtseff. This Ukrainian-Russian
girl died aged twenty-five, thus becoming even more romantic than
Barbellion, who ran to thirty-one years. The tempestuous Marie
loved herself, hated herself. Misery excited her: it was something
to pour into her many diaries. And she discovered as others have
done that she was really two people.

'At present I am vexed, as if for another person.

'Indeed, the woman who is writing, and her whom I describe,
are really two persons. What are all her troubles to *me*? I tabu-
late, analyse, and copy the daily life of my person; but *to me,
to myself*, all that is very indifferent. It is my pride, my self-
love, my interests, my envelope, my eyes, which suffer, or weep,
or rejoice; but *I, myself*, am there only to watch, to write, to
relate, and to reason calmly about these great miseries, just as
Gulliver must have looked at the Liliputians . . .' *(Paris, May 30th
1877.)*

Copying out these sentences now, I recall that for a brief period
I lusted for this amazing emotional girl, long dead. I heard her satin
skirts sweeping the Second Empire carpets, her voice at the piano, I
empathised with her intense longings, feeling we would be a perfect

match for one another, a consummation and a disaster waiting to happen.

Of course I was ashamed of these feelings. In this callow, shallow period, I was ashamed of all feeling. Much like the divine Marie, I could not tell how distraught I was. When I did have a real girlfriend, I dared not by a flicker of the eye reveal as much to my parents, or even to Betty, who might have *told* Dot.

Impossible to admit that I had a sex life. They would have murdered me. Or, worse still, laughed at me.

In some ways, it became more comfortable to be at school – though there was always the dread of leaving home, of feeling that I was being kicked out. I never shed tears – except when I said goodbye privately to Tiny, who was growing old.

Ours became an excellent form as we moved steadily up the school. We laughed a lot. I endeavoured to read every book in the moderately well-equipped library. This was when I started on Freud and Gibbon and Eddington and anything to do with astronomy or the workings of the human mind. My mind was already giving me trouble. The novelists we much admired were Evelyn Waugh, Aldous Huxley, Eric Linklater and J. B. Priestley. Graham Greene came along a little later.

Buckland was and is a sporting school. We played Chivenor, the nearby RAF station, at rugger, as well as various other public schools such as Blundells, outside Tiverton. All that strenuous exercise prepared us not only for the Army, but for life, to endure its hard knocks.

At the beginning of the autumn term, lorries arrived to collect the senior part of the school and drive us out to new agricultural developments on Exmoor, where heath had been turned into farm land. Acres and acres of potatoes were being grown. We worked from early in the morning until late, digging up long rows, turning up nests of those smooth vegetable eggs, while the sun sloped low towards the Atlantic.

It was backbreaking work. Our reward was to be driven home to school for mass baths, all grubby naked bodies steaming together, followed by a meal in hall of sausage with piles of mashed potatoes, *our* potatoes.

We also held drives for the Forces. At one time, a group of us, wearing clean rugger togs, pushed the school barrow around Swimbridge, collecting waste paper. We knocked on people's doors. Sometimes they invited us in and plied us with cups of tea. Generously they gave, throwing out valuable books, sets of Edwards' Birds, first editions of Anthony Trollope's novels. But, 'Us'll keep us bound volumes of *Punch*, because them's real valuable'.

What was really worthwhile went out with the rubbish. The mediocre was saved.

As in an inverted morality play.

III

The School

Suddenly, after a long silence, he began to talk . . . 'A man goes to knowledge as he goes to war, wide-awake, with fear, with respect, and with absolute assurance. Going to knowledge or going to war in any other manner is a mistake, and whoever makes it will live to regret his steps.'

Carlos Castaneda
The Teachings of Don Juan: A Yaqui Way of Knowledge

We held a 'Wings for Victory' fair on WBS rugger field, the Huxtable. It was a great event. Our vendettas against local farmers were set aside so that we could borrow their carts. I turned what had been shameful into satire against myself and became Adolf for a day.

Some years previously, one of the innumerable Framlingham bullies, a creature with the skin of a bullfrog and hyperthyroid eyes to match, grabbed me and declared that I resembled Adolf Hitler. Dragging me into his foul den, he pulled a lock of my hair down over my forehead and painted a moustache of black boot polish on my upper lip. I was then made to goose-step round a senior common room, giving the *Sieg Heil* for the delectation of all the other bullies – many of whom would doubtless have given their eyeteeth to dress up in Nazi uniforms, rape Slav women, and bugger each other while strangling Jews.

By Buckland's 'Wings for Victory' day, I had sufficiently recovered from this degradation to put the act to good use. Suitably uniformed, I mounted one of the farm carts and addressed all and sundry in gibber-German, looking remarkably like Adolf. Or so my friends and admirers told me later.

Hitler still exerts an awful attraction. He has proved to be many things to many men. Hugh Trevor-Roper captured something of the truth when he described Hitler's mind as 'a terrible phenomenon, imposing indeed in its granitic harshness and yet infinitely squalid in its miscellaneous cumber – like some huge barbarian monolith, the expression of giant strength and savage genius, surrounded by a festering heap of refuse – old tins and dead vermin, ashes and eggshells and ordure – the intellectual detritus of centuries.'

Well, that does sound fascinating . . .

It is terrible to think one should still hold Hitler in mind. And I once imitated him! Even the young and innocent are fascinated by wickedness. I suppose it helped prepare us at WBS to be soldiers.

To Crasher Fay I owe more than mere learning. For English classes, we had to produce an essay every Monday. I was excused. Crasher permitted me to present a story instead. A gratifying privilege as we trudged towards the School Certificate . . .

By this time, the writing of short stories had become a continuous occupation. Our form enjoyed, shared, quoted, laughed aloud at Sellar & Yeatman's *1066 and All That*, as well as their less famous books, such as *Horse Nonsense* and *Garden Rubbish*. I wrote 'Invalids and Illnesses'. It was sanitary enough to take home, where my mother read it. I overheard her saying to someone, after reading out a funny bit about diphtheria, 'You may not like it, but it is clever.' Eavesdroppers seldom hear good about themselves; I felt she had summed me up.

Most of my stories were less sanitary. They were mainly planetary adventures, dirty SF, crime, or dirty crime. Screwing featured largely. I often wrote in the dormitory, under the bedclothes by torch-light. The stories always remained first draft. Penny-a-read was the nominal charge. Nobody paid, everyone read. It was gratifying. A superior fellow in the Sixth, a horn-rimmed Harrison, said, 'Aldiss, these tales of yours are ridiculous and badly constructed.'

He was probably right. But I wrote compulsively, and risked beating and expulsion if they fell into the wrong hands.

I also wrote and illustrated a series of comic tales, 'The Jest-So Stories'. At term's end, Bowler and I put all the manuscripts in a Huntley & Palmer's biscuit tin and buried it in a rabbit burrow in the Plantation, from where we retrieved it the following term.

I became prolific. At one of my more acceptable sardonic stories, presented as a Monday offering, Fay took offence. After reading parts of it aloud, he stared hard at me and said, 'I warn you, Aldiss, if you

go on like this you'll become another Evelyn Waugh.' Never had I
heard such praise.

Bowler was a great character. He, Saxby, and I were jokers-in-chief.
Don Smith was a more sophisticated type. He brought a wind-up
gramophone and played jazz records. We heard for the first time
Tommy Dorsey and Orchestra playing 'Getting Sentimental Over
You', and, ah!, Jimmie Lunceford and his band playing 'Blues in the
Night', with the Johnny Mercer lyrics:

> From Natchez to Mobile
> From Memphis to Saint Joe,
> Wherever the four winds blow . . .

And wherever those cities were, there I wanted to be. I saw the
movie *Blues in the Night*, which features Jimmy Lunceford, eighteen times over the years, in England and abroad. Almost as many
times as *Citizen Kane*. As an adult, I sang the song in duet with
the philosopher A.J. 'Freddie' Ayers.

End of term. Back to that dreary Bickington shop on the corner. And
now great excitement. Following Pearl Harbor, the United States
of America had entered the war. On our side. What was more, an
American regiment was to be flown over to Fremington.

Fremington was next to Bickington; one village straggled into
the other along the main road. Under Dot's guiding hand, the
Bickington Women's Institute decided to give the Americans a
slap-up reception. Music and dancing would be the order of the
day. There would be food and soft drinks. No alcohol, since we
had heard the American forces *drank* – unlike, of course, our boys.
Everything was made ready.

The American regiment arrived. It was black. In those days, the
US segregated its soldiery by colour.

What a fluttering in the dovecotes! Committee meeting! A sensible decision was arrived at. Black Americans were in the war just
like anyone else, and would soon have to fight in Europe. The slap-up
reception must continue exactly as planned.

So black troops poured into Bickington, and the party went ahead.
It was a roaring success. The music veered from the hot—

> I'll be round to meet you in a taxi, honey,
> Better be ready 'bout a ha' past eight—

to the sentimental—

I'll be your sweetheart, if you will be mine

The Bickington ladies, including Mrs McKechnie, were delighted with their own wisdom. The black Americans were charmed to find themselves in a country without any colour prejudice . . .

At school, we made a discovery. Mr H. G. Wells was still alive! It amazed and cheered us. We were accustomed to reading books by dead authors; the books we studied were by the illustrious dead, from Hillard & Botting onward. But the great imaginer was living in London, a city more devastated by German bombs than by his Martians.

I read and wrote. Most eagerly I read *Astounding*, in which, to my mind, the future was being born. Chicken Coupland caught me reading an issue in class. Seizing it, he tore it into small pieces, damning it for rubbish. I had been in the middle of a Theodore Sturgeon story.

My difficulties with Sammy continued. The one master on my side was my housemaster, Harold Boyer. Harold was of mixed English-German descent, and hence presumably not allowed to serve in HM Forces. He arrived at the school in 1940 and went on to become a governor of the school and an HM Inspector of Schools.

Harold could teach anything. His manner was somewhat theatrical. He would prowl before us, slapping one hand in the other. 'Facts, facts, you must have facts.' He was making reference to the School Certificate exams, which began to loom over us.

He became head of the house I was in, and showed a genuine interest in our lives. Like Crasher Fay, he rarely if ever beat people. He was a humorous man. After I had left school I discovered just what amusing company he was. Harold then revealed a bawdy subversive streak, whereas in the form room he could resemble a one-man version of the Holy Roman Empire.

Like the other masters, Harold shared Buckland's general discomfort. Unmarried masters generally had rooms within the school. Harold, being married to Isabel, and having three daughters, lived in a cottage two miles away in Charles Bottom – always known as Charlie's Arse. Sometimes we saw the dark-haired Isabel pushing a pushchair up to school; this sight caused some excitement among the sex-starved.

Finally, our form came to the test – School Cert., later to become GCE. Although my militaristic spirit was rather more pinko than khaki, I had passed Cert. A, the OTC exam, a necessity for becoming an army officer. I was less confident about School Certificate. At that precarious stage in life, one's whole future appeared to depend on the wretched exam. And I had not always paid the greatest attention. Was I not 'Foo', the demon humorist of the Middle Fifth?! ('Foo' was a favourite expletive used in Bill Holman's prize surrealist comic strip, 'Smokey Stover'.)

Sammy did everything to make life difficult. On the morning of the first exam, tension was high. We were to proceed into the memorial hall to widely spaced desks. On the way, I dropped my inkwell. Ink splashed over the stone passage. This Sammy seized on in a fury. Here was a chance to humiliate the comedian!

I was made to go down to the kitchens, fetch a bucket of hot water, and swab up the mess. One of the menservants could easily have done the job. As a result I entered the hall late and flustered. When I made a return visit to the school after the war, I observed a faint blue stain still marking the site of my accident: the Aldiss Memorial Blob.

We went through the exams, playing tennis between times. A week in limbo, isolated from the rest of school and from the future. At the end of term my report reached home. Sammy wrote on the bottom of the report that I had behaved so badly I did not deserve to pass the exam.

It was a low blow. Bill was furious. Was this all I cared for all their sacrifices? He mentioned in passing how much money he had wasted on my education. As usual, I stood before him without defence. Not for the first time I wondered why, when I admired my father so, I was mute in his presence.

After the ticking off, he and Dot were hardly on speaking terms with me. I could not explain. Before the most patient interlocutor I could not have explained the difficulties of matching two conflicting sets of interests, education and growing up. Indeed, these difficulties remain hard to reconcile. You strive to become adult, which means rejecting the control of your elders; yet to become educated you must submit to their discipline.

'Your father is really upset,' was all Dot would say when I tried to approach her. 'You didn't work, did you?' She too suffered from conflicting loyalties.

That was always her role in our little army: the NCO between the Commanding Officer and his tiny conscripts.

Bill and Dot were an incompatible pair. Whatever had occurred between them in the early stages of their marriage, during the wartime years and afterwards, they stood together. When things were most trying for them, at the Bickington store in particular they saw the necessity for solidarity, even at the expense of their children. However greatly they had once disappointed each other, they remained loyal and devoted. Over all, they set Betty and me a persuasive argument for marriage and its loyalties – an argument I later found myself unable to follow.

Under the shadow of Bill's silent disapproval, my fragile morale evaporated. Only at school had there been friends to turn to. I slipped under the ever-threatening shadow of my own disapproval. I took to climbing apple trees and falling out of them, but received only bruises rather than the desired broken neck. Even there I seemed to lack determination.

Successes glittered occasionally amid the prevailing shades of failure. I persuaded Betty to scale the north face of the roof and enter the deserted bakery with me. We established a museum in our old disused stable, filling it with stones, fossils and sheeps' skulls found in nearby fields.

It was during this period that Mussolini was arrested and killed. We were treated to newsreel footage of him hanging upside down, like a pig's carcass. How dare I make anything of my sufferings when the great world was undergoing a kind of death agony, and millions were dispossessed or dying? Who am I to cry out? No great religion has ever proposed that life is a bed of roses.

Those summer holidays were a sickness. The days wasted away, one by one. Exam results were due to arrive by post on 5 September. The day of my complete humiliation drew nigh. On 3 September, the anniversary of the outbreak of war, I woke early, cowering in bed, listening for the sound of the postman. I was determined I could not face the parents at the breakfast table. In the end, I felt driven to go downstairs.

The post had brought no communication.

Next morning, anxiety roused me. I sat hunched up in bed, listening for the postman, to crawl downstairs when I knew breakfast had come and gone and Bill was in the shop.

On the following morning, worn out by worry, I overslept.

I was awakened by both parents rushing into my bedroom, waving pieces of paper. A modestly brilliant result! I had passed the School Cert. exam with five credits out of seven, and thus had matriculated. So delighted – and shamed? – was Bill that he thrust a cheque for ten pounds into my hand. So astonished was I that I took it.

All my past is accepted. Yet still there remains regret that I did not reject that conscience money. I had never possessed ten pounds before; but it was my submissiveness that led me to accept the cheque so meekly, and smile while doing so, without a word of reproach.

The incident smoulders still. It seems to epitomise much that was wrong with my parents' relationship with their lad – and the lad with them.

At the beginning of the next school holiday, I returned to the shop to find another change. The shop was still there, but Bill had bought a bungalow, Meadow Way, half a mile away, on the main road to Fremington. The accommodation was better and Bill could walk up to the shop every morning.

Such memories as I have of that bungalow are entirely neutral. It was bought, taken over, and we lived there. The pieces of furniture we possessed were arranged in rooms. There was no sense that anything might be improved; we had to take the place as we found it. Nowadays, having bought a house, one expects to make all manner of alterations; conservatories are added, rewiring is done, or perhaps an attic room is created. The place is redecorated. Such ideas never entered our heads as far as wartime houses were concerned.

In the same way, clothing had no style. I wore Bill's cast-off sports jackets, and grey flannel trousers. I suppose everything we owned looked shabby, but we were unaware of it. In the evenings, after work, Dot and Bill padded about the place, smoking, in pre-war slippers.

On Christmas Day, there was Bill, at the ironing board, ironing out the wrapping paper from our presents, to preserve it in a cupboard safely for the following December. Parsimony was a kind of patriotism.

There was no going off on holiday in wartime. Betty and I walked all over the place and sketched and painted together. Betty attended an art school in Bideford and was already inclining towards costume. Unknown to us then, a pathway to the BBC was opening up ahead of her.

Dot was altogether a more cheerful person. She laughed a lot. Over the breakfast table, she would regale us with her ludicrous dreams, which generally centred around sexual embarrassments. She would lose her corsets during an important meeting at the post office; or she would be caught by a farmer relieving herself in one of his haystacks.

Much listening to the radio went on. Everyone's memoirs of the war years include a compulsory reference to Tommy Handley's *I.T.M.A.* We too listened devotedly, and spouted all the catch phrases. One benefit the war brought was an importation of American radio shows. So we learnt of Duffy's Tavern, Where the Elite Meet to Eat, and became addicted to the *Bob Hope Show* with its signature tune 'Thanks for the Memory'. Bob Hope was a master of one-liners. His description of a totalitarian state is classic: 'It's where they name a street after you one day and chase you down it the next.'

Another favourite show was Jack Benny's, with his black servant, Rochester. We heard later, in the time of Martin Luther King and the raising of black consciousness, that Rochester came to be regarded as an Uncle Tom. However that might be, he was the character we liked best on the show.

Woods and fields surrounded Meadow Way, in which Betty and I strayed. We could also, with difficulty, get down to the rolling river Taw. I wrote and illustrated a book about our adventures, real and imaginary. One golden summer, possibly 1942, we picked blackberries from July until October.

Bill still liked to shoot. Rats in the store certainly. Also rabbits for the pot. Rabbit stew with dumplings remained to our Norfolk-bred tastes. On one occasion, Bill invited me to go with him, to a glade not far from the bungalow. I took my .22. As ever, I was nervous in his presence. He seemed so to despise everything I did.

We moved quietly down a tree-shaded lane. I was anxious to prove myself in his eyes. Rabbits sported some distance ahead. He signalled to me not to fire yet. I was a pace or two ahead of him. He wanted to give me a chance.

Happening to glance back, I saw that two or three rabbits had hopped out of the bushes only a few yards behind us. Without thinking, I raised my .22 and fired.

The bullet missed Bill's ear by little more than an inch.

'You silly sod,' he said. I had never heard him swear before. 'You silly sod. You could have killed me.'

We returned home. I was still trembling and pale. I went to my bedroom and could not emerge again that day. Added to my own crass act was the shock of hearing Father swear. In those more polite days, the harshest words were 'blinking', 'blithering' and 'confounded' . . . possibly 'ruddy'.

* * *

Back at school, after the dull Bickington holidays, the times were still improving. When we entered the senior forms, we were allowed to join the Home Guard. It accustomed us to wearing khaki uniform, to working with men, and to travelling further afield. Sometimes we carried out exercises on those parts of Saunton Sands that were not mined, firing at each other with blanks.

The only real shooting carried out on that beautiful coastline was for British films. Shaw's *Caesar and Cleopatra* was filmed there, as was a scene from the Powell & Pressburger film *A Matter of Life and Death*.

The general Sunday procedure was for a lorry to call at the school early in the morning. About ten of us, kitted out, uniformed, with army boots and rifles, would jump in. The lorry would then drive around to nearby farms, picking up the troops. Very few of them had uniforms. Very few of them seemed to know what was what. We christened one farmer's son the Trout. He did indeed look like a fish. One Sunday, the Trout climbed into the lorry with a poker sticking out from the muzzle of his Lee Enfield. He had used the implement from his hearth to try and clean the barrel of his rifle. There it had stuck.

Life in the Sixth Form is remembered with affection. After nine years – more for some poor wretches – at boarding schools, we had climbed to the top of the pile. There came a sort of breathing space in which to be semi-civilised, to enjoy music and the art club, even conversing with, rather than thumping, each other. We valued the artist Mr Lyons-Wilson, who drove over from Exeter once a week to talk to us of Botticelli and Gainsborough. Although Lyons-Wilson was not without his affectations, his own watercolours were masterly. Also we liked him because – as was the case with Harold Boyer – he was on our side. And amusing.

Most of us belonged to the Phoenix Debating Society, which brought the privilege of a separate reading room. We gave readings of plays and stories for the rest of the school. I argued about religion and was permitted to make funny speeches. We formed a school jazz band in which I was the vocalist, encouraged to yell out the lyrics to 'In the Mood'. We inclined towards the Don Smith mode of jazz: that is, very bluesy.

> You can take my meat and ham gravy too—
> But I draw the li-ine when it comes to you.
> Yeah man, yeah man, yeah man

*   *   *

The school's four houses decided to put on house concerts to celebrate end of term. As ever, my situation was uncertain. I had passed School Cert. and was supposedly to study for A Levels, in preparation for my future career. The plan was that, since H. H. Aldiss had been shot from under us, I should become an architect and join my Wilson uncles' firm in Peterborough.

I was inclined towards the idea. For that purpose, I had given up Latin in order to study German, because only with German went Higher Maths (the vagaries of the educational system were strange, then as now). But Higher Maths under Mr Coupland proved as far beyond me as had Lower Maths. You need the Higher stuff in order to become an architect. I coasted in that last year, and was therefore available for things more amusing than calculus.

Like the house concert.

Bowler was in charge of the Grenville concert, I of the Fortescue concert. With the assistance of Harold Boyer, I wrote all the sketches, poems and catches, and performed in many of them. It was my term. For once my labels, Foo, The Comedian, came fruitful. And instead of Sammy trying to destroy me, there was Boyer to encourage me, and to laugh.

Fortescue House won the contest. Applause and congratulations. Sammy kept out of the way, smoking on his Gold Flakes in his airless study. It was my finest hour, or at least half-hour, for the nursing sister Veronica Talbot was so delighted that she invited me to her room, gave me gin to drink – and kissed me. Yes, Veronica Talbot kissed me on the lips!

My last term at Buckland. Military service loomed. Several of our Six Formers sought for ways to escape call-up. Schemes for further study incurred exemption, if you were clever about it. I wonder how some of my friends who were clever then, and escaped war service to retreat to the sinecure of Edinburgh University or other seats of learning, feel about their strategy now. Confused I might be, but 'dodging the column' was never my style.

To adolescent anxieties was added one peculiar to our generation. We were caught in what Harold Boyer taught us to call a Morton's Fork of a dilemma. By 1943, the tides of war were turning in Britain's and the Allies' favour. I became eighteen years old in the August of that year – ripe for cannon fodder. The question was, would the struggle soon be over? Would we be drawn into the dreadful mêlée, possibly to die on some alien battlefield? On the other hand, would we in fact miss out on the great male initiation rite of the century? These alternatives, both fairly ghastly, lived with us continually. We wanted neither, needed both.

We were standing shivering on the brink of a chilly sea, unable to take the plunge. I felt I had little to lose. During the holidays, I went to the Recruitment Centre in the Foresters' Hall in Barnstaple to volunteer for the Army – for the Royal Corps of Signals. The sergeant told me that the Signals required no more men.

'Why not join the Royal Navy, lad?'

It's a man's life. Sir Francis Drake, a Devon man, and all that stuff. There's lots of promotion in Submarines, lad.

You bet there was. I left the Centre, in part relieved. No one, even at eighteen, when testosterone is swishing vigorously round the circuitry, actually wishes to be shot or drowned. Drowned, not. Shot, okay.

During that last term, an official letter in a khaki envelope came to say I was to report for a pre-conscription medical check in Barnstaple. Sammy gave his approval and issued a day's exeat for the expedition. When the morning of 29 July dawned, I felt ill, but ascribed it to cowardice. After dragging myself down to Filleigh station, I caught a train to Barnstaple. It was a beautiful summer's day. Like a slow poison, the war gave no sign of its existence.

The Forester's Hall in Barnstaple High Street was occupied by the medical board, and divided into various booths, in each of which one physical attribute – height, urine, eyesight – was tested, as in a Kafkaesque fairground. The hall was strangely lit, I thought. Everything seemed glaring, yet remote. No one was making particular sense. I undressed as instructed. In the various booths, as each intrusive medical test was carried out, the doctors looked at me strangely. It was so cold. Some conferring went on among the medical fraternity. Someone thought to take my temperature. It was running at 106 degrees.

A senior doctor advised me to go to hospital. He was annoyed that I had appeared before them in such a state. When I told them where I had come from, they ordered me back to school immediately.

I could have caught a bus home; it was only two miles away. Instead, I caught the next train back to school. Again the three-mile walk up the valley from Filleigh station. I felt a bit odd. Half-way to Buckland, the school car arrived to take me the rest of the distance. *The school car!* Sammy must have sent it. Obviously, some sort of trouble was brewing.

But not at all. The medical centre had rung the school and strongly condemned them for sending me when I was so ill. Something like a hero's welcome awaited me. I was bundled into the sickbay to a concerned Sister Talbot; Doctor Killard-Levy pronounced that I had pneumonia in one lung. I got into bed in a pleasant little ward, otherwise unoccupied, turned on my side, and fell asleep.

At that period, I found myself misrepresented as a hero. I had gone for the medical only because to have pleaded ill that morning would have laid me open to the charge of cowardice. Everyone was sensitive to such imputations in the middle of war. Still, this misrepresentation was enjoyable – and, after all, I had not bolted for home.

As far as I was concerned, it was all rather a joke, a fuss over nothing. Ridiculous to catch pneumonia in mid-summer. And in only one lung!

During the night I became feverish and cried out in my sleep. Into the ward came Sister Talbot, in flimsy nightie and wrap. Without switching on a light, she got on to my bed and wrapped her arms about me in a gentle embrace.

Responding, I went to put an arm about her, but slid my hand inside her nightdress and clutched her naked breast. The delight of it! That beautiful breast . . . It is the desire of every writer to be able to speak of things for which there are few words. It is particularly difficult to talk about sex, that ocean of sensations, where what is carnal seems sacred. There's secrecy about bliss, just as there's bliss in secrecy.

Soon her little nest of spicery, as Shakespeare calls it, was hot in my hand. It's sufficient to say we then became lovers. It sounded such an adult word when I whispered it to myself. When I was recuperating, I was able to go up to Veronica's little rooms, where much of the school linen was stored, to make love to her.

It was the great redeeming pleasure of all those years at school, a more meaningful kind of matriculation. And for some years after I had left, after I had come out of the Army, she and I sustained a pleasant relationship. She was fifteen years my senior. That too added a poignance, and a reassurance that there was no formal commitment between us, except that of pleasure and affection.

Oh yes, I was to discover what a fantasist she was, how deception was her defence against a wounding life. That I reported in my partial portrait of her in *The Hand-Reared Boy*. It made not a jot of difference to my feelings for her. If she needed me in ways I could not fathom – well, that applies in many affairs of love.

After all, I was also a fantasist, in believing myself to be her only lover. That was so greatly what I wished to believe that no opposing thought entered my head. Later, I found this not to be the case by a long chalk. That too – after the first shock – made no difference to my feelings for her.

So that last summer term passed, with friends, lessons, cricket, debates – and Veronica. Though I failed to realise it, all was in place for me to become a writer. A certain detachment, a facility, a store of reading, curiosity: everything was there except experience. A sense of my own inadequate personality kept this knowledge from me. I was content enough to go to war. As far as I recall, I didn't much care what happened to me.

It was the final day of term. We had practised not swearing or smoking. The Sixth broke up casually as usual. Farewells were brief. Bowler and I had buried my stories in their biscuit tin in the Plantation as we had done previously, for posterity to discover. The usual eagerness to get home overtook us. Most of the school tramped down the road to Filleigh station. I remained behind. Someone I knew was coming by in a tradesman's van to pick me up and give me a lift into Barnstaple.

My thought had been that I would leave Buckland without regret: or, if not Buckland, then those painful years of adolescence. Standing outside the front of the school, its buildings now all but empty, I felt the weight of an ending heavy on my shoulders. A phase of life, with its wearying sequence of lessons, punishments, discomfort and incarceration, had seemed to drag on for ever. In the last two years, it had provided its successes, had even become pleasant. As to what the future would bring, I had not the slightest idea. Prophetic gifts are rare; in wartime, one is all too aware of the fact.

Warfare is a whale, swallowing up its young like krill. Even as I left WBS for good, British and American forces were fighting their way through Sicily. Sinister railway trains with their packed cattle trucks were proceeding eastwards from Germany to the extermination camps.

The historian A. J. P. Taylor said of World War I that it was imposed on Europe's statesmen by railway timetables; that that war was the climax of the railway age. In World War II, wickedness fuelled the trains that ran eastwards with their doomed thousands from the Nazi-occupied countries. The climax, not of the railways, but of human beastliness – so far.

Back at Meadow Way, I received my Enlistment Notice from the Ministry of Labour and National Service. I was called upon for service in the Army, and was required to present myself, on 18 November, 1943, to No. 52 Primary Training Wing, under the aegis of the Royal Norfolks, at Britannia Barracks, Norwich.

A travel warrant and postal order for four shillings in advance of service pay were enclosed with the demand.

Failure to report on time would render me liable to be arrested and brought before a Court of Summary Jurisdiction.

So Britannia Barracks it was – quite a distance from North Devon. By coincidence, it was the same barracks to which Bill had had to report in 1914, twenty-nine years earlier.

Even the feeblest children grow up to become soldiers – for good or ill.

IV

The Old Business

The burden of the long gone years: the weight, The lifeless weight, of miserable things Done long ago, not done with: the live stings Left by old joys, follies provoking fate, Showing their sad side, when it is too late . . .

Lionel Johnson
Experience

A time of war is comparatively easy to describe. One's personal details can be crosschecked against grand external events. And an adult memory, working on adult time, has filed away its record, for good or ill. But to return to childhood, to the Permian mud of infancy, is to enter a more questionable area. We may see certain distant events with clarity. But on either side of the event, fogs roll in. And were those events in fact the events as they are 'clearly remembered'?

My uncomfortable advantage is that I see – *believe* I see – much of my first five years of life with clarity. For when I am five years old, something happens to me resembling the fall of a guillotine blade, severing past from future.

Those early formative years can roll like a film and are as untrustworthy as a movie, however sincerely truth is attempted, for the movie has been edited by time.

It is mid-August, two o'clock of a summer's morning. The newborn infant lies in its cot in that eternal present tense preserved in memory. It is a boy, with the slight blemish of a port wine mark on its forehead. It will be christened Brian Wilson Aldiss, thus bearing the names of both sides of the family. It cries a little.

It is born at home, in its parents' bedroom. Its mother lies exhausted, a nurse hovering over her. She also cries. She had hoped for a baby girl.

The boy is a disappointment, and will be made to feel that keenly. It lies listening to its mother's muffled sobs. The curtain of its life goes up; but, as in an Ibsen play, there is already a terrible past history awaiting revelation. One day, someone will knock at the door and then the whole charade of normality will fall apart.

Already deception is brewing like a thunder cloud about the infant. The deception will masquerade as truth for many years, and devour tissue like a cancer. The mother, almost without willing it, is brooding on a consoling fantasy which will survive undetected for sixty years, and accumulate a burden of anguish meanwhile.

This is the story of how, for much of that time, I was not so much living as being entangled with life.

Such is often the case with first-borns: but should I count myself a first- or second-born? For sixty years, that too remained a puzzle. No wonder the infant cried a little!

The name of the mother sobbing comfortably in her feather bed is Elizabeth May Aldiss, née Wilson, generally known as Dot. She is married to Stanley Aldiss, generally known as Bill. Bill and Dot always address each other by these invented names.

Something of their history is in order before the camera of memory turns its lens towards the newcomer in its cot.

The sepia deepens as we sink back into the late nineteenth century.

Dot is born in Peterborough, on 1 June, 1884, the fourth child of Elizabeth and Allen Wilson, the other three children being boys.

The Wilsons are a jolly lot. Their origins are humble, but Allen has one great advantage to set against his 'lack of background', as people used to say. He has great charm of character. Unlike many charmers, he is industrious. He becomes a builder and rises out of poverty. A. W.'s and Sarah Elizabeth's four children largely inherit these pleasing traits. In order of seniority – the children are christened Allen, Herbert (Bert), Ernest and Elizabeth May. Elizabeth May is doted on by all the family, the family's dear little spoilt girl.

Although the film is blurred, we perceive that the Edwardian period is good for the Wilsons. The family moves to a bigger house, a solid semi-detached in a respectable street, which A. W. has built. My grandfather, prospering, never works after lunch at this time. He smokes cigars or plays billiards. He now owns four houses in

Park Road, and becomes secretary to the active Baptist Church at the bottom of the street. He breeds pigeons; pigeons of all kinds and colours, pigeons with puffed-out breasts, pigeons with none.

Allen Woodward Wilson Esq. becomes President of the All England Pigeon Fanciers Association. After his humble beginnings, he is happy to feel himself to be a man of some substance. On the occasions when he goes away on business, A. W. wears a top hat and employs a small boy to carry his case to the LNER station.

The film is a silent one. Now comes a card bearing the ominous caption: '*The Great War*'.

In 1914, the brothers are of an age to join in the general slaughter. Off they go, Allen, Bert, Ernie, waving gallantly from the train as they leave from Peterborough station. The boys' mother weeps as she waves until the train draws out of sight; A. W. raises his top hat. Their sons are starting a journey that will take them to the mud of the trenches on the Western Front, and captivity in a German oflag. At least they will all survive the slaughter, and live to tell a small part of the tale.

Allen becomes a lieutenant in the 8th Battalion of the Northampton regiment. Bert becomes a lieutenant in the 23rd Northumberland Fusiliers. Ernie joins the Royal Air Force.

The first German words I shall learn will be inscribed on a slender white enamel sign: **Rauchen Verboten**. The uncles will remove the sign as a souvenir from a compartment in the train which, in 1918, will bear them back to liberty and the rest of their lives.

The history of the Aldiss family cannot be told in great detail. There have been rumours of connections with the Norfolk Bullen (or Boleyn) family, who yielded up a wife for Henry VIII. This connection remains unsubstantiated.

More certain is that an old etymological dictionary gives our name as a corruption of 'alehouse'. It sounds appropriate. The Aldiss family has always struggled through the centuries between alcoholism on the one hand and teetotalism on the other.

The progeny of a John Aldous, the first of whom was born in 1697, are variously registered as Aldhouse, Aldes and Aldus. The first undisputed Aldiss is Thomas Aldiss of Beccles (christened 1726), who became a blacksmith and married a butcher's daughter, Susan Creme of Diss.

A Thomas Aldiss was born in Lowestoft, on the Suffolk coast, in 1759, probably a son of the similarly named Aldiss of Beccles. He lived long and, like my paternal grandfather, like me, he ran to two wives. Thomas was a blacksmith. Evidently he prospered, or else married 'above his station'. While his first marriage took place in Lowestoft, his second marriage, rather more grandly, took place in St Paul's, in London.

Thomas handed down to posterity a few anvils and a number of progeny, six by his first wife, five by his second. One of the children by Thomas's first marriage (to Elizabeth Brame) was Robert. Robert Aldiss continued the blacksmith and gunsmith trade in Lowestoft. He married Sarah Ann Goulder on the last day of January, 1830, and between them they produced eight offspring.

Their oldest son, William, was born in the year of their marriage, in December 1830. This William Aldiss was my great-grandfather.

Draper William married Ann Doughty, of a well-known Norfolk family, in Swaffham in 1860. They had six children, of whom the oldest, Harry Hildyard, became my redoubtable grandfather.

H. H. was born in a house on the market place in Swaffham in 1862. The house still stands. He struck out on his own as a draper. In 1885, after the most dignified of courtships, H. H. married Elizabeth Harper, a farmer's daughter. I have a Holy Bible H. H. presented her with, which has survived the storms of the years. His message in it is brief. It reads 'Lizzie Harper. From H. H. A., as a token of his love. May 6th, 1881'. The message comes printed in gold, now faded, on a red label, increasing its air of formality.

My grandfather remains vivid in memory. He is a short, stocky man with a good, strongly featured face. His values are Victorian; above all, he is stern but just, his stern side ameliorated by a sense of humour – as when, in his role of JP, he fined his gardener five pounds for allowing his dog to chase a neighbour's chicken. After the case, he slips his gardener a fiver, saying 'After all, the dog was mine, and I couldn't very well fine myself.'

From this time on, families are becoming less large, as health and sanitation improve. Elizabeth and H. H. had four boys: Reginald; Harry Gordon (my uncle Gordon); Stanley, my father; and Arthur Nelson, known as Nelson. There were two years between the birth of each child, Reginald being born in 1886, in Horncastle, as were his brothers.

Reginald died in the year of his birth. A stone stands to his memory in East Dereham churchyard.

The move to Dereham came some time before the First World War. There H. H. bought a failing drapery business and rapidly expanded it, assisted by his two surviving sons. H. H.'s youngest son, Nelson, was dead.

He died tragically. Mother often told us the story – we never heard of it from Father. Like Father, Nelson was educated at Bishop's Stortford College. He was due to play in an important rugby match when he experienced severe stomach pains. He reported to the college sickbay, only to be told not to malinger. Next day, he collapsed on the pitch and was carried to hospital. There he died of a ruptured appendix, aged fourteen, another victim of the public-school spirit.

Perhaps H. H. and Elizabeth found there was no competition in the thriving little market town of Dereham. Certainly the firm of H. H. Aldiss Ltd prospered for some thirty years, from before the First World War until the Second. After the Second World War the business was sold off by Gordon's son.

Yet the childish imagination experienced the Aldiss business as something as permanent as Stonehenge: and possibly remains affronted at its disappearance.

The premises stood in the High Street, looking up Norwich Street. It was in those premises that both my sister and I were born.

So the movie starts up again. It is 1925, still in the era of the silent film, and I come to the task of describing my own infant life.

My first five years are sealed in a time capsule. The capsule opens on the day of my birth, to close on 30th April 1931, some months before my sixth birthday.

As consciousness reaches out for the world beyond the cot, I find myself in a large flat above my father's department of the shop, which is to say, the gents' outfitters. Two of our rooms look eastwards, towards Norwich and the rising sun; they are above the front of the shop, facing up Norwich Street. Their windows are remembered as being many yards above the pavement. An astonishingly long corridor connects with a lounge at the rear. This lounge overlooks the shop's busy yard and one of the entrances to the furnishing department, over which my uncle Gordon rules.

Near this rear end of the flat are clustered, on one side, a bathroom, a lavatory and a maid's storage compartment (dark, polish-smelling, exciting), which contains a separate lavatory for the maid. The lavatory I unwisely invade at the age of four while the maid is enthroned – all in the interest of scientific curiosity. She is furious and later gets her own back.

On the other side of the long corridor are the kitchen, the pantry and another room, sometimes serving as a breakfast room, sometimes as a bedroom for a live-in maid. Further along the corridor towards the front of the flat are two bedrooms, the main bedroom, where my parents sleep in a double bed, and where a cot is sometimes accommodated, and a smaller room, all but attached to the larger. These two rooms are of immense importance: the centre of the universe, and therefore worth a pause as we look round them.

Both of these bedtime rooms, the larger and the smaller, face north. Like blind eyes, they have no view worth speaking of. In fact they look across the side entrance to the shop premises towards the uncommunicative sides of an old building.

The parental bedroom is where I am and, later, my sister is born. Between its two windows is a grate, where sometimes a coal fire is lit, for instance when I am ill. I have a memory of one such occasion when Dot has wrapped lumps of coal in newspaper during the day, so that she can add them to the fire silently during the night, without disturbing my sleep. The floor is covered with a shiny lino, cold to the feet. The lavatory is some distance away, so chamber pots wait under each side of the double bed. In this room, terrible infantile dramas take place. I will have to listen to screams of anguish from my sister as she resists having vests with tapes at the neck pulled over her head. Even darker things happen in this room, as will be related.

I am moved at an early age from my cot in this larger room to a bed in the smaller one. The bed remains in memory as almost insuperably high. At head and foot, its four posts are capped by elegant squares of wood. On the wall for my delight is a Rowntree study of bluetits among stalks of corn. A Price's nightlight is provided for me, to stand guardian at night on the chest of drawers at the end of the bed.

It may be assumed from this that I was a pampered child; I was certainly a carefully guarded child; precautions were taken to keep me confined to the flat, and against this restriction I was in constant rebellion.

To the fortunate child (on the whole I was a fortunate child, though remarkably slow to realise the fact), the mother sings lullabies and nonsense songs. The child thus becomes acquainted with poetry and rhythm from the start. This is presumably how it was at the beginning of human life on Earth. The mother follows an archetypal pattern. In every literature, poetry precedes prose.

It must be understood that one's bed takes some climbing into at first. Also that all doors are built unnecessarily tall, so that their handles are unreachable. All rooms are vast and full of strange smells and heavy objects. The corridor is so long that one can pedal up and down it madly on a red wooden scooter-affair.

Leading off the long corridor is a steep stairwell winding down to the shop and the outside world. At the top of this stairwell, a gate has been affixed, following an exciting incident when the red wooden scooter-affair has plunged with its rider down to the half-landing. On that half-landing stands an object of chinoiserie, an octagonal table with sharp legs, ebony, inset with slivers of mother-of-pearl, some of which have fallen out, others of which can be picked out.

In the front room, looking up Norwich Street, stands an iron-frame upright piano, given to Dot by her father on her wedding day.

This front room has a pleasant window seat from which to gaze at life as it moves in and out of the shops of Norwich Street – the butcher's, the grocer's and Mr Fanthorpe's music shop. We do not discover until later years that Mr Fanthorpe also has a son, Lionel, who will grow up to be another science fiction writer.

The most interesting features in this room are its pictures. Framed in gold, here and in the long corridor, are desert scenes. Palm trees wave. Steely-eyed Bedouin gaze over dunes into scorching distance. Camels gallumph in camel-like fashion across the Sahara. Every-where is golden sand, exactly the colour of the frames. Bill has been in Egypt during the war, that war to which constant reference is made.

Before I am very old, I find this home imprisoning. As I go from room to room, I am followed, talked to, instructed. Dot still lives out the nightmare of having lost her previous child, that paragon of daughters; this may explain the tense family atmosphere. I struggle against the unremitting surveillance under which my mother places me. I know that all about us, unseen, the necessities of commerce, the intense life of the shop go on, crammed with people, circum-stances, adventure.

The window of the room which is sometimes a breakfast room, sometimes a bedroom, has a special attraction. I can slide it open silently without Dot hearing, and climb out on to a slippery roof. From there, proceeding with care, I can make my escape across a second roof. A jump, a swift heave, and I enter an open window some distance away from the flat: a small forgotten window . . .

Ah, now this is exciting – forbidden and therefore, of course, *naughty* . . . I am standing inside a room stacked full of big cylindrical cardboard boxes. Nobody knows where I am. In fact, I have arrived just above H. H.'s millinery department, situated over the drapery, the very hub of my grandfather's dominions.

The millinery department comes to hold an irresistible fascination. This room into which I have climbed was once the sitting room of a person or persons unknown. Beyond the room is a little uncarpeted staircase. Breathless with bravery, I creep up the stairs. The boards creak beneath my sandals. The stair twists up to two attic rooms.

The shop fades away. The tide of its boxes has not reached this high. A little sad narrow deserted house remains. Its walls are covered with floral paper, much faded. On one wall, a framed sentimental print still hangs; a girl clutches roses to her satin breast. Each room permits views of unknown roofs. Each possesses a grate with a mantelpiece crowned by a cloudy mirror. If I drag a horsehair chair over to peer into one of the mirrors, I can see myself, pale and interesting, ghostly. Who am I? Am I a different person for being in this phantom place?

The chair is black and leathery, punctuated with big leather studs. There are gas mantles beside the mirrors. The whole place must have come out of History!

And no one lives here!

Over the years, I often visit this phantom house. It becomes one of my secret refuges.

Occasionally, one of the young ladies from the millinery department tiptoes up the twisting stair and catches me. She likes to give me a scare. This is a skittish slender teasing type of person, wearing a neat black velvet dress and shining patent leather shoes. Everything about her is pretty. She has black hair and red lips. Her eyes are dark and lustrous.

When she catches me, I pretend greater alarm than I feel. She seizes and embraces me. I am pressed against her gentle velvet-clad bosom. While I am small, she sits me on her knee. Later, we will cram together into the big chair. She kisses me, teases me intolerably, kisses me again. Ah, her kisses! Everything about her I admire. This diversion will continue for some years; what is mainly her amusement certainly becomes mine as well. The power she has over me is the power women have over men.

Was I ever again, in all my years, so tortured and delighted, made sad and raised to ecstasy, encouraged to dream, to pursue a scent, to feel more than myself, caused to sing and run about, and to cry – was I ever again to be so over-brimmed with emotion, so excited, so enchanted, or so crazed with longing, as I was by that dark-haired young lady from the millinery? Oh yes, indeed I was. Many a time.

*　　　*　　　*

As the slow years pull their compartments along, I learn that this little phantom house, almost entirely devoured by trade, is where Bill and Dot first lived when they were married. This knowledge adds to the attraction of the silent rooms: they are part of the secret life my parents led before I was even thought of . . .

Dot always said that when they were first married, she and Bill used to lie in bed between those walls with the floral paper and the cloudy mirrors and listen to the rats running – 'like greyhounds' – overhead.

The union of Wilson and Aldiss families resulted in a commission for my uncle Herbert Wilson. H. H. employed him to reshape and reface the shop. A thorough restyling of H. H.'s premises resulted. This would have been in 1921. Bert was responsible for the comfort of my parents' new flat, above Bill's outfitting department. Their first flat became absorbed by the millinery. He created a graceful façade for the shop. It featured large windows of curved glass, while an 'Aldiss' legend was set in mosaic at the entrance. Although the shop was eventually sold and carved up, Bert Wilson's façade has been preserved.

Dot tends towards shortness and plumpness, is fond of saying she 'suffers from Duck's Disease – bottom too near the ground'. This contrasts with Bill, who remains tall and thin throughout life. Dot has brown hair. She keeps it under a hairnet at night because it is always trying to escape her.

Dot is a homebody, content to remain indoors or at least to linger in her garden, tending her mignonette. Bill, on the other hand, retains a longing for outdoor life. There is always this dichotomy, he wishing for the Great Outdoors, she for the Small Indoors. Many a time, when Betty and I are drawing happily at the dining-room table, Bill in passing will say, 'Why don't you go outside?' His way of bringing up children is largely admonitory.

In her East Dereham phase, Dot is generally 'poorly'. Dr Duygan arrives briskly with his black medicine bag, to prescribe whisky-and-soda and a lie-down after lunch. Teetotal though she is, Dot obeys to the letter. She keeps cachous in her handbag for when she goes out. This is another way in which you tell the sexes apart: men never suck cachous.

Suffering from teeth problems, Dot's face becomes swollen. Gazing at herself in the glass, she complains, 'I look more like a pig than a woman.'

Four-year-old son, brightly, placatingly, 'You make a very pretty pig.' Flattery will become his stock-in-trade.

Dot is amused. All is well, therefore.

Later in life, I come to realise not only that Dot suffers from depression at this period, but that she combats it by a method her son unconsciously imitates: she cheers herself up by making others cheerful, by jokes which often include making fun of herself. It is a kindly fault.

My role in life, according to Dot, is to remain by her side until I am old enough to be sent to Miss Mason's Kindergarten, where middle-class Dereham kids are instructed. Yet I can easily give her the slip, to escape into the shop, becoming lost on the premises and beyond.

Downstairs in our hall are two doors, one to the outside world, where the step is scrubbed white with Monkey Brand, one into Father's outfitting department. This department is immense, a cavern filled with many places for a young subversive to hide.

Rows of coats and suits, enormously high; ranks of deep drawers, oak with clanky brass handles inset; long counters; islands of dummies wearing the latest slacks in Daks; disembodied legs and feet displaying Wolsey socks; heavy bolts of suitings, wrapped about a wooden core; a repertoire of felt hats; much else that is wonderful.

And, above all, the staff. I have complete confidence in their entertainment, as they in my distraction, value. Betts, Cheetham, Beaumont, Norton and the rest. Their names over the years have become a litany.

They work long hours and must be frequently bored; nothing is as tedious as being a shop assistant (but at least they are not part of the dole queue that forms regularly down Church Street). They all wear suits. To look extra alert, they sometimes stick pencils behind their ears, points forward, or a number of pins into their lapels, or else they drape a tape measure round their necks. Safe from the dole they may be, but time hangs heavy; so the intrusion of a small hurtling body, ideal target for a knotted duster, provides a welcome diversion. Oh, what glorious scraps and chases among the fixtures! What laughter!

There in his little empire, Bill is at his most content. He is on good terms with his staff. Although he runs an orderly business, he too seems to welcome me in the shop, allowing me to run about as I will, providing a little amusement for the chaps.

His office is tucked at the far end of the shop, next to two fitting rooms. Here he sometimes interviews commercial travellers. When I published an article on the shop in a newspaper during the eighties, one of those travellers, long retired, wrote bitterly to me, saying how little he earned, and how H. H. Aldiss always paid as stingily as possible for his suits. He slept in his car when on the road, to save money.

As the slow Dereham afternoons wear on, a tray of tea is delivered to Father's office. It comes from Brunton the Baker, a few doors away. Brunton makes the most delectable pork pies; it also does teas for businesses. Father's trays include a small selection of buns and tarts. Any young hopefuls hanging about just after four are sometimes permitted to snaffle a jam tart.

Every evening at closing time, the bare boards of the shop are watered from a watering can and then conscientiously swept. Dust covers are thrown over the stock. The staff, young and high-spirited, departs, whistling into the night. The whole place becomes gorgeously spooky, and would pass muster as an Egyptian tomb.

So let me continue the tour of this lost Arcadia, to the front of the shop, past the little window of the cash desk, where a pleasant cashier called Dorothy Royou sits, past my uncle Bert's front entrance, down a slight slope, into the drapery. We will proceed round the property in a clockwise direction.

The drapery is the domain of H. H. himself. He rules over about fifteen women assistants, all dressed in black. I call him H. H., but everyone – including his sons and my mother – addresses him and refers to him as 'The Guv'ner'. The Guv'ner he is, monarch of all he surveys.

I am not welcome in this department. One does not fool about here. The ladies are far more respectable, and less fun than the men.

At the front of the drapery is the door into the street. Ladies entering here have the door opened for them, and are ushered to a chair at the appropriate counter. With their minds grimly set on fabrics at four and three farthings a yard, they certainly don't wish to see a small boy skipping about the place.

To the left of the front door as you enter are grand stairs which sweep up to the millinery, presided over by sombre ladies. To the right, is the very citadel of H. H.'s empire, the keep of the castle. This is where Miss Dorothy Royou sits secure, with her little windows looking out on both the men's and the ladies' departments, receiving payments, distributing change. And behind her cabin, on to which she has a larger window, is the Office. The Office is situated in the heart of the building. Miss Royou can communicate with anyone in the Office. The Office is dominated by a safe as large as – and slightly resembling – the front of a LNER locomotive of recent design. Near this safe sits H. H. himself, cordial in a gruff way, impeccably shaved.

Every morning, H. H. walks to his shop from his home, 'Whitehall', buys his morning newspaper from Webster's in Dereham town square, and then enters the establishment next door, the shop of Mr Trout the Hairdresser. H. H. sits in one of Mr Trout's chairs and is shaved with a cut-throat razor by Mr Trout himself. He hears the gossip of the town before leaving and walking at a leisurely strut to open up his premises for the day. Bill is already in his department.

Before leaving H. H.'s office, you must notice the door on its rear wall, seldom opened. The old premises are riddled with more secret passages than you ever heard of in *Boys' Stories*. The passage behind this door is dark, and leads – miraculously, to a youthful mind – back into Bill's part of the shop, where you can pop up unexpectedly behind a counter, to the feigned astonishment of Betts & Co., who stagger about as if they have seen a miniature ghost. It always takes them a minute or two to recover from their fright.

To add to the fascination of this passage, it contains a *blocked-up window*. It is clogged up to knee-height by old sales posters and cardboard effigies of men in striped suits looking sideways.

Leaving H. H.'s office in the regulation way, you are back in the drapery. At its far end are two doors, one a sinister, battered, mean affair, probably stolen from Norwich prison. The other is more of a doorway: its double doors, painted dove-grey, have inset windows of frosted glass, adorned with traceries of flowers and ferns, and birds having a good time.

The criminal door slams closed when you struggle through it, while the ladylike doors remain always open, welcoming customers into an elegant showroom, where there are grey Lloyd Loom chairs in which ladies sit while sucking cachous and trying on gloves or whatever it is ladies try on.

You fight your way through the criminal door. SLAM! it goes as you pass into night.

Another secret passage! This one enormously long, so dark that it could be in the bowels of the Earth. Lit only by one light, half-way along.

The far end of the drapery tunnel is not the end of all things. A bizarre room without windows is situated there, all wood, all drawers, with things hanging. Too scary by half to enter. Take a right turn at a run and daylight gleams ahead. You can escape into the yard, and freedom.

Or you can climb a mean flight of stone stairs, which rises just before you reach the yard door. At the top of these stairs, you come (but not very often) into a huge echoing room under a high pitched roof, its stresses held at bay by transverse metal bars. It is a vast room, like a hangar for light aircraft. Several people work here, on either side of a long battle-scarred table. Sewing machines whirr. They are presided over by a huge woman dressed for all eternity in red flannel, matching the flames in her face.

'What do you want, boy?'

'I came to see how you were getting on.'

'Well, keep quiet, then.' The kid's the boss's son, ain't he?

The red flannel terror has a gas ring burning by her side, guillotines being hard to come by in East Dereham. Things steam, pudding-like, but do not smell like puddings. Flat irons of antique brand and purpose heat over radiators. The denizens of this department are making felt and other hats and goodness' knows what else. The red-faced Queen of the Inquisition has wooden heads which split in twain at the turn of a wooden screw. Pieces of material are strewn everywhere on the huge central table, as if laid for a banquet of cloth-eaters. The gas hisses. The pale-faced people stare, saying nothing. They have lived here for ever, their existence controlled by the huge terror in red. I turn to leave.

'And shut the door behind you,' yells the terror. She roars with laughter at what she mistakes for a joke.

There is someone else in the aircraft hangar, a man, the only man. Father calls him 'Perpsky'. Perpsky dresses in a pin-stripe suit snappier, darker than anyone else's, and manages to wear the tape measure rather flashily round his neck. He is bald and cheerful. He likes to sit me on his knee and tickle me. Although I do not care for this, I am too polite to say so. Father tells me to stay away from Perpsky. Later, Perpsky leaves H. H. and sets up on his own as tailor and outfitter.

So now you are in the yard, in the middle of the topographical tangle, with buildings all around, each devoted to different aspects of the retail trade. Removal vans come and go, the name 'H. H. Aldiss', complete with a curly underlining, large in mock-handwriting upon their sides.

Here is a giant Scots pine, which you can see from the sitting-room windows. It grows outside Bill's garage. The Rover is kept here, square and black, inside its house with mica windows. It sulks if not driven regularly and its batteries go 'flat', although I detect no change in their proportions. To start up the vehicle, Father produces a double-angled key, inserts it under the front bumper and with enormous effort produces a faint coughing from the engine – polite at first, then furious at being disturbed. Exciting blue poisonous gas fills the garage. I love the smell of it and inhale deeply. The car runs on Father's favourite petrol, Pratt's High Test.

Behind the garage stands the engine room, where the shop's electricity was once generated. Here is a huge brutal machine with pistons, levers and gauges, all unmoving and unmovable. It is silent now. Its day has come and gone: after the dinosaur, company electricity.

The outside passage to the left of the engine house is narrow and threatening. On its other side is a slim-shouldered wooden door, set in a crumbling brick wall. Once the door was painted red. Now it is a sort of shabby rose, and flakes of old paint can be picked off with a fingernail. It has a funny wooden bobbin latch – all part of a bygone day we cannot decipher.

Go through this door and here's another puzzle from the past. A narrow lane with a gutter running down the middle, which ends in a brick wall; it is a little street leading back to Victorian times. To the left is a high brick wall, the wall marking the end of the drapery department. And to the right . . . a row of low, two-storey terraced cottages, three of them, with bobbins at each door. Creepy though it is, the brave can still enter the cottages, can even venture up stairs that creak horrendously as you go, to peer out of the tiny upper windows.

Not only are the cottages almost certainly haunted, they are stuffed with ungainly goods. Black enamelled bedsteads, for instance, wrapped about with twisted straw, babies' cots enclosed in sisal. Here too reposes a huge old wicker Bath chair with two yellowing tyred wheels. The cottages are now stores, demoted and outmoded.

You creep away and come back to the yard. The yard is wider here, leading to the stables. On the right is the Factory, built, Norfolk-fashion, of knapped flints interspersed by rows of brick which mark its three storeys. Against the factory walls is my sandpit where I play. I build castles with tunnels sweeping through them. I use woodlice – 'pigs' – as the inhabitants of these fortifications. Sensing that they may not entirely enjoy this occupation, since I have woken them from cosy sleeps under stones, I make a vow to the woodlice that, if they will play with me, I will be kind to them for the rest of my life, and never kill a single one.

Over sixty years, I have kept my vow. Indeed, a tribute to 'pigs' is paid in *Helliconia Winter*, where they are called *rickybacks*, a more friendly name than woodlice. Rickybacks survive for thousands of eons on Helliconia, as woodlice have done on Earth.

There's a fence opposite the Factory. Behind this fence is our garden. That is to say, Dot and Bill's garden, some way distant from the flat, but much enjoyed by Dot. Father has bought her a summer-house. It looks across the lawn towards the row of cottages.

These old cottages were built for the live-in staff, not of H. H., but of his vanished predecessor. Conditions in those little rooms must have been primitive. The gutter in the middle of their lane indicates as much.

Dot is fond of the garden and spends some time there, occasionally sighing and wishing she were as free as a bird. When her mother, Grandma Wilson, or Cousin Peggy comes to stay, we sit in the summerhouse. Grandma in still in her widow's weeds, and remains that way until her death. I practise reading to her.

Dot furnishes it as if it is her doll's house. She subscribes to *Amateur Gardening*, which gives away colour prints of flowers, generally flowers flopping about in bowls and vases. At least once a month, one blossom is seen to have fallen from its bowl on to the surface of a highly polished table. Mother cuts these pictures out and frames them in passe-partout – words to which I am for a time addicted, learning the eccentric way in which they are spelt. Dot hangs her pictures in the summerhouse.

My cousins and I are naughty. If The Guv'ner catches me, I get a yardstick across the back of my bare legs. Sometimes Bill gives me a more ceremonial whacking. I do not cry. What I most dislike is that afterwards he squats down to make me shake hands with him and announce that we are still friends.

God also gets fed up with my naughtiness. As gods will, he devises more subtle tortures than any mere father can. In the garden stands a low-growing thorn tree. I rush into the garden one day, shrieking. Possibly I am three, a peak shrieking time. I find two of the yard dogs there, growling furiously. They have chased one of the yard cats into the thorn tree. The cat crouches on a branch, looking down at the dogs, just out of reach of their snapping jaws.

My arrival startles the cat. It decides to make a run for it. Leaping from the tree, it has gone only a few feet before the dogs are on it, baying with fury.

Next moment – in the words of Handel's *Messiah*, 'Behold, I show you a mystery . . . we shall all be changed, in a moment, in the

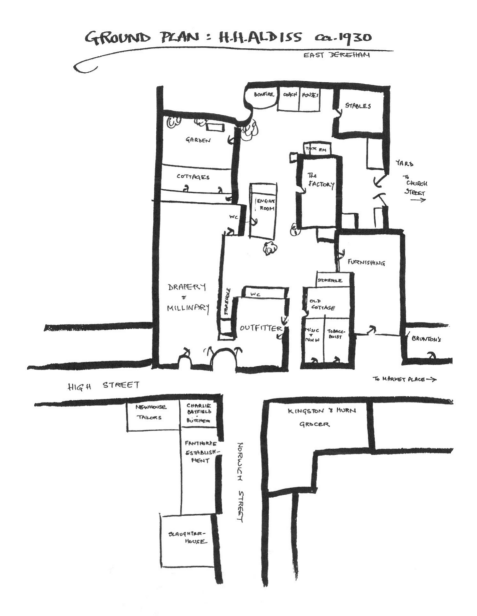

GROUND PLAN : H.H.ALDISS ca.1930

EAST DEREHAM

twinkling of an eye, at the last trump.' The cat is changed in the twinkling of an eye. It becomes meat. It becomes an incoherent red mess, stretching, stretching, as the two dogs rush past me, each fastening on to a strand of flesh, running off growling in parallel.

For many months this terrifying image, and the guilt attendant on it, dominated not only my waking hours.

For ever after there was to be,

> . . . that sorrow at the heart of things
> which glides like water underneath thin ice,
> Bearing away what is most innocent
> To darkness and the realm of things unseen,
> Lending our joys a meaning never meant.

Dogs were everywhere.

Bill and Dot, in their carefree days before children overtake them, keep Airedales. They breed them and at one time have fourteen. At shows around Norfolk and Norwich they win prizes. These are their happy times, before my arrival, even before the steel-engraving angel. Just beyond my standpit stands a shed, later to be a tool shed, in which Dot boils up sheep's heads and oats with which to feed the dogs.

Occasionally, after closing, Bill and Gordon would organise a rat hunt in the outbuildings, and send the dogs in. What a fury of barking! Into blackest corners rush the terriers, emerging with grey bodies clamped between their jaws.

The dogs are sold off one by one. Only an old lady, Bess, is kept as a faithful pet. When I am an infant of no more than a year, Bill and Dot are busy. I learn to walk – this is family legend, not a real memory – by clinging to Bess's tight curls. Patiently the old dog goes forward, step by step. Step by step, I stagger with her.

When Bess dies, Dot buys a smooth-haired terrier we call Gyp. Faithful Gyp! He can be induced to pull a big wooden engine down the length of our corridor.

H. H.'s premises are a child's ideal adventure playground. Full of horror as well as pleasurable excitement. I can be wild for a whole hour before tea time. My favourite film actor is Tom Mix. Tom Mix, the great cowboy star, and his horse Tony perform an amazing stunt. I talk about it for months.

Mix is being pursued by a whole gang of bad men in black hats. They are drawing closer, but he might escape by galloping across the railroad. Unfortunately, at that moment, along comes a freight train with many trucks, winding slowly across the prairie. It looks as if it's all up with Tom Mix.

But happily – in the nick of time! – there's one, just one, flat truck in the middle of the train. Without a pause, Mix spurs on Tony, crouches low over the gallant animal's neck and – wowee! – they jump right over the moving flat car and are away to safety.

Much as I admire Tom Mix and other cowboys, I want not to be a cowboy but an Indian. For one birthday – but perhaps this lies on the far side of the Five Year Abyss – I am given a Red Indian suit, plus head-dress with coloured feathers (far too bright for realism, I think), a tomahawk, and a bow and arrows.

What I do with the arrows gets me into hot water. But an Indian brave can always climb and trees are meant to be climbed. There are two favourites in the garden and another just outside, crowning a rockery.

The trees inside are a laburnum and an elder. The laburnum slopes in such a way that I can swarm up it and on to the top of a brick wall to hide among the foliage of the second tree, the elder. He lies there, elegant and at ease, yet a threat to all baddies, until danger passes.

The tree just beyond the garden is much bigger, a full-grown elm. I find a way of climbing it. All things considered, it is wonderful. I have no fear of heights. Up I go. Elms become easier to climb the further one goes. I am able to gain almost the topmost, outermost twig, far above the ground.

This is a sort of paradise, to be above the world and its troubles, to be among the birds and rushing air. It's easy to be up a tree. You hang on and make yourself comfortable. Everything below is transformed, amusing.

One thing cannot be escaped, even in the crown of an elm: one's characteristics. I call cheerfully to one of the staff passing below, proud of my newly acquired skill. The staff takes fright and runs to tell my mother. She rushes from the flat, to stand under the tree in her apron and beg me to come down before I break my neck.

'You don't love me.'

'Of course I do. Come down at once.'

'Tell me you love me, then I'll come down.'

'I love you, you idiot, I love you. Come down or I shall fetch The Guv'ner.'

I climb down. I have discovered a secret weapon.

*   *   *

We still have a way to go to complete the tour of H. H.'s premises. Now we are far from the street, where a bonfire of discarded boxes burns almost continuously. It is confined within a low stone wall. My cousins and I dare each other to jump in. We wonder if this is the Mouth of Hell we hear so much about in church.

Next to the bonfire, the old coach houses, black-painted, now repositories for hay and straw, and the rat Utopia into which Bill and Gordon's terriers are occasionally thrust. We are in the area of the stables, at the far end of the property. Here are cobble-stones underfoot, to allow horse urine to drain peacefully away. Just opposite the coach houses stands the tack room, while further ahead are the stables where the horses are confined.

This region is presided over by one of the shop's great characters. His name is Nelson Monument. Monuments still live in East Dereham. Nelson is the stable man from the late twenties onward. On ceremonial occasions, he wears a top hat and tails. Most of the time he is in cords, leggings and a big rough coat. His hasty temper is legendary. He has earned himself the nickname of Rearo. For this reason he, and particularly his shiny top hat, have become targets for the wit of Betts & Co. Rearo cannot enter the outfitter's premises without catching one of those notorious knotted dusters on the nut. His furious response, as he looks about for the culprit, is always greatly enjoyed.

'Oh dear, did something hit you, Mr Monument?' Betts enquires.

Rearo retreats in dudgeon to his little tack room, sweet with the stench of horses. There a little fire burns, except in high summer, to dry out the harness.

The tack room stands next to the tool shed where Dot once cooked sheep's heads. You can climb on to the roof of the shed and from there leap on to the tack-room roof. If by chance you have with you a sack soaked in water, you can lay it over the top of the chimney.

In a minute, reliably, Rearo will be smoked out of his den, and rush furiously into the yard to see *what blighter done it.*

There is no one in sight.

Outside the tack room stands a large metal water bin, wheeled. Occasionally it contains not water but bran. In the bran lies a chunk of rotten meat. The whole bin crawls with maggots, swarming from the meat. The stink is bad, the sight curiously fascinating. We do not, in those early years, entirely grasp the connection with human mortality. These maggots, full of blind life, are destined to be impaled on hooks and drowned in one of the Norfolk Broads during Bill's and Gordon's fishing expeditions.

Mortality is one of the mainstays of the stable area. The great black horses in their wooden stalls, where they stomp and kick restlessly, and look down with disdain on visiting boys, are funeral horses. All they see of the outside world is the road to East Dereham cemetery and back. Their destiny is to pull a glass-sided hearse.

On such occasions, the horses wear black plumes, and are preceded by my uncle Gordon, transformed into a comic figure of piety, dressed to look as black as the mares, complete with top hat instead of plume on head.

Like a Communist state *a parvo*, H. H. Aldiss will look after you from cradle to grave.

By the rear gates, we come on one last place to explore. A narrow exterior flight of stairs leads up into the top floor of the Factory. Here is a series of small wooden rooms in which the tailors live. Some sit cross-legged on a low bench. They mark their suitings with soapy triangular pieces of chalk.

These men are miserable. One is crippled. They do not wish to talk. They work long hours in poor light. It is too late to speculate upon their home life.

Everything in H.H.'s domain connects with something else. There is an escape route from the tailors into the Factory proper. The Factory is the major storehouse for all manner of items. A whole floor is given over to rolls of linoleum. They stand solemnly together in a leafless lifeless forest. The carpeting forest is more amenable. On the ground floor is a coconut matting forest, a very hairy forest, inhospitable to juvenile life. Yet in the middle of it is a secret nook, a hidey-hole among the prickly orange trunks. Here I take Margaret Trout, whose father shaves H. H.'s cheeks every morning. When we are snugly concealed, I kiss her.

She sits tight. I propose marriage to her. She agrees. The union is sealed with a toffee. Much mockery from Dot and Bill when they hear about it (from someone else, not from me; even at that early age, I know how to keep my affairs to myself). But that event is on the other side of the great Five Year Abyss. The engagement is broken off when I witness Margaret Trout being violently sick at school, just outside the front door, by the holly tree.

Another picture from this time. It illustrates a serial story in the children's department of our daily newspaper The picture shows a small boy sitting by the hut where he lives. The sun shines brightly. He forms the shadow of his two hands into the silhouette of a duck. Unfortunately, the duck flies away. Thus, the boy loses his shadow.

Losing one's shadow is like the loss of one's reflection, as happens in Offenbach's *The Tales of Hoffmann* and elsewhere. It is equated with losing one's soul.

The boy travels the world in search of his shadow, to find it eventually in China.

The picture holds a grand mystery for me. I colour it, and wish to go to China myself. From then on, China becomes a permanent flavour in the stews of my interior thought. Impossible though it would have seemed to Bill and Dot, their son will in time mingle with Chinese people, and will go to China. He will wonder if that story was the first step along the way.

Now we have come to the end of our tour of The Guv'ner's domains, except for the furnishing shop. The furnishing shop has staff doors opening on to the central yard, though its customers' arcade and entrance is on the High Street. This is Gordon's province and boys are unwelcome here.

We say nothing of what goes on underground. Two stokeholds feed the central heating of the various parts of the shops. Ferocious men shovel coal into boilers. Here, too, boys are unwelcome, in case they catch fire.

This great various place, the property of my grandfather, H. H. Aldiss, is where I passed my first five years of life, imbibing all its joys and terrors. It remains vivid to me, a complete little bubble of existence. To be exiled from it was to experience a burden of inexpressible loss. Of that loss I could speak to no one.

V

The Small Town

The tale of East Dereham cannot be understood without glancing occasionally at the wider backcloth of English history which commenced in time out of mind, and is still in the weaving.

Noel Boston & Eric Purdy
Dereham, the Biography of a Country Town

East Dereham is a peaceful place. Sleepy, some might say. It is a small market town, of some importance in the district. In the twenties and thirties, the cattle market was much alive. The bellowing of ill-treated animals filled the town every Friday.

When I was bustling through it with hoop and top, Dereham still had about its chops the brown gravy stains of the Victorian era. The High Street was illuminated by gas. As night fell, the lamplighter trudged along with his hooked pole, to catch one of the two rings on the gas jet which, when pulled, lit the mantle. The pallid gaslight was like an apparition: ghastly the faces of all who passed beneath.

The magnificent George Borrow, who was born in Dumpling Green, speaks of East Dereham as a 'dear little place'. It is also a place with its share of horrors. Opposite the façade of H. H. Aldiss's emporium, two shops stand on either side of the corner of Norwich Street. One is a butcher's shop, run by Charlie Bayfield (admired and scorned by Bill in equal amounts); often drunk. On the other corner is a grocer, Kingston & Hurn, much frequented by Dot.

Just up from Bayfield's is Fanthorpe's music shop, where The Guv'ner buys me a wind-up gramophone for my sixth birthday. The gramophone comes with six records ('Impressions on a One-String Phone Fiddle', etc.). Beyond Fanthorpe's stand the huge double wooden gates to Bayfield's slaughterhouse. I watch as cattle are driven – whacked – down Norwich Street towards the gates of hell. Men shout at the animals. Although I am repeatedly told that cows never suspect what is about to happen to them, I remain un-reassured.

In they go, poor beasts, hooves slipping on greasy cobbles in their haste. They are forced inside the abattoir. The doors close behind them. Bellowings are heard. Scuffles. Thuds. Silence. All is over. Then blood begins to flow in a torrent beneath the double gates into Norwich Street. A red stream, a tide carrying pieces of straw with it, rushes in the gutter towards our shop. It disappears into a drain outside Charlie Bayfield's sawdusty door.

Again a sense of incredulity. Could that stream be poured back into the cows, to make them live again?

Dot takes me and Gyp shopping. We meet someone Dot knows. The two women are immensely friendly. As they stand chatting, I bask in all the benevolence flowing between them. Dot is happy for once. This is how life should be. They part, seemingly with reluctance. Directly the other woman has gone, Dot is vicious.

'Oh, how I hate that woman. What a hypocrite and liar she is, what a snake in the grass!' So Dot cannot be trusted. Appearances deceive.

You cannot distinguish between adults telling the truth and adults lying. I do my best to faint. No luck.

Dot is friendly – or she pretends to be – with Nellie Hurn. She often takes me through the pleasant-smelling grocery shop, through a mirrored door, into Hurn's private hall. Nellie, like us, lives upstairs. The stairs are dark. Everywhere is stained brown, adding to the darkness. I enjoy the thrillingness of this, and kick the brass stair rods that hold the stair carpet in place as we go up. Dot reproves me. She calls 'Coo-ee!' as we ascend. Comes a faint answering cry.

Nellie Hurn lives in the front room, which is entered through a bead curtain. It is like coming suddenly on the Orient. The beads hang there, multicoloured rain suspended in mid-fall. They are strange, confusing, as we push through them. Inside a dark room sits Nellie – sits or rather reclines in an adjustable chair. Nellie is pale from playing too much patience at a round brass Benares table. She smokes a black paper cigarette while gazing frequently out of the window.

I too gaze out of her window while the women talk. There stands our shop, H. H., with the windows of our flat above. So supposing

I could get back there very quickly, *terribly* quickly, would I be in time to see myself staring out at myself at Nellie Hurn's window?

Dot and Nellie sip tea from delicate cups with serrated edges. Dot takes her tea with sugar and without milk, whereas Bill takes his with milk and without sugar. For some years I believe this to be a sexual difference: all men do it one way, all women do it the other.

I never see Nellie outside her dark room, exempted from the world by that curtain of suspended raindrops. We visit other women in the town who also spend their years reclining, as though some nerve in their minds has been fatally sprained.

Kingston & Hurn specialise in teas. Dot buys it in packets which are made up at the counter. The tea is weighed, poured on to a flat piece of paper. The assistant smartly knocks this paper up into a box, folds it, seals it neatly, Bob's your uncle. I long to have a try.

On one occasion, Kingston & Hurn promote Mazawattee tea. In their window they erect an advertisement which moves. There, larger than life, but of painted wood, sit Alice, the doormouse (asleep) and the Mad Hatter, at the tea table. The Mad Hatter pours tea from a huge red teapot. Alice holds out her cup then drinks from it, smiling with satisfaction. She then holds out her cup for more, and the Mad Hatter pours again. Alice drinks, still smiling.

She will drink and smile for ever. The Mad Hatter will pour for ever. He is relentless and will forever pour, and she forever drink, the tableau like a ghastly parody of John Keats' Grecian Urn, the tea and they

> For ever warm and still to be enjoy'd,
> For ever drinking and for ever drunk . . .

I stand there, nose to the glass. Dot drags me home. But I can run upstairs to watch the display across the road. From our front window I get a good view.

They are still at it. The big red teapot is still dispensing its pretend Mazawattee. He still pretends to pour, and she to drink, pour and drink. The model works by electricity. But I think to myself that possibly Alice and the Mad Hatter have feelings: since they look human, perhaps they feel human. Perhaps they are forced to pour and drink, pour and drink – and all the while, smiling, they don't wish to.

The existential dilemma overwhelms me. I cannot think my way out of the riddle. This enforced behaviour – all this enforced smiling – has wider and uncomfortable implications.

Of course I understand that this advertisement is simply a construct. But the incident of the cat torn apart 'in the twinkling of an eye' shows how narrow is the threshold between living and non-living things.

So supposing the figures are thirsty and want real drink while having pretend drink forced on them from that hideous red teapot...

And after all, we humans go on day by day, doing the same things automatically. Supposing we merely think we are real, the way Alice does in Hurn's window. Suppose our feelings, like Dot's, are insincere...

Are we stuck in a window with God outside, watching us go through the motions?

I am haunted by the Mazawattee Tea Paradox, Schrödinger's Cat made flesh, or at least three-ply.

Dereham appears to be a God-fearing place. The religious habit in the late twenties and early thirties of the century is bound up with memories of the war, still fresh in people's minds, and therefore with the social life of the country, and so with a patriotism that is now, at the end of our century, greatly diluted – probably for the better, the xenophobic element being also diluted.

In the United States, religion, or at least a frequent reference to the Almighty, is similarly bound up with social life, patriotism and big business (What's good for God is good for General Motors). A kind of official optimism is also involved. Whereas in Britain the prevailing mood is more one of scepticism. It suits us better. The garment is cut according to the cloth.

This is well illustrated on Armistice Day, 11 November, commemorated with due ceremony.

The film is here an old documentary. For its viewers it is over in a few seconds; for those involved it is a caesura in their lives, rendered more weighty by that sense of time dragging its feet which important events engender. It is raining slightly. Dot puts on her cloche hat and her coat with the part-belt below her bottom. She scrutinises herself in a mirror before slipping a cachou into her mouth. Snowfire has already been applied to her chapped hands – the Snowfire pot bearing a brave image of a brazier of coals flaming away in the midst of an icy waste. She turns to her son and crams his arms into a small red mackintosh. We go downstairs. Taking up an umbrella from the stand in the porch, she leads the way to the market square.

Other people hurry in the same direction. All wear hats, the men with caps or soft felt hats or even bowlers, the women with various confections, some from H. H.'s millinery, their offspring perhaps in berets or 'tammies'. Since I am only a little tacker, I also wear a tammy.

A considerable crowd has already gathered in the square. Uniforms, medals and banners are among them. People stand, solemn-faced, saying little. They are roofed by black umbrellas which make soft drumming noises as the rain falls on them. Everyone waits.

A silver band plays. Solemn marches and hymn tunes are the order of the day. At eleven o'clock, maroons sound.

Everything stops. Time itself dare not utter a word.

The men remove their hats or, if they forget to do so, have their hats knocked off. Heads are bowed. Traffic halts. In H. H.'s shop, customers and staff will remain in suspended animation for the Two Minutes Silence. All over England and Wales and Scotland and Northern Ireland, the United Kingdom, silence prevails. A silence of mourning and thanksgiving.

The maroons sound again. Once more, normal lay life resumes. Hats go back on heads. The inhabitants of East Dereham close their umbrellas, shake them, and return to work.

'Mummy, what are you supposed to be thinking in the Silence?'

'You can thank God that your father survived the War.'

But if he had been killed, I begin to think, then I . . .

The church in Dereham is dedicated to St Nicholas. In the middle of the nineteenth century, its benevolent vicar was Benjamin Armstrong, extracts from whose diaries have been published. But of greater interest to the world of letters is the smaller church in the market square, squeezed between two shops. It is as ugly as if built by Thomas Hardy in his architectural phase. Its ugliness proclaims that no beauty has meaning, except the beauty of God (see inside). One cannot think that any Eastern religion would embody in stone such an absurd thought.

This is our church. It commemorates the poet William Cowper, who died in East Dereham in the year 1800. We are Congregationalists. If the documentary film is left running, it will catch us every Sunday entering this place of worship, Bill, Dot and Brian, in their Sunday best. We are greeted by our vicar, a small lively woman, Edna V. Rowlingson.

Our pew is at the rear of the church, on the left as you go in. The Guv'ner will be here. Also, in the pew just in front, Gordon's family, his sharp-nosed wife, Dorothy (née Childs), and their three children, Joyce, Derek and Tony. Not Gordon. Gordon is the organist. The Guv'ner will read the first lesson. Bill is 'linesman' with Mr Fox, and will move down one of the two aisles, taking the collection in a shallow wooden plate. The Aldisses really have religion buttoned up.

The interior of the church is different from anything else I know at that time. Not comfortable, with the seedy brown-sugar comfort of the Exchange Cinema, rather echoing voids and dumb surfaces, the solidity of pillars either being or resembling marble. The pulpit, into which our little reverend climbs to preach to us, is of the stoniest stone.

Miss Rowlingson is not shy. She speaks forthrightly, never forgetting she has children in her audience. All the same, we children are sinners like the rest of the congregation. Hell fire awaits us too. Oh, she's convincing, with that terrible inarguable faith also resembling marble. For years and years to come, I shall wonder, Is it true? The first lie, the first wank, the first shag in Calcutta: Is it true about hell fire? Am I to suffer eternal damnation?

To capture the attention of her congregation, the Revd Rowlingson leads into her terrible themes with the beginnings of an interesting story. She might open the sermon by saying, 'Last week, I decided to go into the country. I was walking in the fields near Swanton Morley, when suddenly I saw I was in a meadow with a large bull. The bull began to approach me from the far side of the field at an increasing pace. Temptation is rather like that bull . . .' We are back with damnation, which may gore us at any moment.

A scarcely audible sigh of disappointment escapes the children in the congregation. There are three characters in this fragment of story, the person, the bull, and God. Of these three, God is the least interesting. We don't know what the person and the bull may do, but God has made his position perfectly plain.

The bull has more options than God. He can charge at Edna and toss her, he can charge and funk it at the last moment, or he can simply walk about looking slightly down in the mouth, in the manner of English bulls.

It's the person who has the most options. She or he can walk stealthily away in the direction of the gate; or they can run like billyo for the gate; or they can try jumping over the hedge; or they can stand their ground and address the bull courteously, as the man did with the lion in the fairy story, hoping the bull will turn away, unable to think of an answer; or they can quickly

build a china shop in the field, whereupon the bull will pass into
it.

Pondering such questions, I find the sermon passing pleasantly.
For those expert with the divining rod, here may be divined the seed
of my science fictional habit. I have always preferred to write about
people than about bulls and other alien creatures.

Hymns with repetitive lines or meaningless words like 'Hallelujah!'
are most boring. I like the ones with geographical reference. 'From
Greenland's icy mountains/From India's coral strand . . .' Even better, 'Before the hills in order stood/Or Earth received her frame . . .'
What a vision that conjures up. I imagine the world as a jumbled
mess, swept by enormous waves.

At home, religious references are frequent, although often used
sarcastically. If one sulks or asks for sympathy, Bill is always ready to
intone, 'The noble army of martyrs . . .' On rising from bed, he greets
rainy days with 'Hail, smiling morn!' Dot enjoys a misquote: 'Just
as I am, without one flea'. (We are rural; fleas are not unknown.)

The church has its claims upon us. One claim is particularly life-
threatening. Visiting pastors come to stay with us over the weekends; we are so conveniently near the Cowper Memorial Church;
or perhaps Bill is low man on the Aldiss totem pole. They visit; we
house them.

The visits of pastors need much preparation. Dot and Diddy, our
favourite maid, are in the kitchen by Thursday, wondering what
they should cook for the weekend. How fussy is he? They work
on the assumption he will be pretty fussy, and are often right.
By Saturday morning, Dot makes a house search. As a religious
family, we are forbidden packs of cards, 'The Devil's picture book',
and all that. But there are incriminating signs of our lack of genuine
holiness which must be concealed.

The *Radio Times*, the paper containing lists of the week's wireless
programmes, is contained in a sort of stiff fabric jacket, on which
Dot has embroidered marigolds. It must go. Far too worldly. My
toys must be hidden away. Only Noah's Ark, my beautiful shining
Noah's Ark, may remain, in view of its exonerating connection
with the Old Testament.

What gets hidden under the sofa cushions is the *Passing Show*,
a weekly family magazine. The contents might include a new way
to cook a cake, how to make a perfect dovetail joint, an article on
a celebrity such as Gordon Richards, the jockey, or Sir Malcolm
Campbell, the world's land speed record holder, readers' letters, a

short story, a cartoon strip and a serial. The serials include two of Edgar Rice Burroughs' *Venus* stories.

These serials are illustrated by an artist called Fortunino Matania, whose individual style tends towards the female breast. For all I know, his real name is Joe Smith. The Italian name licences him to give vent to tits at a time when they are still suppressed.

It is tits the visiting pastors cannot abide. So *Passing Show* goes under the sofa cushions.

Sometimes the pastors prove to have more whimsy than Wesley in them. Come Saturday evening, they have settled in, and sit companionably round the fire with the parents. The atmosphere becomes a little less stiff. The preacher ventures a joke. Perhaps he ventures to ask if Mrs Aldiss would be greatly offended if he smoked a pipe.

Why, no. Of course. Yes. Do. By all means. She will fetch him an ashtray.

And would he by any chance like a little something with his pipe?

Well . . .

Well, it happens we have some elderberry wine in the cupboard. Home-made, of course. Bill finds a little sip now and again is good for him.

Well. If you're going to have one . . . I don't mind if I do, Mrs Aldiss.

Please call me Dot.

The Lord has spoken against all alcoholic drink but, in His mercy, has made an exception for home-made elderberry wine. The berries come from the tree in the garden under which the Red Indians lurk.

All this delicacy, this hesitation, these taboos, may sound amusing to a later generation. No funnier than violence on the streets and hooliganism at sport and aggressive coarse language today is going to sound to the citizens of AD 2050. Nothing is really funny about the life of past generations: they had their problems and their pleasures, as we do today. It is simply that the problems in small particulars are different.

The caution not to offend, the delicacy over drink, the hospitality my parents offered (under whatever social pressure), the prurience over the innocuous *Radio Times*, even the dedication of these men who came and preached week after week – all that was how it was in 1930 in East Dereham. Yes, I am amused now; but that is my entitlement because I lived through it. And through it all runs something tender, a sort of unguarded wish to be better, kinder, decent, God-fearing – virtue as well as hypocrisy.

Poor Bill and Dot, how greatly they care, how greatly they are bound to the mores of time and place, as we all continue to be. For the *Zeitgeist* largely glides snake-like through our mortal lives, sloughing a skin now and again. And how greatly one of them at least rejoices when it befalls that they are exiled from this small town where the mores are particularly exacting.

But that crisis lies on the far side of the Five Year Abyss.

The *Passing Show*, with its pleasing title, lies on the far side of another gulf, the World War II Abyss. Its day is done. There is no family magazine like it now. But then, the family itself has disintegrated, if you are to believe the higher journalism.

How much brighter magazines are today. How they proliferate. How they specialise. Six on yachting. Seventeen or eighteen on cars. Twenty, thirty, on cooking and dieting. Fifty or more on PCs. On the upper shelves, rows of tit, bum and cunt magazines. No family magazine. Don't laugh at the thirties, okay? Among major gains, something has been lost.

Little conformist that I am, I do not mind the itinerant pastors, since my parents seem to like them. I come greatly to like Edna V. Rowlingson. I recognise in this bright, sparrow-like lady a real goodness; of course, at the time I do not phrase it in these terms. I know only that it is pleasurable to be with her. Although I am only one of her flock, she likes me. She cares about people. For this reason, she makes a splendid preacher. Perhaps if you really know her, you will find she is truly concerned to think we shall all go to hell. I am sorry when Bill jokes about her behind her back.

William Cowper is part of the mythology. The ugly little church that bears his name is built on the site of the old house in which he died. There is much in that very English poet to love – not only his poems but his letters, which display a gentle personality.

Cowper believed in eternal damnation, as I did. This is one way in which the national mentality has changed over the course of a generation. We can no longer believe that after death, if we have sinned, we shall enter hell. Hell has been acted out here on Earth in the time of Nazi Germany, when even the innocent went in their millions to a hell that beggars the imagination. A profound change in attitude has come about as a result.

*   *   *

The film continues, an 8mm epic. Year by year, I begin to discover more of East Dereham. At the far end of the market place is the Cabin. It stands behind the newly built war memorial. You climb a stair to it, hence its name. Inside, Dot and her son eat iced cakes. A few doors away, conveniently, is Mr Toomey, the dentist, who profits from the sale of the iced cakes. I am rewarded with lead soldiers whenever I visit Mr Toomey and do not make a fuss. I never fuss.

The reason why we all keep Mr Toomey in business is because of a habit of Bill and Dot's. By their bedside stands a tin of Callard & Bowser's Olde Mint Humbugs. At bedtime, they pop these corrosives into their mouths and their son's mouth. By the time the son is twelve, both parents have to wear false teeth.

Just beyond Mr Toomey's torture chamber is the entrance to the cattle market, past the Cherry Tree pub. On Fridays, this market fills with life. To me and my cousins, it seems to sprawl for miles. Some animals arrive by lorry, others by horse-drawn carts. Many are treated with cruelty, made to hurry, to be herded into metal pens. They slip, try to escape, are heartily beaten. Cows, bulls, sheep, ewes, a few goats, some with kid. All are kicked and cursed into appropriate pens. Blood, excrement, straw, fly everywhere.

Into small cages are crammed many kinds of living thing. Ducks, geese, hens, cockerels, several types of rabbit, stoats, ferrets, their cages marked with a warning not to touch. The ferrets fling themselves in a fury at their bars.

Perhaps rural life is always like that. Respect for animal life is not high.

My grandfather, The Guv'ner, is a JP in the time I know him. I like to go and play in the grounds of Whitehall, where my grandmother lies upstairs in bed. Whitehall looks vaguely Italianate. Wide eaves and a tower, sitting in the middle of the building, account for that. Its windows are large, their sills on the lower floor coming to within a foot of the ground. An ornate verandah runs along the front of the house. The place has a peaceful and generous air as it sits foursquare at the end of its long drive.

The gardens run a good way back, past the asparagus beds, the vegetable beds, the two sunken greenhouses, each of which is patrolled by age-old toads, the fruit trees, to a wide lawn fringed by sheltering trees and shrubs. Spinks is H. H.'s loyal gardener, and Spinks's loyal companion is H. H.'s dog, Spot. Spot is a wire-haired terrier. Three enormous black cats live at Whitehall. H. H. spoils them and talks to them, lowering his habitual guard.

H. H. bought Whitehall before the First World War in his cool offhand manner.

He is travelling back by train from London on one of his buying trips when he falls into conversation with another passenger. This passenger says he is leaving Dereham to live elsewhere and intends to sell his house. The Guv'ner says he happens to be looking for a suitable house.

The passenger says his house is fairly large, with good gardens and a field, the recreation ground, attached.

The Guv'ner knows the house.

By the time the two men reach Dereham station they have shaken on it.

Grandma Aldiss, the farmer's daughter, once Lizzie Harper, is bedridden for as long as I am about. Dot knew her when she was well, and cherishes some of her recipes. One favourite recipe is for Pork Mould, a dish made with pigs' trotters. When cold, it is turned out of a mould rather resembling a child's sand castle. We eat it with Colman's mustard, and plain brown bread on the side.

I do not recall Bill ever going to Whitehall to see his mother. Dot often goes, and takes me with her. Dot will carry fruit or cornflour buns in her basket. She will be in her cheery mode.

We proceed upstairs to a room at the rear of Whitehall. Here long windows on two walls look down the length of the garden and across to The Rec, as the adjoining field is known. Lizzie lies patiently in bed, year after year. Self-effacing in the background, a nurse attends her, wearing a starched cap, uniform, and black cotton stockings.

Provided I do not make a noise, I am allowed a grape or two from the fruit dish by the side of the invalid's bed.

Why do I remember the room so well, with its long curtains with wooden rings on mahogany rods, and a wash stand with basin and jug on it, and the swan-neck brass light fitting over the bedside table, and the grey patterned carpet, and the general grey stuffiness of the room – and yet cannot call to mind a single feature of Lizzie, or anything she said? Or anything Bill ever said about her?

What has gone wrong? Two of her four children died. Is there some great disappointment in her life? She leaves no record. As far as I know, she makes no complaint. She dies in 1930 or 1931. I fail to remember the event.

Every Christmas, we go up to Whitehall for Christmas dinner. It is a serious commitment. Beforehand, Bill and Dot become anxious.

Also present will be the rival brother's family. Gordon with his sharp-nosed Dorothy and their three children will outnumber us. I, by contrast, skip about, because I shall receive a present from The Guv'ner, and it might be a Hornby train. He always knows what young boys like.

Despite a roaring fire, the dining room at Whitehall is cold. There is no central heating. Dot always complains beforehand, applying Snowfire and cachous to their appropriate stations. I know without being told that she fears Dorothy's sharp nose, which bores holes in Dot's fragile self-confidence. I know without being told of the rivalry between Bill and Gordon. H. H. ignores these tensions.

In the room above the dining room lies Lizzie. She is not brought down, perhaps cannot be brought down, to join the fray.

We are seated, nine of us, round the table. The maid brings in the turkey. And I disgrace the family.

This humiliating memory must date from Christmas 1927, when I am twenty-eight months old. If it dates from the next year, then it proves I am a backward child. For a christening present, the Roddicks, family friends, give me a silver pusher. I adore the pusher. It is a miniature hand-held bulldozer. The pusher has a loop for a finger to go through and a tiny shovel blade. With this, food is pushed towards a spoon held in the other hand. It is a device to simplify eating for the infantile or retarded. This I employ on The Guv'ner's turkey, which in consequence has to be cut up for me.

One of Dot's great triumphs is to have delivered me into the world ten days before my cousin Tony is born. This, it is felt, is definitely one up on Dorothy.

But – here is Young Hopeful on one side of the table, still having his food cut up, still using this babyish implement. It is a gift to the opposing team. On the other side of the table, his cousin is already using a knife and fork, although not wisely or too well.

The contrast is immediately noted.

Oh, Brian still has his food cut up, does he, Dot?

Sometimes, yes, Dorothy. It's quicker, really.

You don't find the turkey at all tough, do you?

It's very tender. How is yours?

He's quite good with his little pusher. Tony has been using his knife and fork for some months now, haven't you, dear?

Yes, Mummy. Smarmy merriment.

It is a bad moment. More than a moment. I am out of favour for several days.

*   *   *

The contrast between H. H.'s two surviving sons is marked. Gordon is large, hearty, almost bald. He looks out at the world through owlish spectacles. The cashier, Miss Dorothy Royou, long after she has taken up another occupation and another name, tells me how Gordon persuades her on a drive into the country in his car and tries to seduce her. She refuses. He kicks her out of the jalopy and she has to walk home. Other young ladies in the shop, she informs me, suffered from the same tactics.

Gordon also keeps in touch with events at Newmarket and frequently absents himself from the shop to go down and watch the horse races. On Saturday, he takes his boys over to Norwich to watch Norwich City play. He is a sporting man, and can be found pretty often in The King's Arms in the market place.

Bill is of different build and habit. He is neat and spare, humorous, good-looking, less tall than his brother. He never in his life goes into a public house, and is teetotal for most of his years. He works hard in the shop and does not molest the ladies – or so the historic record asserts. He does not bet. Only once do we go to Newmarket with Gordon. Once a year, Bill and Dot will put a pound on the Irish sweepstake. God goes easy on the Irish sweepstake, perhaps because the Irish are so Catholic.

Bill does everything his father asks of him, is submissive, dutiful. Whereas Gordon has been known to cheek The Guv'ner and please himself.

On a wall in our long corridor, next to the photograph of Bill in a pierrot outfit, hangs a photo of Gordon and Bill as boys. They sit companionably on a rug together, with two terriers standing by. They wear caps and have guns tucked under their arms. Once they were friends. The photograph must cause Bill pangs of regret.

The traitorous thing is this, that I quite like Gordon and Dorothy. I occasionally go round to the Corner House where they live, where Dot never sets foot. They appear much richer than we are. Their house is better furnished. It is a puzzle. Also Dorothy has a huge folding tray table with raised edges, made especially for jigsaws; we work together amicably on a huge landscape which includes huntsmen. I labour under the impression that Dorothy is nice to me. I like my cousin Derek. And Gordon is generally genial if overbearing.

Tony and I kick a football about in their garden. He sends it through a window and bursts into tears. So I am one up on him. I would not cry.

Dorothy tells me a joke I am supposed to riddle out: 'The Queen reigns over China'. I know she does not reign over China, but eventually we tease out the word-play. She rains every night, into her china chamber pot.

We are all convulsed with laughter. Fancy thinking that of haughty Queen Mary! The mere idea of Queen Mary peeing sends us into fits.

I go home and tell the joke to Dot. She is far from laughter. It is disgusting and vulgar, not a joke at all. Like an earlier queen, Dot is not amused.

My picture of Dereham, which we leave finally when I am twelve years old, is coloured by the attitudes of my parents. Only later do I realise Bill's dependence on his father: he was my hero, and I thought he depended on no one. I perceive his dislike of Gordon, his brother, I soon realise how Dot suffers from paranoia.

She loves to accuse everyone of *backbiting*, while indulging in it herself. She is sweet to everyone's face, cruel when they have gone. She is nervous. She consults Dr Duygan, whose advice to drink a whisky-and-soda after lunch every day has not entirely resolved her unhappiness. She suffers from being overweight, so that we visit Yarmouth to buy Dr Scholl's shoes. Her largely unarticulated view of Dereham is that it is a kind of prison. Narrow-minded, she calls it.

She takes books from both Webster's, the bookseller, and from Starling's Lending Library. Starling's books come in a protective cardboard jacket on which is printed a legend: 'A Home without Books is like a House without Windows'. Dot often reads the legend aloud to me. 'How true!' she exclaims. Or perhaps more mysteriously she will say, 'Too true, O King!', quoting I know not what.

Gorleston on Sea figures large in our lives. From Dereham to Gorleston is about thirty-five miles. Gorleston is beautiful, a small, elegant seaside resort, with a bandstand and a pierrot show in summer. While I like everyone in the pierrot show, my favourite is the comedian ('I'm the one who makes you go ha-ha,' he sings as he comes on). Later we shall live in Gorleston for a while, as reported, until war breaks out, and the world we know falls into little bits, and the jolly rude picture postcards blow away down yesterday's beaches.

Before the Five Year Abyss opens at my feet, Dot escorts me every September to the Dereham fair. On one occasion, I escape from

Dot and rush to see a sideshow where a man stands bare-chested, swallowing watches offered by his audience. He gets hold of a turnip watch on a gold chain. He tips back his head and gulps it in, lowering it into his insides link by link, as if sinking an anchor into the North Sea.

He beckons me out of the crowd. Horrified, I go forward. I am forced to place my ear against his chest to give a sounding. I hear the watch ticking, entangled somewhere among the sea wrack of his lungs.

The watch is hauled up again, glittering with phlegm.

Another time, Dot plays the Wheel of Fortune, to win a yellow Norwich canary in a cage. She bears it home in triumph.

The bird becomes a favourite and 'sings its heart out'. Considering how it is imprisoned and can never fly again, the phrase seems appropriate. It (or she, rather) lays many eggs, which Bill blows, to keep the shells bedded on cotton wool in a tobacco tin. Both Bill and Dot are baffled by this sequence of eggs.

One day, Bill gets up to riddle yesterday's cinders and lay a fire in the grate, when he discovers the canary supine at the bottom of the cage, claws in the air. Alarmed, he takes it out and administers brandy to it on the tip of one of its feathers. The bird makes a full recovery, and continues to chirrup its song for many a year.

Bill, incidentally, is an expert on birds and birdsong. I stand with him, mute, on the edge of a great field. He waits under a tree, gun at the ready, for something for the pot, a rabbit or a pheasant. He wears plus fours and a cap at a rakish angle. I wear a tammy and rubber boots. A strange creaking note is heard distantly.

'That's a corncrake,' he tells me. It seems a curious name for a bird. Nowadays, I fancy, modern methods of farming mean that the song of the corncrake is no longer heard over Norfolk farmland.

The fair comes to East Dereham with the ripe apples of harvest time.

While we in the Congregational church are lustily singing that 'All be safely gathered in, Ere the winter storms begin', the fair people are gathering in on the outskirts of town, waiting to invade. Tony and I mingle with the gypsies, their dogs and horses – and probably Alfred Munnings RA. The large caravans, the big rides, the big roundabouts are pulled by traction engines. The engines whistle and scream as the lofty monarchs are stoked into life.

Here the film is unreliable. Clever editing suggests that every year I run in to town beside the turning wheels of one of these machines, along with other urchins. I do so at least once. The hint of perpetuity remains, so great is the delight.

The ground shakes as our traction engine rolls towards the market place. A savage man with a red kerchief round his throat shovels in coal, standing high above us, a god with a black face. The great painted wheels turn, the twisted brass barley-sugar sticks that support the roof gleam, the furnace looks like the entrance to hell, while the smoke tastes like a whiff of paradise. We run yelling beside it, drinking in its power, all the way to the market square.

At the far end of the square, the Dodgems rink goes up rapidly. Once, with my friend Buckie, I discover a half-crown in a car recently vacated. We rejoice in our luck.

A visual treat is erected at the H. H. Aldiss end of the market place. The big roundabout is built round the traction engine that powers it. Under the striped canvas roof, a parade of monstrous bright animals, cockerels, tigers, spirited white horses and dragons, dances round and round, up and down, barely restrained from breaking out into the crowd and freedom.

How the staff of H. H love the fair! During their lunch hour, their one brief taste of liberty during the day, the young ladies of the drapery department, like a flock of blackbirds in their dark dresses, fly towards the attractions, sweeping me up with them as they go.

There's my flirtatious millinery lady, all tease and flame! She shows her legs as we climb aboard the roundabout. Already the music starts, the platform begins to glide! I am lifted high by her, by her giggling friends, up, up on to the most Chinese of dragons. It seats three people. It begins to move. Up, down, up, down. The young ladies clutch me. I smell their perfumes. We all shriek. The music plays. The day shines and blurs.

Ah, the music of the big roundabout! The wheezing lungs of the boiler blow breath through unfolding punched paper, creating a din as powerful as the music. They play 'Destiny', 'The Sun Has Got Its Hat On', 'You Can't Stop Me from Dreaming', 'The Skater's Waltz', 'Alexander's Ragtime Band', and many more tunes.

At night I am put to bed. Dot kisses me goodnight. The fair is still going. It's getting rough, now that dusk closes in. Drunks are about. Who knows what's happening as crowds are drawn to the excitement from distant Toftwood, Shipdham and Swanton Morley – chaps with girls and whatever they do together. As I fade away into sleep I hear its music in the distance: 'You Are My Lucky Star', interpreted through that randy, wheezing music.

* * *

When I am older, I have a small sister to take to the fair. She loves it as much as I do.

The fair people come into the Aldiss shop, often dragging their curs with them at the end of a piece of rope. The men buy new suits, spending generously in heaps of small coin. By the time the fair is over, its stalls folded away, its glitter packed and gone, the rubbish and droppings swept from the market square and Church Street, the town is fairly hopping with fleas.

Dot stands my sister and me in the bath. She pulls off our clothes. She searches every inch of us for fleas and squashes them with a thumbnail, one by one.

VI

The Parents

My father told me . . . that mine was the middle State, or what might be called the upper Station of *Low Life*, which he had found by long Experience was the best State in the World, the most suited to human Happiness.

Daniel Defoe
Robinson Crusoe

T he film continues, in that eternal present of memory.
Dot at this period of her life is a moody person. She is in her early thirties when I am born. She has yet to recover from the death of her daughter in 1920, confronting her naughty son with the perfections of the dead girl, with the result that this phantom little person preys heavily on his state of mind. Studying an illustrated edition of Bunyan's *Pilgrim's Progress* – a copy of which no serious household was without – I see a picture of a man pestered by a small angel fluttering round his shoulders: there is absurdity and menace in it. From then on, the dead sister becomes 'the steel-engraving angel'.

Dot has other problems. Bill's health is one; his difficulties stem from the war.

He enlists in the Army on the outbreak of war in 1914, aged twenty-four. In May of 1916, he is transferred to the Royal Flying Corps (later to become the RAF). His number is 26047.

One period of the war he tells me about is the nightmare of a Channel crossing in a ship transporting mules to France, presumably to the British Expeditionary Force. A storm hits, the mules break loose below decks. Bill has to control them. I picture lamps swinging and blinking, hardly illuminating the dark fetid stables. Great black animals plunge in fright, showing the whites of their eyes. Amid the noise, the stamping hooves, Bill fights to keep the brutes steady.

Bill serves in Salonika. Later, he is gassed. He is sent to Egypt to recover. The dry air is considered good for his lungs. He is admitted to the 19th General Hospital in Alexandria, where he suffers from malaria. He flies with 113 Squadron in Mesopotamia.

Faded sepia photographs, kept in an old cardboard box, tell part of his story. Here he is in Luxor, among the ruins. Here he is by the Nile. Here he is in a topee, washing his socks. In most of these photographs he is perky and cheerful, as I first remember Bill – and puffing away at cigarettes. A photograph survives of him standing by an old Sopwith Something, leather flying helmet and goggles on his head, the image of Biggles, smoking.

He is involved in the Dardanelles débâcle, Gallipoli. But I cannot put a timetable together. Eventually, at the end of April, 1919, he is discharged from what has become the RAF.

When approached in 1990 for details of Bill's military career, the Ministry of Defence is helpful, but can, after so many years, produce only two brief documents. One of these documents shows that Bill is mentioned in despatches and awarded a pension of eight shillings and sixpence for seventy weeks. Presumably this is a disability pension.

Some time during the Second World War, when we live over the shop in Bickington, I discover a key which fits an old desk. Daringly, Betty and I unlock. In one drawer, to our mutual embarrassment, we discover a collection of washable condoms. In another drawer we find a document, written in Bill's neat hand. It is an account in verse of his military career. Since he is something of an artist, he has illustrated it with sketches in pencil. We hear someone coming. Guiltily, we close the drawer.

What happened to this manuscript is a matter of guesswork. Sadly, it was not preserved.

Legend has it that when Bill's ship bringing him back from the East docked in Southampton waters, he was so eager to get home that he dived overboard and swam ashore. He married Elizabeth May Wilson almost as soon as he had dried off.

Theirs is a modest wedding in Peterborough, with my uncle Bert as best man. It seems that even his father, H. H., on whom he so depended, was not present. Gordon, by contrast, marries in style in London.

Bill's ill health continues. He is prevailed upon to lunch with

Mother and me at a small table in their bedroom, at which, on doctor's instructions, he drinks a bottle of Tolly's Brown Ale every day. On the label of the bottle is a figure holding a torch aloft; perhaps it is Mercury. The novelty of this arrangement is appealing. On a Monday, it is generally mince, with triangular slices of toast.

A severe winter comes. Is this 1928? It snows at Christmas. Uncle Bert is staying with us. Bill is well enough to venture out for a walk. I am wrapped up like a small parcel. We walk into Dereham market place. All is silent under its white cover; there is no traffic. The horse trough by the war memorial is filled with a solid chunk of ice. But this is not a real memory. This is a photographed event. The film of the past has been edited.

What is real is the crunch of impacting snow under red rubber boots, the taste of air like a chilled wine, the wonderful sense of the world transformed. The knowledge that everything is miraculous can never again visit us as vividly as when we are three, and it is Christmas Day, and we are wrapped up like a small present.

But Bill coughs. It's the gassing or the smoking, or probably both. I am frightened in the mornings by the terrible harsh noises he makes as he gets up and washes.

Poor Bill becomes unwell. In 1929, Dr Duygan says to him, 'Stanley, if you want to survive the winter, you'd better go to a warmer climate.'

He books a passage on a liner and sails to South Africa for six months – rather a long winter.

Mother stands by the chest of drawers in their bedroom and weeps. I go to her and clutch her legs, the only part of her I can reach.

'Don't cry. I'll look after you.'

It proves to be the sort of thing I am to say to women ever afterwards. Dot merely weeps harder.

She closes the flat. She takes me to stay with her mother in Peterborough. Uncle Bert is fun. Lions and tigers is our favourite game.

This is an exciting time in Peterborough. Dot's brother Allen is getting married – rather late in life. He is to marry Nancy Perkins. I am to be their page. This responsible post is marred only by the fact that you have to wear shiny patent leather shoes with *buttons*.

After the ceremony, we all adjourn to Woodcock's Restaurant, opposite the cathedral, for a wedding feast. This includes champagne. Considering that all the Wilsons are teetotal, this must represent a Perkins innovation.

Indeed, Aunt Nancy enjoys the good life. She is fun, and looks very pretty and stylish – perhaps the snappiest member of a family whose Achilles' heel may be lack of style, at least until my sister Betty gets going. Nancy often trots up to London and buys herself a smart new dress, which we all admire. Her belief in jollity is perhaps a shade firmer than Allen's. Of course, she is twenty years his junior.

Aunt Nancy becomes a favourite. She and uncle set up house in 'Grendon', which is north of Park Road, by the eponymous park. One spring, a robin nests by the latch of their side gate; the gate stands open for weeks, so that we don't disturb it. Whenever I go to see Aunt Nancy, she puts her heels up on a chair, smokes and tells me jokes. Sometimes she tipples sherry. Later, fruit salad is served and I get all the halves of cherry.

Other important things happen while Dot and I are at Brinkdale that winter. We both get flu. Grandma worries. She remembers the great flu epidemic of 1919, when so many people who had survived the war died.

Brinkdale has its scary elements. On its upper landing, just where you have to turn the corner to go to the lavatory, hangs a sepia print of a Roman sentry in uniform, holding a spear, while behind him through a gloomy archway people are dying as flaming chunks fall from the smoky air. The sentry's eyes roll upwards in a frightful way, as if spotting something disagreeable just behind me.

Grandma, to calm my fears, tells me that this is Poynter's famous 'Faithful Unto Death'. The doomy title does little to cheer me.

I must say something of that kindly and frail-looking person, my maternal grandmother.

Sarah Elizabeth Wilson is about fifty when Dot and her small boy stay with her in the winter of 1929. She is long past the climacteric when, in the eyes of small boys, people cease to be People and become a different species, the Old. It's the difference between the frisky Atlantic and the Dead Sea.

Grandma wears elaborate widow's weeds, and has never been out of them since her husband died. Her black dress is decorated with black beads and reaches to the floor. A frilled white collar fits tightly about her neck, much as Anne Boleyn might have worn when approaching the block.

Her face is almost fleshless, certainly colourless. Her grey hair is swept back and controlled by a velvet arrangement. She is a serious person. I am never able to warm to her. For this, I condemn myself. She is kind and patient. She will later play endless games of halma with me. And yet. Perhaps it's the smell of lavender and mothballs . . .

Grandma has it good. For her, none of the struggle to live and keep heads above water which the rest of us experience. She has a cook and a maid and a mobcapped washerwoman with sharp elbows and a boot boy to help her. They all have their separate nooks in the rear of the house. Being a farmer's daughter, Grandma is also an expert cook. Succulent home-cured hams, tremendous Christmas puddings and other delicacies hang in muslin like silkworm cocoons from the rafters of the cellar.

On her generous table are items of silver, cleaned once a week by the maid. There is a sugar sifter of particular fascination. She eats Grape Nuts for her breakfast, and takes the *Daily Graphic*, which she reads after breakfast. In the *Graphic*'s pages, I follow the adventures of Pip, Squeak and Wilfred, and Squeak's villainous uncle, Whifskoffski, who carries a round and smouldering bomb in his pocket, and is my favourite character. Whifskoffski is an old grey penguin and, though I know it not, a comment on the extraordinary events taking place in the Soviet Union.

When Grandma is ill, nurses march in, starched and proper, to sit by her bedside and command everyone with their Midland accents. She has a large family to worry about her every cough and sneeze. When she is well, there by her side is her faithful and jolly son Bert to escort her to the car, wrap her securely in a rug, and drive her about the countryside. She is never pushed from the stage of life by a younger generation. She remains always in control – though during World War II she once consents, but once only, to hide from German bombers under her solid kitchen table.

Dot and her son spend Christmas of 1929 at Brinkdale. All that remains of that occasion (but what a wonder that anything remains!) is a little Christmas tree in the back room, the drawing room, and the present of a drum. A bright tin drum, which the little drummer boy belabours exuberantly with two wooden drumsticks until he drives all concerned mad and is forbidden to play with it.

On one occasion Uncle Bert drives us to Milton Common, outside Peterborough. The uncles always tried to keep us amused. They throw away their dignity for the sake of a joke. No wonder we adore them – and behave ridiculously in return.

On Milton Common I find a small branch from which the bark has been stripped; it gleams white; I tell everyone I have found a mammoth tusk. Uncle Bert pretends to believe me.

We are there because the sun is about to go into total eclipse. We stand in the open, waiting. Gradually, a hole is bitten in the blazing buttock of the sun.

We drop our tusk.

The bite grows bigger. And now a mighty shadow gallops across the open ground towards us. We are swept up in it, as by a chilly tsunami. An eerie silence falls. Everyone is transfixed.

Then, in a minute, silver bursts forth on the right-hand side of the black disc. The sun is winning its struggle. Birds begin to sing again. Normality, swiftly returning, seems a disappointment. We walk back to Grandma Wilson, who has remained in the car, snug under her rug.

Eclipse or no eclipse, Grandma's life is governed by pleasant routine. She walks down to the shops once a week, to Ross the Grocer and elsewhere, where she is received by men in clean white aprons, who listen reverently to her order as if to the Nunc Dimittis, and despatch her wants by errand boy that very afternoon.

Bill returns from South Africa with photographs of Table Mountain and is in better health.

Bill and Dot resume their life above the shop. Business occupies his mind. He must make it up to The Guv'ner for having been away. In the evenings, he and his wife sit by the coal fire talking business. Their faces are grave. They talk in the code of the shop.

Suppose we buy double K yards of it at U cis DX. With a mark up of B plus we can reckon on A cis BA, maybe, let's see, A dat double C . . .

I hate this whispering, hate this code. It excludes me. Later, I take to Kafka like a duck to water. For the time being, I play with my Lotts' Bricks and first Meccano set. I build a house for Uncle Bert to live in.

Bill has a repertoire of tricks with which to amuse me at table. He sticks his napkin ring into his eye socket for a monocle and adopts a highfalutin voice. When he jokes, I am happy and think how wonderful he is.

Shortly after Bill's return, in the spring of 1930, I am standing in our living room in the sunshine. The door is open on to the flat roof, built over Father's offices in the shop. It is announced on the wireless that a new planet has been discovered. The name of the astronomer involved is Clyde Tombaugh. The planet is to be called Pluto. It is the outermost planet of the solar system, and conditions there are bound to be pretty cold and dark.

I am thrilled. Though I would not have put it in such terms at the time, it is an extension of our imaginations. A whole extra new world that no one knew about. And how long had it been there . . . ?

Not so very much later, I am reading books by Sir James Jeans. Who, in 1931, could resist a book with the title *The Stars in their Courses*? Jeans speaks of Pluto as being 'so far out in space that its journey round the sun takes about 250 years to complete, and so far removed from the sun's light and heat that in all probability not only all its water but also its atmosphere, if it has one, must be frozen solid.'

Frozen solid. Its *atmosphere* . . .

Gosh, I'd love to go there!

Like all good astronomers, Jeans deals with time as well as space. Near the end of his book is another reflection that extends the imagination: 'We realise that we are, in all probability, at the very beginning of the life of our race; we are still only at the dawn of a day of almost unthinkable length.'

I told an interviewer recently how greatly the discovery of Pluto excited me. She said, 'But you were not five years old . . .'

But before schools and jobs are inflicted upon us, the universe is ours.

As related in *Bury My Heart at W. H. Smith's*, I was early subject to strange ontological dreams. More than once, I dreamed I had been a great wizard in a previous existence, perhaps in France. I had been burnt at the stake for my beliefs. Sometimes the stake with mc lashed to it would crash into the blaze. I would awaken screaming. Mother would bound across the passage from her room to comfort me.

There are other dreams of falling, to be accounted for only years later.

We are now coming towards the September of 1930, when I am given a new pullover and sent to my first school. The Five Year Abyss lies over the horizon, rumbling closer.

For school I am well prepared. I can read and write. The two abilities are almost synonymous. They are greatly encouraged by Dot, who assists my reading by the making of little books. My first stumbling adventures in the alphabet are taken up with my crude drawings and bound together. The books are covered with pieces of wallpaper, cut to size, remnants from the furnishing shop.

At the age of four or five, I am on good terms with the tracklements of the main meat dish of writing: the pens, scissors, pictures, rulers, bindings, and above all the white paper.

How I love these little books! Dot is in a good mood and does not sigh too much when we sit together at this occupation at the dining-room table. She finds me a ready pupil. The books get bigger and more eloquent. Crayons are used. I win another prize.

So school comes round.

It's not too far. I walk from the flat through the market place, past a haunted house, which stands empty at the top of Swaffham Hill, and up Quebec Street to Miss Mason's Kindergarten. On the way, we play conkers or marbles or tag or anything. Someone has a slowworm in his pocket. He scares the girls with it.

Miss Mason is tall and severe, with red cheeks on which capillaries map the delta of the Nile. She is assisted by two other teachers. One is a fat panting lady, who comes to school with an ugly little pug dog, and has to have an inflatable cushion on which to sit in class. Her name, suitably enough, is Miss Payne. The other teacher is a trim and elegant lady who wears tweeds and has pearls in her earlobes to denote her superiority. Her name is Miss Ida Precious. I would learn Higher Calculus for Miss Precious. She never takes the remotest notice of me. I think to myself, Better that way.

We have French lessons almost at once. C H A T. CAT. With a picture of a cat, just to make sure. The two words are similar. No problems so far. We're in deeper water when they try to tell us that C H I E N means DOG. On the face of it, the idea seems unreasonable. Education entails learning a number of unreasonable things.

We chant our multiplication tables as if they were psalms. Twice two are four, twice three are six. Only when you get to the seven times table do you start to wonder if teachers really know what they're about.

It is in one of the breaks that Margaret Trout is dramatically sick, thus shattering our engagement. The promise to love someone for ever rests on the understanding that they will remain forever loveable.

There are other attractions in the playground. It is easy to tell girls from boys; they are the ones who tend to kick you less. Some are also beautiful. I am fond of one whose name has disappeared down the rabbit hole of time; she has short dark hair and wears a mustard-coloured cord dress. She is quiet and has a half-smile. She lives in the country, Toftwood probably. Jammed with me behind a sheltering water butt, she lets me look up that mustard-coloured skirt. Oh, the days when we ask – and receive!

As it must have done to a greater degree to parents born in

Victorian days, it seems extraordinary now to recall how much sex goes on in Miss Mason's playground. It was purely pleasurable, without guilt, the sort of playfulness one imagines Gauguin hoped to find when he arrived in the favoured isles of Melanesia.

One game is called Cows and Milkmaids. The boys are cows. They line up and the milkmaids come along and 'milk' them. It's a colossal hit! Everyone loves it, except for little Clara Cream, who is regarded as too objectionable to be permitted to play. The cows moo with delight, the milkmaids work away. Scrunch scrunch scrunch in the trousers.

So enraptured am I with Cows and Milkmaids that, eager to share, I tell Dot about it. Dot flies into a morality fit. Horror is not the word. Sex is a bit of a sore point with her. She bids me sit perfectly still and not move. She phones Miss Mason. It is not enough. She dons coat, cashmere scarf and hat, and goes off to confront the lady personally.

I have no idea what the fuss is about. Which does not stop me feeling an uneasy and all-pervasive guilt.

What have I done? How frequently children must ask themselves that.

Just supposing Dot tells Miss Rowlingson . . .

So the game of Cows and Milkmaids is stopped. The interest remains. We were only exercising a natural curiosity in each other's bodies. It's a curiosity that lasts throughout life, and powers much of our art.

When I graduate to Miss Mason's upstairs room – but this episode is on the far side of the Five Year Abyss – a gorgeous girl called Rosemary locks the door, tears off all her clothes, and dances naked upon the central table. We stand there enthralled, gazing upward. Rosemary is celebrating the attainment of puberty. Dark hair curls on her body, a special little wilderness among the barren slopes of her thighs. For days we beg her to do it again, but there is only that one performance. Perhaps someone else was fool enough to confide in their parents.

Every morning, as I set off for school, Dot comes to the flat door with me to see me on my way. This is what she says:

'I may not be here when you come back.'

Perhaps she feels that this phraseology is insufficiently precise. Then she will say something even more dreadful as she gives a final tug to straighten my cap. The words are for my ears only; no one else hears what she says. What she tells me is the most dreadful thing anyone has ever said, though perhaps I will become accustomed to it when it is repeated.

'I may be dead when you come back.'

After school, I drag my heels down Quebec Road, linger in the market place, in two minds about going home, about ringing the bell, about seeing if anyone answers. The steel-engraving angel is heavy at my shoulder.

I call the premises of H. H. Aldiss a paradise. So I was to think of it for many and many a year when we were exiled from it. But there is no earthly paradise; the Revd Edna Rowlingson was right there. Moments of beatitude certainly, but no long continuance.

If Bill is unwell, Dot also has her suffering, and much of this she passes on to her son. Something weighs upon her spirit. Winter depresses her, first spring flowers – the snowdrops, modestly hanging heads – elate her. She sighs and repeats that she wishes she were as free as a bird.

Worse, she would pretend to weep if I did something wrong. Why could I not be more like that dear dead little sister of mine?

> What are little boys made of?
> Slugs and snails and puppy dogs' tails—
> That's what little boys are made of

Her weeping, hand shading eyes so that face could not be seen, is a convincing performance. Only when Betty comes along is there someone robustly to reject this pantomime, this hypocrisy.

Worse still, Dot has a way of governing me. She has a threat far worse than Bill's thrashings. When I misbehave, she delivers the threat.

'I shan't love you any more if you do that.'

This poison, too, she must have felt, lacked some precision. She developed a variant which I found more lethal.

'If you do that again, I shall run away and leave you.'

I have lapsed into a past tense. The film of childhood is breaking down. Time is on its destructive course.

When these threats are issued, I am made ill. I am a robust and jolly little boy, rarely sick. However, I have what Dot calls 'bilious attacks'. Dr Duygan is summoned, with his old black bag. He can find nothing physically wrong. The attacks are a mystery, to me as much as anyone else.

The attacks earn me a groat of gratitude: I am always sick into the lavatory bowl. Not a drop is spilt elsewhere. It shows commendable control.

Decades later, as a grown man, I face a similar crisis, and yield up a similar response. So I perceive the true nature of those puzzling childish attacks. They are a nervous response to Dot's threats; attempts to spew out the poisons she pours into my mind. They are not 'bilious attacks'. They are violent physical responses to emotional attacks.

My agony of mind is great. I resolve that if things become too bad, I will go down to the shop and tell Bill. He will make Dot stop. He will understand I cannot help being bad. But I never put it to the test.

I take to running from the house. I hide in the shop. I climb trees. I trot about Dereham streets. After dark one evening, I am run over by a bike. The man dismounts and calls anxiously. But I rush limping away, hiding in an alley until I'm better. I go home with dirty clothes. Dot is plaintive when she sees the mud.

This time she really will leave me if I continue to be naughty.

She adds details. She will run away up Norwich Street and never come back.

I go into the lavatory and throw up. Yet another 'bilious attack'.

It is convenient that I now go to school. It gives Dot more time alone. Bill works downstairs in the shop, coughing his dry cough.

Dot takes it easy upstairs. She is pregnant.

I have no knowledge of this aspect of the universe, which later will interest me greatly. I do not realise that Dot is growing larger. I can summon no recollection of her sorrows and sufferings during those months.

What remains in mind is that I am induced to kneel by her side and pray with her every evening.

Dear God, you know how I suffer. This time, *this time*, please let it be a girl.

I kneel by her side, hands clasped together, eyes tight closed, less than the dust. I know I am her mistake.

1931 dawns. I am still taking the *Rainbow* and following the exploits of Mrs Bruin's Boys, but my mental horizons are widening. Dot likes to be driven by one of the staff to Norwich. She takes me with her for company, so that she can keep an eye on me. She likes to lunch in a restaurant overlooking the market square.

She cheers up over a good meal and tells me stories of her childhood, which are many. Dot is also a good overhearer. She eavesdrops on other tables and can hear the most intimate confessions even while yielding up her own.

On one occasion, a little downtrodden woman is eating alone at the table next to us. The waiter in his white tie serves her condescendingly. She is timid. She orders chicken. When she has finished, the waiter returns and enquires if she will have any sweet.

'Oh, no, thanks,' she says. She pauses, then confides in a rush, 'Yes, I'll have the rice pudding. You see, I'm *out for the day.*'

The waiter retreats. And a new catch phrase is added to the Aldissian repertoire. 'You see, I'm out for the day.' It serves for many occasions.

The poor woman was evidently a domestic on a rare day off. Dot always finds this saying immensely funny and (I hope) immensely touching.

After lunch we may shop in Norwich shops. More to my liking, we may go to the cinema. Was it called the Haymarket or the Maddermarket? In any case, it had about ten years to go before the *Luftwaffe* blasted it out of existence.

In that cinema we see George Arliss as Disraeli. There is also Erich von Stroheim in *The Great Gabbo*. Very intriguing. The ventriloquist is taken over by his dummy. We see films featuring Tom Walls and Ralph Lynn, with Gordon Harker. I like Harker. He is hard-faced, and it rains a lot in his films, not always very realistically.

A horror film is showing. All the men wear evening dress. A husband is regularly away in the evening. His wife, who is very slender, determines to find out where he goes. She dresses in evening dress, disguising herself as a man. She enters her husband's club. To maintain her deception, she is forced to accept a cigar, which makes her almost faint.

She attends the club theatre. A magician comes on and asks for a volunteer. The woman's husband goes up on to the stage. He is changed. He sprouts a terrifying lion's head, all mane and teeth.

This film, name completely gone, ranks for many years as one of the best films I have ever seen. I am a bag of nerves for weeks afterwards.

When we leave Cowper church on Sunday mornings, we are never allowed to look at the stills outside the Exchange Cinema on the opposite side of the market place, where they put a big cardboard Charlie Chaplin outside whenever one of his films is showing. Not to look at the stills is a refined torture, because on Sunday they advertise the programme for Monday onwards.

We enjoy our own version of The Movies at home. Occasionally, Bill will shove away the great mangle which stands against one wall of the kitchen – the mangle in that I am exhorted every day of my life not to catch my fingers. On the plain wall, he projects slides from a magic lantern. They tell a story about pirates. The pirates glare bloodthirstily from their bright, crudely coloured discs. In a series of stills, they swing from the rigging and hack each other to pieces, in the manner of all pirates.

It is tremendously popular.

VII

The Exile

Discontinuity and nostalgia are most profound if, in growing
up, we leave or lose the place where we were born and spent
our childhood, if we become expatriates or exiles, if the place,
or the life, we were brought up in is changed beyond recognition
or destroyed. All of us, finally, are exiles from the past.

Oliver Sacks
The Landscape of his Dreams

The spring of 1931 draws on.
It is the time in which to tell of my *life dream*. More than
a dream, a vision of the kind which helps to shape one's future.

I was five years old when the dream visited me in its first and most
powerful form.

I am walking along a lane. The lane is long, long and straight,
stretching into the distance, with fields on either side. The sun is
low and red, round like a fireball, for the day is nearing sunset. I
know I have a long way to go.

As I continue on my way, I see two people in the distance, standing
in the middle of the lane. They are dressed in black; their clothes are
stiff and old fashioned, belonging to another age. I approach with
some apprehension.

The couple are evidently man and wife. They are waiting by the
entrance to a church, which stands on the left of the lane.

The church is clear in the dream. It has a square tower, like
many Norfolk churches. There are three arched windows, filled
with stained glass, in the long wall of the nave. It stands at right
angles to the lane, with its tower overlooking the roadway. I see

no sign of a graveyard. The old man and woman appear friendly, and invite me into the grounds. We enter from the far side of the church.

Now it can be seen that the building is actually a ruin, the tower alone remaining intact. The body and roof of the church have collapsed, leaving only one wall standing – the long wall I saw as I approached. Using the fallen stone, persons unknown have constructed a humble dwelling – a cottage which utilises the remaining wall as its rear wall. The couple live in this subordinate lay building.

They welcome me into the cottage. I am weary and untrusting.

As the cottage door swings open, I see within a bright fire burning, and an aspect of homeliness.

Before I can cross the threshold, I wake up.

The dream is full of dreamlight – the light that never was on land or sea.

So impressed was I by this dream, and its vividness, that I painted the scene. It remained clear in every detail. So delighted was Dot with this painting that she showed it to all and sundry. I painted or crayoned the scene several times. It held apotropaic power. At one crisis of my later life, when I was leaving my children, I painted the scene again, and gave it to them, hoping it might bring them comfort too.

Such a special dream, a 'lifetime dream', such as many people have experienced, is open to many interpretations. There is no definitive interpretation, is not meant to be. On that first occasion, the dream radiated consolation. Later, it was open to more sophisticated reading. Nowadays, I see it as a prodromic dream, the dream of one who has a long way to go . . .

The paths of our lives cross and recross. At West Buckland School, there hung in the dining hall a framed reproduction of Hobbema's 'The Avenue' (properly titled 'The Avenue at Middelharnis', painted in 1689). All we see is an ugly road, with lopped trees and flat banal scenery, but what a cross-referencing of reflection it awoke in me.

Later, in a print shop, I happened on one of Piranesi's 'Vedute', his imposing views of Rome. It depicts the mausoleum of Helena, mother of Constantine, in ruined splendour. From its fallen stones, citizens of a later generation have constructed a humble villa. The villa stands within the embrace of the grander structure. Nightshirts hang on a washing line suspended from one of the windows. Here was my church again, in a more pretentious interpretation.

So paths of our inner lives cross and recross. And we have to recognise that though they may be magical for us, to others they will seem as banal and blank as Hobbema's avenue. While writing of my own long avenues through life, awareness prompts that others have trodden them, others will tread them. Such is common human experience. It is common too, to wish to record the feelings that went with the events, just as we may suppose the Dutch artist in the seventeenth century was moved by the very ordinariness of his avenue.

In those early years, vivid dreams choked my sleep. I like to fancy they were the footfalls of a strong psyche coming into being, welcome even when rigged with alarm.

One Blakeian dream is mentioned in *Bury My Heart*. It is all light and flux, grand, impossible, implacable, the dream of a terrible thing in robes and fires advancing down our long corridor to where I remain helpless behind a closed door. The personage comes to seize me! He advances at infinite speed. Yet the corridor is also infinitely long. So, as in Zeno's paradox, he is always arriving, never getting there.

This dream occurred more than once, perhaps between the ages of four and seven, then not again.

One interpretation is that this was a dream about being born, the long wait in the womb revisited, with intimations of movement about to become actual. A reading that fits more comfortably with my current preoccupations is that the foetus, as we know, recapitulates in its growth the phylogenetic history of our kind; so the time must dawn, at about the thirtieth week of gestation, when the assembling foetal brain gains sufficient complexity to generate a measure of consciousness – much as must have occurred at some period to our proto-humans as they gazed across their Pleistocene landscapes.

In that moment of profound shock, a man could look about him and realise he was, however little he desired it, a thing apart from his environment and from his mate. An individual.

This realisation – which I suppose marks the birth of *Homo sapiens* – finds its echo in the womb. We can hardly be surprised if a necessary acclimatisation to this puissant knowledge still takes place in dreams after birth, since dreams are a mode of communication with ourselves, and less subject to the foreshortenings of time as experienced by our waking selves.

I must not choke this book with dreams and imaginings, as humanity has choked its world with dreams and imaginings. When we, or our representatives, arrive on Mars, to walk those desolate distances in their spacesuits, they will find themselves on a globe empty of gods and demons – and will then proceed to cram it full with them. The shadowy Martian sunlight will surely encourage strange states of being, and phantasms.

Whether we shall then terraform the Red Planet, as many SF writers predict, to fill it with polytechnics and politics, remains to be seen. Perhaps Mars might be allowed to remain swathed in its own solitudes, an astronomical Ayers Rock, to be visited for meditation or honeymoon. And other harmless purposes.

So to that ominous spring of 1931.

The world's economies are in a rocky state; later in the year, Britain will abandon the gold standard. Dot becomes more passive. Our evening prayers intensify. This time, *this time*, please let it be a girl . . .

A cot is brought over from Gordon's furnishing department and rigged up as for a girl, with pink ribbons.

More and more of my time after school is spent among our maids.

Our maids are always of interest and sometimes of discomfort. Behind the respectable façade of church-going Dereham lurk many strange things. People sprout lions' heads.

Our cleaning lady is a Mrs Rushden. She hails from Baxter Row, an old part of town, considered by all at Cowper Congregational Church as a Tobacco Row. Mrs Rushden is a dignified woman with a sharp face and sharp tongue. She has two children. Her motto, often quoted by Dot, is *Nothing's a trouble for the stomach*.

She announces to Dot, early in their acquaintance, that she is not a washerwoman. She is *a lady wot obliges people*. Another one for the repertoire.

In later years, when Dot is older and wiser and we can discuss sex, she tells me that the father of all Mrs Rushden's children is in fact Mrs Rushden's father. 'That's Baxter Row for you,' she says.

Much younger is Abigail. Perhaps she is only sixteen, teetering on the verge of middle age. She is pale, blue-eyed, of scrubbed appearance. She is the maid on whose privacy in her lavatory I intruded. I am curious about her in a way I cannot articulate. Possibly this is reflected in her attitude to me. She takes me out for walks. Something between us makes me edgy, part attracted, part repelled.

It is hard to tell whether she likes or hates me. I am Master

Brian to her, keeping me at a distance, yet there is . . . whatever it was. Something like an unwilling conspiracy which neither of us needed.

Relationships are usually subject to development. Sometimes, though, they seem to exist beforehand, snapping full-grown into being when a pair meets. Only a glance is needed. It is this kind of decision, made without intellect, that leads people to believe in Fate. You may prefer genetics; an inexplicable thing still remains between people, luring us on.

One day, Abigail takes me for a walk and directs our footsteps towards her home in Baxter Row. I am reluctant. The row is very narrow. We enter a small house. I am unsure whether it is Abigail's home or someone else's.

Other people are there. They leave. They look back over their shoulders as they go. I have an impression of a bare room, through the window of which the house opposite looks too close. A girl remains in the room, younger than Abigail, blue-eyed, mischievous. Perhaps it is her younger sister. Perhaps I never knew. The younger girl endeavours to make herself pleasant. I remain alert. Abigail tells me to take my shorts down.

I say I do not want to.

She takes me gently by the arm and tells me to do as she says or she will tell my mother.

So I take my trousers down.

The younger girl comes near and stoops close to see what I have to offer. She does not touch. After a moment I am allowed to pull up my trousers.

It is curious to feel simultaneously humiliated and powerful.

To write of East Dereham with nostalgia would be easy. Yet it was no paradise. The shop was my marvellous playground, full of friends and enticements; for years I was to miss it dreadfully. On the other hand, there remained the abattoir, with the blood running in the gutter, where cows, like Jesus himself, were giving their lives that Man should live.

And what of that crude doctrine of punishment by eternal fire then being preached? Had anyone in Dereham ever had a new idea since George Borrow decided to speak Romany? And there remains the case of the Michelin man.

The Michelin man is dropped by van into Dereham market square. He parades about, advertising those excellent tyres. He is encased in the familiar Michelin trade mark. He's a little fatty made of white tyres, with old-fashioned motoring goggles for eyes. All he can do is strut, or rather waddle, from one end of the town square to the other. A gaggle of boys, of which I am one, follows him about.

The man grows nervous and tells us to clear off. We persist. One of the bigger boys throws a stone. It bounces harmlessly off the pneumatic waistline. At this signal for violence, all the lads begin to shower stones at the unfortunate man.

He tries to run. We follow.

At first it seems like fun. But the man's terror is palpable, as perhaps hounds pursue a stag because they scent its fear. The man runs into a cobbled side street. Here is a better supply of stones. I never throw one, but wait to see what happens next – the writer's guilty role in life.

The boys have the man cornered. His fat arms wave helplessly.

They close in like a wolf pack. Bigger boys appear from nowhere, as at any unpleasant scene bigger boys have a habit of doing. They kick the man until he topples over. Boyish laughter, cackles, more kicks.

He lies in a corner, rolling from side to side on the cobblestones, like some unutterable crustacean washed up on a Permian beach.

'Quick! Someone's coming!' A shout from one of the lads.

The boys clear off. I stand there. No one comes.

I make no move to help the Michelin man, indeed am frightened of him. I clear off in my turn.

I never speak of this unsettling incident to Dot, any more than I can tell her how Abigail made me expose myself. She might leave home if I did so.

But no. Dot is in the last stages of pregnancy, wandering heavily about her bedroom, sighing, applying eau-de-Cologne and cachous. A nurse is engaged to tend her for a fortnight or two. It is Nurse Webb again, sober as a judge, starched from stem to stern. And I have a misfortune that is to cost me dear.

I catch whooping cough from someone at school.

Whooping cough was common in the days before there were inoculations against it. It is extremely infectious. If babies catch it, they may suffer brain damage or die.

It is somehow typical of me to be ill at a crucial time, when Dot is about to give birth. It is the last day of April, the next best thing to the Ides of March.

The maids keep me in the back room. Trying to stifle my coughs, I listen as they read *Alice in Wonderland* to me. I am more or less aware of people in the rest of the flat, tramping about as if this were a boarding house. Nurse Webb, of course. Doctor Duygan, with his black bag. Bill, up from the shop. The baby is delivered in the middle of Chapter Six.

> Alice caught the baby with some difficulty, as it was a queer-shaped little creature, and held out its arms and legs in all directions, 'just like a starfish', thought Alice.

It is a girl! Praise the Lord! *This time*, it is a girl! No tears from the mother this time. Our united prayers have been answered with unusual efficiency.

Bill enters the back room, flustered and uttering a series of short, sharp edicts. I must get some shoes on. He is going to take me to Grandma Wilson immediately. I cannot stay in the house in my infectious state.

A little suitcase is already packed.

I am bewildered.

But why—?

I just told you. Come along.

I am allowed as far as the threshold of the maternal bedroom. Dot is in bed. She lifts up in triumph a little wizened howling thing. A cursory glance suggests it is much like Alice's starfish. Its mouth is open and bright red. Scarcely less red is the rest of it.

Elizabeth Joy, my sister Betty, has emerged successfully into the world and looks none too pleased about it. She sums up what she sees in a shrill bawl.

Only a glimpse is permitted me. It is enough. Peering back into the past, you find some episodes are written in mist, some on stone. Here is stone enough to last as long as life. The overheated room, those windows looking out to blank walls, the nurse in the background with her starched bosom, the rumpled bed, the triumphant, sweating woman in the bed, the scarlet babe, howling as it is held aloft like a banner – only a glimpse is needed. The tableau is going to remain for ever.

I have no words.

Bill gets me downstairs and into the car. I clutch the suitcase. We head for Peterborough.

When will I come back home? I ask Bill. Bill does not know.

The film ends.

John Bowlby, who died in 1990, was a towering figure in child psychiatry and psychoanalysis. His monumental work is in three volumes entitled *Attachment, Separation: anxiety and anger* and *Loss: sadness and depression.* They appeared respectively in 1969, 1973 and 1980. I could not read them properly for the overwhelming sense of sorrow they conveyed.

In one of his other books, *Child Care and the Growth of Love,* Bowlby has this to say:

> It is common in Western communities to see in the removal of a child from home the solution to many a family problem, without there being any appreciation of the gravity of the step and, often, without there being any clear plan for the future. It is too often forgotten that in removing a child of five from home direct responsibility is taken for his future health and happiness for a decade to come, and that in removing an infant the crippling of his character is at risk.
>
> From all this the trite conclusion is reached that family life is of pre-eminent importance and that 'there's no place like home'.

So, in an extreme state of bewilderment, I was dropped at my grandmother's house. There Bill left me.

My grandmother's house was to me what the blacking factory was to Charles Dickens. So greatly did that enforced stay fill me with guilt and dismay, that I dared speak of it to no one until I was well into adulthood.

The Five Year Abyss swallowed me up. I stayed in Peterborough in Grandma Wilson's house for *six months* before being allowed to return to Dereham.

Wait. That is untrue. That is what I believed for many years, until I was adult and out of the Army, sufficiently hardened to look back into that exile. There were details I could check. Whereupon I found I was kept away from home not for six months, but a mere *six weeks*.

I could scarcely credit it. How long did Charles Dickens spend in the blacking factory? We know the humiliation of that episode in Dickens' childhood went so deep that he was unable to speak of it until he was a middle-aged man.

And supposing it had been six months. The exile seemed to stretch for ever throughout boyhood, parching it like a bitter wind. Nothing grew. At night I lay awake, mute, alone.

The woman still lay in her rumpled bed, grinning as she held aloft a screaming child.

At last I had been replaced.

On that last day of April, snatched from home, I was simply stunned.
I recall Bill's hasty leave-taking, as he deposited me with Grandma
and Uncle Bert at Brinkdale and then turned back for home and his
wife and new child.

> Here we are again, happy as can be—
> All good pals and jolly good companee . . .

It was one of uncle's many snatches of song he liked to sing on
any suitable occasion. And how well he and Grandma looked after
me in those weeks.

And how ill I was. The chest X-ray showed no complications. The
doctor held up the misty mysterious plate, where for the first time
I could look into the seemingly empty interiors of myself, or at any
rate of a person resembling a ghostly mummy. There I saw a section
of my skeleton, waiting patiently for its true birthday in three score
and ten years' time, when it would emerge from entombment in
the flesh.

In the year that H. G. Wells' *The Time Machine* was published in
London, a paper was published in the city of Würzburg by Wilhelm
Roentgen, entitled 'Uber eine neue Art von Strahlen'. The new rays
were X-rays. The ghostly outlines of Frau Roentgen's hand may still
be seen, complete with a ring on one bony finger. The plate is as
precious an artifact, in its way, as the great Tiepolo ceiling adorning
Würzburg Residenz. The human body, resplendent in the vision of
the Venetian artist, garbed in fine raiment, has become transparent,
without colour, shadowy, permeable.

And shadowy and permeable I felt. My illness was not merely
physical. It was the illness of a child, in Bowlby's words, crippled.

No teddy bear ever accompanied me to bed. Instead, a golliwog
called Peter played sentry to my soul through the night watches.
Peter was an invention of Dot's. He was black because he was constructed of the tops of one of the maid's cast-off black stockings.

Peter's soggy shape was clothed in garments Dot knitted or made
up from pieces of felt. Two linen buttons such as served in the
1920s to secure underpants were used as Peter's blind, staring
eyes. The mouth was a curve of green wool, the hair a startling
red crew cut. Small wonder I have had a taste for the macabre
ever since!

And the first night I was tucked between Grandma's sheets in a small feather bed, sick and homesick, I whooped and vomited all over Peter.

My faithful golliwog was taken away and destroyed.

My cousins Peggy and John sometimes waved to me on their way to school, as I watched through the window. They were allowed no nearer for fear of infection. Peggy's sweet round smiling face was something to be looked for. When I ceased to be infectious, this dear cousin would take me by the hand and lead me about Peterborough. I never knew her other than gentle. Yet there was a shadow over her and her brother John's life: their mother, May Wilson (née Schofield), had died a year or two earlier of tuberculosis.

A compound of illness and remorse, I had been sent away, unwanted boy child, as soon as the girl child had arrived. I had much offended in ways beyond my comprehension. My mood was one of self-abnegation – and yet I could not help throwing up all over Granny's house.

I was not getting better. The doctor came again. The sticky medicine I had been given – 'A Tablespoonful at Bedtime' – had completed the work begun by Callard & Bowser's Mint Humbugs. My milk teeth were rotting and would have to come out.

Uncle Bert took me to his dentist. The dentist produced a sort of dunce's cap made of flannel, which he soaked in chloroform. Instructing me to count to a hundred, he placed the cap over my face. I looked up into it and began to count . . . and when I woke, twelve of my teeth had been extracted. Uncle carried me back to the car in his arms. A limp and gummy sight I was.

Although I wanted to die in peace, the life force of which George Bernard Shaw spoke so highly asserted itself. I sat up in Grandma's narrow front room, surrounded by framed photographs of my grandfather's champion pigeons and the certificates they had won, and ate a little white fish for supper, garnished with fresh blood.

One consolation of living with Grandma was access to 'the Fireby-Wireby Book'. This was the name I gave, at a very early age, to A. Moreland's *Humors of History: 160 Drawings in Color*.

Despite the spellings, the book was entirely English. As the title page states, the pictures were 'Reproduced from originals from the *Morning Leader*'. Its ferocious drawings depict scenes from British history, larded with anachronisms.

My devotion to this book – and Grandma's copy has sailed through the storms of time to be with me to the end – must have been inspired by the sinister aspect of the characters depicted. People are forever having their eyes poked out or being poisoned. Henry I dies of a surfeit of lampreys, his agony well illustrated, while the butler looking on can barely suppress a snigger. A marvellous book indeed, calculated to nip in the bud any hope of being sentimental about the past of our glorious isle.

Grandma Wilson presided over a Victorian house. She preserved in it Victorian ways; she must have been born at about the time of the Great Exhibition. Her tastes had set in concrete, or at least gutta-percha, at that time.

Monday was a very uncomfortable day, when a puritanical purging of dirt took place. I felt in danger of purgation too. Grandma employed a fearsome washerwoman of square shoulders and square everythings who set to work with a dolly and tub to beat garments into a pulp, before stringing them up in the garden on a line like so many drowned criminals.

Everything about the house that could be elaborate was elaborate. One sat in the lavatory on a toilet encased in mahogany with a lever to one side, resembling a Jules Verne ejector seat in a giant airship. The bath, similarly encased, had a grill like a set of gnashed teeth into which water was sucked with agonised noises, like Brown Windsor soup through a moustache.

Furniture in sitting and living room was designed to intimidate. Most of it was carved wherever carving was possible, reminiscent of the Cattermole engravings in Dickens' *Barnaby Rudge*, which my uncle Ernie used to read to me.

The flimsiest furniture was in the drawing room, where anti-macassars were the rule. Expressly designed to counteract childhood was a freestanding china cabinet on spindly legs. It contained dozens of small white china souvenirs. To venture within a yard of it was to awaken cries of 'Mind out!', or even 'Mind out, now!', as though one had not minded out only the day before.

Family photo albums with dangling tassels were stowed in a revolving bookcase. A snarling fox, lifelike feat of taxidermy, stood above the door in its glass case, ever threatening small boys that it might jump out and attack them.

All light switches protruded like brass replicas of Hottentot breasts. They were tipped with little vague levers for nipples; instead of the customary brisk On-Off of normal electrical equipment, they featured a Yes-No-or-Maybe function.

A large blacklead grate dominated the breakfast room. The coals imprisoned there glowed with resentment. In the cellar, smelling of damp muslin and pulped mushrooms, hung some of the fruits of Grandma's labours. She was an industrious little woman, an over-baker by conviction, so that she could distribute cakes, concealed beneath tea cloths, to poor relations dotted about town, in the Dogsthorpe Road and elsewhere.

I was taken with her into these cottages, which poverty had preserved in an even earlier Victorian mode than prevailed in Grandma's house.

A particularly overpowering parlour in the Dogsthorpe Road contained huge black chairs on castors with bird's nests of horsehair sprouting from their seats. Afraid to sit on these semi-sentient objects, I remained obstinately standing in one corner of the room. The chairs were always in such a bad mood they overpowered what conversation was to be had. I recollect only my grandmother standing there saying – it seems now over and over – 'Oh, I *am* sorry, dear' – though what about, and to whom, if not to one of the chairs, I have no idea.

She and her two sons, Allen before his marriage, and Bert, inhabited this residual Victorian world, content to all appearances. Never did I hear any of them utter a harsh word. Although they attended the Methodist church with unfailing regularity, their main concerns were with more solid things of life; waistcoats, shoes, puddings, paperknives, hairnets, spectacles, chess sets, pipes, feather beds, the behaviour of the boot boy, the arrival or otherwise of the milkman. They had no patience with infinity or any of that stuff. Was it because of a lack of imagination they were such thoroughly decent people?

Although Grandma's house still stands in Park Road, a transformation has taken place. It has been divided into flats. We have evidence on all sides that the nuclear family is breaking up. So now presumably solitary people inhabit fragments of the family home. Perhaps they are happier, better people. Or perhaps not.

When the whooping cough abated, I was able to enjoy something of Peterborough. It was then a quiet old cathedral town, the sort of place in which the Cattermole who illustrated *Barnaby Rudge* would have painted happily. Planners came along in the sixties and transformed Peterborough into a New Town. But when I knew it at the age of five, stalls of live eels, trapped in the fens, were being sold in the marketplace outside the cathedral, as if in some old print.

My uncles' offices were close by the cathedral, up three flights of stone stairs. There I examined their precise architectural drawings, laid out on special architectural paper. As in an alchemist's den, the offices contained all kinds of instruments of unknown usage.

I was quite excited, and had to be sick into a metal wastepaper container.

In the beautiful cathedral, with its noble west front, reposes the body of Catherine of Aragon. Many a year on, Margaret and I visited the queen's birthplace in Spain, in Alcala de Henares. The uncles took me on to the roof of the cathedral. From there, on a clear day, you can make out distant Ely cathedral, another fossil of a vanished age of faith.

When Uncle Bert went about his architectural business, I often accompanied him. We ranged far beyond Peterborough, beyond Dogsthorpe, Whittlesey, Twenty Foot River and Hobbs Bridge, towards Wisbech. He took me to inspect ugly little churches he and Allen had designed. He drove me out into fenland.

Here, the Wilson partnership had designed sluices to drain the land. Water ran, it was hoped, according to an orderly scheme, through the flat lands to the Nene and thence out to the Wash.

Another of Bert's treats was to drive us to March. March is the sort of place where the Flat Earth Society probably meets. The grand LNER railway ran through March, on its course between Liverpool Street station in London and Waverley station in Edinburgh. When the LNER was setting up speed records, the miles about March were where the recording took place. Bert and I stood at the level crossing to watch the trains rush by, straight as a die, horizon to horizon.

When The Flying Scotsman hurtled through Peterborough station on its way north, screaming its contempt for all immobile things, the station vibrated, together with everything in it. The noise seized and shook us. Such power would not be felt again until the first rockets climbed into space. I made a resolution – common to boys at the time – that when and if I grew up, I should become an engine driver on a steam locomotive.

At night, as I lay in my small room trying not to cough, I could hear the distant noise of trains. Marshalling yards sprawled not far behind Grandma's house. The noise of shunting was comforting, as a whole cacophony of trucks and carriages, in obedience to Newton's laws, connected one after the other. A sound now gone from the world.

And another place in Peterborough, prized as greatly as the station: the museum. Here, along with many stuffed animals, were preserved souvenirs of a war before the Great one. I used to stare into glass cases containing structures built by French soldiers in Napoleon's army, imprisoned locally in Norman Cross. Using little but bones from their prison meals, they created ships, palaces and prisons, often with ingenious moving parts.

I was captivated by the idea of a prison growing within a prison. Insert a penny and this one worked. Guards emerged through a door into the courtyard. With them was a prisoner. A bell chimed. Before you could say Jacques Robinson, the prisoner was hanged.

You could save his life by refraining from inserting a penny in the base of the model.

Something else in the museum proved even more compelling, though made of the same material, bone, as the prisoners' structures. In the longest glass case I had ever come across lay the skeleton of an ichthyosaurus, dug from Nene mud beds. I walked all round it – a mile this way, a mile that. So such things really existed! I had read of prehistoric monsters in an encyclopaedia, and here one was. The word made flesh or, rather, bone. From then on, I was addicted to the wilderness world of dinosaurs and their predecessors.

These streamlined creatures, inhabitants of the warm Triassic and Jurassic oceans, came into being perhaps 200 million years ago and had a long swim for their money. But there was the mystery of their coming-into-being and their extinction.

Were there any ichthyosaurs nowadays? I asked my uncles. They thought not, but were vague. None, in fact, none too interested.

If a million years was a long time, so was six weeks. I never ceased to be homesick. No, more than merely homesick: crippled by my banishment.

Slowly my health improved. Following my infectious stage, I was able to seek the company of my kind Wilson cousins. I accompanied them to the swimming pool. I was a strong swimmer, and the splendid pool improved matters.

Peggy and John took me to the cinema. John's tastes were agreeably lurid. Only a little later, in 1936, he took me to a cinema on Broadway, long since demolished, to see a piece of history: two British melodramas starring the grand old ham, Tod Slaughter. Tod Slaughter! – a name once calculated to make a youngster's hair twitch with fright! The films were *It's Never Too Late to Mend* and *Sweeney Todd, the Demon Barber of Fleet Street*. Between the films, Slaughter himself came on stage – Slaughter, a little long in the tooth now – and acted out the famous Demon Barber scene, where his customers are tipped from their barber's chair down into the pie shop below!

Cousin Peggy was less fortunate with me. I could tolerate any ghastliness the cinema could create – except on one occasion, when

Peggy took me as a treat to see Harold Lloyd in *Feet First*. For some reason – inexplicable at the time, comprehended years later – I was reduced to intense fear by Lloyd's antics, as he dangled out of windows over an immense drop.

Peggy had to hurry me from the cinema – which she did without a word of protest.

One incident gives me an insight into a permanent feature of my character. I was playing with my clockwork tank in Grandma's front room when a car stopped near by and hooted its horn. I mistook that noise for the sound of our car horn.

Bill had come to rescue me!

I jumped up and went to the window, peering out hopefully.

Grandma entered the room at that moment and asked me what I was doing.

I knew by her tone what was in her mind. She did not want me to be homesick.

'Oh, I just saw a dog run by,' I said airily.

I was protecting the lady, not wishing her feelings to be hurt. Such consideration was to get me into trouble later.

At last the six weeks were over. I was delivered home. I met Dot at the bottom of our stairs and collapsed weeping into her arms. But of course it was all different now, on the far side of the Abyss.

VIII

The Decision

There is a power in the human mind which is at work in our everyday perception of the world, and is also at work in our thoughts about what is absent; which enables us to see the world, whether present or absent, as significant, and also to present this vision to others, for them to share or reject.

Mary Warnock
Imagination

B etween scribing the last chapter and this lie many months, during which I turned my attention to other matters. To continue the narrative was too painful. I could not, even in the interests of frankness, bring myself to set down in any detail the anguish of mind into which I sank when finally returned to the bosom of the family, to witness how definitively the maternal bosom was occupied by my infant sister, Elizabeth Joy.

At first, I tried to get close to mother and baby, to cuddle them when the latter was being fed. I came too close, and was banished from the bedroom, that little room where so much of the tone of existence was decided, for each of us – the Paternal Bedroom.

The result of these banishments was that I in part reverted to infancy and became a great trouble to all, including myself.

Scenes remain from that time when I had returned from Peterborough. Rushing in impotent fury into the bedroom and kicking the chest of drawers. Waking dismayed to find I had wet the bed, and Dot saying, when she discovered it, 'If you do it again, I shall tell Diddy' – Diddy, the much-loved maid, who held the shreds of my self-respect . . . And, of course, doing it again, and Diddy being told . . . And running down to the garden and climbing high in the highest tree.

So the little animal grows into an English individual, separate and largely isolated. Widely known for his sang-froid . . .

Vexed by my behaviour, Dot took to giving me a Good Talking-To. My response was not favourable. More blubbing.

'You don't love me any more . . .'

'Don't be so stupid. Of course I do.' Words accompanied by a Good Shaking.

Dot and Bill put up with tears and tantrums as long as they were able, which is to say all of eighteen months, before packing me off to boarding school.

Why did I make such a fuss? That I asked myself from my dormitory bed, reflecting on how worse had succeeded bad through my own actions. Then, as now, I regarded myself responsible for my own behaviour. I saw how *reasonable* it was that an infectious child should be sent away from home in order to protect a vulnerable infant. But the grounds for my intense anxiety state had been well prepared: all those earlier threats of Dot's – that she would go away and leave me, that she would soon be dead – had made my banishment to Peterborough seem like a fulfilment of destiny, or at least the fifth act of a tragedy. What she had presaged became actual. The fulfilment of those threats was more terrible than I could have imagined.

Now, in my disturbed state, I was again exiled – more thoroughly, to more complete exclusion, among strangers, unpredictable boys noisy in bare rooms, to shortages, stinks, and incomprehensible rules.

'Work hard, old man,' Bill said, in a kindly tone. Bill shook my hand and left me in the front hall of St Peter's Court Preparatory School for Boys in Bacton, Norfolk. The generous bulk of the headmaster, Mr Humphrey Fenn, loomed over me like a toad over a slug. Bill wasted no time to be gone. I listened to our car retreating down the gravel drive.

For what, foreigners might ask, did preparatory schools prepare us? Why, to be little frigid English gentlemen!

St Peter's Court was a brick building standing in spacious grounds. To one side of it was a playing field which we came to know well, to the other a vegetable garden. Behind these premises, hidden by a wall of knapped flint in approved Norfolk style, was a lane that led directly to the beach and a chilly North Sea – in which we were sometimes commanded to swim.

At the core of my grief lay a serpent of a dilemma, demanding resolution. I had to ask myself, in that scrubby little bed in that scrubby little dormitory, Why had they sent me away again? Did Dot love me? It was a way of enquiring whether I was worth the loving.

At six years of age, one is ill equipped to debate metaphysical questions with oneself. The scales of justice are unfairly weighted: one sees no wrong in parents and plenty in oneself, much as a dog still loves the master who beats it.

I worked over the questions for many hours and many days. A longing to end uncertainty finally decided that *No, she did not love me*. Then I wept into my pillow. Just a few sobs. No, she did not love me: and the corollary was that I was not worth the loving; now that the desired baby girl had arrived, I was rejected.

For biological reasons, a child enters the world with confidence. Its demands are few, and mainly concerned with the breast and the love that goes with it. Soon, it becomes aware of problems to be faced. These can be negotiated with the support of parents. Every challenge resolved increases inborn confidence. Too many challenges, too many set-backs, and that confidence withers.

A child's outlook is subjective. If its all-powerful parents appear to disapprove of it, then the child feels the fault is its own. Happiness is partly a matter of attitude. If we see that the circumstances shaping our lives are largely random, rather than a matter of sin, that perspective makes for a more cheerful life. But a six-year-old is incapable of such musings.

The decision taken in that little box of a dormitory proved to have a far-reaching effect on my life.

Some relief followed from my decision, painful though it was. It became a component of my character until I failed to notice it was in place. The corollary remained in place also: that I was worthless.

So our perceptions of the world are formed. Guilt and self-blame do not make for a sunny view of the world.

One particular piece of evidence decided the verdict in that tormenting debate. The latest of Dot's repertoire of mean tricks had been to desert me.

Something I had done – what dreadful crime had I committed, I wonder? – provoked her into executing that threat which came so readily to her lips, the threat to leave her child.

She put on her coat and hat. She attached her fox fur, with its little vixen face, about her neck, while I, mere jelly, begged for forgiveness. Although I slavered at her feet, she would not listen.

She dressed her innocent baby for outdoors. Still I wept, still she would not listen. She was leaving me for good.

I still pleaded. I blubbered. I cast myself on her mercy. What would I tell Bill?

'You will have to tell him how bad you have been.'

'When will you come back?'

'Never.'

I watched from the sitting-room window. I saw her go. She walked briskly up Norwich Street, with Betty in her push-chair. She disappeared in the direction of the railway station. I collapsed on the floor, under the window, longing to be dead – more than dead, never to have existed, never to have been known among the living.

Some hours – or years – later, in the early evening, Dot sneaked back, before Bill could find out what she had done. No matter that she returned. She had gone. I had longed to die, to be more than dead. Never could I forget it.

Dot had carried out what she had long threatened. The desertion had been enacted, and I was stricken – as intended. No, she had no love for me. She could not possibly love me or she would never have been so cruel.

During that first term at Humphrey Fenn's forcing house for young gents, I continued my career as a bed-wetter: a disgrace which could not be hidden from the other boys. My judgement that Dot did not love me was reached reluctantly, after a sense that I had weighed the evidence to the best of my ability. I was, of course, mentally disturbed.

A part of me understood well enough how confused I was; taking the decision, wielding the knife, at least removed uncertainty; from now on I was on my own and might act with some clarity.

My admiration goes out to that beleaguered boy. Given the circumstances, his decision – erroneous though it was – was valuable, sparing him destructive emotional conflict. It marked him out as capable of judgement, of debate within himself. For this reason, self-respect held a toe-hold along with self-contempt.

The misfortune was that this decision, a saviour of reason despite all the undertones of disgust, was to prevail over future years – too poisonous to examine. Of course the boy did not judge his mother as in any way guilty. He continued hopelessly to love her as before. It was trust her desertion had destroyed.

I take a leap across the years to demonstrate how the upsets of childhood can scar the sufferer: and not only him or her, but those near by. When my first daughter was born to my first wife, the Peterborough trauma returned in gale force. That old exile sought to re-enact itself. It proved the last straw, the last spurt of flood water, in a marriage already disastrously waterlogged. Ten years later, my second daughter was born to my second wife. This time I was intellectually prepared for the dangers; my defences rested in a loving marriage. Yet the ancient disgrace came boiling up again, throwing me off balance. The births of my sons caused no such turbulence.

I paint a poor picture of myself in this chapter, yet have felt constrained from depicting fully the absolute wretchedness I had to contain within my frame in those prep school days. Pushkin, setting out to write, said he wished to *lay waste the hearts of men*. How I admire that ringing phrase! So I would have done, so I would have done, had I not discovered within myself the fatal art of entertainment.

That must be told in its place. Suffice it here to say that I became an avid creator of paper mazes while at Fenn's school. The mazes grew more elaborate, term by term, uncurling over multiple pages, glued together, the wonder and puzzlement of the class. Through the little winding tracks, coming up against dead ends, doubling back, finally – finally – reaching The End, went pencils or grubby fingers belonging to my classmates.

Why did I do it? Why did they endure it?

If ever there was art as therapy, imagination as salvation, life's puzzlements reduced to metaphor, there they were, in the carefully drawn entrails of my mazes . . .

Edna V. Rowlingson taught us that the House of God had many mansions. Evolution developed the mind without forethought. The brain has been less deliberately drawn up than were my mazes, at least in respect of unity. As a result, the brain also has many mansions, to my taste more fascinating than those in the House of God.

Often enough, one mansion scarcely seems neighbour to another. There's mercy in that. For in almost the same neighbourhood as my anguish, construction was taking place, doors and windows of learning were opening. I was able in this period to develop many creative traits which lead to a fulfilling life. But before we attend to them, a marriage must be arranged.

IX

The Refuge

Look, he said, I bring you happiness where men do not expect
to find it. You mean, on earth?, I asked, doubting. Not earth,
he said, but on sand.

Kharnabhar: The Winter Season

One evening in the summer of 1932, a fault of San Andreas
proportions opened at the feet of Bill and Dot.

The Guv'ner had a soft spot for Dot, the less abrasive of his two
daughters-in-law. Occasionally he would come upstairs from the
shop into our flat on a Saturday evening to drink a cup of tea
with Dot before walking home to Whitehall. By this date, his
bedridden Lizzie had died, to become more permanently horizontal
six feet underground. H. H.'s house cannot have been particularly
cheerful.

On this special evening, when he had cashed up with a new cashier
– Dorothy Royou having left his employ – The Guv'ner came to see
us. He was his usual level and amusing self; he was about to take
his annual week's holiday. After the cup of tea, I, having just been
tipped sixpence, accompanied Bill and The Guv'ner to the stairs
down into the shop.

'Don't bother to come down,' The Guv'ner said cheerfully. Bill,
ever obedient, obeyed. We stopped half-way down the stairs, well
positioned for The Guv'ner's bombshell.

'By the way, Stanley,' he said, pausing at the shop door and
glancing up, 'I may get married while I'm away.'

The Guv'ner was regular in his holiday habits, staying in hotels
in Torquay one summer and Gibraltar the next.

'Wait a minute,' Bill said, for once raising his voice to his father.
'What's that you say? You're getting married? Where? Who to?'

'I didn't say I was going to get married. I only said I might. Good-night, Stanley.'

And with that, the old blighter slipped away into the night.

What a schemozzle! Bill was in a fury. Dot could not believe it. One went red, one went pale. Bill was upset enough to ring his dreaded brother and tell him. Gordon said the old fool must be stopped.

The Guv'ner was then seventy-one. He went neither to Gibraltar nor Torquay. Instead, as we later discovered, he went to the Palace Road Congregational Church in Fulham, London, where, on 2 July 1932, he married Dorothy Florence Royou, once his cashier.

So there was a new Mrs Aldiss in Dereham, in Whitehall, and a very imposing lady she was, quite as quick of wit as her Harry and seemingly an ideal match for him, for all their difference in age.

Gordon's and the Corner House Dorothy's fury at this unexpected match did not abate. The thought must have been in their minds that the new tenant of Whitehall would inherit the business. They did not consider The Guv'ner's happiness. Unlike Gordon, Bill did not defy his father. When Christmas loomed, he and Dot decided they should go to dinner at Whitehall as usual on Christmas Day. A deal of whispering had to take place before Dot was egged on to phone the new Dorothy, Dorothy R, to say they would turn up, if that was acceptable. It was. Bill then phoned his brother to tell him what he intended to do.

'Do what you like. Go to hell for all I care.' So said Gordon.

So we turned up as previously for Christmas dinner, and the Corner House did not. I had ceased to need the aid of a pusher by this time. The Guv'ner was given a new biography of Scott of the Antarctic. Certainly Dorothy R was happy to greet us, and remained our good friend until her death, many years later. Our family addressed her, rather euphemistically, as 'Aunt Dorothy'.

Bill now decided to leave the flat over the shop and move to a regular house in Norwich Road, 'The Beeches'. I recall sitting on newspaper on a bare kitchen floor in our old flat, amusing a by now bouncy little sister and thinking that here came – yes, another end of an epoch. I grew up collecting ends of epochs like cigarette cards.

The Beeches did not last long. Bill sold to a mad purchaser at a profit. While we lived there, he installed two guardian geese in our orchard. These white birds, at once beautiful and faintly ridiculous, became friendly, even towards Betty and me. When we walked in their enclosure, the birds took our little fingers in their beaks to accompany us wherever we went. Benevolent birds! Their eggs were considered a delicacy on the breakfast table, too.

Reverting in part to his countryman persona, Bill also bred rabbits in a way that seemed to me enormously clever. On the south side of the house lay a considerable space between house and parallel fence. First, Bill dug a trench below the fence in order to build a submerged wall, beneath which the most industrious rabbit would not burrow. Next, he constructed two low walls at each open end of the space, setting a gate in one of them. Thus a grassy square was formed, on to which the kitchen looked – fittingly, since the rabbits were intended for the kitchen.

For most of the year, I was away at school. This separation meant the end of my long continuous familiarity with the men and ladies of the shop. I went there very little. The phantom house over the rooftops was lost. Shyness had overtaken me. Nor was I at ease with Bill and Dot; there was a sense in the holidays that reluctant space had to be made for my tenure. Cowper puts this feeling well in his poem 'Tirocinium', a hymn against public schools. After the miseries of term, the pupil returns home:

> A disappointment waits him even there:
> Arrived, he feels an unexpected change,
> He blushes, hangs his head, is shy and strange,
> No longer takes, as once, with fearless ease,
> His fav'rite stand between his father's knees,
> But seeks the corner of some distant seat,
> And eyes the door, and watches a retreat,
> And, least familiar where he should be most,
> Feels all his happiest privileges lost.

Undoubtedly there is consolation in finding in poetry something one has experienced oneself: a case of what oft was felt and often well suppressed.

While I was discovering Cowper, I was also discovering Frank Richards, that indefatigable chronicler of imaginary schools, real name Charles Harold St John Hamilton. His best-known school remains Greyfriars, starring the chums of the Remove, although my preference was for the less parodic St Jim's, where Tom Merry & Co spent their days. The St Jim's stories were written under the *nom de plume* of Martin Clifford. They appeared weekly in a magazine to which I subscribed, the *Gem*, and also in square paperbacks, The Schoolboy's Own Library, published every month at the price of fourpence.

As Owen Conquest, Hamilton wrote of Rookwood School. All told, he invented over one hundred schools, and wrote by hand over one hundred million words, for which he was ill paid.

His one rival was Edwy Searles Brooks – rather an unreal real name – who created St Frank's. Chronicles of St Frank's were published in the Nelson Lee Library and the Boy's Friend Library. Both Brooks and Hamilton also wrote for *Modern Boy*, the weekly magazine I read from 1934 until almost the outbreak of war.

Such innocent pleasure these partly forgotten writers gave, at a time when the genre of public-school stories did not seem bizarre.

Bill sold The Beeches to a man eager to own the property. What happened to the geese and rabbits I know not. I was away at school.

This experience gave Bill a liking for trading in houses. He could always find the creaky board to stand on while negotiating, the window that stuck, the ceiling that sagged just a little, the tap that whistled and juddered when turned on.

He bought another house, nearer the shop. This one was haunted.

While we were in this new house, 'St Withburga', misfortune was to befall Bill. But for a short while at least the sun shone for him, while the San Andreas Fault prepared itself for action.

There were still country pursuits. Norfolk was, and still is to a lesser extent, plagued by rabbits. Rabbits could eat as much as a tenth of a field of wheat. So at harvest time, it was reckoned good sport to shoot them. The Guv'ner owned at least one farm near Dereham. I was taken out there with Bill, The Guv'ner and Seeley, our van driver, a friend of Bill's.

Rooks are cawing in the tall elms, sensing something is about to happen. Every living thing in the field is alert, from the various rural folk who line its edges, to the birds and animals hiding in the wheat. Everything waits.

What moves is the clumsy harvester, centre of our attention. It lumbers slowly around the four sides of the field, working from the outside in, so that the standing corn is an ever-diminishing rectangle.

The men lining the field are in gumboots. Some of them wear waistcoats, despite the heat. Their miscellaneous hounds are restrained in case they get shot by accident. All the men carry guns, tucked under an arm. Bill is among them, gun in hand, pipe in mouth. I stand by him.

Women are here too, clustering in a group, watching to see what happens. They are sturdy, and hold small children, or clutch the hands of urchins wriggling by their sides. Some are wearing aprons.

I stand in my rubber boots with some bigger urchins, all pretty ragged and brown. We boys heft stout sticks, ready to clobber any creature which, in desperation, attempts to break from the diminishing shelter of the crop for a nearby hedge.

Time goes by.

As the harvester makes its slow progress, devouring the wheat, it sends a fine gold dust into the air. Rabbits, partridges, pheasants, the odd hare, make sudden dashes for safety. Few of them gain the hedges. When the animals fall, still kicking, boys rush to snatch them up.

The rectangle of corn grows smaller. The distance between it and the safety of the hedges becomes greater, the animals' chances of survival less. Now we can see the terrified creatures between the thinning stalks. Shooting is more frequent. The guns crack, the rooks scream.

The machine rolls on its way, great blades turning.

Now the wheat is but a thin strip, decreasing more rapidly. The distressed wildlife looks about anxiously, undecided in their final moments of precarious shelter. As their cover is eaten away, there is nothing for it but to run or fly.

How the guns barked! Everyone was caught in the excitement. The pheasants flew, to fall dying to the ground almost immediately.

A frightened rabbit scuttled in my direction. Bill called to me to get it. As the creature ran towards me, I raised my stick and, by luck, caught it a glancing blow on the head. The blow carried away the creature's fur on the side of its skull, revealing blood and bone.

I was immediately sickened, and could not strike again.

The wounded rabbit ran into the undergrowth and was lost.

'You nearly had it, man,' said Bill, turning away in disgust.

Afterwards, we trudged back to Seeley's cottage. Seeley slit open the body of a dead hare. Its intestines poured into a bucket. Seeley's tot of a daughter, clad in pinafore, was barely tall enough to peer over the side of the bucket and watch the grey mess slither into the bottom. She stuck out a grubby hand and stirred it in wonder.

*   *   *

In the early thirties, much of the coast of Norfolk was wild and untenanted. Of the traffic on its quiet roads, most was local, and horse-drawn at that. The coast to the north of Gorleston and Yarmouth was fairly deserted until one reached Mundesley.

This coast, lacking cliffs, was constantly being eroded. Winterton, where Bill liked to swim off its beach, while Dot ate sandwiches by the dunes, itself briefly enters English literature, in Defoe's wonderful story. Before gaining his famous island, Crusoe is aboard a ship that is struck by a great storm in the Yarmouth yards. When the ship is driven ashore at Winterton, Crusoe experiences his first shipwreck. The crew survive and walk by night all the way to Yarmouth, where they are hospitably received.

Farther to the north of Winterton, beyond Happisburgh and its lighthouse, lie Walcot and Bacton, perched on the edge of the sand. It was in Walcot that Bill and Dot discovered and bought a small pebble-dash bungalow. The bungalow stood at the road end of Archibald Lane, a sandy track leading only to the sea. The name of the bungalow was 'Omega', the last of things. Nowadays, you would have to go to Iceland to find a place as remote as Omega seemed then.

Bill was a good carpenter. He constructed an outside privy, furnishing it with an Elsan, adorning it with trellis and honeysuckle. Dot worked inside, redecorating everything. They were content.

Two small bedrooms led off the living–dining room, which was comfortably large. Its panelling was stained glossy dark brown, the wall above painted cream, in the taste of the time. Dot covered chairs and sofa with striped orange fabric and had curtains to match.

This colour scheme was carried outside, where rows of wall-flowers, orange and yellow and cinnamon, were planted along the top of the low turf banks that walled the garden from road and lane. On the other side of the lane, cornfields stretched all the way to Happisburgh. In those distant days, before modern weedkillers arrived, red poppies and blue cornflowers flourished within the cereal crop, making the field a thing of beauty – and, no doubt, giving to bread a flavour different from its present one.

All this I remember well, for Omega was Dot's new excitement, a rival to the enticements of Gorleston. Often she would get one of the assistants from the shop to drive us during the week the thirty-odd miles to Walcot. There the two of us would stay, and she would frame a print of calendulas in a bowl in passe-partout, to hang on the cream wall. She would make another sausagey cushion for the sofa. Bill would join us at the weekend, to execute some of his famous rustic work on the verandah.

Omega became beautiful in our eyes, and Uncle Bert arrived to stay.

I was allowed to run on my own up the lane to the sea – that wondrous drowsy tame lion of a sea, the trouble it had given Robinson Crusoe long forgotten. So it appeared in the long hot summers with which the thirties were blessed, as if to compensate for the war clouds forming.

When that sea withdrew at low tide, it left behind a mile's width of pebbleless beach which held in its brown palm numerous puddles, lakes and miniature rivers winding out to join their mighty parent. The lakes were wonderfully warm and secure – ideal for Betty when she, closely supervised, was brought to the beach. In those lakes lived shrimps, crabs and small fish.

The lakes contained within the sand were known as 'lows'. The sand thereabouts might be perfectly smooth, smooth as piecrust: or it might be imprinted with an elaborately repeated pattern. This artistry, good to walk over, was never explained. And although sand patterns are now comprehended in terms of water and air activity, they remain, whenever I am on a Norfolk beach, a source of mystery. Perhaps the physical laws of the universe delight in themselves, as we delight in life.

In those Walcot days, I was allowed to be alone, at peace. At high tide, the territory of lows and brown sand was covered. When the tide again retreated, you could splash out, following the defeated waves, to reclaim the new ground. It proved as wonderful as the previous day's.

You were the sole explorer in a continent free of complexity, where the odd white pebble, still gleaming with moisture, was as precious as a pearl. Little fish darted in the shallows. All day, the mumble of the sea sounded, the arch of sky zinged overhead, and scarcely another soul was about. Just you and tiny tickly crabs. Never a road in sight and, though I searched the horizon, never a cluster of black Arab tents either.

It must have been on Walcot beach I learnt to swim; I cannot recall a time when I was unable to swim: just as my first children, Clive and Wendy, living in their turn on the fringes of the sea, cannot. Nor was there ever a period when days seemed more timeless, as if the distant murmur of waves extinguished the tick of clock: until at last the sun began to slope towards unseen Hunstanton, turning bronze as it did so. And by many cunning subterfuges the tide started to renew its acquaintance with the low cliffs.

When the first sly finger of water curled about their battlements, my castles would be abandoned. I would gather up my shrimping net and bucket full of shrimps, and wend my way back down Archibald Lane to Omega. Dot would toss the shrimps into a pan of boiling water. In no time, we'd sit together in the orange and brown room and eat the shrimps for tea on brown bread-and-butter. Soon the world would become drowsy-dark. Whereupon the brass oil lamp was lit, its wick turned up until the milky glass shade was glowing like a moon. Cosy in bed at night, we could hear the sea promising another fine tomorrow.

We stayed in Omega in the winter too. When the fogs rolled in from the North Sea, I would lie in bed listening to the moan of a foghorn, for all the world like the cry of a great prehistoric beast calling for its mate.

On the road from Dereham to Walcot, we used to pass a Bacton preparatory school, St Peter's Court. So the idea of sending me there entered easily into Bill's mind.

X

The Transcendence

D ot cooked happily in Omega, just as she did at home. We never
at any time ate out in restaurants, except for occasional 'treats'
in tearooms. There, in those tearooms, behind leaded windows and
chintz curtains, under low ceilings, we were decorously served with
Shrimp Teas or Devonshire Cream Teas.

Those little tearooms, with their inglenooks and sentimental
pictures hanging on the walls, were usually run by ladies who had
found no men to marry in those post-war years. In order to make
ends almost meet, they had developed sufficient culinary skills
to run a 'Teas with Hovis' establishment. Baking had overtaken
watercolouring as an occupation for the middle-class lady.

Dot was an excellent cook who enjoyed practising her art. Pastry
was something at which she excelled. She could be relied upon to
produce at teatime glorious moist cakes and several sorts of buns. In
our mellow teas at the Walcot bungalow, Surprise Buns, which had
a spoonful of raspberry jam concealed within them, and Melting
Moments (made from cornflour) featured large.

At home, Dot produced a noble line of pies. Blackberry and apple
pie was favourite; we had picked the blackberries ourselves. Every

fruit in its season presented itself on our table under a roof like a circus big top, supported in the middle by a ceramic blackbird, the lung of the pie. That pastry roof would be decorated with pastry leaves or, possibly, imitations of the fruit below, and was surrounded by a deckle edge like a wedding invitation card. The pie dish itself would be presented well dressed, in a white paper ruff.

To be served with a portion of such a pie was to know you were in luck. It would be accompanied by baked egg custard and a serious helping of double cream.

There was always cream. The Dereham milkman did his round every morning. Dot or Diddy would go down to the front door with two jugs, one for the cream and a larger one for the milk. We possessed no refrigerator, so the milk jug stood on the pantry floor, covered with a cloth. The milk frequently went 'off' when the weather was hot. It was never thrown out. Instead, it was allowed to clot before being tied in a muslin bag, through which it dripped to make cream cheese, a delicious cheese eaten with a sprinkling of pepper and salt on brown bread-and-butter.

Jam-making went on in season – plum, gooseberry and raspberry. The aroma of fruit cooking filled the house. It was boiled in a special stainless steel jam pan. The results were poured into Kilner jars and sealed up with care.

Dot's pies sanctified meat as well as fruit. Her star turn was rabbit pie. Under a big top similar to the one the apple-and-blackberry wore, richly glazed with egg yolk and tanned by baking to exactly the right second, lay chunks of rabbit, nestling by cubes of ham, little onions, shallots, carrots and squares of potato. The world will never taste such a dish again.

Nor was it pies alone that proclaimed her virtuoso touch. The steak and kidney pudding was perfection, even better than the steak and kidney pie. The meat came with a balancing amount of kidney, all encased within a thick and yielding suet jacket. Liberal dollops of Colman's mustard went with it.

When were our plates not passed up for a second helping?

Apple dumplings were another speciality: Apples in Jackets. Large cooking apples the size of babies' bottoms came incarcerated in pastry, juicily awaiting release. Bountiful stews arrived on our snowy tablecloths, containing Norfolk dumplings large as snowballs with fleece like a lamb's.

While we still lived over the Dereham shop, this parade of glorious food emerged from Dot's primitive Valor. The actual oven, a long metal box with charred mica windows, was heated from below by three burners coffined in three blue chimneys. These burners were fed from the shallow tank full of paraffin on which they stood. I look back in memory at this contraption and marvel – that it proved so infallible in Dot's hands, and that it never exploded and set the house on fire!

The family ate well, even in wartime, ate well and ate almost everything. None of us was a faddist. Dot's food was allowed to provide its own flavour. Not only did she not use garlic, she avoided such patent flavourings as Bovril and Oxo. However, she was partial to a flavouring she shook out of a small packet, a dry gritty substance called by the fine old Victorian name of Edwards' Desiccated Soup. Great was my delight in later years when, on reading James Joyce's *Ulysses*, I found in those pages a mention of Edwards' Desiccated Soup. At last the Aldisses had achieved some small connection with the world of literature!

The food at St Peter's Court was less good – less good to the same extent that the hills of Norfolk are inferior in altitude to Mont Blanc. We poor boarders, never more than fifteen in number, were forced to eat everything set before us. Happily, a toilet and wash-up stood across the hall from the dining room; we could rush across to vomit, provided we then returned and swallowed some more mouthfuls of the over-ripe meat or under-cooked sago, or whatever it was our young stomachs found intolerable.

I wrote about Humphrey Fenn's school previously, when I found little to be said in its favour. With age, I become less censorious. At the time, I carried humorous reports home in the holidays, making light of the shortcomings of the place. There was a slight auburn-coloured Mrs Fenn who, by whatever means one hesitates to guess at, produced a child for Humphrey. The Fenn baby's napkins, when sufficiently worn, were used in the kitchen as drying-up towels. Our family esteemed this a great joke.

Yet the school had some points in its favour. We were taught carpentry and I learnt to turn a lathe and to chisel out a mortice-and-tenon joint. So that in due course I constructed and stained a wooden footstool. This little monster still stands about in various corners of the house, unbreakable and uncomfortable. But all mine . . .

There was no way in which I could ever warm to boarding school. I regarded it as an inflicted punishment. When Bill dumped me at Fenn's door, it served as a reminder of the time he had dumped me at my grandmother's door. For ten years I was to endure that 'punishment' in three schools.

*　　*　　*

Bill discovered to his annoyance that only he and one other parent were paying Fenn the fees demanded in his brochure; everyone else had done a deal. This error bought me a privilege, for I was the one boy at St Peter's who was allowed out on a Monday to go and have riding lessons with a Mr Mace who had a stable near by.

Mace was a casual man. He allowed me to gallop a pony along the sand at low tide, thus passing over the stretch of beach where so recently I had played at liberty in my swimming costume. The exhilaration of trotting through all that glittering light, reflecting from sea and wet sand, was a tonic.

After one term, however, I was forbidden to leave school grounds, and the riding lessons stopped. An incriminating book had been discovered in my desk; it was one of Martin Clifford's St Jim's stories, *The St Jim's Barring-Out*. To a demented mind, it may have looked like a revolutionary tract. I had infringed one of Fenn's insane rules, and from then on was doomed to remain in school.

When daily lessons were finished, we stayed confined to the schoolroom. There we were left, to construct our own characters as best we could. Or, if the weather was fine, we might be sent out into the field. On the mornings when Fenn entered the schoolroom and announced that we were entitled to a day's holiday for good work, we groaned, for then we were confined to the field and not allowed back into the building until sunset. Fenn, doubtless, was 'having a rest'.

To my eyes the field was immense. Here we played football and cricket in season. The road swept by it in a broad curve – that road which led from Mundesley and Bacton round to Walcot, passing Omega only a mile further on, that road which represented liberty. When I lay in the dormitory bed at night, with a framed engraving of Landseer's 'Stag at Bay' hanging on the wall, I used to listen for a certain car to drive along the road.

The car sped past from the direction of Mundesley. As it began to approach the school curve, its headlights flooded into the dormitory, lighting the stag, chasing round the room briefly in the direction opposite to the one in which the car was travelling. Rounding the broad curve by our field, it had to slow. I listened for the sound of its double de-clutch. Then it charged merrily on again, on to something exciting, on to freedom.

Memory is an extraordinary thing. Why do I still remember that car, still speculate about its owner? The recurrent meteor of a car was a symbol of rebellion, of a free spirit.

While it is true that one is marked by childhood events, we have within us the impetus to free ourselves. Those autobiographies which begin with early childhood can give a wrong impression. My strenuous attempts to throw away the ill parts of my boyhood were eventually successful. On several occasions, I have felt that my life was rising anew like a phoenix. Certainly that was my inward knowledge as I climbed up the gangplank of the *Otranto*. H Deck was never as bad as the Bacton dormitory.

Church was another snobbish Fenn infliction. Unlikely though it may sound, we few boarders were made to dress on Sunday in little Eton suits. The shame of it! The sheer Englishness of it! Wide stiff white collars, black ties, black shoes, a pinstripe suit and, crowning indignity, *a straw boater!* Thus we were disguised as sons of gentlemen!

In this garb we marched in crocodile down the road, through Bacton, to Mundesley church. The merriment this caused the local lads almost did them injury. They peered over walls at us, they ran before us and behind, they whistled, hooted and guffawed. They put on airs and threw stones, or pretended to faint. Never were so many Trabbs' Boys assembled together!

Oh, the humiliation of that walk! From Fenn's point of view, we were a living advert for the virtues of his school. And when we shuffled with relief into the church pews, we were supposed to be advertisements for purity. But I fell for the policeman's daughter.

The policeman's daughter was about my age, seven or eight. She sat with her parents in the pew on the opposite side of the aisle to me. When we knelt for prayers, I could observe her through folded hands. After the service, she marched out with a saucy side-glance at me, understanding perfectly how I felt. Women develop their antennae at a tender age.

The impossibility of touching or even speaking to the policeman's daughter was always in my mind. It charged the delight in merely setting eyes on her every Sunday with turbulence. She was the one friendly element in a hostile local population. She was undoubtedly the cause – it was the Policeman's Daughter, rather than God the Father – of my out-of-body experience in that church.

The service was droning on, we were at prayer, when I found myself looking down from a great height on the vicar and the congregation.

The 'I' of myself was floating serenely under the carved beams of the roof. There I remained, gazing down on the congregation. I was hardly surprised, certainly in no way frightened. Serenity was in everything.

'This is an eternal moment.' So I told myself. Many people do not recognise such para-consciousness as 'real'; yet the oxymoron 'eternal moment' seems to acknowledge the paradox as verifiable.

When practising pranayama many years later, I achieved states of meditation, setting mind and body to one side. The eternal moment was much like a meditative state; both were beatific. All was well and all was eternally well.

If only one could always remember that, setting it against the discomforts inseparable from the human condition . . .

Imagination was not involved in that eternal moment. Imagination is an active principle, whereas the transcendence was purely involuntary. If consciousness is a function of physical forces, then physical forces are other than we currently conceive them to be.

But what of the policeman's daughter? Alas, there's nothing more to be told of her. We never even spoke. I once touched her coat as we filed from the church. It was pink. She may now be living happily, a granny with grandchildren, in Mundesley. On that I can cast no light.

Consolation of a more mundane kind lay in a book I discovered in my first term and read at the beginning of every term thereafter. It was a sub-Dumas story of Huguenots, entitled *Prisoners of the Sea*, written by Mrs Florence M. Kingsley. There is comfort to be had in a book one knows almost by heart.

Stuck in the St Peter's field during one of Fenn's days off, we had nothing to do but chatter, run about aimlessly, make train noises, or garden.

At midday, Fenn's boy would come out from the house, bearing a toffee tin full of sandwiches. We were on bad terms with this lout, who seized on every possible opportunity to assure us we were worthless scum. One day when we knew Fenn was away, our head boy, Ian Keymour, took this varmint on. They fought barefisted on the landing and stairs, and Ian won after a long fight. The varmint left Fenn's employ and was never seen again.

As for the sandwiches . . . the gristly meat was disgusting. We slung it over the hedge, and filled the bread with produce from our gardens. These 'gardens' were narrow strips with a flint wall at their back, while just in front of them stood neglected apple trees. We guarded our individual strips jealously. When not working at them, we sat at the rear resting against the wall on 'thrones', flat stones.

In the spring term, we were allowed to visit a small shop next to the school – Miss Abigail's. It was a little old-fashioned shop selling bars of Milky Way for a penny, and much else besides. Miss Abigail also sold Bees' and Carter's vegetable seeds. By sowing these seeds in our gardens in March, and weeding scrupulously, we stood a reasonable chance, when returning to school in April, of finding little crops of carrot, lettuce (Webb's Wonder), or radish thrusting up, to be eaten sparingly during the summer term, augmenting our diet.

Whatever may be said against Fenn's preparatory school, it was certainly character-forming. I have enjoyed growing vegetables ever since.

With my first seven years behind me, a new psyche was born within me, and a positive and lively force it proved. Although we were not allowed toys, I took with me to school an excellent small microscope, to which I was devoted. I examined many things under its lens, copying what I saw into a sketchbook. My mazes grew in size and complexity; the largest consisting of six foolscap sheets of paper joined together.

I began to write stories and compile small books. One story concerned a wonderful machine which flew to the moon. I drew the machine. It had many windows. Beyond them was a spectacle too good to miss, the spectacle of space, with its paradox of glittering darkness.

As though formal lessons were not enough, I also gave lessons in 'Prehistoric Monsters' to the other boys. Dinosaurs were not the vogue then that they later became. While I knew little about the subject, my audience knew less. We learnt the names of the past ages of the Earth by heart. These were exciting new things, for the antiquity of the Earth was still being extended, just as the galaxy was still expanding.

My main textbook, such as it was, bore the grand title *The Treasury of Knowledge*. Bill and Dot gave it to me while we were living at The Beeches; it came free after you had collected a hundred tokens from the *Daily Mail*. The sections that held most interest were those dealing with the solar system and its formation, the beginnings of life, the ages of the great reptiles, and what the book called The Perilous Adventures of Early Man.

What I wished to convey to my self-selected class was the excitement that this knowledge brought – all contradicting anything the Revd Edna Rowlingson taught. So we learnt a litany of names not found in our Bibles: trilobites, the Carboniferous Age, archaeopteryx, tyrannosaurus rex, Pliocene, evolution. We studied the atmospheric paintings of the creatures of the Jurassic by Charles R. Knight. We learnt how one age succeeded another. Cro-Magnon ousted the Tribes of Judah.

This body of knowledge was then comparatively new, and still being supplemented. Archaeology and the mighty panorama of existences before man was one positive heritage of the nineteenth century, along with less desirable things.

We boys were pleasant with each other. Learning to integrate with your fellows proves ultimately a more useful skill than a knowledge of algebra or how to parse a sentence. In the main, we supported one another – surprisingly, for small boys are not particularly amiable creatures. At the school to which I was next sent, bullying and sadism were the order of the day. But there were so few of us incarcerated in Fenn's little prison, and Ian Keymour was a head boy of excellent character and influence.

However, we did have a scapegoat. Edward Augustus Bode. I cannot recall why we disliked him. Perhaps it was a question of pheromones. Bode was a brave surly boy who, during our days cast out in the field, spent his time perched out of harm's way, in the top of one of the apple trees.

We knew nothing of sex. At the beginning of one term, Peter Spiers, who was our star batsman, arrived breathless from Cromer, to announce he had learnt a great secret. Women had a place in them where eggs were born and from these eggs babies were hatched. We were so disgusted with this unlikely story that we beat Peter with his own cricket bat.

This myth Peter had hold of made no mention of the man's role; among early humankind, too, the male role in conception was not understood.

Fenn himself inadvertently introduced a sexual note into our lives. In my penultimate term at St Peter's, he hired a matron of astonishing beauty to supervise our bedtime. This young lady represented something new to us, with her dark curly hair and red lips and high spirits. She was all that women can be, magic, seduction, loveliness, the unknown, garbed in a natty white apron. Her arrival spelt the end of my unconsummated affair with the policeman's daughter. I believe we all fell in love with the neat little matron without understanding what that kind of love meant. If we were particularly good – or indeed, if the whim took her – she would clasp and kiss one or other of us good-night. How wonderful those kisses tasted to emotionally starved ten-year-olds! Our behaviour became excellent as a result.

And then foreign boys arrived at St Peter's. A German lad came first. I suppose he was German Jewish, like the Boxbaums. This was 1935, when Mussolini invaded Abyssinia and the swastika became Germany's official flag. We nicknamed the foreign arrival Killy-Kranky. His real name has faded from memory. Killy-Kranky was a born survivor, lively and amusing. We believed him to be more intelligent than we. With his mad version of English, he was immediately welcome. He taught us to say *'Du bist ein alte Kamel'*, assuring us it was a deadly insult. We adored it.

After the fugitive from Hitler came the fugitive from Mussolini. He was less charitably received than Killy-Kranky.

He was a small boy, only five years old, timid and vulnerable. He arrived after summer term had begun. His father drove up in a swagger car. The father, as we peered from the schoolroom window, made an unfavourable impression. He was a dandified man, with slicked-back hair, light-fawn clothes, and a pronounced *air* about him. After some conversation with a Humphrey Fenn at his most Uriah Heep-like, the Italian pressed a comic on his son, kissed him on the forehead, and drove away in a shower of gravel.

Of course we never were told what dreadful drama had stranded this small denizen of Rome at a refuge in Norfolk. Some refuge! The boy spoke in the faintest tones, which we immediately imitated. He folded up his comic – that precious parting gift! – and tucked it defensively inside his blouse. His *blouse*? Only *girls* wore blouses!

We had no mercy. He was soon shown what fascists Anglo-Saxon boys were, that monsters did not flourish only in Italy or Germany. For many a year afterwards, I grieved to think how we tormented the little chap, how even Ian Keymour teased him by snatching that treasured comic away.

One last image of that dismal chapter remains. Bode in the field on another of those compulsory days off, climbing ape-like up into his apple tree, taking with him the Italian boy, nursing him to keep him from harm. There they stayed all day. Bode held the boy, and read to him from his comic.

The child did not come back for a second term.

Other dramas went on over our heads. Fenn's assistant master, the peppery Mr Knowles, refused to get up one morning. Keymour was despatched to the attic where Knowles slept to rouse him. Knowles would not come down. Keymour was sent up a second time. We sat at our desks, breathless. Keymour returned to report the same result: Mr Knowles refused to come down.

Knowles was sacked and not replaced. Peter Spiers cried as we watched Knowles cycle off down the drive. I wondered why. Knowles was as bad as Fenn, and more ready to tease and humiliate us.

Henceforth, Fenn took all the lessons, except for Religious Instruction, for which a Roman Catholic priest, Father Snowdon, drove over from North Walsham. By special dispensation of the Vatican, he had, it appeared, retained his milk teeth well into middle age. He spent most of the lesson uttering prayers to himself with a sibilance for which the milk teeth had providentially equipped him.

And the most awful drama of all. Bode did something wrong. Bode offended. We were not told how he offended. He could not tell us because he was locked away in an attic room, out of sight and hearing. We speculated, but speculation is always limited by what one knows or can guess. There was little we could guess; had Bode stolen something? Had he gone out of bounds?

Or had there been some ghastly human failing totally beyond the cognisance of our innocent thirties minds? Had he, for instance, attempted some amateur form of sexual intercourse on the Fenn infant? Sometimes these cogitations still amaze the troubled midnight, not to mention the noon's repose.

Fenn, clad in specially oiled hair, announced that Bode was to be beaten and expelled. We were to sit at our desks. Fenn's prisoner was brought, pale of face, into the schoolroom, wearing only his pyjamas. Behind him came Fenn, armed with a big stick, with Mrs Fenn in attendance – not clutching the baby. Fenn proceeded to roll up his sleeves.

One of the boys, Mickey, made a dash for the door and was called back. We sat there (the jury?) to witness Bode (the convicted?) being brutally beaten. How vigorously Fenn (the judge?) laid about him! Mickey (the verdict?) was violently sick over desk and floor. Bode then disappeared from everyone's life. No explanation given. As far as we were concerned, Bode had left the planet.

Before this disturbing event, we had regarded Humphrey Fenn merely as a sort of natural force, something that happened inevitably while you were growing up, like blackheads. From then on, we hated the man. We were never the same.

Yet people are not consistent. Fenn was not consistent. It was 1935, the year of the Silver Jubilee of King George V and Queen Mary. Celebrations and holidays were in order all over the country.

The school closed. All the boys were hauled off by their parents for the day, except for Killy-Kranky and me. Goodness knows where his parents were – or mine, come to that.

I was aggrieved that they did not visit me that day, but hid my feelings in order to keep Killy-Kranky in his usual cheerful mood. Fenn and the auburn wife, plus infant, drove over to a grand fête in Mundesley – and took us two boys with them.

It was a happy occasion. The Fenns were kind. They bought us tea in a marquee and gave us both souvenir mugs. Perhaps I thought, regarding my parents, that here was something else to store up against them. They had given me the cold shoulder again.

Summer holidays arrived at last. In August Bill drove us from Dereham down to Walcot and Omega. As we passed by the school, driving along that broad curve taken by my speeding nightly car, there stood Killy-Kranky in the field, all alone, clinging to the wire-mesh fence and looking wretched. My sympathies went out to him. I could imagine being stuck there alone all the eight weeks of holiday, with *Prisoners of the Sea* re-read in the first week. He stood by the fence, staring blankly out at the road.

I said to Bill, 'Can you stop and let me speak to Killy-Kranky?'

He answered contemptuously, without slowing, 'What have you got to say to him?'

In this portrait of myself at my first boarding school, I have drawn an odd character, or so it seems to me. A divided boy – with all the traits that would leap up in the adult like Jack's fairytale beanstalk: the love of learning, the adventurous nature, the spirituality, the romantic streak, the anxiety, the creativity, the depression.

XI

The Ghost

One night the mirror people invaded the earth. Their power was great, but at the end of bloody warfare the magic arts of the Yellow Emperor prevailed. He repulsed the invaders, imprisoned them in their mirrors, and forced on them the task of repeating, as though in a kind of dream, all the actions of men. He stripped them of their power and of their forms and reduced them to mere slavish reflections.

Jorge Luis Borges
Fauna of Mirrors

Why was St Withburga haunted? How was it haunted? It is contradictory not to believe in *ghosts*, despite objective evidence that one at least existed and probably still exists.

In the days when I was at least partly mad myself, I received for review a book by the psychoanalyst Charles Berg, posthumously published, called *Madkind: The Origin and Development of the Mind*. The thesis expounded is, not to put too fine a point on it, that humanity is insane, that we are neotenous apes, clinging to a mass delusion which is not reality. The human mind has not been constructed to deal with reality – by which Berg means the revealed truths of science.

Our sacred institutions, our sacred cows, are one by one driven to Berg's slaughterhouse. Education, marriage, hygiene, religion, architecture, class, sport, war: one by one the knacker's man kills them off as symptoms of a deep-seated malady.

To quote:

Society still clings to its unfounded superstitions, its unfounded beliefs, its unfounded moralities, its unfounded customs and ways of behaviour. When I say unfounded, I mean unfounded upon anything real, on any scientific knowledge or accuracy. It is founded upon an age when there was relatively little or no science, when everything was unknown. So environment was, as it were, created in the image of man, and of his mind and his projected phantasies and impulses. In other words, an entirely erroneous reality was postulated, believed in and clung to. The point I want to emphasise is that it has been clung to ever since, and is still being clung to. That is the reason I have for naming this book *Madkind*.

Berg's arguments appealed to me. They applied in part to my own existence; unwittingly, I had fashioned an erroneous reality for myself. There is evidence for the insanity of humanity all round us; this century has proved an absolute showcase for the fact. I used Berg's book as curare for the tip of *The Dark Light Years*, my flight of sixties fancy.

Berg bears down hard on the notion that a man born in Nazareth should have the power to make the dead rise and live in some other imaginary but ill-imagined sphere.

If you did not believe in God, surely it was beyond reason to believe in *ghosts*?

In East Dereham, Dot was full of good works. Like her mother before her, she went about town with a basket on her arm, dropping in nutritious pies and cakes on members of that undiminishing class, the Poor. They were always with her. These congregational duties took her to a house then called St Withburga. There lay an old bedridden lady christened Bessie, on whom Dot lavished trifles and sympathy.

And when Bessie died, Bill – casting about for a home after his profitable sale of The Beeches – bought Bessie's house.

If I read a 1757 map of East Dereham correctly, the house stands on the site of an old inn, long since demolished.

Much renovation was needed when Bill took over St Withburga. Rotten wooden sash window frames were removed and new metal Crittall windows, then fashionable, installed. A rickety rear staircase was taken out. New fireplaces were put in.

The Guv'ner came round to see what was going on. But The Guv'ner was preoccupied with his new marital status. Dorothy took him away on a cruise of the Mediterranean in the RMS *Orontes*, during which time they visited Cairo and Luxor. But, sadly, The Guv'ner's health was failing.

The next time I returned from school for the holidays, the family was installed in St Withburga. Delivered back into the family circle, I went up to my room, flung myself down, and read in luxurious peace. Dot was vexed by my unsociable nature. Little she knew of the racket that continually assaults you in school. Nor did she know Cowper's line about the returning scholar who 'seeks the refuge of a distant seat'.

Our new home had three front bedrooms. They looked out towards the church of St Nicholas, the graveyard, and St Withburga tower. Betty who was now a bouncy girl, humorous, defiant, a companion, slept in the largest of these three rooms, then came the landing, then my bedroom, and then a narrow little room, towards the rear of which were two steps down to a door into a boxroom.

The arrival of the ghost remains clear in my mind. It was mid-evening, and dark outside. Betty was peacefully asleep upstairs and Bill and Dot were sitting in the living room below. I was with them.

From the ceiling overhead came the sound of footsteps, so heavy they jarred our central light bowl, suspended from the ceiling by three chains. Father dropped his newspaper and sat up. The footsteps went towards the window. Then came the screech of a sash window being thrown violently up.

'We've got a burglar!' Bill said. Seizing the poker from the grate, he rushed upstairs. I followed with the coal tongs.

Everything in Betty's room was quiet. She was asleep. The window was closed. We retired downstairs, baffled.

The sound effects, we agreed, were of a sash window being thrown up. Yet the replacement windows were metal and side opening.

'It's the ghost of old Bessie,' Dot said. 'She died in that room. She won't hurt us. We were always kind to her in life.'

Dot's calm was a cause for wonder. She was a nervous person, rarely calm. I would go further, for my researches at school had just turned up the word 'neurotic'.

The ghost was a cause for alarm to Betty. Soon, Betty was running screaming on to the landing in the middle of the night. A lady had approached her bed, holding a candle, bending over her and asking if she had been a good girl. She refused to return to her room, and was taken into bed with Bill and Dot in their rear bedroom.

The parents hit on a solution to the trouble. Betty would sleep in my room and I in hers. So I became subject to Bessie, and fell asleep propped up, to stare uneasily at a linen room, narrow and with a window, which opened into the bedroom.

When I could not take it, I was moved into the narrow bedroom with the steps into the boxroom. I became very nervous; if I woke in the night, I would put on the light and read, not daring to close my eyes until light showed at the windows. So began half a lifetime's habit of insomnia.

No rational traffic can be had with a ghost. You can confront it or run from it. Communication is impossible (*pace* the ghost of Hamlet's father) because the apparition is a chord, as it were, from its own past, perhaps from its moment of death. Although it seems to have movement, it comes from somewhere beyond speech. All it can do is replay itself.

This does not explain why it fills us with such alarm as to bring us out in cold sweats. We can only suppose that as the invisible scent of lilac fills a room, so an apparition emanates a pheromone like fear.

From all the muddle and melancholy I extracted a benefit. Telling the tale of Bessie to the other boys, after the lights went out in Fenn's school, and the little scudding car that had double de-clutched round the curve of the field, I began a career of oral story-telling. I could induce them to retreat in terror under the bedclothes, begging me to stop. I had found my first audience.

'Shut up, Aldiss, you bastard!' – the abuse was a mark of my success.

Later, at Framlingham, I became the dormitory's champion story-teller, spinning my tales – often serial stories – night after night. I had my roots where story-telling had its roots: the dark, the loneliness, the solitary magician with a tale by which to hold the listeners. Many a time my reward was a beating, six strokes of a malacca cane across my pyjama'd behind. But of course I was incurable.

In Dereham during the day, life went on almost as usual but posters inviting men to Join the Modern Army broke out round the town.

In the holidays, Dot and I would walk up Church Street to the shops. On the opposite side of the street, a line of poorly dressed men queued for the dole. Dot then would clutch my hand so tightly that I felt her fear.

With Bill, I drove out to Gressenhall Workhouse. H. H. Aldiss supplied cheap suitings to the male inmates. A great forbidding place it was (now a museum), with sorry old broken people tottering about its grounds. Bill left me in the car while he went to negotiate. He came back gloomily.

'We may all end up here ourselves, one day, eating bread-and-pull-it.' He often made such remarks, adding his insecurity to our own. The shadow of the workhouse haunted many men of his generation. Perhaps they saw war or the workhouse as alternatives.

While I was away at Framlingham, going every day in fear of my life, the next act of the family drama was played out.

The Guv'ner became increasingly ill. There had been a time when Bill had driven to the Norfolk and Norwich Hospital with me beside him, to visit The Guv'ner in his sick bed. The old man, dogged as ever, recovered and had got himself back on his feet. But the illness, which I presume was lung cancer, struck again.

Dot later reported his last words. Bill had said to his father, as H. H. lay in his bed, that he hoped he had made provision in his will for the shop premises to be divided in two, since The Guv'ner knew his sons could never agree on anything.

'You'll have to fight your own battles, Stanley, from now on,' The Guv'ner said.

He died early in the morning of 11 March, 1937, the day before Bill's birthday. Mother wrote to school to tell me of the death. I could not come to terms with the fact. I had not realised he would ever die. How could I say how sorry I was? Words would not come. When I wrote my statutory weekly letter on the following Sunday, I made no reference to my grandfather's death. The failure shamed me for many a day.

Photographs of the funeral have come down to me. All of East Dereham mourned. Blinds everywhere were drawn half-down as a token of respect. Immense numbers of people followed the funeral cortège on foot to the cemetery.

What followed was disaster for Bill. It all happened off-stage for me, like slayings in a Greek play.

Bill never said a word to his son about his troubles at the shop. He was probably too bitter to speak of them. Only through Dot did the son learn later of his discovery of misappropriation of funds, of items unaccounted for, of incriminating memos. Bill fought his last battle with his brother Gordon, and lost. Gordon bought Bill out.

There was little for Bill in Dereham now but the ignominy of defeat. He sold St Withburga and its ghost. On 28 February, 1938, the *Dereham and Fakenham Times* carried the following news item:

DEREHAM FIRM CHANGES

MR STANLEY ALDISS TO LEAVE THE TOWN

It was learned this week that Mr Stanley Aldiss has disposed of his interests in the firm Messrs. H. H. Aldiss & Sons, of Dereham, in which business he has been in partnership with his brother, Mr H. Gordon Aldiss.

Mr Stanley Aldiss has decided to leave Dereham, and he will do so probably in a month's time.

The business will then be carried on by Mr H. G. Aldiss.

Mr Stanley Aldiss has been connected with the establishment for about 30 years, since leaving Bishops Stortford College. In Dereham, he has been associated with many activities locally. For a number of years he has been secretary and a deacon of the Cowper Congregational Church, and in his earlier days he took an active interest in local football clubs.

At one time he was chairman of the Kennel Society.

During the war he served with the Army and Royal Air Force, and saw service in Gallipoli, Salonica, Egypt, and Palestine.

Mr Stanley Aldiss was a member of the Cowper Guild in connection with the Congregational Church.

His departure from Dereham will be greatly felt by his many friends in the town. A tribute to his work for the Congregational Church was paid by the Rev. Edna. V. Rowlingson (minister) in an interview, who said that Mr Stanley Aldiss had been a very loyal and enthusiastic supporter of the church and worship, and the loss sustained through his departure would be keenly felt.

Mrs Aldiss has been secretary of the Ladies' Working Party for years, and has done a great leal of zealous and hard work.

Mr and Mrs Aldiss have two children, a boy and a girl, one of whom is at school and the other at home.

While I was still incarcerated in the Suffolk penitentiary, I had news of all this. Dot wrote a letter saying that we were leaving Dereham, and that from now on we were going to be very poor and would have to be careful with every penny. I cried over the letter. Leaving Dereham? Was I supposed to feel nothing at the news? Leave my friends, leave the shop, leave that ever teasing lady in black velvet, leave everything?

Yes, apparently so . . .

Dot's letter left unanswered a rather important question: how was I to get back to Dot? Would she and Bill leave me for ever at the hated Framlingham, as Killy-Kranky had been left at Fenn's school?

Bill sold up Omega. When the end of school term finally came, I was to go to a small terraced house, one of a row of six, near the seafront in Gorleston on Sea. Once more, everything was changed.

* * *

The connections with Dereham were severed. Bill and Dot never went back, and it was many a year before Betty or I returned.

The family maintained connections with 'Aunt Dorothy', widowed after only five years of marriage to The Guv'ner. She had the misfortune to be stranded in Dereham with the side of the family that hated her. Soon she too left, to live elsewhere with her mother during the war. Eventually she came to Oxford to live with a widowed Dot. Dot relied on her, yet something of the old jealousy remained until Dot's death. Aunt Dorothy lived on into her nineties, a stoical example to the whole family. Margaret and I looked after her in her final years.

Old Bessie was another story, although that story too, I believe, is about to close.

As soon as I had access to a library, I searched for rational explanations for apparitions. To my mind, Bessie's manifestation was linked with the family situation, with all its repression, memories and disappointment. I wished to know that Bessie did not exist. Support of a kind came from some Freudian writings, showing that poltergeists centred about teenage girls. Perhaps a small girl and a neurotic mother would serve equally well as a focus.

Dot certainly had a special relationship with Bessie. During what, it transpired, were to be our final weeks in St Withburga, Dot was alone in the house one autumn afternoon, pottering in the kitchen. She heard footsteps overhead in the bathroom. Bill, she concluded, must have come home early and gone up to wash his hands; it was unlike him not to call out when he came in.

Dot walked into the hall and called up the stairs. 'Bill! Is that you?' Silence.

'Bill?'

The steps emerged from the bathroom. They came to the top of the stairs, paused, and then proceeded to descend. Dot remained rooted to the spot. The steps passed her eye level, got to the bottom of the flight, turned, and advanced towards her. They died away as they reached her.

Released from the spell, Dot ran through the front doorway into the lane, and waited until finally Bill came home from the shop.

'If Bessie is coming downstairs, I don't want to live here any more.'

This crisis took place in the shade of the bigger crisis, when Bill was facing the fact that he would have to give up his share of the shop.

From all this, I deduced at an early age that the apparition was in some way a projection of our troubled family spirit. With this conclusion, a doubt entered my mind: I wondered if I had ever seen Bessie myself, or if that was not just a dramatic detail I had added to make my dormitory tale more horrific. Such is the untrustworthy nature of memory that I cannot to this day decide whether or not I saw the ghost. Certainly I heard it. Certainly it cast upon all of us that fear traditionally associated with such apparitions.

If Bessie had been some kind of subjective phenomenon, as I had supposed, her legend would die with our leaving. We quickly sold St Withburga and left town.

The years passed, long war years, years of my first marriage, the deaths of Bill and Dot. Still Aunt Dorothy survived, dying in 1984, almost half a century after her husband. Her request to Margaret and me was to have her body interred in the cemetery in East Dereham, next to Harry. We obeyed her wishes. Many of 'our' side of the family attended. There was no one from Gordon's side.

After the ceremony, when I had settled everyone in the only tolerable place in Dereham in which to have lunch, I walked round to look at the house in which Dot had met with the apparition and Bill had met with misfortune.

St Withburga was no longer a home. It had become council offices. I went in in my sombre funeral clothes. A strange feeling it was, to find that our breakfast room, where Betty's doll's house had stood on her birthday, was now divided into three consultation compartments. After a while, I was introduced to an elegant lady in her thirties, who seemed interested to know that my family had once owned the building as a private home. No, she said, she did not like working in the place. Why was that?

'Because the building is haunted by an evil spirit,' she said.

The other women supported her tale. They had forced the council to agree that they would not work there in the winter after dark.

That apparition was surely older, darker, more malevolent than the mild Bessie. I thought about the old tavern that once stood on the site. Someone was flinging open a sash window which no longer existed. You could imagine some unfortunate, upstairs in the dismal provincial inn, awake long into the night until his candle guttered out. Dismayed, drunken, damaged, furious with life's disappointments, he had flung up the lower window and jumped into a greater, starless darkness.

The elegant lady told me that she had been working upstairs late in the previous year, after night had fallen. Her office was the room in which Bessie had died. She heard someone coming upstairs and, thinking it to be her boss, had called his name.

No answer. The steps came nearer. She turned. The steps approached her, fading away as they reached her. Horrified, she rushed from the building into the lane, and could not nerve herself to go back in. It was Dot's story over again.

This was objective proof of the ghost's reality.

I got in touch with the Revd Harry Tate, the vicar of St Nicholas. He wrote to me some time later to say that, somewhat against his own inclination, he had performed an exorcism ceremony in the building. As soon as he opened his attaché case to bring out the Bible, there was an almighty explosion and a stink. He completed the ceremony, convinced that the spirit had vanished for ever.

Something more ancient, more evil, some hagridden thing may have possessed that site even before the days when the old inn stood on the spot, so close to Bishop Bonner's Cottages. The Bishop's Shadow? Whatever it was, is, it holds for me a metaphorical implication, a reminder of what Carl Jung says in one of his lectures in *Analytical Psychology*, that 'the ego is only a bit of consciousness which floats upon the ocean of dark things'. Could this dreaded St Withburga *thing* be in some way a projection of the shadow side of human life, of unhappiness, as the oncoming war might be seen, among everything else, as a projection of European misery?

One can only say that as yet science has tunnel vision and cannot see or explain many manifestations, such as mind itself, which do not submit to instruments.

Or, indeed, to Bibles! Some while after the exorcism, another letter came from the Revd Tate, announcing that the foul thing had returned to its haunt. Now no one will work there.

In this year in which I write, Margaret and I returned to East Dereham. We found that the building now stands deserted. Whatever resides there, it has won.

It is time to turn our backs on Dereham.

XII

The Enchanted Zone

These reflections led me to the conclusion that the jungle,
with its resolute inhabitants, with its chance encounters, its
accidental meetings, its not yet elapsed time, had taught me
far more of the essence of my art, of the profound meaning of
certain texts . . . than the reading of so many books that lay dead
for ever on the shelves of my library.

Alejo Carpentier
The Lost Steps

Happily, the whole family drama, the mysteries and unspoken
things, were left behind while I was in India. There we could
stand up and be men. We said goodbye not only to England and
family, but – it proved almost the harder thing – to books, which
are practically another life.

Mhow hardened us to a tropical climate. After we had been
inoculated once again, after we had been lectured once more upon
the perils of having sexual intercourse with native women ('Stick to
the old five-fingered widow, lads'), after interminable parades, after
the whole rigmarole of the long-established British-Army-in-India
routine – after, as I say, six weeks of getting brown and being browned
off in Mhow, we were despatched in various directions to various
units. Some went to be *base wallahs* in Delhi, some to the Signals
centre in Ahmednagar, some to join the excitements of Burma.

Twelve of us boarded a train at Mhow station, heading eastwards.
We were loaded down with kit, with rifles, and with sacks of stores
for the journey. It was difficult to turn round in the Hard Class
compartment, which bore an order on a small ivory notice: *To
Accommodate not more than Eight Indian Passengers.* For the

succeeding sixteen days, we were ensnared within the complexities of the Indian railway system. It was a long train ride.

We slept as we could in our compartment, on the seats, under them, up on the wooden luggage racks. Or on station platforms, or in transit camps *en route*. We were besieged by beggars and sometimes by monkeys. We were shunted into a siding in Allahabad station, there to remain through most of a scorching day. A monkey jumped in through the window and snatched a precious loaf of bread from our sack of provisions. I climbed on to the roof of the train after him. Running as if in an Olympic event, I had almost caught up with him when, with a bound, he swung himself up into an overhanging tree, and was safe with his booty.

It was fun.

I was no longer the lad of last chapter's events, no longer the youth leaving West Buckland with some little achievement behind him. Give a young man a gun, train him to shoot, dress him in whatever uniform, put him among similar young men, and he becomes that archetypal figure, *the soldier*. He may be the lowest of the low, yet he sees himself as a Lordlet of Creation.

Those sixteen days on the train were part of the hardening-off process – seen even then as a journey with legendary aspects, a progress towards war. But I have written of it at length elsewhere, and so will rush on at a better pace than was achieved by the train to Dimapur, the gateway to the conflict in Burma.

Legends generally include the crossing of a river. In our case, it was the mighty Brahmaputra, the very name of which is like a sluggish Hindu dream! We made the crossing in a shallow-draught paddle-steamer, sitting crowded on deck with other troops. Evening was drawing cloud across the sky. A storm arose. The boat had to heave-to in mid-stream, from whence we could see neither bank. We lay in the middle of a muddy sea. Darkness came on. Constant sheet lightning played over the water. We were surrounded by flashes, ghostly, unaccompanied by thunder. Waves splashed up at us – puny waves, but we sat only a foot above the water line.

The great display of light seemed determined to continue for ever. We fell asleep where we were, huddled, heads resting on packs. We woke into a chilly dawn. The storm was over, the steamer was pulling into the eastern shore.

A tinpot train waited to take us to Tinsukia, a village at the end of the railway line which straggled north from Calcutta.

On Tinsukia station we stood for five hours, smoking, complaining, instructing beggars to bugger off, while darkness fell. Darkness with its sudden Indian fade swept across the sullied plain. A thousand little oil lamps winked on in protest. But to the north of us, immutable, the long bastions of the Himalayas remained in light. Easy to believe in the gods when gazing on that sight!

The evening deepened. Those vast white memorials to a collision between two continents slowly turned as pink as the toes of lotus-eyed Lakshmi. In the state of mind induced by such a vision, one might levitate or, alternatively, sink into the amber arms of a willing goddess. But we were foreigners – the train came grunting and puffing in at last, to bear us off to our duties.

Feeling, as our patois had it, *chokka*, we arrived at the end of that long journey in Dimapur, dusty, second-rate Dimapur, which stands at the fringe of Nagaland. Orders had not come through: we were not expected at the camp. For our first night there, we had to sleep on mess tables out in the open.

The Dimapur transit camp was one of the worst ever encountered. These camps, dotted all over the subcontinent, werc almost autonomous, little Fort Zindeneufs at the mercy of their commandants. Guardian of the gate at Dimapur was a massive ape, signifying that this was Kong country.

The ape was permanently chained to a dead tree stump fifteen feet high, and in consequence was in no mood to trifle with visitors. From its perch, it would shin down in an instant, to dash out, roaring, to the full length of its chain, eyes blazing with hatred, eager to grab and dash to destruction anyone or anything within reach.

Beyond grabbing range of this terrifying guardian lay the camp itself, a series of tumbledown *bashas*, filled with wretched men who somehow managed to avoid – if only for a day or two – moving any further eastwards towards Burma.

Our contingent was diminished in number. Of our original party of twelve, five of us only remained, the rest having been posted along the route to different units. We had run out of money and provisions. We were dirty and starving.

Before us on the mess tables were placed hunks of bread, and open cans of butter and jam, around which flies buzzed incessantly. For them, it was but a short buzz from the fetid latrines.

While waiting there to go forward, my pal Bloomfield and I were commandeered to fly in Dakotas on supply runs. Our troops in

Assam and Burma had to be supplied by air; only water waggons took the overland route.

Americans flew the Dakotas. The Dakota was one of the finest planes ever built by Douglas. It was very stable, even at low speeds, serving as cargo or passenger plane.

Since the camp at Dimapur was not expecting us, I went to the CO and volunteered to work as a radio op in Chunking. Chunking lay over the hump of the Himalayas in China, the wartime HQ of Chiang Kai-shek. I knew that everyone in Chungking lived in holes in the ground while Japanese planes bombed them continuously.

I had seen a chance of getting into China, dreamed of ever since boyhood. The CO dismissed the idea – and me.

'You want to get out of the fighting, Aldiss?'

'There's fighting in China, sir.'

'Dismiss.'

Twice more, during my overseas tour, I volunteered for a China posting. In 1946, I was to get as near as Hong Kong.

A 3-tonner arrived at Dimapur transit camp. With four others, I climbed into the truck and we started along the Dimapur road. The road led to Kohima and Imphal, through the small Indian state of Manipur, across the Kabaw valley, into the parched heart of Burma.

That extraordinary road, winding some ninety miles towards Kohima, represented the triumph of mankind over extreme adverse conditions. Every mile of it had been gouged out of afforested hillsides, by Indian, Chinese and Naga labour. To sustain it on one level, the road writhed from one direction to another, a snake in dying agony. At our very elbows, the hillsides fell away to a thread of river far below. Lorries had driven over the *khud*, and lay broken, down in the distant water.

The sunshine swung from one side of the lorry to the other as we negotiated the twists and turns. I stood by the tailgate with my mate from Catterick, Ron Ferguson, being violently sick over the edge, as travel by any road had made me sick when a boy.

It was indeed a journey to another personality. Realisation dawned, as we rattled along, that I had become prone to travel sickness only after Bill had driven me into exile in Peterborough. Fear and self-disgust had induced the sickness thereafter, for over a decade. This understanding came clear and uninvited. I vowed to myself on the Dimapur road I would never be travel sick again. I was a man now.

So it came about. My sickness disappeared, never to return. The triumph of mind over muckiness.

*   *   *

The 3-tonner delivered us to Milestone 81.

There I was signed for like a parcel, to become a humble item on the XIVth Army's payroll.

There I was swallowed into the British 2nd Division, always referred to as '2 Div'.

There I was given the divisional Cross Keys insignia to stitch to my uniform and bush hat. Strangely enough these keys of St Peter had also been the symbol of Fenn's prep school. I tried not to think about that; for all its shortcomings, Milestone 81 was to be preferred to Fenn's establishment. My new bosses had sensible objectives in view.

Milestone 81 was the designation of a resting place for Div Signals. It perched on the side of a sheer mountain, up which the unruly jungles of Assam swarmed. The assorted soldiery lived in tents improvised from tarpaulins, in various degrees of discomfort. The hillsides above us yielded the odd boulder, which came crashing down in the night, often incurring not death but a general stand-to, so near were the Japs, so fraught everyone's nerves.

Crowning the top of the mountain, unseen from below, was a Naga village, strictly out of bounds. Every day, we watched the lithe Nagas, men and women, climb a mile down to the valley, immense wicker baskets strapped about their foreheads in order to leave both hands free for the climb. There was nothing else to watch. The limited pleasures of Dimapur were inaccessible: the marvellous, terrible road was for supplies alone. Naga women were similarly inaccessible. It was rumoured that any man attempting conjunction with one would find a deftly wielded *kris* parting him from his military member.

The sole washing facility for the unit was a large-bore pipe issuing from the mountainside, spewing out, night and day, a jet of ice-cold water. One stripped off in full view of all – including any distant possible Japs – and strove to maintain a toe-hold on slippery concrete while receiving the full blast of water on the chest. It arrived like a shot from a cannon.

Food was severely rationed at Milestone 81, but letters home remain resolutely cheerful:

> The mountains here are wonderful. But I find it hungry work, living at 4300 feet . . . The grand scenery here produces a great sense of calm, and seems to reduce war to the useless squabble it really is.

* * *

Very philosophical, and designed for home consumption. Not a word about feeling *chokka* . . .

Living at approximately the height of the peak of Ben Nevis, we were hot by day, chilly by night. I was given a place in which to make a bed just inside one of the improvised tents. The trick was to stretch a groundsheet across a rectangular structure consisting of four poles lashed together with signal wire. This was raised off the ground on empty jerry cans. On sloping ground, it was at best a precarious arrangement.

A mosquito net had to be secured above this contraption. It hung limply over the bed like a moth-eaten flag at half-mast. When I climbed in to sleep, the net almost touched my nose.

In the night, it did touch it. Rats turned the tent into a miniature greyhound stadium during hours of darkness. One leapt on top of the net, in so doing landing on my face. Jerking angrily awake and sitting up, I upset the balance of the jerry cans. I was tipped clear out of the tent, to roll naked down a section of hillside.

My swearing elicited no sympathy from the other occupants of the tent. They told me to *Chibar-ao!*, Urdu for 'Shut up'.

The hillside had been honeycombed by Jap bunkers, making their occupants hard to dislodge. Only a few weeks before my arrival, flame-throwers had been turned on them. The Japs had perished horribly in their burrows. The entrances to the bunkers had been sealed off, leaving the charred bodies inside to rot. Rats had then enjoyed the fortunes of war.

My new mates were unfriendly. I was merely a reinforcement, untried. They had been through the hellish battles raging round Imphal and Kohima. In the battle of Kohima, 2 Div had lost 2,125 men. I was a pale white young thing; they were tanned the colour of a mule's backside. I knew nothing; they knew everything and could say nothing.

To their contempt was added a general weariness and disillusion. Many of them had already served three years in the East, and saw no prospect of returning home. They called themselves the Forgotten Army.

Looking back fifty years, we regard that war as an imperial war. The troops, as troops will, served on without questioning the larger issues. We were treated in a cavalier, imperialist way, sent out in stinking, overcrowded troopships, often housed in tents and huts abandoned after the First World War, badly fed, and – above all – given no sort of promise that we would ever be returned home. Terms could hardly have been harsher had we enlisted in the French Foreign Legion.

At the time, such reflections did not enter my head. I concentrated in burning myself brown – protective coloration. And, because everything was new, I remained in a state of subdued excitement.

One new thing was the Fullerphone, on which I was delegated to work. This little object, a marsupial of the pre-electronic age, was a line instrument on which one tapped out Morse to whoever was at the other end. In our case, this was generally the Brigades, in forward positions.

In this respect, I was a useful reinforcement for 2 Div. I could send Morse code at the rate of eighty words a minute and read as quickly.

The Fullerphone was a small black metal affair about the size of an early answerphone. It worked on batteries and emitted, when in operation, a low threatening buzz as if about to take off like a hornet in the direction of one's throat. Maintenance on the little brute included opening up, putting two fingers across the terminals, cranking a handle, and getting a shock. This was the machine I was to operate for the next six months.

The day came when we were assembled on the hillside. Our commanding officer addressed us. He was armed with a map and a pointer.

'Well, men, we are at last going into action, you'll be glad to hear. We're going to sweep the Japs right off the map. We've got them on the run and we aren't going to let up now.'

He wielded the pointer. 'We shall move across these mountains here, cross the Chindwin River somewhere here, cross the Irrawaddy approximately here, and re-take Mandalay. Here's Mandalay. After that, we sweep southwards towards Rangoon, and nothing is going to stop us. We have good air support from the RAF and USAF, and tank brigades on the ground. We've got the Japs licked, and all we have to do is maintain pressure.'

This sort of talk has since been parodied, but it was serious at the time. Everyone understood the code. The CO concluded by quoting Henry V's great speech at Agincourt,

> And gentlemen in England now a-bed
> Shall think themselves accurs'd they were not here,
> And hold their manhoods cheap whiles any speaks
> That fought with us upon Saint Crispin's day.

At Shakespeare's words, many a case-hardened eye was piped. I've always been proud that that oratory was used on that occasion. It was a portion of being English.

Before we moved forward, much preparation was required. André Malraux declared that the purpose of war was to ensure that as many fragments of metal as possible penetrated human flesh. In Burma, matters were somewhat more absurd. Many things penetrated human flesh, including ticks and mosquitoes. Casualties from malaria were always high, despite the mepacrine tablets we were forced to take, making us look as yellow as the enemy.

DDT was then a new thing, at least in our theatre of war. We were issued with gallons of it. First we dyed everything we possessed green, including underpants and towels. Then we soaked them in DDT. The seams of our trousers were specially treated. We knew we were entering a water-free zone, where insects would be in good supply.

Our bedding too was treated. That was easy enough. Bedding consisted of one American-issue blanket. It was a smooth brown blanket, unlike the hairy and uncomfortable British ones of the period. I liked that blanket even when it grew to stink of sweat, and was sorry when the time came to part with it.

Early in December 1944, we began to roll.

This was a further journey into unknown lands. The sixteen days of rail travel had been a self-contained saga. Now, compressed into four days and nights, was a saga of a more traditional kind, to be experienced once only in a lifetime – the saga of an army moving into action.

Our vehicles drove on improvised roads. This being the dry season, dried-up *chaungs*, or river beds, which churned to dust under rolling tyres, served as our highway. With much revving and changing of gear, the convoy traversed the broken series of escarpments which made any advance in that region such misery.

The narrow thread of vehicles stretched for miles. When our S Section lorry was labouring to the top of a crest, we could see the thread of vehicles far away behind us, below clouds; conversely, when we were in a valley, we could look up through clouds and see that thread continuing far ahead of us, climbing the next series of heights.

Field-Marshal Bill Slim, Commander of the XIVth Army, describes this territory: 'You must hack and push your way through the clinging, tightly packed greenery, scramble up the precipitous slopes and slide down the other side, endlessly, as if you were walking along the teeth of a saw.' One admires the use of the very English word 'greenery' in this context. Later, flying over the area, Slim says, 'As we roared over these endless, razor-edged ridges, covered to their very summits with the densest jungle, they gave the impression of a thick-piled, dull green carpet, rucked up into fold after fold.'

Over this carpet, our convoy struggled.

This thin caterpillar of warfare, creeping forward, towards the east and the Rising Sun, carried with it clouds of dust, surrounding it as if we were about to go into a cocoon stage. Between the lorries rolled Jeeps and guns. Despatch riders weaved perilously back and forth along the column, carrying messages. We maintained radio silence.

We travelled in darkness or in light. To be part of this insect of war was most thrilling after dark. Dim headlights scarcely penetrated the muck we threw up. We could scarcely see the taillights of the vehicle ahead. Speed was down almost to walking pace. The impression of an animal bent on traversing a strange planet was at its strongest. On either side, unknowable, thrilling, fearsome, stood the jungle, pale as a ghost jungle in its layers of dust.

Our lorry was packed with stores on which we had to sit. Between cab and body, where the spare wheel was stashed, was a bale of barbed wire. I found that, by climbing on to the wire – it was no more painful than a bed of nails – I could prop myself on the cab roof and gain a better view of this hell-like cavalcade.

Unfortunately, I fell asleep there.

'You, man, *you!* What the hell do you think you're playing at? Get up at once.'

Shouts awoke me. It was daylight. A sergeant was shouting at me, and I was upside down.

Having fallen asleep, I had slipped and was lying head downwards between cab and body of the lorry. Only the barbed wire, digging into uniform and anatomy, had saved me from falling under the wheels of either our vehicle or the succeeding ones. In the night, no one would have seen anyone run over in the deep dust of a *chaung* . . .

On one night of the advance, S Section was required to camp by the roadside. Bivouacs were pitched among thickets of trees. The trees stood limp, awaiting the rains of midsummer.

The moon was bright. Filled with excitement, I could not sleep. I climbed out into the silvery dark and stood among the thin trunks. Not far distant lay the improvised road. The vehicles of the Forgotten Army were rolling ceaselessly onwards, all noise muffled by the dust which shrouded them – dust which made their shapes uncertain, their headlights dim as tiger's eyes.

How long I stood there I know not. *Nobody knew where I was.*

The trucks in their shrouds of dust resembled a kind of gloomy lifeform, inhabiting a world where their sun was the silver globe shining overhead through the trees. As in some weird tale by Ambrose Bierce, I might have fallen from the flanks of one of the creatures when asleep, have died, and was now in the grey and noiseless world beyond life.

Although we were thrown much together, and bound to cooperate, it took some while for the other members of S Section to accept me. At one waiting place along the route, a canteen opened unexpectedly. Perhaps it was to mark Christmas Day. I see from a letter home that 'I bought canned peas, canned pears, and Post Toasties . . . The pear tin was the size that we four used to have for tea. But I had no one to share it with.'

I have no memory of this. I do recall being always hungry. For the rest of the campaign, we were on half-rations.

We passed Kohima's smouldering remains, and what was left of Imphal. These names, so famous, so charged with pain and heroism, the very places where the Japanese advance on India was halted, designated mere villages lost in trackless bush. Perhaps ancient Thebes and Troy were no grander.

The Burmese had welcomed the Japs, seeing them as liberators from the British yoke. But the Japanese had treated them with their usual brutality and, when the tide of war was turning, so the Burmese became less hostile towards the British. The clever and courageous Aung San turned the Burma National Army against the Japanese, though not before he had informed the Japanese of his intentions.

In May of 1945, Aung San presented himself to General Slim at the HQ of the XIVth Army in Meiktila, dressed in the uniform of a Japanese major-general, complete with ceremonial sword. By then the war was almost over, and the deeds of the remarkable Aung San pass from military to political history. Aung San was to sign an agreement with PM Clement Attlee in 1947, guaranteeing Burma's almost immediate independence; later that year, he, whom the British had spared, was murdered by Burmese thugs.

So the Burmese were never entirely trusted during these campaigns. By and large, they made themselves scarce. Our entry into deserted towns like Imphal stood in stark contrast to the scenes in European cities liberated from German occupation by British and American troops. There, agreeably excited ladies swarmed on the streets, offering flowers and kisses – and who knew what else – to the troops. If we saw anyone in the dusty townships we passed through, they likely as not sank back into shade and safety. No sign of welcome came from them, no girls ran out to be kissed.

Once the convoy had wound its way through the mountains, the plain was easier going. We were now, at least nominally, in Jap-held territory.

The road became worse. Huddled in the back of our truck, we of S Relief could only hang on. Sleep was impossible. My resolve never to be travel sick again held. When we halted for a while, for one of those inexplicable waits which attend armies, everyone walked about like corpses, covered with the talc of the roads.

When the dust was red, then the foliage on either side was red for at least a hundred yards in; when the dust was grey or white, then the jungle took on a funebral aspect as if, instead of heading for the Chindwin, we had, in our muffled movement, day and night, become like that dead dream army in Alexander Lernet-Holenia's supernatural story 'Baron Bagge'.

And I am now talking of a dead army, advancing in a country no longer even called Burma, over half a century and many minor wars ago.

At an area on the map labelled Yzagyo, our section of the convoy made camp. The country seemed part desert, part forest, with melancholy trees no more than eight feet high, spindly, and widely spaced. The desolation was punctuated from here to Mandalay and beyond with white marble pagodas.

The pagodas are what one remembers most vividly, with their reminders of a native love of beauty married to religion, in contrast to Dereham's Cowper Church.

As our vehicles circled and parked, we climbed to the ground, beating the powdered dust from our clothes. A trickle of river flowed near by, with a particularly large pagoda dominating the landscape. NCOs marched about, shouting orders. A group of officers stood by the river bank.

A shot rang out. One of the officers fell. More shots. Everyone running, throwing themselves flat, setting rifles to shoulders with little idea at first of what to aim at.

The shots came from the top of the pagoda. A Japanese sniper had been walled up in it, with a cupful of rice and a gun, to await just such a moment as he had chosen.

A mortar was brought and the top of the pagoda blasted off, the hidden assassin with it.

In Yzagyo I saw my first live Jap. He was trotting along the river bank, almost naked, quite a perky little figure. What kept him going was the BOR (British Other Rank) behind him with a bayonet at his back.

Once the signal office was established, we dug slit trenches for our bivouac. I was ordered to share a bivouac with the least friendly member of S Section, a Lancashire man called Bradbury. We worked with picks and entrenching tools. The trenches had to be a minimum of eighteen inches deep. Roots of trees had to be hacked away. The ground was like rock. This procedure was carried out, day or night, every time we camped.

Bradbury and I had achieved a good deep trench when we struck a white ants' nest.

'I'm fooked if I'm digging another fookin' hole,' said Bradbury, flinging down his entrenching tool and marching off in disgust.

I started again, a few feet away. When it was finished, the bivouac fitted over the top. It was just big enough to contain two *charpoys*. By now I had devised a more comfortable *charpoy* from two boughs resting on either end of the trench, kept apart by bits of planking and crossed by strips of parachute harness from one of the air drops.

By the time all this was done, grime was plastered over my body. Beside a nearby road was a stream in which lay an upturned Bren carrier. I joined a group of sepoys *dhobi*-ing their clothes, and enjoyed a wallow.

We went through Burma in bare buff, wearing slacks, puttees and boots. No hats, except after dark – they were considered womanish. We trailed the fragrance of sweat.

Describing Yzagyo in a letter, I wrote:

When we first arrived, we found quite a dignified area covered in low undergrowth, but in the last forty-eight hours a great change has been wrought. Hosts of miniature tents have arisen, crouching between piles of brown earth. Branches and foliage are cast about everywhere in an attempt at camouflage. Everywhere, tree stumps, tent cords, pegs, and wires. Even the brilliant moon doesn't save you from the occasional concealed trip.

From the trees go clothes lines, hung with blankets, slacks, pants, shorts, and towels, all green. It's a strange-looking area. Here we live and move and have our being – fifty or so soldiers who are linemen, drivers, operators, or mechanics in 'business hours', and in their spare time cooks, story-tellers, washermen, and navvies – or chaps writing home. There's an *atmosphere* about this place, and not a bad one.

*   *   *

I also complained that the drinking water was heavily chlorinated. It was all conveyed in tankers from distant sources.

Since I was writing after dark, I said that 'soon the varieties of parachute-cords-in-paraffin and ropes-in-petrol and electric torches and storm lanterns and candles will wink out, one by one'. And we would be left with darkness and the great Burmese moon. In memory, the Burmese moon is always full, always low above the landscape. All that magical moon lacked was a girl to go with it.

But we had entered an enchanted zone – a place of evil enchantment, if you like. You could not buy a ticket to get where we were. Several kinds of people were forbidden entrance. No women were allowed, or hairdressers, or any kind of extraneous occupation. Lawyers, entertainers, politicians – all were prohibited.

Two American officers drove up in a Jeep loaded with fire power, having come all the way from Calcutta to get 'a smack at the Nips'. Even they were turned away. To attend this show, you had to be young and male and part of the British Empire.

We had Australians with us, and East Africans near by, and many of the war-like Indian nations.

One evening, the members of S Section decided to have a meal. Our resourceful corporal-driver, Sid Feather, had scrounged a duck from somewhere. As the man in charge of our Dodge, he was able to undertake private missions. Other members of the section had canned vegetables and fruit. They had lit a fire. I heard them arguing as to whether I should be invited to join them. Bradbury was against it.

'What's he ever bloody done? He's got nowt to contribute. Leave him out. Fook him.'

'I'm not having anything to do with it if we're leaving him out.'

That was the reasonable voice of Lou Grey. Lou was a farmer from somewhere near Pinner. I greatly respected him, and we became friends.

Because of Lou's intercession, I was invited to the feast. I took along my canned peas, pears, and Post Toasties. From then on, I was accepted as one of the group. And quickly I became as schizophrenic in skin colour as the rest: almost boot-polish black above the Plimsoll line, startling white below.

Lou had a game eye, which gave him a look of maimed wisdom. Sergeant Leigh was a round-faced man with a pouting lip, who delighted me that Christmas by saying, 'I wish I was in a boardinghouse in Skegness, in bed with some low woman.' Leigh could be sharp. Corporal Dyer was a large bland man, never hustling, forever yearning for his family, still as homesick as he had been when first shipped out to India, three years or more earlier. Most remarkable was our orderly, Steve, a nice gruff man with a walrus moustache, avuncular towards me as a youngster, but slowly going *puggle*.

Many unfortunates in the Forgotten Army professed that with the heat and long service they were slowly going *puggle*. It was in part despair, in part romanticism. Steve Mantry was a genuine case. He spent many hours, when off duty, drilling himself outside the bivouacs.

'Private Steve, Har-ten-*shun*! As you were. Smarten up there, man. Private Steve, har-ten-*shun*. Better. Keep your chin up, man. By the right, qui-i-i-ck MARCH! Lep, lep, lep, ri', lep. Swing those arms. Plenty of bullshit now. Har-bout TURN!' etc. Tirelessly.

This routine often continued after dark. Back and forth Steve marched, rifle at the slope. A gentle chap, but round the bend. Hardly surprising in the circumstances.

In the enchanted zone there was no fixed front. As we advanced, pockets of Jap resistance remained, to be mopped up later. We never knew where they were. Some died of starvation in the jungle rather than surrender. S Section moved every few days, when our office and line connections, forward to Brigade and back to 33 Corps, had to be rebuilt. Often we were out in the wilds and did not know how close the enemy was. Despite fatigue, there was fascination in reconnoitring each new halt. Sometimes we were there for no more than a day; at other times, we remained for a week, as the advance met with enemy resistance.

For several years after I returned to England, I tried to memorise all the places in which we stopped; but inevitably they have faded to a blur.

What remains is the beauty of the day, bringing a sense of sorrow as the sun set. Tousled heads of trees would be silhouetted against the bright western sky as if cut from metal. The scene was mercilessly remote from man's ordinary affairs. Then darkness came on. You could not help expecting the lingering twilights of English summer evenings, where one sat out on the terrace, an old house at one's back, talking in quiet voices, until the stars shone. Burmese dark comes down like a shutter, full of winged things. It is a chargeable offence not to roll down your sleeves against mosquitoes.

The nights were nervous. Little nocturnal things scurried about outside the bivouac. They might be birds or snakes or Japs. We dozed under our mozzie nets with our rifles by our side.

Danger, though it never really materialised, remained present as a threat. Always there was the balm of being continually out of doors. Almost as soon as we left Yzagyo and pushed towards Kalewa on the Chindwin, the climate became hotter. We crossed the Tropic of Cancer. At last, the true tropics!

For the first week or two in action, I was starving. Half-rations drove me to risk a court martial offence. After our midday meal, I found it was possible to cut through the trees to another mess, possibly a REME mess. Here I queued for a second meal, wolfing it guiltily down from my mess tin. According to King's Regulations, this is 'stealing another man's rations'. I had to have it, whoever the man concerned was. Gradually my body adjusted to half-rations and forgot to be hungry.

At one point, Base sent us down large tins of biscuits and cigarettes. The supplies had evidently been hoarded since the end of the Great War, locked away in some dim quartermaster's stores. The cigarettes were de Reszke; only the paper was brown: the tobacco was green with age. We smoked them just the same. But the old stale hardtack was rejected by everyone but me. The rest of the section laughed as I crunched my way through them.

My simultaneous fear of and rapport with our surroundings was strange. Many decades later, I came to believe that if Nature itself has a prompting towards self-awareness, then we are its fallible instruments. I found myself opening up to the wilderness, and dreaming, as I have so often dreamed since, of landscapes through which I must travel, in accord with my *life dream*.

So there was phylogeny as well as ontogeny in the *life dream*, for our species too seems to have no beginning, except in journeying – down from the trees, into open ground, or out of Africa. For the first time, I was in something at least resembling that primeval landscape in which humankind walked without trailing its knuckles on the ground. Who knows but that the blind promptings of evolution do not come from the whole biomass we call Nature? In trying to explain how I felt then, my thought is supplemented by the white pagodas whose bells tinkled in the slightest breeze, tokens of a religion that seemed to be in harmony with nature.

The business in which we were occupied was a twenty-four-hours-a-day job. Our network of communications became continuously more busy. DRs – despatch riders – roared up to the office with messages. The messages were either encoded or sent in clear to their various destinations. A constant flow of instructions circulated in all directions. When our shift went off duty, another shift took over. Nothing halted the flow of messages under our fingers, through our ears. Sometimes we remained working while the other shifts moved forward. Then it would be our turn to leapfrog forward.

At night, the nature of the traffic changed slightly. Long opreps and sitreps (operation and situation reports) came down the cable from forward areas, to be retransmitted to Corps HQ. Morse was forever chattering in our heads. On duty, we had no time for anything that might be called personal thought. All communication was impersonal, our reason for being.

One day, I walked through what resembled an orchard. The trees were no more than eight feet high, stunted, and growing apart in the poor soil as if planted by a gardener. This orchard was a mortuary. The trees did not bear fruit. The kind of birds I saw there did not sing.

I came on this place through a burned-out village, in an off-duty hour. Bodies of dead men lay about under the trees like fallen branches. Poultry of a kind moved among them, white scavenger birds, alarmed by my approach. They had feasted in the orchard until they were almost too fat to fly. Only with a great struggle did they get themselves into the branches of the trees. There they sat, mainly on a level with my head as I passed. I could have killed them with the butt of my rifle, had I been so inclined. Instead, I went quietly by.

These were not the vultures to which Indian life had accustomed us, saturnine birds with red wattled necks and severe ecclesiastical airs; what these most resembled were ordinary hens of the barnyard, White Leghorns and Wyandottes, bloated beyond reason. Their snowy plumage was disconcerting. It was hard to come to terms with the knowledge that they were full of human flesh. When I had passed, they fell out of the trees like so much heavy fruit, back on to the dead bodies.

There were times when I sweated from fear. To be alone without the protective truck, just with the Fullerphone, left under a tree, miles from anywhere, not knowing where the enemy was, hearing an imagined footfall – then I was overwhelmed by terror. When everything seizes up, intelligence cannot force the body to be brave.

Later, you hate yourself for cowardice and pray no one ever sees you in that state.

Our signal office day was divided into three shifts. The easiest shift was the morning one, from 8 a.m. to 1 p.m. The afternoon shift ran from 1 p.m. till 6 p.m. The night shift ran from 6 p.m. to 8 the next morning. As a rule, those who did morning shift took the afternoon off, then did night shift, with the afternoon shift next day. It was demanding work. Often the flow of traffic meant no escape from the headphones and the Fullerphone during the entire shift.

Occasionally, the night shift slacked off for an hour or two in the hours before dawn. Then it was possible to get your head down, often resting it literally on the table before you, or sometimes lying, dead to the world, boots pointing up to the sky, on the floor of the signal vehicle.

Periods off duty were filled with sleep whenever possible. More frequently, we might have to man a Bren post or to dig fortifications or, most likely, move camp a few miles farther forward.

The habit of reading became marginal. I carried in my kitbag a copy of Palgrave's *Golden Treasury*. I read Peter Cheyney and Ian Hay and P. G. Wodehouse. And one other mighty book, to which I will refer later.

When our forward units reached the Chindwin and met with opposition, then Signals units were most stretched. Sid Feather might drive me and another BOR to some forward position under a tree, leaving us with a day's provisions before he drove off. We would have no notion where anyone else was, friend or foe. We would then work the wireless, a 19 set, turn and turn about, while the other man kept guard, gazing out among the trees at the plains trembling under their own weight of heat – the plains with their pagodas, distinct whirls of whipped cream in the brilliant light.

We'd smoke and clutch at our prickly heat, and hope that someone would come back for us before nightfall.

Most of the pagodas on the plains were no more than ten feet high, topped with a little open metal crown, from which depended bells so ethereal the slightest touch of breeze would set them tinkling. Sometimes these pious monuments were protected by *chinthes*, the ferociously grinning Buddhist dog with the sharp teeth which gave its name, distortedly, to the Chindits. The Chindit motto also was a compound of languages: *Numquam wappas* – 'Never back'.

Inside the pagodas was a shrine, generally a marble counter on which had perched images of the Buddha. Most of the Buddhas had been stolen, to repose in the backpacks of British, Indian or Japanese soldiers. On the slab would lie flowers, fading in the heat, a mouthful offered towards the hunger for peace.

XIII

The Advance

Burningly, it came on me all at once, This was the place!
Robert Browning
Childe Roland to the Dark Tower Came

E veryone likes to conform. I conformed, seeing survival in it, and
was accepted by the Section. We sweated and swore the same
oaths together.

We bumped everywhere in our Dodge truck, that product of the
United States' massive automobile industry which so greatly helped
to win wars in West and East. As we lurched through the narrow
chaungs to reach the map reference where we were next to set up
shop, we would pass the PBI, the Poor Bloody Infantry, marching
their way across Burma. Our dust smothered them. They plodded
on. We were ashamed at the ease of our life.

'Thank God we aren't in the real fucking army,' we said, making
a joke of it.

Some of the infantry carried items of loot on their backs. The
pickings were poor here, often compared bitterly with the loot to be
had in France, in Belgium, in Italy and Germany. I saw one soldier
of the 2nd Royal Norfolks bowed under a heavy old Jap typewriter
lashed to his back, and wondered what he would do with it. Maybe it
was *pegdo*'d (discarded), or maybe even now it adorns the front room
of a house in Happisburgh or Swaffham.

We found little loot. There is curiosity value, though, in coming
to a deserted Japanese camp with items of kit strewn about, pages
of a Jap newspaper, perhaps a photograph of parents or a girl. *These
bastards were here only the day before. You'd be dead, had you
turned up then . . .*

What would it be like to kill one of them, shoot them? Not bad, eh? Not too bad. Bloody good, probably.

In off-duty hours, we tramped into Burmese houses, built up on short stilts, perhaps with beautifully carved verandah walls in teak. Inside, all peaceful and shadowy, full of an atmosphere of a time already taken apart. And our infantry had been in and wrecked the place for the sheer joy of destruction. I stood in one grand little house, which listed to one side as if it were a sinking ship. Someone had hacked away one of its stilts for the pleasure of doing so.

That sinking room embodied the wastage of warfare. I picked up a photograph, spilled in haste as the owners left. It showed an old man in a saffron gown, sitting in a wicker chair with two sons squatting at his feet. The photograph is still in my possession.

In war, the Shadow side of human character gets a real run for its money. Perversely, the destruction of property felt more shocking than the killing of men. Houses had not harmed us, whereas the Japs were the reason for our being in this benighted bit of the globe, far from home.

We worked on. The Signals motto is *Certo Cito* – 'Swift and Sure', but translated in the ranks as 'Shit or Bust'. However weary we were, however *chokka* with soya links for breakfast, we had our own motto: 'Bash on Regardless . . .' That we did, for much of the time in a fog of weariness.

Sightseeing was low on our list of priorities. We viewed the country from the back of the truck as we were shunted to the next post. When the brigades, 4, 5 and 6 Brigade, as they were imaginatively called, reached the Chindwin, Jap opposition stiffened. Traffic over the Fullerphone to the Dorsets, the Durham Light, the Norfolks, and the Royal Welsh increased as opreps came through. At least all the messages were now in clear. Matters were too urgent for the cumbersome five-letter cipher blocks which suffered the delay of decoding.

Above the mosquito whine of the Fullerphone, we could hear big guns pounding across that celebrated river. The slam of shells was like the banging of a heavy castle door. Their flashes were clear at night, signals from disputed river crossings. In the course of nine nights, we were working six of them, flat out, all night without pause; or in a respite we would fall into heavy sleep for half an hour, cheeks pressed against the metal of the truck floor, till someone shook us awake. At dawn, we staggered away, into a pallid world where that door still slammed like an overloaded pulse.

We collapsed after shift in our sweltering bivouacs, to dream of *kyfer*. But the infantry – they were doing the real job.

Though fatigue had us staggering, we were frequently unable to sleep. An accursed bird that lives on the Burmese plains chirped Morse instead of singing. 'Dit dit dit, dit dah dit dit, dit, dah,' with variations, on and on, from the height of a great palm. I have rushed out naked, screaming and cursing, and have seen other men do so, to scare away a wretched bird sending us messages our tired brains were forced to receive and decode.

As for *kyfer*, the rumour went about that three sepoys from Dagger Div had caught a Burmese woman and raped her by turns. When they were exhausted, she is supposed to have said, 'Come on then, I was just getting interested.' Possibly this was true, possibly apocryphal. Men's minds fasten on the subject of women when none is present.

Once across the Chindwin, the way to the Irrawaddy and Mandalay was clear. Schwebo and Ye-U lay ahead. Slim planned to rid the Schwebo plain of Japs before pressing on to the old capital, where the Japanese commander was preparing to defend his positions to the last man.

Our section crossed the Chindwin near Kalewa. We drove across the world's longest Bailey bridge, waved on cheerily by REME. We were treated to an ENSA concert party that week. There were white women, shipped in from England, prancing on a stage. As though to emphasise our single blessedness, a little vamp in a frilly dress came on and coyly sang 'Especially For You, I've been selected . . .' and so forth. It was a form of torture. Soon S Section was singing my version, 'Let's get connected'.

The stage on which the party performed was improvised in the middle of a *maidan*, so that as many men as possible could crowd in and sit on the baked ground to watch the proceedings. It was night. A great moon presided over everything. In the middle of the show, there was an air raid. All the lights went out. But the performers went on with the act, singing, dancing – clearly visible in the moonlight as three Jap Zeros flew overhead.

Later, the 'Sweetheart of the Forces', Vera Lynn, flew out to entertain the troops. She insisted on going to the forward areas. We bumped over to Brigade in Sid Feather's Dodge to see her. Diarrhoea had struck the poor lady. Twice she had to leave the stage in the middle of her act, but back she came, undaunted, to sing 'Yours to the end of life's story, Here or on far distant shores . . .'. This spirited lady, the apotheosis of the ordinary, tuneful and full of courage, has achieved a kind of mythic status, a kind of Queen

Mother of war. She trots out from retirement whenever trouble is brewing, once more to sing – rather ominously in context – 'We'll Meet Again'. The Falklands war saw her back in strength. After the nastiness with Saddam Hussein in the Gulf, the comedian Ken Dodd joked, 'I knew there was going to be a war – as I passed Vera Lynn's house, I could hear her gargling.'

We were now deep into the plains. The temperature rose. One of our temporary destinations lay in the midst of elephant grass, nine feet high. The temperature reached 136°F. The signal office staff dripped sweat on their message pads. Among the insect allies of the Japanese were ants, of which Burma spawns a great variety. The small ginger ones had a vicious bite. They came climbing up the guy ropes of the signal tent. Nothing could deter them. Once inside and swarming over the roof, they had a habit of dropping down on our necks.

We came upon the road to Mandalay, long ago made famous by Rudyard Kipling.

It was a good macadamised road, almost suburban in appearance. Fortunate were those who had travelled this road from India to enjoy the pre-war glories of ancient Mandalay. The trees grown for shade on either side of the route had their trunks painted white.

Along this highway, running straight across the plains, thousands of men, women and children had thronged in 1942, seeking to escape from the invader. It was mainly a civilian exodus, such as all wars bring about. Fleeing Indians, Burmese, Chinese, British had headed westwards, hoping to reach India. They had to cross those 'ridges like the teeth of a saw', of which Slim spoke, which stand between Burma and the desired railway line at Dimapur which runs to Calcutta.

Not the terrain alone but an oncoming monsoon impeded their efforts. Some were assisted by Assam tea planters. Nevertheless, it has been estimated that perhaps as many as 50,000 people perished in the retreat from Mandalay.

The suburban aspect of the road formed a disconcerting background for the metal carcases that lined it, mile after mile. Among the rusting skeletons of cars were remains of bullock carts, almost eaten away by termites. Together, they formed a macabre parody of a long traffic jam, in which all radiators pointed towards the west.

In these vehicles, the more fortunate had travelled, jostling from Mandalay and towns near by, until petrol gave out or the overloaded bullock died of exhaustion. Heat, insects, illness and fatigue had overtaken many of the travellers. They died by the roadside or in the ever-devouring jungle.

With them had died this component part of the British Empire. When all's said, the enchanted zone was a terrible landscape of loss.

Shaving in half a *piyala* (mug) of cold water, squinting into a square of mirror propped on the bonnet of Sid Feather's Dodge, I thought of Bill. He, thirty or fewer years ago, had done much the same thing in Egypt. I recalled the sepia photograph of him washing a pair of socks in a bowl of water in the middle of the desert.

The parade of rusting vehicle skeletons grew thicker as we approached Mandalay. The scene would stand today for a science fiction film or a sequel to Jean-Luc Godard's movie *Weekend*.

By now, the promise of victory was almost fulfilled. Morale since Milestone 81 had improved. Lord Louis Mountbatten, C-in-C SEAC, came to speak to us on a lightning tour of the troops. I stood within a yard of him. He was immaculate, handsome, an embodiment of the ruling class. No doubt he smelt better than we did; for him, civilisation, showers and *dhobi-wallahs* were only an hour away by plane: we had weeks to endure before we saw even an improvised ablution. He told us we were doing well, were going to smash the Jap and regain Burma for Britain.

We were very pleased to hear this. We gave him a cheer as he flew off.

The grandeur of our situation: the beauty of the country, the intense heat, the dimensions of global war, the horror of it, and the excitement of winning: all this was an intoxication. I wanted everything every day to remain on this grand scale. The pettiness of the chat around me seemed out of key. But I had a book to read which more than matched the scale of events.

I was waiting for injections against typhoid, tetanus and cholera. The MO had installed himself in a well-furnished tea planter's bungalow. One wall of what had become the Medical waiting-room was filled by the planter's bookshelves. On those shelves I discovered W. Olaf Stapledon's *Last and First Men*. This visionary book tells the story of humanity over the next two billion years, of how it evolves to live on Venus and Neptune. My spirit thirsted for Stapledon's news, and his conclusion: 'It is very good to have been man.'

Stapledon is one of a line of English visionaries like William Blake and Charles Doughty, who try to create their own legend to live by. He is neglected, sadly, because science fiction has become divorced from the main flow of English literature. I owe a debt of inspiration to Stapledon's book, published in the early thirties, although Stapledon went on to create a yet more magnificent vision, *Star Maker*, at the end of the thirties.

A copy of Eric Lomax's *The Railway Man* has just come to hand. He too served in the East, to be captured by the Japs on the surrender of Singapore. He too mentions reading *Last and First Men* on a train winding up the Malay Peninsula, taking him to labour on the Death Railway.

Doris Lessing too read Stapledon's book in what was then Southern Rhodesia. She asks, 'What made this extraordinary man? What star shone on his cradle?' The imaginings of a religious atheist will always find an audience – not least in time of trouble.

Our section of 2 Div now became part of a pincer movement closing on Mandalay. We set up our bivouacs near Ye-U. Still all our supplies were dropped by air. The Dakotas flew low, releasing their colour-coded freight. We had all grown wild. Our bodies were burnt almost black. Our hair was long. Our bush hats were decorated with *pugarees* of parachute silk, red, yellow, blue, green, which trailed down our backs. We were a new sort of pirate.

Wherever we went, the Pioneer Corps was just ahead of us, digging latrines. Latrines were always situated near the cookhouse. A rectangular trench was dug, perhaps as much as ten feet deep. A tree was felled, its trunk laid along the trench, just over the edge of the pit. You hung your behind over this pit and got away as fast as you could. Sometimes half-a-dozen men would be there at the same time. Lime was flung regularly over the rising contents. You might not exactly like it, but that was how things were.

When we moved on, the Pioneers had the task of filling in the pit again. No doubt flourishing knots of palm trees mark our route, even to this day.

We were at full stretch in Ye-U. But Sid Feather, ever resourceful, found us a river, the River Mu. It was so long since we had seen water, that the Mu was preferred even to sleep.

That wonderful, sacred river! Even in the dry season, the Mu is magnificent, forcing its green-white foaming way to the Irrawaddy. It flows in Burma for all its length, and makes up for this shortcoming by speeding through steep banks of sand – pure, yellow, hot-to-the-touch. We could not swim against its strength. We stripped off, flung ourselves in, and allowed ourselves to be washed rapidly downstream. The Mu whizzed us round bends as if we were taking a bobsleigh ride, ducking us and roaring on its way.

Then, where the water became shallower, we could bask, before climbing out and hurrying back upstream for another immersion.

I still have two of Lou Grey's photographs. One shows our naked figures tiny against the spread of the river bed, the shrunken river cutting a channel southwards. In the background is one of the railway bridges British engineers built in peaceful days, for a single track running East–West. The bridge spans the width of the Mu in flood. When the Japanese invaded, locomotives and carriages were driven on to the bridge, and the central span was blown up. Such a valuable asset could not be allowed to fall into Jap hands.

Three years later, a locomotive was still dangling over the gulf, suspended by its coupling to its ruined coaches. Lou and I trudged upstream to stand below the great brick pillar of the bridge and gaze upwards. Above us hung a symbol for the decline and fall of almost everything.

The other photograph shows most of S Relief wallowing in the Mu shallows beside a smaller engine, a shunter, which has fallen into the stream. The metal of the engine is too hot to touch. It will be drowned deep under water again in another couple of months, when the monsoons arrive.

The signal office moves to Schwebo. Schwebo has been a fine town, as Burmese towns go. Now it is devastated. We enter a splendid large pagoda which has had its top blown off. Inside lies a large Buddha, horizontal in marble. His pale hands are clasped together in the *namaste* attitude. His great feet are bare. His garments are gathered about his knees. His eyes are half closed by heavy eyelids. On his face is an expression of post-coital satisfaction (so unlike the agony of Jesus, half dead on the cross). The jewel once embedded in his broad forehead has been stolen.

British soldiers stand before this recumbent figure uneasily. They cannot decide if or how to mock.

Here we saw *pungyi*s, the Buddhist monks with shaven heads, and dressed in saffron robes. They were bolder now that it was easier to see which warring side was going to win the struggle. They passed barefoot with their begging bowls; the troops, being kindly men on the whole, often gave them something. Certainly there is an air about those dedicated men, so gentle in manner, having put away aggression, which touches the heart. But we were in no position to learn from them.

What was it like to visit this country in times of peace? That option was quite beyond rankers; there was no way in which we could visit Burma, except to serve our country in case of war. And this paragraph is being written on Tuesday 22 August, 1995 –

or rather after midnight, when Margaret and I have been enjoying a candlelit alfresco meal with Wendy and Mark in the garden of their Oxford home. Strange that one of our main topics of conversation was Burma ... that haunting country where Wendy and Mark spent part of their honeymoon and where Mark's father served with Wingate's Chindits. So this fragment of the past thrusts itself into North Oxford, as distant times transform our everyday.

For S Section, our position outside Schwebo was unusual. We had to erect our bivouacs around a splendid tree festooned in all manner of climbers and epiphytes. Lianas thatched and barricaded it. To get to the trunk without hacking your way in with a *kukri* would have been impossible. Happily, we no longer had to dig slit trenches for the bivouacs, since the Jap air force had been all but wiped out. From this site, it was a mile's walk by a jungle trail to where the signal lorry and adjoining tents stood, camouflaged, in a small clearing. There was much work to be done, the Fullerphone still buzzed and whined all night, as the sitreps and opreps proliferated.

Our selected site made us uneasy. We looked across the *maidan* towards an old canal. This open space had to be guarded. Parties of Japs who had evaded mopping up by our brigades were still active. Much of our off-duty time was spent manning Bren guns, peering out across the crackling landscape.

An abundance of wildlife moved about by night. Once the sun had gone down, and its brief funeral service was veiled in darkness, small animals and birds scuttled through the dry undergrowth. Advancing Japs, bent on a last suicidal charge, might sound no differently. Nobody wants to be bayoneted in bed; it lacks dignity. We fell asleep under the stifling mosquito nets, clutching our rifles and wearing our boots.

And then Steve, ordering himself about as usual, observed something moving in the crown of the splendid tree under which we sheltered. We stared upwards. It seemed as if the tree top was infested with snakes. Rather large black snakes. Snakes preparing to rush down the tree into our bivouacs. We soon realised, however, that what we were looking at were not snakes but *tails*. And that black-and-white masked faces were peering down at us.

This was our first encounter with any wildlife larger than scavenger birds, rats and snakes.

Night fell. The great gong of moon rose. The scuttlings in the undergrowth increased. Some of these scuttlers ran right through the tent, which was no more than a fold of canvas overhead. Bradbury slept on.

After a while, a more senior scuffling was heard, followed by a positive crashing. The animals were coming down from the crown of the tree.

'Brad, wake fucking up, will you?' Tense whisper.

But Brad slept on.

Gripping my rifle, propping myself up on an elbow, I could see out of the bivouac through my mosquito net. We had raised the structure on stilts to avoid having to crawl in. First one then a second animal swarmed down to the ground. In the moonlight they were quite distinct.

One of the animals approached my bivouac. It was about the size of a wolfhound. Slowly, with a sort of careless stealth, it entered the bivouac ... I dared not move to fix my bayonet on my *bandook*, instead remaining crouched inside the net. I glared out at the animal. Its eyes flashed scarlet. It half turned its head, as if to acknowledge my presence, but without pausing. For that moment, our heads were on a level. Then it passed. It left through the rear of the tent.

To the best of my knowledge, these beautiful and alarming creatures were clouded leopards. Their long tails and the ease with which they climbed trees indicated as much.

We came to no harm from the leopards. Nor, more remarkably, did they come to harm from us. No one suggested shooting them. 'Live and let live', was the general verdict. Very English in its mild way.

There would have been food for the creatures in the vicinity. In fact, we were camped by a village – a village from which, unusually, the inhabitants had not fled. The Burmese tolerated us, and were neither friendly nor unfriendly. We stood and watched them threshing grain. We eyed the women with particular interest. Some of them, as the sun declined westwards, stood with arms akimbo to smoke long white cheroots.

We took Sid's rhesus monkey, Minnie, with us across the *maidan* to inspect the old Schwebo canal. Its waters in the dry season were about eight inches deep, and flowed very slowly. After the energetic Mu, the canal was a disappointment.

I was the only member of our section who bothered to revisit the canal, since it was some way from the camp. Whenever I had a spare hour, rather than sleep, I would take Minnie to the canal across baking fields full of tall dead grasses. Its solitude held a great attraction. I would lie basking, a strange parti-coloured fish, buttocks and legs white, torso deep brown, in the shallow water. Minnie would swim close by, before settling contentedly on my shoulder.

We could see nothing but the clear blue sky overhead, the clear water below, flowing over its gravel bed, and the grassy banks of the canal, on which an occasional low tree grew. We watched a blue kingfisher plunging, a splinter of sky, into the water, to emerge with tiny fish in its beak. It perched in one of the stunted trees to swallow down its meal.

There is no quiet like an interval of quiet in a war. The war, army, work were far away. On the Schwebo canal, peace had been declared. Perhaps it is still maintained over that pleasant scene.

> I see what was, and is, and will abide;
> Still glides the stream, and shall for ever glide.

XIV

The Forgotten Army

And in all this journey he finds no habitation or shelter, but must carry his stock of provisions . . . The inhabitants live very high up in the mountains. They are idolators and utter savages, living entirely by the chase and dressed in the skins of beasts. They are out and out bad.

Marco Polo
The Travels, translated by Ronald Latham

In the enchanted zone, there was an intense comradeship. We had abandoned the civilian habit of privacy. We had even done away with many traditional army habits, such as haircuts and rankers having to salute officers. We submerged our differences and tolerated the differences of others. We were good at our jobs.

Our friends were more than that, they were our *oppos*. Or more than that they were our *mates*. Or even more closely, they were our *muckers*. We mucked in together.

We could tell who was at the other end of the Fullerphones. We recognised them by their style of sending Morse. They too were our mates.

Members of S Section formed a close community. Some were sons of men who had fought in the Great War and had been unemployed for most of the thirties. The Welsh lads were particularly bitter; they hated Churchill – who was supposed to have ordered troops to fire on striking miners at Tonypandy – and they hated the English. Some Irish also hated the English. They were *our* friends, just the same. Although I had a natural predisposition towards the Scots and the Cockneys (a race apart!) I enjoyed friendships with a great variety of people, always wanting to hear about their backgrounds.

I admired a certain carefree quality about the dog-poor, and a certain generosity. Whereas, in the case of some of the most bitter men, it was plain they had forged themselves a cast-iron channel of complaint down which their natures would always run, narrow and turbulent as the Mu, unable to escape.

During the campaign, we bumped into the rest of the company mainly at meal times, at the cookhouse. The cookhouse was, of course, pitched in the open air. Arrangements were very rough and ready. Each man had his own 'eating irons', the army issue knife, fork and spoon, two mess tins, and a *piyala* for *char*. The cooks, greasy and well-fed men, stood behind their barricades of dixies on trestle tables, dishing out *khana* (food). The half-rations were the cause of much complaint.

You took your rations, whatever they were, and ate them hastily, standing or squatting, or sitting on any nearby log. Officers, of course, fed apart, at mess tables. Hunger was no longer a perpetual torment. Although I was unaware of it, I was growing throughout the campaign, a plant flourishing on poor soil.

Who were more hungry than we? The Japanese. Both armies operated at the ends of greatly extended lines of supply. We relied for every particle of food on air drops, while the Japanese lines of supply were even more problematic. But the Japs had cannily learnt to live on wild nourishment found in the jungle.

The sense of common purpose, the satisfaction of being accepted as the member of a tribe, overrode other considerations. After ten years at boarding schools, Burma was no real hardship. I was the only public schoolboy (I kept quiet about that) in the section, and the youngest. Hardship was a way of testing, of improving yourself. The glorious sun ruled us.

Life in the enchanted zone has a mythical quality. Dragon-slaying with Dodge trucks. Besides, we are going to liberate a city with a magical name – Mandalay! I try to remember every detail of life. I keep a secret and forbidden diary, writing at night in the almost-dark, straining my eyes while Bradbury snores.

One evening, as we went in single file through the jungle to the signal office, I felt less than healthy. My head ached and I was oddly weary. When I opened up the Fullerphone to Brigade, an idiot operator came on duty at the other end. He was sending what we called square Morse. Which is to say that the dashes were scarcely longer than the dots, or the *dahs* than the *dits*. I fell into a fury with him, hammering the key and shouting and raving in a manner unlike me – and of course forbidden.

The officer on duty ordered me off the instrument. I cursed him as well as I knew how. Sgt Leigh hauled me outside the tent, telling me quietly that I would be shot if I carried on like that.

Everything was confused. I fought with everyone. They were gentle with me.

Someone gave me a jab. When I woke up, I was lying in something approaching a bed, in the tent of a field hospital. Despite all the mepacrine, I had contracted malaria.

Anyone suffering merely from malaria was treated without much compassion – with good reason, since there were badly wounded infantry among us. The heat in the tent seemed to have jellified the air, rendering it almost unbreathable. Men were brought in on stretchers, to lie groaning. The badly wounded did not swear, emitting only an aspirated, 'Oh dear . . . oh dear . . .' at intervals. Only those like me, in a high fever, cursed and blasphemed.

In my dreams, the Japs charged us with fixed bayonets. This was my fear. We were prepared for such a charge, and would answer it. We were not prepared for death. We were mild and non-militaristic. Whereas the Japs were prepared to die. Who would win – who could not fail to win, it seemed – in such an encounter? In my fever combat, they never lost.

On the second day in hospital, our tent came under mortar fire. We could only lie there while the shells made a dull underwater kind of roar near at hand. When I was strong enough to get up and put my boots on, I was given light duties by the hospital. This entailed chopping down a palm tree with a *kukri*. Such hard work could be likened to hacking an elephant's leg off with a table knife.

When discharged as fit, I had to make my own way back to my unit. I felt well again; but malaria is a strange malady: for many a year, back in Blighty, the malaria recurred, to prostrate me every time. I stood by the track, wondering where S Section might be, after moving on from Schwebo.

A man in a Jeep told me he could give me a lift some of the way. He seemed to have some idea where 2 Div Signals was. He was the kind of soldier we knew as a 'buckshee', the term derived from the Urdu *baksheesh*, meaning free. Buckshees would not pull their weight. They were free souls, determined not to fit into Army regulations. Such was this man. Once I was in his vehicle, he was in no hurry to get anywhere.

We sat beside his vehicle at sunset, brewed up some tea and ate

K-rations. We were on a great plain fringed by tousled heads of palms. We stayed clear of pagodas, behind which the enemy might conceal himself. The buckshee boasted about the things he would achieve after the war. This was not particularly to my taste: survival was as far as I got when thinking of the morrow.

My buckshee friend had managed to *puckerao* a service revolver. He slept on one side of the Jeep, I on the other, both keeping a sort of provisional watch for Japs. Bells of a distant pagoda sounded, as if the canopy of stars rang with interstellar cold. Above our heads, it was a glorious night, as it had been for billions of years. I slept undisturbed by Japs or mosquitoes.

We drove on in the morning, sometimes sighting British tanks or trucks. These, the buckshee avoided. At a certain point, where a sandy track appeared, he made hasty excuses, dropped me, and charged off in a fresh direction.

His Jeep vanished in a cloud of dust. I stood alone on the plain. There was still a little water in my water bottle. My *bondook* was slung over my shoulder. On the whole I was not displeased.

It was early in the day as yet. I set my course eastwards, towards the sun, and marched towards distant trees. As I drew nearer, something glinted between their trunks. I held the rifle at the ready.

After some minutes, it became apparent that a river flowed among the trees, reflecting light. My nervousness was in vain.

So I came to the banks of the Irrawaddy.

That great highway running from north to south of Burma rises somewhere in the chilly fastnesses of Tibet. It winds its way southwards for one and a half thousand miles, towards Rangoon, where its mouths empty into the Anderman Sea. South of Mandalay, the river receives massive infusions of water from both Mu and Chindwin.

The flood was low when I came on it, shortly before the arrival of the monsoon. Its present shores were choked by sandbanks. Finding a place of concealment among bushes, scanning it for snakes, I lay down and took up a firing position. Nothing alarming was to be heard. After some minutes of watching and listening, I got up and stripped off. My rifle I placed pointing away from the river, on top of my clothes. I launched myself into the embrace of the waters.

Gin and tonic may consist of warm gin and cold tonic. The Irrawaddy consists of warm Mu and cold Tibet, the contrasting streams remaining separate but entwined, so that a swimmer is by turns warmed and chilled.

In the middle of the river lay an old steamer. It lay half submerged, canted on one side. At this low-tide season, the deck was above the water line; in a few weeks, come the monsoons, everything would be covered again.

I hauled myself up on deck. Bushes grew by the wheelhouse. I went to investigate. Something rustled in shadow and sped away. I looked over the rail, to watch a cobra swimming, thrashing its body towards the shore. Now I alone was captain of the vessel! I sunbathed on the sloping deck. The dark entwined streams of warm and cold water flowed by, with a litter of bubbles along the surface, breathing a last memory of Himalayan snow. No one knew where I was. I did not know where I was.

How often in memory have I returned to those moments of peace and isolation . . .

Later in the day, back in uniform, I secured a lift from another passing Jeep. The driver was a ferocious man on an errand for a 2 Div officer. He drove like fury into Myingyan, which S Section had reputedly reached.

The town of Myingyan stands on the flat plain south-west of Mandalay. Sections of it resembled a garden suburb in Surrey, with substantial two-storey houses, often with mock-Tudor timbering, set apart in parched gardens. But this was Surrey after a Martian invasion. Many trees and houses were still-smouldering ruins.

Touring what had once been suburban streets, the Jeep driver and I came across a wall built of dead bodies. The driver stopped his vehicle.

The bodies had been stacked neatly, much as one would build a wall of logs. To the best of my belief, they were Koreans, who fought beside the Japs. In their neat stacks, boots towards the street, they had turned black and purple in the heat. Some seemed to have burst. They were awaiting the bulldozers which would plough them into the ground, far from their native land.

'I need a new pair of boots,' said the driver, jumping to the ground.

A low continuous humming came from the wall, as if those who comprised it were murmuring the words of the Tripitaka even in decay. As the driver approached, an immense swarm of bluebottles rose, disturbed, then settled again.

The stench was very bad – a frightening smell, warning the living to stay away. I sat tight in the Jeep.

The driver investigated the wall. He kicked a sow that was gobbling a swollen leg. The animal dragged its heavy belly away, almost too bloated to move. When my friend pulled a boot off one corpse, the foot came with it. He flung it aside and tried again. After two or three attempts, he found a pair of boots which suited him. Strapping them on, he left his old boots by the roadside.

He was returning to the Jeep when a redcap roared up on a motor bike. He told us to clear off. He also instructed me where to find my unit. I walked the rest of the way, through the reeking streets, past all those bijou residences where no one would go again.

Mandalay once stood at the centre of the universe, or so Burmese astrologers believed in the nineteenth century. Previous reckonings had been slightly mistaken. The enlightened King Mindon moved his whole court to Mandalay, to establish his capital there. Mandalay flourished. It became one of Buddhism's great religious centres. A forest of pagodas and stupas surround it, climbing to the hill on which Mindon, and later his less puissant successor, Thibaw, lived in a colossal palace.

The palace was bombed by the Japs and later pummelled by British artillery. Only its walls remained.

The palace was a city within a city, rather like Diocletian's palace in Split, in the palmy days of Jugoslavia. In this glittering palace lived King Mindon, clearly not in utter sanctity, since he had over fifty wives and twice that number of royal children.

A Lord White Elephant also lived within the palace, pampered and protected, revered for his wisdom. This captive ruminant, when young, enjoyed the privilege every morning of a fairly unusual ritual. Ranks of young Burmese women bared their bosoms. The elephant moved slowly along the line, sucking milk from each dripping breast in turn.

Mandalay seemed much like Myingyan, a place of the dead. There were no crowds of the grateful liberated to greet the XIVth Army when they entered it, as happened with the victorious Allied armies in Antwerp, Brussels, Tours, Paris and dozens of other European cities. In this broken city, Slim held a parade with some of his commanders, and the Union Jack flew once more over Fort Dufferin.

Again the blackened dead were piled up to await the bulldozers. Lines of Japs were marched at bayonet point to prison camps. We heard, too, that flocks of Comfort Girls – women of many nationalities forced into whoredom for the Jap troops – were being sent downriver to Rangoon to be freed: to the disappointment of some of our troops.

So we reached the successful conclusion of our campaign.

We were given a ration of beer with which to celebrate. Soldiers are great singers. We sang many sentimental songs, such as 'Keep Right on to the End of the Road', a Harry Lauder favourite, and 'The Mountains of Mourne', as well as bawdy songs which combined as much lechery as possible. These latter songs formed no part of the way in which Bill and Dot had brought me up – a reason to revel in them.

The Japs were in retreat southwards, heading for Rangoon. That would mean more fighting – but not for us. Our part in the scheme of things was over. It was time to leave the enchanted land whose enchantments had drained away.

The supply problem had grown with distance. Now 2 Div was to be flown back to India.

It has been estimated that the war in Burma, from late 1941 to August 1945, cost the lives of 71,244 British and Commonwealth troops. Surprisingly, the number of troops of UK origin killed was under 5,000. The cost was much higher for Indian troops, who lost three times as many lives. As for our enemy, the Japanese, some calculate they lost – according to the total given in Louis Allen's book, *The Longest War* – 185,149 men. Three-fifths of the soldiers despatched from Tokyo never returned.

Throughout this account, I have referred to the Japanese as Japs. That is what we called them, 'Nips' being a little-used alternative. Some claim the term *Jap* to be offensive – though I observe that the British these days are sometimes content to refer to themselves as *Brits*.

The Jap treatment of their prisoners and subject people was barbaric. Yet, as Churchill said, 'In Victory: Magnanimity'.

'Harp of Burma' is a story, by one Japanese, Michio Takeyama, of how Mizushima remained behind after the war, disguised as a monk, to gather the remains of his old comrades and give them burial.

I shall not return to Japan. I have made a pledge to stay behind in Burma. Dressed as you saw me, I shall travel all over this country, into its mountains and along its rivers. There is a task to be done here. I cannot leave until I have finished it. Years from now, when my work is done, I may try to return to Japan. Or perhaps I may spend the rest of my life here, now that I am a monk, a servant of the Buddha. Whatever I do, I shall obey his will.

I have been taking care of the Japanese dead who lie scattered throughout this country. I dig graves for them and bury their whitened bones, to give them a final resting place. Hundreds of thousands of my young countrymen were drafted into the army, only to be defeated, routed, killed – and now their remains lie abandoned. It is a tragic sight. Once I saw it, I felt I had to care for these forgotten corpses.

This reveals a very different side of the Japanese character to the one British prisoners knew.

Once hostilities were over, the British set the War Graves Commission to work. These men travelled the East, identifying and memorialising the dead. One result of their work is the immaculately kept Kranji War Cemetery on Singapore Island, where all nations involved in the conflict have the names of their dead displayed, 24,000 names in all.

At Kohima, where the tide of war was turned, a simple memorial was erected. On it is carved the epitaph:

WHEN YOU GO HOME, TELL THEM OF US AND SAY
FOR YOUR TOMORROW WE GAVE OUR TODAY

The gallant lines speak for all wars, all warriors. Ours was to be almost the last war of the old British Empire; for that reason, I have thought it worthwhile to record my impressions of it. Yet exactly what purpose it served, except for the political one of convincing the Americans that their enemies were our enemies, is hard to say. Whose is the Tomorrow the epitaph addresses?

Was it worth all those lost lives, Indian and British, not to mention Chinese and Japanese? And for each of those lost lives, other lives were lost at home, women and children, lovers . . .

The men might complain, but complaint served only a sort of choric purpose. The truth was that most rankers expected little from life, had been brought up to expect little. And received little.

Tolstoy has something to say of this matter, in Part II Chapter Six, of *Resurrection*: 'The people perish, they are accustomed to the process of perishing.' He goes on to say, 'Customs and attitudes to life have appeared which accord with the process – the way children are allowed to die and women made to overwork, and the widespread undernourishment, especially of the aged. And this state of affairs has come about so gradually that the peasants themselves do not see the full horror of it, and do not raise their voices in complaint. For this reason, we too regard the situation as natural and proper.'

Although Tolstoy was speaking of peasants in last century's Russia, the force of the remark remains.

We freed Burma from a cruel invader, and shortly afterwards gave it independence. But we had ruined much of it.

Almost as soon as the Union Jacks were hauled down from the flagpoles of Mandalay and Rangoon and elsewhere, the country became involved in civil wars. It plunged into Communism and a totalitarianism from which it still suffers, half a century after liberation.

My novel, *A Soldier Erect*, is the only novel of that war in Burma written by a BOR who served there in the Forgotten Army.

Our leaving Burma held none of the romance of our entering. No exhilaration. No convoy. No Shakespeare.

Returning by that toilsome road to India, the way we had come, was impossible. The way from Dimapur was now busy with one-way traffic, bringing in supplies to Burma and China. Our transport capability was to be left in the Mandalay area for other users on their way south.

We were split up into small groups to be flown out. I was on a rear detail with Steve and a recent reinforcement, Chota Morris. The three of us camped under the branches of a giant tree, alone on a wide plain. There we remained, isolated, for three days. There was nothing to do. No information was to be had.

Steve still drilled himself up and down tirelessly in the heat. 'Private Steve, by the left – wait for it, man! – by the left, qui-i-i-ick MARCH! Keep your dressing there. Swing them arms, Private Steve. Lep, lep, lep, ri', lep. Bags of bullshit now. Har-bout TURN!'

We lived on K-rations, while winds of ill omen blew up, died, and then revived. The monsoon was on the way, with dust and cold its forerunners. Some great anonymous thing was closing down.

Though, for companionship's sake, one part of me was as disillusioned as my mates, the part that has never been disillusioned was saying to me, 'So you're regretting that you never faced a Jap in hand-to-hand encounter. Regret nothing. Maybe the experience has had ragged edges – but you enjoy life served with a slice of lemon. You've been lucky.'

Another voice said, 'You think it's all so wonderful. This is what young men have always done – war with another tribe.'

I lay looking up into the tree, watching the legions of unforgiving ants toiling on their patrols.

But the thought remained: 'This wasn't as good as the war Bill had been in, and my Wilson uncles. It wasn't as good as the Great War. You saw the dead, fine. *You never saw anyone actually getting fucking killed.'*

It was over now, as far as you were concerned. It would never happen again. The rest of your life was going to be played out on a lower key.

On the third day, a Jeep drove up with an officer sitting primly in the rear seat. He called us to Attention. We saw he was not one of our outfit; his whole manner suggested it pained his sensibilities to address men in the ranks. He told us that he would convey us to Map Reference so-and-so to await an airlift to India. Our kit must be reduced to – whatever it was. Sixty pounds, maybe. Bivouacs must be left behind.

'What about my books, sir?'

'Sixty pounds and no more. You heard what I said.'

'Sir.'

The time had come for another *pegdo*.

When all you possess in the world is about one hundred pounds of kit, it is hard to reduce it to sixty pounds. We all swore various oaths as we stacked scruffy treasures under the tree. The fruits of victory were proving a negative crop.

The wind blew harder, with an uneasy chill in its throat. The three of us piled into the Jeep. As we bumped off across the *maidan*, we looked back at our sheltering tree. Leaves and dust blew. The wind was whipping through the pages of a book I had had to leave behind, perhaps an Eric Linklater. From the bushes were stealing *dacoits*, thieves emerging from nowhere, who could not wait until we were out of sight to pillage our belongings.

'There goes my bloody dress cap,' Chota Morris said.

The problem of getting us out of Burma was a considerable one. The difficult supply situation meant we had to be gone as soon as possible. Resources had to be diverted to the units now actively engaging the enemy.

Steve, Chota and I were issued with fresh ration packs and dumped on the edge of an airstrip. The Jeep disappeared. We were told that a plane would pick us up within forty-eight hours. We grumbled a little, but at least we were left with a wireless set, the old 19 set, and a call sign. My days with a Fullerphone were over.

*   *   *

We stood by our kitbags and watched the vehicle that had brought us drive away. We were nowhere. No sign of habitation showed in any direction; not so much as a pagoda relieved the monotony.

This was another of Burma's varied micro-environments, this one as simple as a child's drawing. The old airstrip was a giant swathe cut from dense forest, stretching for miles. A lank soft grass which grew to a foot high covered the strip. The wall of forest on either side consisted of tall trees of uniform height. Above the forest sailed a cloudy sky. No other feature broke the sombre landscape, no flag, no windsock.

The wind blew fitfully. We dragged our kit to the margin of the trees. At night, the three of us slept there, not venturing into the forest.

By the afternoon of the second day, our water bottles were almost empty. Every hour, I switched on the wireless set and gave the call sign. Never any response. We were low on someone's priorities.

The pre-monsoon wind blew more strongly. The monotonous view did not change, except for a pall of distant smoke. Night was dense, moonless. We slept huddled in monsoon capes.

On the morning of the third day, when the rations gave out, the smoke was much nearer. With it came a roaring, as if lions were approaching. We stood uneasily in the middle of the strip, watching, wondering. In the near distance, the whole forest was alight.

Powered by wind, the fire was coming in our direction. Twin waterfalls of flame, one on either side of the strip, advanced like a bad dream. Forest fires move onward rapidly, carried on vectors of intense heat.

The fire was bearing down on us on either side, two great walls of fire like a pair of William Blake's avenging angels' wings. We could not run.

All we could do was shoulder our rifles and kit, and wait in the middle of the clearing. We stood our ground as the conflagration raced down upon us. So great was the heat that the grass burnt too, its flame always keeping pace with the bow wave of fire. The air filled with smoke and furious roaring. We half closed our eyes against the intense heat. The line of lighted grass rushed at us. As it reached our boots, we jumped over it.

Behind the band of flame lay only blackened ground. The grass was too thin to sustain a blaze. It burnt and the flame passed on, transforming the landing strip into cinder as it went.

As for the great torches to our left and right, terrifying as they were, they too rushed furiously onwards. Behind them stood black, smouldering trunks. The great green world disappeared. A smoky black world took its place.

The fire roared on like a madman, into the distance.

We stood where we were for an hour, kitbags on shoulders, waiting for the oven to cool.

A Dakota finally arrived with an American pilot.

'Get in, Aldiss, and look sharp about it.' Ah, a friendly voice!

It was Sgt. Leigh. The rest of S Section was aboard.

The flight was bumpy, as we flew low over the hills. There were no seats. We huddled on the deck with our kit, glad to be back together again.

As we disembarked, the pilot complimented us. 'None of you guys threw up! If you had been Yanks you'd all have thrown up, every man jack of you.'

'We don't have anything to throw up on, buddy. We haven't eaten for days.'

The Yanks ate better than we. The Indians ate less well. The Chinese even worse. The world is built upon such pecking orders.

From the landing field, we eventually got a train to Chittagong. Lou Grey took a photo of Chota and me standing on the engine platform. I look skeletal, ribs showing clearly under the stretched brown skin.

A remarkable fact emerges from the campaign. We had had to subsist on half-rations. As my battered pay book, carried with me through my years in the Army, shows, I was five foot eight inches tall when I reached Dimapur. Barely six months later, when I reached Chittagong, I was six foot one and a half inches tall. In my nineteenth year, I had grown almost six inches. Truly, a late developer . . .

Piecing my life together, trying to see what was meaningful, what was dross, I wonder at the store I set by that period in Burma. Of course those were brave days. Of course they provided young men with an initiation rite into manhood, very satisfying in terms of the archetypal experience of our kind.

But something more. Under the umbrella of 2 Div, we were back in the wilderness, the wilderness rejected by civilisation. Great psychic satisfaction was to be gained, living hard in that hunter-type environment. Burma embodied the conditions under which our species has lived out about ninety-five per cent of its existence. 'The two-million-year-old Self' – to use Dr Anthony Stevens' colourful phrase

– received gratification. The small wild urchin in a Red Indian suit was freed again, to run naked on the sands of the Mu.

No doubt many others felt as intensely as I did, but were – like me – unable to articulate. Olaf Stapledon's detached view of the human experience helped me. My comrades were 'hardened troops'. Yet somehow the Ancient Self got through, as it always will, and spoke in its romantic, troubled voice by the very name they called themselves: the Forgotten Army . . .

XV

The Bomb

Bliss was it in that dawn to be alive,
But to be young was a very bugger . . .
[*After*] William Wordsworth

The monsoon that gathered when we flew out of Burma was in full spate. It drove in upon us in a majesty of black and gold cloud formations. As excess is beautiful, there was beauty as well as madness in rainstorms that could last for two days and a night without cease. We often waded thigh-deep in water along flooded streets. Fortunately, the heat helped one dry off rapidly. Rain was just one more factor to be endured, like mosquitoes, a part of life.

Because I had read about monsoons, in boys' papers, in Maugham, in Conrad, I found them – is *romantic* the word? To lie on one's bunk listening to the heavy-footed rain smashing down on the thatch of the *basha* above induced a freakish turn of mind, pleasurable in a masochistic way. The melancholy continuous drip of soggy thatch on mud formed a rhythm of something huge and meaningless. As the weeks wore on, the permanent dampness of everything become hard to take.

The British Army itself contributed to Indian squalor. Although the peacetime barracks in Mhow were excellently designed, many of the impromptu wartime camps were deplorable. In Kanchapara for instance, outside Calcutta, where the weary army rested and put on a little fat after Mandalay, we were housed in rotting pre-war tents. Wood and rope were issued to us, with which we constructed our own *charpoys*. The impression was that no one cared a jot for our welfare. We had done our job and were now a part of the great War Surplus . . .

Kanchapara's hastily constructed lavatory – the shithouse, in Army parlance – was something out of folklore. Over a deep pit, a wooden sixteen-seater had been constructed, in two parallel rows of eight holes. This wonder was housed in a grey rectangular building on the camp's perimeter.

The roughest of men dislike, the most scrupulous of men adapt to evacuating themselves in public, which makes the arrangement no less degrading. Sitting there, one was in danger of one's sweaty back coming into contact with the sweaty back of the man shitting just behind. Adding flavour to this misery, the attap and bamboo walls were decorated with warnings against venereal disease, incorporating large photographs of decaying and suppurating knobs.

The halitus of this huge shed – lime, excrement and urine – was fragrant enough to attract flies of all description. To keep them out, mosquito netting had been secured all over the ceiling vents. The flies, however, found ways of entering through the swing doors. Demons of cunning though they were, they could then find no way to get out. Millions of flies, Hindu and Muslim, swarmed up to the light, carrying with them their burdens of disease, only to be frustrated by the netting.

The deep-throated buzz of a million bluebottles made the noxious shithouse audible half-way across the camp.

When the monsoon hit Kanchapara, the insecurely pegged tents were blown from their moorings. The ground flooded, to become one knee-deep brown river.

Men ran naked hither and thither, cursing, glimpsed intermittently in lightning flashes. The chill rain lashed us. Sailors on sailing ships rounding Cape Horn acted much as we did, hauling in whatever the mainbrace was through driving spray. We clung to the guy ropes of tents now billowing like sails. All our kit was swimming in a tawny river of mud. Drum rolls of thunder sounded over all.

Slim's victorious army, brought back from the war zone, was ungratefully treated.

The end of the Mandalay campaign carried with it waves of reaction, psychic equivalents of the rainstorms. As counterpoint to an unexpected relief that one was now safe from the vagaries of warfare came disappointment. My brave hour was over – and the small part I had played in the campaign! And this – *I had never come face to face with a fucking Jap!* In Kanchapara, I realised that I had longed to kill a Jap, just one Jap, riddle him with bullets and see him fall.

Here was another cause for self-disgust. Thinking of it now, half a century later, I know myself for a peaceable, equable man: yet in some old broken-down corner of the mind that regret squats still. It's called the Fruits of War.

Other fruits were to be had. A short distance from the camp, across a side road, was a space which had once been a garden or an orchard. A fence had collapsed, a row of houses decayed quietly near by. Some mango trees stood there, heavy with fruit.

When I showed the place to one of my mates, he would not eat what he called 'wog fruit'. Such were the prejudices of the time.

Fresh mangoes are a delicacy and I frequently took one or two back to our tent. They are delectable to taste when plucked straight from the tree, with that elusive flavour which carries hints of paraffin and French marigold. They used to say that, even on one tree, no two mangoes tasted exactly alike. Possibly the saying contains a sliver of truth. Clearly some fruits receive more sun than others.

Even allowing for prejudice, India was hard to take. That terrible Stone-Age poverty was always there, the beggars and filth were ever present. BORs did not enjoy the defences officers could muster against such things. The children were so beautiful, the deaths in the streets so public. Never were the cruel facts of life – the grinding necessity to earn a crust – so vividly displayed. Like many a young soldier there, I was being worn down. Fine faces. Skeletal figures. Boils. Sores. Missing limbs. Clutching hands – everywhere.

At Kanchapara, sexually frustrated after the chastities of the campaign, the subject of *kyfer* was on everyone's mind. 'Shit, shave, shampoo, and off into town.' Calcutta was well able to supply the need. Whores were cheap, pimps were everywhere with their slimy sing-song blandishments. 'You like my sister, sah'? She only a schoolgirl girl, sah', very good girl. Five rupee. Just here, you come see.'

The girl would be up a side alley no wider than a chair, the alley entrance bearing the crossed red circle meaning 'Out of Bounds to British Troops'.

Sex on bed. So different from sex in bed.

Squalor and disillusion. Bare little rooms like boxes. Flesh greasy, pickled in prickly heat. Hasty transactions: while, beyond the window, trams rattle by, cascading green-and-white electric sparks from their feed arms overhead. Stagnant nights, stench, haggling over prices. Disgust. Quarrels. More beer. Second-hand French letters sold by street vendors. Lust, rupees, booze, bankruptcy.

The great palaces of Calcutta cinemas were air conditioned, but out on the fetid streets drunken British and American soldiers fought each other and were hauled off by redcaps. And the immense trade in female flesh went forward.

All satisfying merely the loins. Past reason hunted, and past reason despised . . . All backed by the extravagant noise of Hindu music, cascading from tinny radios dangling at every merchant's stall.

The deaths, the mutilated beggars. Life led on the streets was full of interest to a curious spectator. In one desperately down-at-heel street, I witnessed the poor supporting each other. Barbers, butchers, stallholders, *char wallahs* had some kind of agreement whereby (I believe) no money changed hands between them. Only persons outside the circle were charged. The barbers – *nappi wallahs* – squatted in the street, and their customers squatted before them to be shaved.

Nothing in Calcutta was ever discarded; yet in that poor street, something was thrown away. The *char wallahs* served their tea in little unglazed clay cups, shallow cups without handles. The customer stood and drank down his *char*. Afterwards, he threw the cup down, to break in the gutter.

In context, how eloquent was the gesture. I have seen insolent Hungarians similarly, after some grandiose toast, toss their wine glasses to shatter into fireplaces.

Stamping down those exotic streets in metal-shod Army boots, in among all the bare brown feet – the Army was a refuge from Thought, yet you could not help wondering: one side or other must be doing something wrong here. Perhaps the boots should be removed . . .

And one remarkable find in Calcutta. Steve and Chota Morris and I took a ferry across the Hooghly, a coracle of a boat rowed by a sweating man in a *dhot*. We passed yachts and steamers, where the officer class lounged on deck with their smart drinks and smart women, playing gramophone records. 'The Waiter and the Porter and the Upstairs Maid' drifted to us across the muddy flow. On the far side of the river lay the Botanical Gardens, a lovely park planted with many species of tree.

It was extremely hot that day – as were most days in Calcutta. Men swarmed up coconut trees to bring down the big green fruits. They sliced off the tops with a *kukri* and presented the coconuts for us to drink. Ah, that cold nutritious liquid!

In those gardens, we came to the Biggest Tree in the World, an old banyan. It crept across the park in all directions, as if setting out to conquer the whole globe. As it went it put down aerial roots from the outer branches. It was a senior citizen among trees, and many a branch was propped by pale wooden crutches. Salvador Dali had turned sylviculturist. We sat there for an hour, enjoying the unlikely tree.

The tree was described in the 1920s. In his essay 'The Meaning of Death', Julian Huxley, the biologist, speaks of the banyan as covering more than two acres of ground. Huxley saw the tree as an example of a single individual able to 'go on living indefinitely' when artificially preserved (from the destructive goat, for example). Well, the banyan is not subject to what, in humans, Huxley calls 'intestinal putrifaction'.

Thanks to its longevity – not least in the imagination – the Calcutta banyan eventually reached England, entered one of my books, and filled the whole globe.

From Calcutta rest-camp, I was posted to Secunderabad. The old XIVth Army, 'Forgotten Army', the Forgotten Army, the army of lost causes, the army of despair and fortitude, the army comprising fourteen different nationalities and more languages – that army had been broken up and its older members at last sent home. I had said goodbye to Lou Grey and the others. We were never to meet again.

In Secunderabad, I joined an Indian division, the 26th, 'Tiger Div'. A repatriation number was issued to everyone. By my number, 57, I could calculate I had still two and a half more years to serve overseas. My first year abroad was practically over. The 26th posted me almost at once to Bombay, after a spell of leave in the cool Nilgiri Hills.

On the Bombay detachment, I was alone, a wireless operator now. My billet was about half a mile from the signal office. The road from one to the other led past the legendary Beach Candy, a generous swimming pool perched on the edge of the Arabian Sea. I lived in a house otherwise occupied by Indians – a military arrangement with a high inscrutability factor, and greatly to be enjoyed. Even stranger, the very road is mentioned in Salman Rushdie's novel *Midnight's Children*.

The house as I recall it was full of carved screens, all covered with animals prowling through forests, punctured by carved apertures through which breezes might travel. Rich furniture of unfamiliar design stood amid potted plants, as if the teak verdure were not enough. Just to be in a house again was overwhelming.

There I had a servant and slept on a balcony with a view of the sea.

*   *   *

Bombay was an improvement on Calcutta from my point of view. When off duty, I swam in Beach Candy, ate delicious egg *fu-yong*s from a pool-side snack bar run by couth Chinese, or sat on the wall by the rocks, watching the sea lap-lap-lap against India. Watching, mind blank, automatically slapping off flies from back and arms.

Especially in the big cities, one had the impression that most of the population was mad. Lunatics roamed about freely, harmless as the sacred cows. Lustrous dark eyes so often contained a hint of some kind of other-worldliness. One was never free of the perplexing religions of India, mostly of a showy kind. It is easy to be spiritual if one has been undernourished from birth.

In the Bombay signal office, a rare pleasure. We had a WAAC (I) working with us, a lady called Mary. The initials, pronounced Wack-Eye, stood for Women's Army Auxiliary Corps (India). Mary was perhaps Anglo-Indian, a Eurasian, to use that now obsolete term which Han Su-Yin, the novelist and author of *A Many-Splendoured Thing*, told me she hated so much. A pretty young woman, meek, Catholic, light of skin, well brought-up. Thrown among rough British troops.

We had a DR who kept coming into the office. His business was to remain outside and deliver messages by motor bike. He assailed Mary with foul language compounded of scatology and racism. He was a little acne-cheeked Welsh jerk, very aggressive in manner.

No one liked to interfere. No one really knew how to treat Mary. But certainly not as Taff treated her.

At last I could stand no more of it.

'If you ever speak to Mary like that again, I'll punch your fucking Welsh face into your fucking Welsh skull. Shut up and get out. Stay outside by your bike.'

It hardly seemed to be me speaking. Perhaps it was a token of deterioration setting in; but I was in charge there. Anyhow, it worked. Taff got out. From then on, he kept his bile to himself.

That evening, when I returned to my smart billet, Mary was waiting for me in the hall.

She held out her hand. 'You were kind to me. I am grateful.'

I kissed her. It took more courage than threatening Taff. Nothing in Standing Orders said anything about being tender. She made no response. Without undue hurry, she left the house, closing the door behind her.

All too soon, I was posted back to my unit. It had moved, and was difficult to find. Again I was at the mercy of Indian railways and the RTOs (Railway Transport Officers) who controlled military journeys.

One of the fascinations of India lay in the long train journeys and the sub-cultures which grew up around the railways. As in Russia, the most efficient restaurants in smaller cities were often to be found on the station. On one occasion, possibly in Jaipur, the station restaurant brought and served me an elegant breakfast on the train. I had some funds that day. The train pulled out of the station before I had finished my toast. My waiter clung to the outside of the train, travelling 200 miles to the next stop in order to redeem his tray. Quite an amusing thing to do, I thought, wiping my lips on my damask napkin.

Monsoon or no monsoon, the decrepit yet vital Indian life went on, afloat on its multitudinous religions. The monsoon is unforgettable. It drums down on tents, on thatched roofs, on whatever it can find – and it finds everything. The rain is the sound of dromedary herds racing across the bridge of booming Sinai, filling your mind with wonder and madness. In its temporary oceans, animals and insects hastily copulate and spawn, toads lie knotted together, bellies upward. Its noise roars on into infinity.

Either alone or in a small detachment, I saw a fair amount of India. I smoked opium in Ootacamund, was chased by baboons in the Nilgiri Hills, stayed in an immaculate little hotel in Mysore, slept one night on Allahabad station, visited a tea plantation in Darjeeling, paid five rupees to watch a mongoose fight a cobra, watched pilgrims ducking themselves in the filthy waters of the Benares *ghats*, ventured into Indian cinemas to see Indian films, lived primitively in an old tent in a small red desert outside Kameredi, slept in dozens of filthy camps straight out of old movies about Devil's Island.

Always, everywhere, poverty, squalor. Also bright and lurid things – clothes, sacred figures of wood and clay. Pretty bright coal-black kiddies with hope in their faces. The beautiful or obscene scents – no easier to forget than the tormented *tablas* of the monsoon. And that vexing quality India holds for a Westerner, reminding him or her that something is missing in them.

Within the ample, scarred world of the subcontinent was contained the world of the British Army – the Army with all its insane restrictive rules, yet, because of the size of the surrounding world, unable to press those rules too harshly. In high places, uncertainty.

India was preparing for Home Rule. When we arrived in India, we were addressed as '*sah'b*'; when we came out of Burma, it was the more egalitarian 'Johnny'. Mahatma Gandhi went about his business, visited England, pressing home his message of *swaraj* – self-government. Dressed in his *dhoti*, discussing with cabinet ministers. Visited Manchester, whose cotton mills he wished to close, was cheered by the workers.

Within the military's quasi-society, men came and went, posted here or there because of a list, a position in the alphabet. Old friends disappeared, to reappear again later in another place. I met up with Ron Ferguson again in some benighted camp on some meaningless plain. He spoke in a dark-brown voice, jocular and wry as ever.

On one of our senseless parades in the burning sun, we stood at attention with our rifles. We were awaiting an inspecting officer, who was probably swilling whisky comfortably in a comfortable mess. An hour passed. We stood motionless. Fergie began to sway. Without a sound, he fell forward, crashing on his face. Stretcher-bearers took him away. His face was badly damaged, and he lost four teeth.

A deadening disorder prevailed. India was a different experience from Burma, far more demoralising. The Indians did not want us. They stole from us. We stole from them. Life had deteriorated. The dedication of Burma had evaporated.

A corpse lying under a sheet, ignored by passers-by in a busy street, was more shocking than a whole pile of dead Japs, pickled in the noonday sun. War has its conventions which are abhorrent in peace – or what then passed for peace in the crowded Indian cities.

My letters home became more and more remote from the truth. There was nothing that could be told. I concentrated on describing the films I saw. In a way, falsehood was forced upon us. It was understandable that in Burma, for security reasons, we could mention no names in our correspondence. But in Bombay, far from the strife, the imposition was ridiculous.

Under the rigidities of service lay anarchy. Britain was to quit India. It would soon regain independence – never soon enough for most Indians. Meanwhile, the war against Japan must be pursued. How could that be done without that great base, that source of supply and expendable warriors, India? How would a now ramshackle empire survive?

The traffic I had been sending and receiving in Bombay was mainly between London and ALFSEA (Allied Land Forces South East Asia). The weary and depleted forces of the region were preparing for a new offensive. Rangoon had fallen and again flew the Union Jack. The Japs had been driven out of Burma. Now Singapore and Malaya had to be retaken – across an ocean too far.

From Bombay, I recrossed the subcontinent to wind up in Madras. The month was July. It was hotter than a Madras curry. Miles of golden beach fringed the Indian Ocean; beach and ocean were inaccessible because of danger from sharks. No swimming!

Despite which, we trained for amphibious operations in rivers and creeks. Jump from the craft, Sten gun – we were issued with Sten guns by this time – above head, 22 set strapped to back, into three feet of water, wade ashore, throw yourself down into shelter, start to operate set, call HQ link, keeping gun at ready. Get heterodyne tone, press pressel switch. 'Able Charlie Dog, come in Able Charlie Dog, over.' FIRE!

The landing craft were old. They had been shipped East from the Mediterranean theatre of war. We hated them and their symbolism that we always got shoddy used goods. The traditions of the Forgotten Army had not gone away. Much of our equipment was worn. Also, we ourselves were old and tired. It was amazing how old one can feel at nineteen.

What we were training for was code-named Operation Zipper.

Zipper's plan was to sail from India across the Indian Ocean, to claim back from the Japs Singapore – the impregnable Singapore! – and Malaya. Not only that. Zipper would 'put on a show' to prove to our American allies that we were still one hundred per cent in the fight now that Jerry was licked in Europe.

The victory over Nazi Germany brought little rejoicing in Madras. We were erecting or dismantling tents, bodies gleaming with sweat which drained into the tops of our trousers, when a sergeant came over and said, 'Right, you men, war in Europe's over. Break off for a five-minute smoke.'

When later we saw newsreels of crowds rejoicing in London, cheering, dancing, kissing outside Buckingham Palace, we felt only the bitterness of exile.

We sat about, puffing on Indian Players, discussing the possibility of attacking the distant Malay peninsula. Our unit had little stomach for it: the Mandalay campaign was sufficient for a lifetime. The thought of an assault on Singapore island and the long Malayan coast introduced a new terror to our lives. The Japanese armies had been driven from or annihilated in Burma, but they remained in strength in Malaya, where their lines of communication were less extended. Their ability to defend, from entrenched positions, the beaches and mangrove swamps with which the west coast of the peninsula was liberally endowed – and to fight to the death – was well established.

In fact, two operations were planned, Zipper for the coastline from Port Swettenham to Port Dickson, and Operation Mailfist for Singapore itself. The assaults were planned for October and December 1945 respectively.

To our anxiety for our own skins was added an anxiety for the lives of the thousands of Allied prisoners in Jap hands, in Changi Jail in Singapore, and in camps elsewhere. In the event of an attack, the ruthless Jap would not spare his prisoners.

This fear proved well founded. Some years later, in Oxford, I talked with a distinguished doctor of tropical medicine who had been incarcerated in Changi; he confirmed that the Japs had prepared chambers, often underground, where they planned to gas or shoot their prisoners if invasion came. More recently, in the early nineties, I gained access to the Department of Oral History in Singapore; among miles of taped interviews, citizens of the island told the same story.

When training for Zipper, we gave no thought to the Chinese. But they, of all races, suffered most at Japanese hands. When I was in Singapore at the beginning of 1946, I was taken by Chinese friends to see a documentary entitled *Blood and Tears of Overseas Chinese*. Brave Chinese cameramen had secretly filmed many Jap atrocities enacted on that pleasant island.

Even had Zipper been successful, it has been calculated, the war would have dragged on. The Allies would have moved towards Japan itself, fighting on the Asian mainland and on every island, as the American forces had to fight, for Bataan and Saipan and Okinawa, with heavy losses. Thousands of lives would have been forfeit, probably millions, if one includes civilians. The US Air Force had been firebombing Tokyo. Early in August, President Truman took the decision to drop the atomic bombs on Hiroshima and Nagasaki. Hiroshima was destroyed on 6 August, Nagasaki on the 9th.

At last the Emperor of Japan was forced to acknowledge defeat. Although some units ceased hostilies within a few days, others fought on. For a while the situation was confused, until the formal surrender on 2 September 1945. Britain regained Singapore on 3 September, six years to the day after the outbreak of World War II. Operations Zipper and Mailfist were mercifully rendered unnecessary. Countless lives were spared.

My correspondence home makes little of this momentous time. In a letter dated 20 August, I wrote 'The Japanese capitulated nicely for my birthday, but since then they seem to have been fighting again. There was no excitement on VJ Day and very little celebrating.'

This flatness owes something to a common puzzled distaste for the Japanese, that a nation so courageous in battle could be so callous in its years of victory. Their religion, their militarism, their loyalty to the Emperor formed a toxic whole Western minds could scarcely grasp.

Yet the Japanese never indulged in the concerted genocide then being revealed to the world, as humanity was confronted with the horror of the Nazi death camps. The Japanese general in charge of the Malayan occupation refused to surrender. Under him were 10,000 thousand men still in good fighting trim. Emperor Hirohito sent a prince to Kuala Lumpur as special royal envoy, ordering him to surrender. Only then did the general lay down his arms.

The indifferent response to the war's end, as registered in my letter home, is puzzling. It was not as if I did not understand the devastating nature of the two bombs. The day after Little Boy flattened Hiroshima, Ted Monks, one of the men I most admired, came over to my bivouac – we were in bivouacs again, outside Madras – and said, 'Major, these bombs – they're the ones they've been writing about in your magazines.' (Ted and I always addressed each other as 'Major'; it was our private rebellious joke.) He was referring to science fiction magazines, in particular, *Astounding*.

Fictional atomic bombs were first dropped in H. G. Wells' *The World Set Free* (1914) – over Germany. John W. Campbell's magazine, then *Astounding*, published stories and articles in the forties and earlier dealing with atomic warfare. The details of one story (Cleve Cartmill's 'Deadline', published a year before Hiroshima) were so accurate that FBI agents called at Campbell's offices in New York, suspecting that the Manhattan Project had sprung a security leak. This event has become legend in SF circles. Rightly so. It stood as evidence that SF was something more than 'that Buck Rogers stuff'.

The Campaign for Nuclear Disarmament, although well intentioned, was based on a mistaken view of human nature. When the Soviet Union had developed nuclear weapons, it would have been folly to abandon ours. To expect a power like the USSR to follow suit was folly. In a school playground as a boy, you kept firm hold on the stick you have found, in case the school bully came your way. By dropping it, you merely encouraged him.

*   *   *

Peace or war, there were matters still needing attention. There was the matter, for instance, of reinstating the pre-war world order. Britain was about to grant India and Burma their independence. Other European powers had no such intention. So, in October 1945, the 26th Indian Division found itself in Sumatra, a Dutch possession, and again on active service.

Not until the summer of 1947 did I return to England, to attempt to make a living for myself.

XVI

The Renaissance

Marcello: I have been a soldier too.
Francisco: How have you thriv'd?
Marcello: Faith, poorly.
Francisco: That's the misery of peace.

John Webster
The White Devil (v.i)

Summer. England. 1947. The weather hot and dry. The *Arundel Castle* docked at Liverpool. Repatriation Group 57 had sailed home to Blighty from Hong Kong. Redcaps stood about on the docks. No crowds welcomed us home. The war had been over too long. Everyone wanted to forget it; it would take at least fifteen years before they wanted to remember it.

The last of my comrades and I collected civvy clothes from a vast store in Woking. A pint of beer in a pub near by, then a handshake and parting. Almost no emotion. Wearing my new sports jacket, woven from coconut matting, I walked to the railway station to wait for a train that would take me, via many changes, down to North Devon. The familiar sense was on me of beginning life anew.

I too wanted to forget the war, to start a new life. The first task was to cease being a barbarian in the service of Empire and masquerade as an English citizen.

Before heading for the West Country, I called on a girl friend and my relations in Peterborough. Grandma Wilson was dead. Uncle Bert had sold the old house in Park Road and was in digs. I slept at 'Grendon', my uncle Allen's house. When my jolly aunt Nancy came into the bedroom in the morning, bringing me a cup of tea, she found me asleep on the floor. I was not accustomed to the softness of a real bed.

As for the imagined softness of civilian life, that too had its hard edges. After ten years at boarding school, followed by escape into the comparative safety and comfort of the British Army, with four years spent in the Far East – why, I was hardly fit for human society. Thus destiny shaped me to be a science fiction writer.

Bill and Dot and sister Betty were living on Sticklepath Hill outside Barnstaple, in Devon. Bill had sold the Bickington store and reverted to his old trade, working in a gents' outfitters in Barnstaple High Street. He and Dot had become friendly with the proprietor and his wife. Dot, doing her garden, found a good friend next door. Betty was pursuing an art course in Bideford. Both parents were happy and well. Their lives had improved. The bungalow had yielded to a pleasant enough detached house, aptly named 'Windy Ways'. They welcomed me and had no idea what to do with me.

Nor was I sure what to do with myself.

There were many English things to which I was unaccustomed. One had to get used to the currency (*florins* and *half-crowns*?), the class system, the bloodlessness, and the correct approaches to girls.

Having sailed from England as a boy, a callow youth, I returned to what was then, and in a curious way has remained ever since, a foreign land.

The place I had left four years previously had sunk below the horizon. My parents were still grumbling because they could not hear the old entertainers on the radio: Suzette Tarri, Scott and Whaley, Felix Mendelsohn and His Hawaiian Serenaders. Bill did not like the Atlee government. Dot could not buy a favourite brand of medicine any more. They were ill equipped, as most of us are, to deal with the great storm of change that had overtaken the world.

My future caused them some concern.

'What are you going to do with yourself now?' Dot asked.

'I want to be a writer!'

'*I* always wanted to write,' she said. It was a gesture of support.

Long military service entitled me to ninety-one days of Demob Leave: days of idleness, possibly. I found that Dot had saved all my letters home, those misleading letters, hoarding them in an old Hoover box. She was busily copying them into a large folio notebook. What dedication! Yet I did not fit under the family roof. I took to playing jazz records over and over, one in particular, compulsively. Chu Berry and his Stompy Stevedores: 'Fan It'. Even better when played for the hundredth time.

*   *   *

I could not talk with anyone of the years away. Yet I wanted everyone to know what that vanished life had been. In particular, the year
spent in Sumatra in 26th Indian Div seemed to me so unusual, so
beautiful and strange; by comparison, English life was thin gruel.

So I began to write what I hoped would turn into a novel.

At least I had a title: *Hunter Leaves the Herd.* I based my story
on a real event. A Sgt Hunter is in the infantry in Sumatra. The
'extremists', as the Republicans were called, are offering a woman
and life in the kampongs to anyone who deserts to them with his
rifle. Several Indian sepoys have accepted. Hunter is the first British
ranker to desert. He drives off in a fifteen-hundredweight, loaded
with Bren guns, Stens and ammunition. The extremists receive
him, and he lives the life of Riley, whoever Riley was, in the jungle
outside the capital.

Occasionally, Hunter organises a shopping expedition into Medan,
driving with woman and bodyguard right into the Kesawan, the
main street.

The Army cannot allow this to happen. Eventually, Hunter's old
mates track him to his hide-out and shoot him down.

It was a simple story, designed to carry a freight of conflicting
emotions and points of view. There were to be those who hated
Hunter and those who admired his courage. But.

But. Although I had produced many short stories, including some
written and set in the East Indies, the form of a novel, its ramifications and subclauses, the sense of an overall meaning, eluded
me. The experience was there, not its tongue. My soldiers on the
printed page could not speak as real soldiers had done. A veneer
of polite speech lay over England at that time, a lingering courtesy
from a more sedate age. Not until the sixties and the trial of D. H.
Lawrence's *Lady Chatterley's Lover* was it to be blown away. For
better or worse.

The self-expurgated *Hunter* was never finished. I flinched from
its unreality and threw it away.

I could not serve out my demobilisation leave in idleness. Looking
back, I realise that I missed the Army, that blue-jowled mother surrogate, missed the rough-and-tumble, missed the friends, Lou Grey,
Ted Monks, George Rust, Ronnie Pine, Harry Dunn, Eddie Edmonds
and many others. England was, for a returning ex-serviceman, an
unfriendly place, where work and routines of work were major
preoccupations.

'Routine' was a concept that held little attraction. But I saw it was time to forget a life of mild rampage and to bite the bullet. One day, I said goodbye to the family, caught a train, came to Oxford, and found employment in a book shop.

The strategy seemed to be:

i)   To forget all about the East
       so that one could
ii) civilise oneself and
iii) fit into society, whatever that was,
       in order to
iv) survive and write.

After the jolly riotous cities I had come to know, the great whoring cities of the East like Hong Kong and Singapore, Oxford appeared a serious place, given over to people enmeshed in learning, grey flannels and ex-service overcoats. Chapels in every college, spires, towers – all the symbols of old Christendom! In those days, every clock in every college chimed hours and quarters. Bells seemed always to be ringing a special Oxford time.

My new employer, Frank Sanders, was originally a Barnstaple man. Of poor origins, he had a deep respect both for learning and for the University which he served (and from which he was excluded). During my first weekend in Oxford, Frank took me on a walking tour, showing me some of the colleges. We walked by the Sheldonian, and past New, down Queens Lane, to Magdalen, to look at the deer park, and then back up the High by Univ and Oriel, which latter college cast its learned shade over Sanders' shop.

Frank Sanders was a small lively man with a rather impudent face and a quiff of white hair across his forehead. He resembled Max Beerbohm's caricature of Arnold Bennett.

He was a complex character, a bit of a rogue, but with a mischievous sense of humour – and an impeccable collection of landscapes and townscapes by Thomas Rowlandson, the great calligraphic artist of the early nineteenth century. His wife was short and portly. He doted on his son, Kingsley, who became a distinguished scientist.

A book shop is a rich but chastening environment for a budding author.

For two and a half years I worked in that shop. It was a prison, dark and airless, after the freedoms of Sumatra. For all that, like the hyacinth bulbs we used to shut in the airing cupboard, I flourished in the darkness.

Sanders' shop was a long, narrow, dark, secretive, overstocked gallimaufry of a book shop, comparing unfavourably in roominess with the crew quarters of one of Nelson's ships. Packed under its low beams was a profusion of ill-sorted stock, the outpourings of the ages. From folios to duodecimos, a mountain range of volumes lurked in obscurity.

Maps, prints, engravings hung wherever there was space. The old maps – Speeds, Saxtons, Mordens – mainly of the English counties, mopped up what light filtered in from outside while remaining themselves beautiful, cryptic and severe in their Hogarth frames. The elegance of those frames!

A twisting stair led up to Sanders' office and, beyond the office, the rare-book room where few customers were allowed. On the staircase was a framed engraving of Dr Johnson short-sightedly reading a 32mo.

Above the till was a window allowing a ration of light into a rear section of the shop. The ration was so feeble that electric lights burned all day. The window itself was partly obscured by an old hurdy-gurdy hanging there. It had to be tucked under the chin like a violin and wound by a small handle. Occasionally, Sanders, a music-lover, would take it down and play a melody.

Oh, yes, a strong whiff of the nineteenth century still clung to Sanders' shop.

Beyond the hurdy-gurdy was a section filled in part by a small office and a packing booth. The books here, tucked at the rear of the shop, were of less tempting varieties. This was the dusty refuge of Classical textbooks, Agriculture and Logic.

Beyond was a door into the rear premises. The shelves here were makeshift, stuffed with books in wild disorder, bought cheap. Idle and unemployed they lay; volumes on brass and beadwork and brassica crops and ballet and the breaststroke and Bastien-Lepage and Brittany and Buckingham and backgammon, to venture no further into the alphabet.

Then came rickety back stairs, where once the maids of Salutation House carried up trays of porter to gentlemen dining in upper rooms. On the stairs, on every step, more books were piled. Some would enjoy the privilege of being catalogued by a shy, charming, poetic man. He was polite, amusing and already a little bald. He was recently down from Merton, and just the company a new assistant wanted. His name was Roger Lancelyn Green.

Roger had written a delicate fantasy or two, some poems and a book on Andrew Lang. He was destined to become quite famous and to marry a pleasant Oxford lady. Later would come his involvement with Lewis Carroll. We leave him cataloguing books on the stairs and peering into a first edition of Douglas Jerrold's *Mrs Caudle's Curtain Lectures*, which were at that time still sought after in Oxford, and regarded by some as amusing.

Turn right at the top of the stairs and you found yourself in Heaven.

This was the highest part of the ancient building, highest and untidiest. Its one dusty window looked out across the broken rooftops of Oxford.

In imitation of the real thing, Heaven was damp and leaky. Here, Dickensian charm and creative vandalism went hand-in-hand.

Many were the old tomes that found their way into Sanders' clutches. Some were fashion or natural history books. Some were of a topographical nature, illustrated by steel engravings or etchings: views of English countryside, foreign views, views of Oxford colleges. They were broken up and the illustrations or maps sold separately, coloured and mounted. The beautiful octavo set in three volumes, Ingram's *Memorials of Oxford*, was cut apart for the sake of the engravings of colleges within. Good complete sets must by now be extremely scarce.

The breaking, the mounting, the colouring were done in Heaven. Here, at benches under a dusty window, sat two ladies, working away with their watercolours. In Heaven sat the cheerful, mischievous Lotte Worms, a refugee from Hitler's Reich.

In the stockroom below you might have come across a set of Peacock's novels in tree-calf, or a complete set of Thomas Hardy's first editions, all bound uniform (but this is the higher vandalism) in blue buckram, together with many other prizes. In huge wooden cases were stored Hogarth's engravings of London life and Piranesi's engravings of prisons and of Rome, in various states. There were also some Rowlandsons. Such Rowlandsons! Country scenes, bawdy scenes, inns, maidens, stage coaches, the whole eighteenth-century world that Thomas Rowlandson's calligraphic line so skilfully evoked.

I had never heard of Rowlandson until I went into Mr Sanders' stockroom, and have admired his work ever since. He was unrivalled as a draughtsman until Beardsley drew. In Mr Sanders' house on the Woodstock Road hung perhaps ten lilting Rowlandsons, country landscapes of the greatest delicacy of line and colour. Over Sanders' mantelpiece hung a pristine print of the painting generally regarded as Rowlandson's masterpiece, *Vauxhall Gardens*.

As far as Rowlandson is known at all, he is valued for his scenes of bawdy, of boisterousness and drinking bouts. But with that subject matter goes a style of transparent delicacy. His creamy young Georgian maids might have stepped out of *Cranford* or an early novel by Thomas Hardy. A travelling print-seller used to come round and sell Sanders pornographic Rowlandsons for his gentlemen clients.

Thomas Rowlandson elegantly recorded an England at once awful and enviable. Just looking at his work made one feel a little more English. The more famous Hogarth is a dour recorder of English life. Rowlandson relishes what he sees and is not judgemental.

Bill Oliver and I were the chief assistants in Sanders' shop. Bill was hard-working, kind, strange. We got on well. Like me, he had been in the Army. He had been captured by Italians in North Africa. Bill practically ran the sales end of the shop.

Our customers were a source of interest. Many famous people entered Sanders' shop, some importantly, some as if they were normal people. All the celebrities of the University, from A. L. Rowsc, Hugh Trevor-Roper, Lord David Cecil and Maurice Bowra downwards, entered our portals.

The visitor I liked least was Evelyn Waugh.

Waugh's early novels were pure delight. Meeting Waugh in the flesh was a different matter, at least if one was victim material, a bookseller's assistant. As I remember him, Waugh was always in a bad mood. Perhaps it was because he was writing *Brideshead Revisited*, where he went off the gold standard. Later, Waugh redeemed himself with *The Ordeal of Gilbert Pinfold*, a brave, funny and perceptive book. Largely autobiographical, I understand.

He entered Sanders' shop like some minor devil, small, bounderish, rosy on the wrong bits of cheek, with a smell not of brimstone but an equally noxious mixture of cigars and lavender water. He wished to see Mr Sanders – so imperiously wished to see Mr Sanders that anyone less than Mr Sanders was hardly worth a glance. A flick of the cigar was all we could hope for.

Sanders would appear in his usual genial way and sweep Waugh upstairs. They would emerge later, Waugh clutching some luxuriously bound volume of landscape engravings, both laughing. I believe he once had a very nice Boydell's *Thames* from Sanders. They would part at the door, glowing false *bonhomie* on both sides. Waugh was a bad payer. And inaccurate with his cigar ash.

Middle-aged ladies flocked to Sanders, just as they flocked to the lectures of C. S. Lewis, who was then at Magdalen College and occasionally came into the shop. The ladies tried to charm Frank Sanders, but Frank Sanders was always more adroit at charming the ladies. Wives of heads of colleges were his natural victims. In the course of intimate conversations, when the ladies were led up to his office, books and money would change hands, valuable prints would turn into more valuable cheques. Sanders would then escort the ladies to the door with amiable courtesy.

Directly they had gone, the mask would fall. He would stomp back into the rear of the shop. 'Oh, that Lady Blank! How she talks, how she wastes my time. I can't bear the woman. She's humbug all through . . .'

Frank Sanders was a self-made man. He began with no advantages in life, beyond the resources of his brain. As a youth in North Devon he sold newspapers for W. H. Smith on Barnstaple railway station. Since I had lived in Barnstaple too, this gave us something in common, and allowed him the opportunity to pay me less than I was worth.

I squinted up from street level at other leviathans of the literary scene who came to the shop. Hugh Macdonald, editor of Marvell's poems and other works, always grumpy, but fun to imitate. Geoffrey Grigson, poet, producer of books, never satisfied with our service. Many celebrated dons, the most engaging of whom was probably J. I. M. Stewart. Stewart was busy installing himself in Christ Church when I arrived in my shabby suit to conquer Oxford. He was writing a series of mock-Shakespearian plays for the BBC Third Programme, then at its cultural zenith. Years later, Stewart must have felt a little rueful when Tom Stoppard tilled the same ground more profitably in *Rosencrantz and Guildenstern are Dead*. But by then he was well embarked on his second or third career as detective writer Michael Innes.

John Betjeman was pleasant. Betjeman would arrive giggling and steaming in an old coat with a fur collar which might once have done duty for Bud Flanagan. His hair was curly and somewhat enveloped in an old felt hat. He filled the shop with formidable goodwill, made himself pleasant to all, and signed a copy of his poems for me.

Betjeman came not to buy but to sell. He was then living near Wantage. He reviewed for the now defunct *Daily Herald*, where he was bombarded by the very sweepings of publishers' lists. Why they sent him such rubbish I do not know, unless Bloomsbury had an exceptionally poor view of the *Daily Herald*. The gaudier the cover, the more likely it was to be despatched to Wantage and a labouring Betjeman.

Betjeman drove up the High in his old van full of trashy books and stopped outside Sanders. He then came into the shop for a half-hour's chat, after which he strolled out again with Sanders.

Sanders would turn the books over and finally say, 'A fiver, John?'

'Well, I know it's rubbish, Frank, but someone must read the stuff. I really have to buy a new set of tyres. Couldn't you make it ten pounds?'

They soon came to an agreement.

The agreement was five pounds.

Bill and I then carried the books into the shop. Betjeman departed.

Sanders kept any books that were at all passable, merging them with our new stock. The rest of the books were crammed into two large suitcases. These suitcases I took up to Foyle's book shop in London, where the buyer in the basement would pay me perhaps twenty pounds.

The only novel I can remember salvaging from Betjeman's collections was Guy Endore's *Methinks the Lady*, which I read avidly while immersed at the same time in Pope's poems and Lewis Mumford's *The Condition of Man*. I still read several books at once.

Mumford I considered one of my best discoveries. He spoke with a voice that held my attention, bringing alive the broadest of schemes with a telling detail. He was a sociologist, engineer and poet. And something more than that.

Mumford wrote *The Condition of Man* in time of war; the book was published in 1944. He talks in the Introduction of those who desire 'a glib mechanical substitute for the painful but rewarding processes of life'. Later, he asks the question I was asking myself – 'What was man's true life?'

Commenting on the grandiose letter Mark Twain sent Walt Whitman on the occasion of his seventieth birthday, Mumford singles out Twain's listing of the marvels of the Victorian age ('The amazing, infinitely varied and innumerable products of coal tar . . .'). He says:

> In the admirable list of inventions over which Mark Twain exulted there was reason to exult – provided reason had governed their exploitation and had made them the servants of man's own higher development. In thinking of the nineteenth century as the century exclusively of mechanical improvement Mark Twain had bowed every other type of invention and creation

out of the picture: he forgot that this was the century of Goethe, Emerson, Tolstoy, Hugo, of Beethoven, Schumann, Brahms, of Delacroix, Goya, Courbet, Renoir, Rodin, and not least of Whitman himself: men who had sought to re-enthrone the human personality and redress the balance between the inner and the outer world.

SF itself, dazzled often enough by technological progress, still falls into the error for which Mumford rebukes Twain.

Oxford is an admirable city, and a good place in which to live, even if one has no privileged position in a college. In part at least, in the shade of an old quad or cloister, it is beautiful. Yet, after the first shock of its academic presence had worn off, I found something missing among its pale stones. The overwhelming diversity of forms of life, of physiognomies, of systems of conduct, of languages, gestures, symbols, the beauty of women and landscapes, which contribute to the vast anthology of existence in Southeast Asia, were lacking.

It seemed that the Great Outdoors was gone for ever. I must resign myself to the Great Indoors. At least my mind need not be imprisoned. In accordance with my strategy, I plunged into reading Gibbon and Max Landau and Oswald Spengler, histories of art and literature, and Boswell's Life of Johnson (the best biography in the world), together with a hundred other items. I discovered Sir Thomas Browne of Norwich, the Beethoven of prose, and tunnelled my way through his writings. 'Half our dayes wee passe in the shadowe of the earth, and the brother of death exacteth a third part of our lives.'

In an endeavour to make myself a less immoral person, I read Browne's *Religio Medici*. Certainly it is a book full of wisdom, strikingly expressed, even if one cannot follow the example set. 'All places, all airs, make unto me one Countrey; I am in England every where, and under any Meridian.'

Less of a new discovery was Thomas Hardy, whose *The Trumpet Major* I had read and enjoyed before my army days. Now I devoured all his novels. Paperback editions did not exist in the late forties. Whenever I was in London, I would scour the book shops of Charing Cross Road, looking for the old Macmillan editions, whose faded print is always remembered, seeming to take on an architectural character in memory of Hardy's first trade.

Particularly to my taste were Hardy's poems, published after he had finished with novel writing. Beyond his lapwing cry of grief was the enchanting twist and flight of his verse forms. Philip Larkin put it well in an article on Hardy's poetry: 'His subjects are men, the life of men, time and the passing of time, love and the fading of love.'

I have a shelf full of books about Hardy, together with criticisms of his writing. Nothing captures the essence of the man so well as Virginia Woolf's essay in *The Common Reader*.

Hardy's poems I read for many a year, along with such writers as William Tenn, Henry Kuttner and Frederik Pohl. They too wrote about men and time; love somehow got left behind in the present, as they looked to the future.

During my early months in Oxford, I wasted my precious half-days off in travelling by train to Reading in quest of a grant. Like an ex-convict trying to shake off the odour of the prison cell, I felt compelled to escape from that atmosphere of monsoon, jungle and bush hat which had made such a mark on me. I attended gloomy offices in Reading, undergoing interviews, filling in forms, waiting in corridors, enduring the snubs that attend such situations.

My chief interrogator was a seedy, yellow-fanged chap, dressed in a crumpled suit – a chap not greatly my senior, but already embracing middle age. As an ex-serviceman, I hoped to qualify for a grant to enable me to attend University (Oxford, of course). Many formal difficulties stood in my way: the jungle of the law had supplanted the law of the jungle. The impression remains that my chief interrogator took a personal dislike to me because I made jokes to lighten the atmosphere; but then, the dyspeptic fellow probably loathed all ex-servicemen; he would be the type who had found himself a reserved occupation the day before war broke out. Eventually, I simply gave up. A prejudice against Reading took some while to dissipate.

Curious inverted images of the dyspeptic chap haunted the streets of Oxford and elsewhere. These were the youths who had just missed the war. Their manhood had to be proved by other means. They became Teds and bovver boys, dressing strangely, acting aggressively – much as we had done in Mandalay.

Sanders subscribed to the *Times Literary Supplement*, later to be known by its initials, *TLS*. I began reading it and became a regular subscriber. I have now been a reader for almost half a century; under editor John Gross it was at its most enjoyable. It remains indispensable, along with *New Scientist*.

My discoveries embraced Franz Kafka's writings and *Hamlet*. Both remain favourites. The prince is something of a Kafkaesque character. In Oxford I was able to attend several productions of *Hamlet*; I have seen the play many times since. It is unfathomable, possibly because it is flawed (for instance, in the way that the Prince of Denmark's age and nature seem to vary from one act to the next), but more likely because we cannot read into it what its first Renaissance audiences saw.

By studying George Sampson's *History of English Literature*, I became acquainted not only with the names of those who had contributed to the richness of English cultural life, but to the continuity of which I, too, hoped to become a part. I am grateful to Sampson's book for much that followed – including an admiration for the early English dramatists.

Living in Oxford, one could see college productions of many pre- and post-Shakespearean plays. The Oxford University Dramatic Society (OUDS) was in full creative swing under Neville Coghill, while most of the colleges also had actors and producers who later made their names in the world. In those first busy years in Oxford, I attended performances of *Gammer Gurton's Needle* – Elizabethan ruff and tumble – *Love's Labours Lost*, *The Relapse: or, Virtue in Danger*, *The Country Wife*, *Venice Preserved*, and Ben Jonson's marvellously funny *Epicoene: or, The Silent Woman*, and harkened to Marlowe's mighty line in *Tamberlane*, and Oriel College's memorable production of *Edward II*. Almost all of the splendidly gloomy plays of Webster and Tourneur were performed by undergraduate actors with relish, if not polish. They proved to be great ranters.

Many of these plays were staged at the end of the summer term, outside, in the college grounds. Often enough, one sat freezing while the sun went down and the old walls of the college hunched up their shadowy shoulders against the cold. Of course one could also reliably see Shakespeare plays, including those less frequently produced. I first saw *Measure for Measure* on an OUDS stage.

As I had experienced it, the East seemed contained within an eternal present. Much of the past was contained in the great archive of Oxford. I loved the smell of it: the past also holds culture shock.

When a grand exhibition of twentieth-century painters was staged at the Tate, my enthusiasm for sixteenth-century Italy waned; de Chirico, Tanguy, Matta, Ernst, and Braque and Picasso in their Cubist period reigned in their stead. From an outstanding period of creative activity, two painters in particular stimulated the imagination, Gauguin and Kandinsky.

On a later occasion, I took a train to London to see a Francis

Bacon exhibition. There were his screaming popes and cardinals! Our generation was immediately receptive to Bacon. I stood in awe before that contradictory genius: his portrayal of agony and disintegration in the sumptuous slimes of paint. I longed to write as Bacon painted.

Those early days in Oxford were very full.

Just as the merchant princes of the Renaissance, who financed the bow-wave of rebirth, sometimes relaxed from worrying about the adornment of churches to enjoy themselves poisoning their rivals, so I too had my fun, despite all the autodidact activities.

Oxford brimmed with eccentrics, many of them finding it hard to settle to the restrictions of academic life.

Charles Parr and his wife Timmie were early friends. I met them in an Italian restaurant, just after my first story had been published in a magazine entitled *Science Fantasy*. Charles was a Balliol man, reading English. We both had a passion for Samuel Johnson. Charles sold his weekly essay to a Dutch radio station under the rubric 'Great Moments in English Literature'. Thus he paid his way through university. I always admired the effrontery of it.

I slept little, reading late in my preposterous digs. Trying hard to be English again, I found the Japs pursued me, haunting my nightmares as they charged with fixed bayonets. The tropics also tracked me down: recurrent fits of malaria hit me for some years, dying away slowly.

Oxford's creative atmosphere was energising. One side of my character told me I was undergoing my own – well, there lay the word for anyone to use! – renaissance. I was buoyed by a general sense that much was possible, that fresh starts could be made. I took to my new role avidly, although the shadow of the old University assures proles they will never learn enough, can never catch up with centuries of learning. The book shop, however, held a more reassuring message for the likes of me, as I sold the set textbooks for the new academic year: that even learning was marketable . . .

For a while I attempted to muster up other talents. In Hythe Bridge Street was a restaurant called The Coconut Grove, or some similarly exotic name. I proposed to redecorate it. The manager was the semi-famous restaurateur, Mr George Silver. While in Medan, in Sumatra, I had decorated a whole theatre, filling it with dusky maidens, weightier Dutch dancing girls, palm trees, suns setting beyond sleepy lagoons and similar motifs, all available for view locally. When I sketched such subjects on paper, Mr Silver approved. The agreement was that I should work late each night, after the restaurant closed. I would be paid nothing, but given meals and drink.

Frank Sanders strongly disapproved of my moonlighting; if I was turning into some sort of a painter, I could not concentrate on bookselling. The scheme petered out, however. When I realised that Mr Silver also intended that I should pay for the requisite paints, the dusky maidens remained unrealised, and the walls of Oxford suffered accordingly. It was all I could do to pay my laundry bills.

Interest in art prompted me to buy John Ruskin's *Modern Painters*. There was a small reawakening of interest in Ruskin in the early fifties, soon to fade. In any case, the interest centred mainly round Ruskin's failed marriage to Euphemia Gray. Poor John Ruskin was shocked by that pretty part of a woman, her mons Veneris; he had not anticipated its thatch of curly hair. Euphemia went off with Millais, who was more worldly when it came to such matters.

Ruskin's greatness, however, has little to do with his sex life. *Modern Painters* was my bedside reading for more than a year. Like *Modern Painters*, his *Praeterita*, an unfinished autobiography, is full of elegant and clear writing, conveying Ruskin's good sense.

Ruskin refers to a time when he was a boy, visiting the Alps with his father, presumably about 1830. It's a thoroughly modern story. Ruskin speaks of the power of mountains to purify hearts and solemnise thoughts, and of the strength he was given by the experience of the Alps. Such sensibility is threatened by 'the populations of modern Europe, first by the fine luxury of the fifteenth century, and then by the coarse lusts of the eighteenth and early nineteenth'.

He was a skilled observer, in the mould of his contemporary Charles Darwin. In that same book, *Praeterita*, Ruskin relates how a sketch he made of an aspen tree became a moment of insight, of epiphany. 'The woods, which I had then only looked on as wilderness, fulfilled I then saw, in their beauty, the same laws which guided the clouds, divided the light, and balanced the wave.' This, says Ruskin, caused him to see a bond between a human mind and all visible things.

In our century, James Lovelock, one supposes, had a similar revelation which developed into his Gaia Hypothesis.

While in my King Edward Street digs, I ate cheaply at British Restaurants. Several survived in Oxford when I first arrived, dinosaurs from more heroic times. The restaurant in the Town Hall served a tolerable three-course meal at a cost of one shilling and three pence.

It proved, with its long, good-natured queues, a useful place in which to meet girls. My determination was to throw away my self-apology and go for the prettiest girl I could find.

Falling in love with red-haired Pamela, I besieged her with poems and plays. How honest she was, how passionate, how elegant! 'I wonder by my troth what Thou and I did till we loved? Were we not wean'd till then?' The portrait of Lady Hamilton by Romney resembles that autumn-coloured lady. I hung a reproduction of the portrait in my room in King Edward Street. She was engaged to an undergraduate. For all that, she loved me. She loved me and I adored her.

Pamela disappeared in the direction of an alien altar, only to live in Middlesbrough. She was too dear for my possessing. Consolation was to be had with an Irish lady of mercurial disposition. She liked to dress in black, and was the first woman I knew to wear black underwear. It was a great success. We used to sit in the rear of the Scala cinema, which had double or snogging seats.

On occasions, that oppressive sense of powerlessness that had overwhelmed me since childhood returned. It was hopeless to remain in Frank Sanders' stuffy little book shop, although I was a success and now entrusted with the ordering – and of course the selling – of new books. That was fun. And there were days when I exulted, when I felt of myself, with Walt Whitman, 'I am large, I contain multitudes'.

Science fiction had something to do with that feeling. Its speculative daring kept open wider vistas than one might expect to see from the grimy window of my lodgings. Sanders' was a storehouse of the past, *Astounding* of the future. The very word 'future' had a talismanic quality.

One of the writers I enjoyed, not least because his style improved over the years, was Clifford Simak. During the fifties, John Campbell published a story of Simak's in *Astounding* called 'Immigrant', in which a young man from Earth travels to a distant planet where civilisation is greatly in advance of ours. There he is to learn all that is within his capacity of galactic culture. Simak's fiction generally had something of the parable about it, and a belief in universal brotherhood.

Such powerful stories appeared to guarantee that a time was approaching when everyone, even the literary critics, would see that here was a new aspect of literature to be welcomed, and its diversity positively explored. Such perception has still not been granted to literary critics – not even to the so-called 'literary editors' of newspapers and journals, of which I was once one.

In those early post-war years, it was easier to become civilised. The public mood, tempered by wartime grief and hardship, was more serious. Fewer trivialities abounded. That benevolent influence on British life, the BBC, launched its Third Programme after the war. It was a bold cultural venture. T. S. Eliot read his *Four Quartets* in a sepulchral voice; Fred Hoyle delivered his lectures on the Nature of the Universe; there were specially commissioned plays by Louis MacNeice and, in lighter vein, the Hilda Tablet plays of Henry Reed.

Meanwhile, as we devised ways of living our peacetime lives, the Cold War developed. The divisions that broke the back of Europe could be ascribed to the megalomaniac policies of the late Adolf Hitler, whose evil influences survive long after his death in a Berlin bunker. An economically enfeebled Britain was caught between two superpowers, the USA and the USSR. It threatened to become Airstrip One, as outlined in George Orwell's novel *Nineteen Eighty-Four*, then being read by everyone who read.

At one moment we were watching Gaumont-British newsreels of our ships setting out from port and pouring weapons and ammunition like gleaming fish over the rail into the North Sea, and at the next we were re-arming . . .

Communism tightened its grip over Eastern Europe, China and elsewhere. Hitler was gone; Stalin remained. Unlike Hitler, he had millions of idolators all round the world. The Soviet Union loomed upon the horizons of our lives, a vast icy mountain, the snows and frosts from which blew westwards.

Human aggressive tendencies, sharpened by a million years of evolution, were fortified by escalating weaponry. Something had gone wrong with the path we had taken. No sooner was the global war over, and the barbarism of Nazi Germany's Final Solution revealed, than fresh wars were breaking out, like boils bursting from a sick body.

In the dull cloddish year of 1950, the Korean War erupted. One black day, I received my papers for 'Z' Reserve. How furious, how miserable they made me! The papers informed me I might at any moment be conscripted back into the Forces and sent abroad on active service. So much for hopes of renaissance!

The idea haunted me then, and has troubled me ever since, that humanity may be a few apples short of the tree of knowledge. When

I read Charles Berg's book *Madkind*, I found there fortification of my fears. Certain theories advanced by Koestler regarding the somewhat jerry-built nature of the brain were also influential. But who, living through much of the twentieth century, needs written proof? In any case, 'Z' Reserve papers, held in a trembling hand, were evidence enough of a prevailing insanity.

One of my hard-drinking friends was a man called Ross. He was a South African who had fought in WWII and was now up at Oriel College. The idea of war haunted him – bloodbaths in South Africa, catastrophe everywhere. He was one of those men who seem always to have private sources of information, in the government, in the secret service, in the War Office. We huddled on Paddington station, drinking whisky on Platform One in a chill winter afternoon, early in 1950, that ghastly year.

'This Korean business is going to get out of all control in a matter of months. We are finally going to have to face up to the Russians. Take it from me, they'll have their own Bomb pretty soon.'

He spoke with some articulacy, and at this point vomited into his overcoat. Brushing some of it away with delicacy, he said, 'Let's get some more whisky. Korea may be the ground where it's all decided. China will come in on Russia's side – two great Communist powers. NATO will have to fight them, and we hope Germany will join us.'

Another cough and a gasp, more vomit, before he said, 'I can guarantee to you, my friend, that we shall be involved in another world war by the end of this year. This time, nuclear.'

We went into the bar and bought more doubles.

But I should have said: Dot came up to Oxford to see me. She put herself up in comfort in the Randolph, Oxford's main hotel, inspected my room, was introduced to Mr Sanders, and met Pamela. She liked everyone and everything she saw, suffering fits of enthusiasm over Oxford itself. Like all middle-aged women, she was enchanted by Frank Sanders.

This was quite a different Dot from the earlier Dot of East Dereham. The cachou-chewing suicidal mother had become an amusing lady always prepared to be amused. On a second visit, she was racketing about the countryside with a man I vaguely knew, a chief light of the estate agency, Carter Jonas. Before anyone even suspected, lo and behold, Dot had *bought a house!* It stood on the outskirts of Oxford in Third Acre Rise, and was called 'Asphodel'.

So Dot, Bill and Betty left the tediums of North Devon to follow me to Oxford. And in the false roof of Asphodel, Betty and I found a trove of twenties dance records with titles like 'You're Getting Terribly Blonde Lately' and 'After You with My Blonde'. Betty at that time did comic impressions of a coloratura singing 'Softly Awakes My Heart'.

To return under the family roof was not exactly to my taste; but, foolishly docile as ever, under that roof I went. My Irish lady friend came under suspicion of 'leading me astray'. To tease Dot, I would sing while shaving in the bathroom of a morning, 'Since I heard your Irish laughter, It's your Irish heart I'm after . . .' But I was not really aiming that high.

Coming home at one thirty one morning, I was not at all pleased to find Bill waiting for me in the kitchen, clad in pyjamas with teddy-bear dressing gown over.

'What on earth are you doing?'

He saw how vexed I was, and backed away from his original intention. 'I thought you'd like some hot chocolate when you came in.'

'I don't want any.' I marched past him, up to bed. It was the first time I had ever spoken back to Bill. The incident marked a shift in our relationship.

The Korean war burned its way through history. The two largest Communist states, the Soviet Union and China, forged an alliance. I was not called up on Z Reserve. Ross disappeared mysteriously. The Amcrican forces under MacArthur used napalm for the first time. I got married to a lady named Olive Fortescue. Bill obtained a job in an outfitters in Oxford. In September of 1951, Russia exploded its first atomic bomb. A dreadful cold froze international relations. Burma by this time had achieved full independence, and was preparing to disappear from human view.

Living the married life in Kidlington (described by Nicholas Pevsner as the worst example of ribbon development in the country), I continued to have nightmares about being killed by Jap soldiers. It was a late reaction to the Mandalay campaign. Malaria was also recurrent, though fading slowly.

Less slow to fade was the regret at having to work at a nine-to-six job. Although the company in the book shop was pleasant, and we managed to squeeze amusement out of the customers, I was oppressed by the confinement, the dull regularity of working hours, the routine.

The book shop job paid badly at three pounds a week. Although my wife also worked, we felt we could hardly live. It was all we could do to pay for our draughty little house. No newspaper – an obvious economy. But there was the new Third Programme to listen to, its talk and its music.

The omens for our poor little marriage were adverse. When Olive, in fear and trembling, wrote to Alice, her tyrannical mother, to announce our engagement, Alice sent us a cutting from the *Daily Telegraph* detailing increasing divorce figures. It proved a self-fulfilling prophecy – after eleven years.

Our neighbours on either side of the Kidlington house might have been set there as examples of a) respectable working class and b) unregenerate working class. There was no doubt which lot had the jollier time of it, the household full of chiming clocks, polished every Sunday, or the dump where they were drunk and merry every Saturday.

The latter family was Irish, the McCrumbs. Mrs McCrumb was a big blowsy lady with untidy ginger hair. I used to listen through the thin walls to her singing, her beautiful light voice a tonic on the dull Oxfordshire air, as she sang of mountains and valleys in Ireland she would probably never visit. A lovely voice she had.

The pub in Kidlington was The Dog. When I could afford to go there – alone, for my wife did not drink or enter public houses – I found it a miserable place, drab and unfriendly. Many years later, as Kidlington became more prosperous, and gentrification was on the march, the pub took a leaf from Morris Motors' book and rechristened itself. The Dog became The Squire Bassett. Much to the family's amusement.

The fizz went out of life for a while. Like my old muckers in Burma, I put up with whatever came along because my expectations were low. Since the days of H. H. Aldiss, my father had fallen low, and I even lower. So I saw the situation. A novel I discovered made a deep impression, *The Ragged Trousered Philanthropists* by Robert Tressell. Tressell was an Irish house-painter; his novel depicts, with humour, the impoverished lives of his fellow workers. I came across nothing so depressingly truthful about working-class life until I read a book by a friend of mine, Nigel Gray, *Happy Families*, published in 1985.

Not knowing where I stood in the Alcatraz of Class, I felt lost to the extent that I despised my own aspirations. Who thought as I did in Kidlington? No one in The Dog.

Through the wall, the sweet Irish voice continued.

As though the world war had been a gigantic binge, which in some way it was, hangover followed. A dreadful aspect of that hangover was the slow continued revelation of Hitler's and Nazi Germany's Final Solution, the destruction of millions of Jews, gypsies and other races. And still anti-Semitism lingers, a psychotic strand of xenophobia.

At first, global response was to blame the German people alone. No doubt the major share of blame rests there. Gradually, a more thoughtful reaction prevailed. Was not a current European mood of anti-Semitism in part responsible, giving the nod to Hitler? I thought of Bill; but his abstract distrust of Jews had been counterbalanced by the help he had wholeheartedly given the Boxbaums, when they took refuge in Gorleston on Sea. No one was entirely free from blame.

Sanders took on a partner, William Chislett, who came down with his wife Muriel from the north. Chislett was a kindly, good-humoured man, inclined to trust people – a fatal mistake where Frank Sanders was concerned. The partnership fell apart. I was an unhappy witness of Sanders poisoning Chislett's name among other booksellers.

By then I was preparing to leave his employment.

I had asked Sanders several times for a rise in pay. He refused. What he dangled instead was the possibility of a partnership in the business when he retired, which, I was given to understand, might be any day.

Then he said, taking me aside, 'You come up and see me on a Friday evening, and I'll slip you an extra pound. You're worth it. Just don't tell anyone else.'

'No, I couldn't do that.'

This reply annoyed him. After work that evening I took Bill Oliver to the nearby Blue Boar Inn. Over a pint, I told him my tale. Bill was completely unmoved. 'Yes, Frank made me the same offer. I turned it down on the same grounds you did.'

'What about the partnership?'

'That's complete boloney. I've heard that tale too. Everyone hears it. The man is a hypocrite.'

After that, there seemed nothing for it but to leave.

By a happy quirk of fate, the sons of both Bill Chislett and Frank Sanders have become my friends.

*   *   *

The dreary years of the early fifties were not wasted. I applied myself
to writing. My wife typed out the short stories on her typewriter.
I also began to write another novel. It was entitled *Shouting Down
a Cliff*. My grasp of construction had improved since the days of
Hunter Leaves the Herd. It was helpful that the characters were
more remote from my own life.

And I tended our little rectangle of garden. Kidlington clay soil
proved very fertile. In spring, cracks appeared down which the
largest runner bean seed might fall yards towards the centre of the
Earth; in winter, the place turned marsh. Yet somehow, in between
times, enough vegetables grew to fill our parsimonious plates. And
in the fields round about – where at first we incautiously made love
– tons of coal-glossy blackberries enlivened the hedgerows all the
way to the canal.

For some years, while my embryo writing stage was developing,
I worked in Parker's, a large book shop which had entrances on
both the Broad and the Turl. I worked at the Turl end, with the
antiquarian and second-hand books. It was not a bad place; the
books and the staff were fine; the customers were another matter.

To walk along the Turl from the High gave pleasure. I seemed to
have many reasons for despising myself, but at least I had levered
myself out of Devon into a civilised town, a town of learning as
represented by the façades of the old colleges with entrances on to
the Turl, Exeter, Lincoln and Jesus – and by the fine horse chestnut
which loomed over the wall of Jesus, to be regarded from my desk
in the shop with some longing, an emblem of the natural world.

One of my tasks was to catalogue books, mainly theology. As I was
going home one evening, I had on my desk, beside a pile of volumes
of the Nicaean fathers, a copy of *Galaxy Science Fiction*. My boss,
Bill Thomas, saw it and said, 'You don't read that rubbish, do you?'

'Yes. And I contribute rubbish to it.'

What a relief when Amis's *Lucky Jim* was published. Here was
someone who felt about authority as I did!

When we could first afford a summer holiday, my wife and I went
south by train to a guesthouse in Freshwater, Isle of Wight. In a
Freshwater newsagent, I bought a British SF magazine, *Nebula*,
published in Glasgow. The stories were so amateur (except for a
story by Robert Silverberg, a new author later to become a friend),
I believed I might do better. I submitted a story called 'T' to the
editor. It was accepted – and published three years later.

Shouting Down a Cliff developed slowly. I wrote in Quink with fountain pen, in two notebooks. The notebooks had marbled hard covers. I filled them while we lived in our cheap Taylor Woodrow house during a draughty winter, and in the garden through two summers.

The notebooks now fester in the Bodleian Library, in the Aldiss Archive, remembrances of things past. The sentences accumulated slowly, page by page. At the same time I was reading Hardy, Hal Clement, Henry James, Proust, A. E. van Vogt and Dickens. The style of my novel swerved accordingly. It was about – what *was* it about, I wonder? Some chaps in an institution. A comedy. Two years it took me to write, but finally it was finished, at a magnificent estimated 80,000 words. Nowadays, the blessed computer counts words automatically!

Writers must develop critical faculties; there can be no better critic than oneself. As soon as the novel was completed, on that day of triumph, I slammed the two notebooks shut. I never read my labours through; nor did I offer them to anyone else to read. I knew it was no success as a novel. Nevertheless, it was a novel, complete with characters and narrative, and not particularly short by the standards of the day. If I had accomplished that much, I could do anything.

So I encouraged myself.

Otherwise, life was proving difficult.

Things are never as bad, or as rosy, as we imagine. In March 1953, Joseph Stalin died. Even from the distance of England, icicles seemed to melt, primroses burst forth in the hedgerows. Throughout his awful domains, the news must have seemed too good to be true. Even better, by the end of that year Stalin's henchman, the thuggish Lavrenti Beria, was shot.

Meanwhile, England remained austere, and we started to hear much about the European Coal and Steel Community. It was the birth of the European Union.

Kidlington was a place separate from Oxford and its stir, separate by a million miles. Life's a sort of rat's nest of things and emotions and vacuums at times. Since I did not know how I felt then, it is useless now to speculate on those feelings. For reasons obvious at least to the family, if not to others, I pass over them masked, shrouded, humping the black tent of silence.

I longed to escape to Europe and its grand cities. A two-pound glass jam jar, standing on the bedroom mantelpiece, began to fill slowly with chunky threepenny bits. When they reached the brim, there might be enough money to finance a trip to Florence. Courtesy of Bernard Berenson, I was still enamoured with Renaissance painting. I wished to visit the Uffizi.

Giorgioni's work generated almost as much enthusiasm as Timmins' covers for *Astounding* or Bacon's screaming cardinals.

The marriage slowly deteriorated. Perhaps there is an undeclared principle in life: when something sinks, something else must rise. The *Bookseller* is the long-standing periodical of the book trade. I went up to London to see the editor, and was given the job of writing – or rather, was permitted to write – a weekly column, 'The Brightfount Diaries'. I used a pseudonym, Peter Pica, a small type. The editor, Edmund Seagrave, was being extremely benign; he had never run a humorous fictional column before.

It was a hit, a palpable hit!

Brightfount's was a provincial book shop, widely based on Sanders' shop and my experiences there. I populated it with a genial and eccentric staff. Readers on all sides of the trade enjoyed the column, which provided a smile lacking amid the gravity of the rest of the journal.

One day, a letter arrived at our Kidlington house. The letter was from Charles Monteith, the new editor at Faber & Faber. He said that all at Faber were fans of Brightfount's. Would I care to turn the columns into a book?

Within the next month or two, I received similar offers from five other publishers. But Faber came first. Faber were undoubtedly the best start anyone could have in publishing, and Charles the best and most genial of publishers. He had already rescued (and rechristened) William Golding's first novel, *Lord of the Flies*, from the slush pile. According to his secretary, Rosemary Goad, I was the first person he wrote to to commission a book.

The Brightfount Diaries fared excellently. It was widely and favourably reviewed and sold well. The book shop – Parker's, now extinct – took a cautious six on sale or return. They sold. Faber persuaded Denis Powell to take one hundred and fifty copies. They filled a whole window, their gallant pink jackets looking out on the Broad. Amazingly, they too sold out. I was on my way.

That was 1955, my *annus mirabilis*. I won the *Observer* prize for a story set in the year AD 2500. It was of great importance to me. Writers connected with the *Observer*, such as Angus Wilson and Marghanita Laski, were among the judges. So I established myself as a writer of social comedy and of science fiction. And in that same year, my first son, Clive, was born.

His coming was miraculous. Though his parents were amateurs at parenthood, he immediately proved practised in the art of being a baby. He was as calm and benevolent as could be, and the smiles he gave us – well, they rained on us as a blessing, for which we stood much in need.

He and I were inseparable. I fixed a small seat to the handlebars of my bike, so that I could take him for rides into the country, along the canal, or through Oxford, to let his eyes rest on good architecture. Indoors, I built him mad castles to be knocked down, or played a number of games about the garden. I sang to him.

He was my joy.

Samsara, the rusty old wheel of death and life, was turning again.

Yet a dreadful shadow of parting loomed. As soon as a little money trickled into our coffers, I sold the house in Kidlington and bought a better one in North Oxford. Then, at a bold venture, I gave up my bookselling job, just as I had always intended.

My literary agent, my kindly publisher, my father, all begged me not to take such a rash step. 'If you want a more outdoor life, become a postman,' my father advised. 'There's a good pension at the end of it.'

The promise of freedom was too great. The success of *Brightfount* had given me confidence. I sat at home in a back bedroom in our house in Victoria Road and wrote two silly little novels – just to be flapping my wings – which were to take a while to sell.

Good things and ill were intermixed. The chill between husband and wife deepened when Olive found it intolerable to have me at home all day. On the other hand, a new opportunity opened for me. I had been reviewing books for the *Oxford Mail* for about a year, in the main science fiction and works on the possibilities of space travel, then appearing like a false dawn. My review of a book called *Freud and Religion* caught the editor's eye, and he appointed me Literary Editor. The editor in those days was a popular and hard-driving man, W. Harford Thomas. The retiring Lit. Ed. was, coincidentally, S. P. B. Mais, who had spent a brief but inglorious term teaching at West Buckland.

I went to see Mais and his wife Jill in their house on the Woodstock Road. He had scarcely changed since his West Buckland days. He was wearing a cap, several pullovers, and a harlequin scarf.

Mais and I became quite good friends. He was a testy man who kept strange disruptive hours, going to bed only when the milkman clinked his bottles on the dawn doorstep. Mais had two stunning daughters, bearing stunning names, Lalage and Imogen.

In the poverty of his retirement, the near-destitution which hangs over most writers, Mais was forced to write quickie books with Jill's aid. These were published by the firm of Alvin Redman. We still cherish our copy of *Round Africa Cruise Holiday* – one of the world's memorable titles. The Maises got free trips on Cunard ships for these jaunts.

The Navy figured large in the case of another of Mais's friends, J. H. B. Peel. Peel mainly wrote of country things, though his Naval career was liable to creep into any subject matter. He had reviewed for Mais. Indeed, they seemed to carve up between them all the books that arrived at the *Mail*. I changed all that, apportioning the best books between members of the staff of the two papers, the *Oxford Mail* – an evening paper – and the weekly *Oxford Times*. One of my star reviewers was Anthony Price. I was always amazed at how much Tony knew about everything.

Books not reviewed went to Oxfam, even then leaving enough money over to finance an innovation of mine, an annual literary dinner at the Elizabeth Restaurant for my reviewers and for H. T.

In the wider world, there were stirrings of a livelier time in the arts. The genius of British art was the unrivalled Francis Bacon. John Wain and Iris Murdoch, with whom I later became friendly, were published. Kingsley Amis's *Lucky Jim* was loose in the world.

'Oh God, Jim Dixon's *me*,' said a friend. We all felt that way, between gasps of laughter.

Over John Osborne's *Look Back in Anger* my wife and I quarrelled bitterly. She believed that such plays should be prohibited, since they only made people discontented. I argued that the play was an expression of an existing general discontent. Of boring Sundays, boring class systems, and many other irritants.

Our argument petered out when Osborne became confused with another of her offending Johns, whose immensely popular novel also destroyed many British institutions – John Wyndham, author of *The Day of the Triffids*. This confusion of Johns, never to be cleared up, was cunningly designed to annoy and baffle.

Bafflement became one of my hobbies.

During this period, Bill fell ill.

His lifelong fear of ending in the workhouse had grown in inverse proportion to the disappearance of workhouses. The money he had received from his share of The Guv'ner's firm had trickled away, the jobs he had been forced to take paid poorly. While I was just a dismal wage slave in a book shop, my sister was leading a more glamorous-sounding life in London, and her life at Delia Collins had to be paid for. Betty was the star of the family, and the future looked rosy for her.

While in Oxford, Betty led a merry life. She became caught up in several fashionable undergraduate circles. One such circle was well known, consisting of Dom Moraes, Ved Mehta and the handsome, cultivated Zulfikar Ali Bhutto. One day Betty boldly invited Ali home to meet Bill and Dot.

The parents were civil and not too stingy with the sherry. After Betty and Ali had gone, Bill said, 'Huh, she's bringing the wogs home now!'

Ali Bhutto later became President of Pakistan.

Incidentally, Bhutto's gorgeous daughter Benazir became, in her turn, an adornment of Oxford. She was later elected the first woman Prime Minister of Pakistan.

Bill's ill health crept up on him slowly. He was not communicative. We never knew when it began.

For a while he continued working in Oxford, in the Broad, at the job he enjoyed. He made a good friend on the staff, John Warwick. Bill said nothing of his first heart attacks. Eventually, he was forced to see the doctor. He was persuaded to retire, was put on medication, and was confined to the little house he had bought, 548 Banbury Road.

In that little black-and-white house, Bill suffered and survived numerous heart attacks. I went to see him regularly. Sometimes he was in bed, or downstairs, sometimes pottering in the small garden. He always greeted one smiling and uncomplaining; but the next attack was never long in coming.

He liked, when he could, to drive a couple of miles down the road to a spot where it was possible to observe the activities on Kidlington airport, a small private airport, busy with small planes. Bill liked to sit watching in the car, with Dot for company. No doubt he recalled the days of his youth, before life became so bleak, when he too took to the air.

One day, Dot took me aside and said, 'Your father would like you to go for a walk with him.' Even to the last, orders came down from the officer, through the NCO, to the ranks. The order, if that was what it was, was alarming. Bill had never said such a thing since the time, years earlier, when I had almost shot him in a Devon lane. All my life, I had wished to be closer to Bill; yet now that an opportunity arose, I was unable to seize it. A familiar paralysis returned. I could not imagine what he would say; had he a terrible confession to make? Would he tell me he was disappointed in me?

As Bill's illness deepened, Dot nursed him devotedly. Instead of complaining, he apologised for being a nuisance. When he was unable to climb the stairs, we arranged a small bedroom for him on the ground floor, the window of which looked westwards – across the road to the cemetery. Dot kept flowers in the window. Betty occasionally came down from London to see him.

When he was well enough, Bill would potter in the garden, pruning the roses, clipping the hedge, or else he arranged things in his garden shed. He had always been a tidy man, scrupulously so, and such traits rarely disappear with age. In the rear garden, not far from the back door, he enjoyed lighting small bonfires, feeding the fire with his rose cuttings and other debris. On one occasion, he managed to keep a fire going for two whole weeks. When hail fell, he protected the fire with an upturned bucket.

When I used to go and see him, we would stand in silence together, watching the thin trail of smoke rise up through the Oxford air and disperse. Occasionally he would throw the fire a twig to gnaw on, as once he had thrown his Airedales a bone.

In Bill's last year on Earth, his roses had never been better pruned.

The nuclear family still held. As Michael Corleone says in the film *Godfather III*, 'Every family has bad memories'. If I could not face the walk Bill proposed through his faithful junior officer, at least I can say I was at 548 when he died.

It was the last day of May 1956, towards evening. Dot and Betty were having a bit of supper in the rear room while I sat beside Bill's bed. He was in his pyjamas, resting, breathing quietly. The last of the sun poured almost horizontally through the little window with its leaded panes. On the following day, it would be Dot's birthday; at Bill's request, I had bought her a card, and he had signed it. The card lay concealed under his pillow to await the morrow.

He died peacefully, my poor dear father, looking out towards the light. I held his hand and felt the grip relax. I called softly to Dot.

'Mother, I think it's the end.'

She came at once, dropping her napkin in the hall, to stand with me, not speaking.

Dusk gathered in the room. Slowly his countenance changed. The lines softened, the wrinkles faded. As the leaden minutes passed, as the summer light died away from the window, he looked more and more like the old Bill, the Bill who had worn the pierrot suit, who had stood nonchalantly in a doorway, a half-smile on his lips.

Dot did not rage at her husband's death. She did not utter terrible cries of pain. I put my arms round her. It was hard to know what to say for comfort. Aware of its insincerity, I said, 'We'll all be with him again one day.'

'I don't believe that,' she said. The following day was her sixty-fourth birthday.

I cycled home to tell my wife Bill had gone. Her grey eyes filled with tears. She wept.

At least he had nursed his grandson Clive on his knee and had been pleased. I had not entirely disappointed him. But of course I had been a disappointment to them both.

Book Two

Permissibles

XVII

The Funeral

Ruby Wax: 'Are you happy?'
Burt Reynolds: 'I been miserable and poor and miserable and
                  rich. Miserable and rich is better.'

Bill's wish was that he be cremated and his ashes thrown to the winds. The brief and hasty ceremony took place in Oxford Crematorium. Now he was gone beyond recall; never again would we look upon him, or catch his wry smile.

His son's marriage was also slipping beyond recall. Years of silence, of coldness accumulated like firn, too slippery to negotiate. George Santayana has a poem which begins, 'A thousand years of silence lies Between the husband and the wife . . .'

I slept in the attic of our house, having been banished from the marital bed. The way there was by a narrow twisting stair. One night, I dreamed, or more properly I had a hypnoid vision, of Bill. He stood at the bottom of the stair, fists clenched above his starting hair. He was furious. Never had I seen a man in such a rage. Hamlet's father's ghost was nothing beside Bill.

For the rest of that night, I remained awake, stricken. All my terrible inadequacies were upon me, my failed childhood, my failed marriage, my lack of success in life. My interpretation was that Bill was violently angry with me for being such a disgrace.

When I became less of a failure, another interpretation emerged – and in these intimate matters no interpretation of a dream is necessarily wrong, or final. I came to understand, let's say, that Bill's fury was directed not at me, or not at me alone, but at those deficiencies inseparable from human life, too many of which had been visited on him. He had made his appearance to me since I was to succeed him, being his only son.

No, it was not an apparition in the old sense, with independent existence; not a terrifying thing like 'Bessie'. Like my dream of the long lane and the church, this was another signal from the ontological depths of being, emerging at a time of crisis, signifying the complexity and wholeness of human life.

Whether Bill 'actually' appeared, or whether this vision was solely in my mind, is immaterial; the world is real enough, but what is more real to us is our perception of that world. Ask any psychotic.

My way has been easier than Bill's. So I move in this chapter from that time of misery to a more recent time, a happier time, when I was married to my treasured second wife, Margaret Manson, and was as without cares as a man can expect to be.

Forty years have passed since Bill's death. If he exists as a spirit, it is only in the memories of my sister and me – and perhaps in his descendants' genetic make-up. There is also the question of the family face. I was travelling on a crowded tube train in London, twenty-five years after Bill's death, when a man spoke to me, saying, 'Aren't you Stanley Aldiss's boy?' At that period, and later, I resembled Bill closely, and was glad to be recognised in this way. Bill in part lives on through me.

Now we are in the 1990s. We travel through 1994 as if it were merely another station on the Underground. It is the occasion of another passing, the death of an ex-landlord of mine, a good man, whose funeral Margaret and I are attending.

You have to grow old before you enjoy funerals. Not only do they become more relevant, but you meet up with old friends, in some cases friends you have not seen for many a year. You reflect on how you have changed, how your circumstances have altered: how you talk, eat, think differently. How the surroundings in which you live have changed. How the city has changed.

Between the date of Bill's cremation in the mid-fifties and the mid-nineties lies a time when many things improved. In Dereham and Devon days, we lived in houses with one or at most two lights in a room, with one phone (in the hall), with one radio in the house. The heating was random. We had not heard of fitted carpets.

In these latter days, we take for granted modern kitchens with many facilities of which Bill never heard, better sanitation, new materials – plastics, nylons, Teflon – vastly safer cars, motorways, more luxurious housing, more various foods and fruits, easier travel, extensive computerisation even in the home, central heating, air conditioning, multi-channel television, safer medical and surgical practices, more music and entertainment, and many other features of material life. I would say, too, more interest of a semi-scientific kind in what makes us human, and what makes us tick.

Those who are old enough for such perspectives would also add more crime, more insecurity, more discourtesy.

In short, how everything has undergone a transformation when you weren't really looking: and for all that remains the same.

And so to my ex-landlord, and another Oxford story, shortly after I was delivered back from Kidlington into the city.

The funeral service for George Halcrow was held on Friday 16 December, 1994, at the church of St Mary Magdalene in Oxford. A sparse body of mourners gathered inside, the Halcrow family arriving last, widowed Penny being supported by her daughter and accompanied by two stepsons, fruits of George's first marriage, and a nephew. Most startling was to see Peter Halcrow, whom I knew as a youth in the sixties: his likeness to his father extending to the moustache and the spectacles. The coffin containing George's body was brought to stand in the middle of the aisle: an abhorrent object, despite the flowers resting on it.

After the funeral, we trooped out to a world now rapidly turning dark. It was 4.10 p.m. In the congestion at the gateway, the composer John Veale said to me, 'Well, so the river flows on . . .'

Margaret and I drove up to North Oxford for the reception. Since we were early, we passed the time by trawling streets full of memories – Bradmore Road itself, where Penny and George used to hold their at-homes; Crick Road, where Margaret was once in digs with a Miss Read; where, at No. 5, a murder took place, ending an interracial marriage – I had to go there to see to the books, and found the whole basement room sprayed with blood, walls, books, bedding; where Tom Shippey lived when he was married to Sue; and next to Tom, David Winfield and his large, dignified wife – Winfield, the expert in Turkish murals and tiles, who had spent one term at WBS before begging his pater to take him away, and who claimed, when we met again after thirty-five years, that I was the only boy there who had been kind to him; Norham Gardens, where Bonfiglioli and his wife Margaret had lived, in a grand Gothic pile once owned by two Anglican bishops who shared as mistress a German princess – Bon never had a penny and borrowed from Christopher Lennox-Boyd, whom he treated as a manservant; and so on, along those quiet Puginesque streets . . .

Then to the Cotswold Lodge for the reception.

*   *   *

Penny had hired a large corner room. I had stood in it before, on some long-forgotten occasion. Quite Victorian and over-furnished, warm, comfortably lit, generously supplied with tasty fingerfood, from sandwiches to small chocolate éclairs. And tea. I looked round at the other guests and suddenly had that odd detached feeling one gets: 'Oh yes, we are English, and this is 1994.' Since the last chapter, I have become more English. It's age.

George died at the age of eighty-five. Penny is younger, but largely incapacitated; she has bronchitis, is lame and cannot climb her stairs. She sat on a low chair by the door to welcome her guests. She had a good clear voice and was in control of herself. I apologised for a cold hand. She said hers were cold too. (But none so cold as George's, said I to myself.)

This lady, whom I had known since 1960, features in a book lying on my desk. It is Margaret Lane's biography of Edgar Wallace, first published in 1938; in it are one or two references, none especially friendly, to Wallace's only daughter, Penelope.

In the twenties and thirties, Wallace was phenomenally famous and prolific. He wrote 150 novels in the course of twenty-seven years; I recall a cartoon in *Punch*, in which a lady going into a book shop enquires after 'the noonday Wallace'. In my early childhood, Bill and Dot took me with them to Norwich to see *The Frog*, *The Calendar* and who knows what else of Wallace's on stage, and later to Edgar Wallace films, starring Gordon Harker. I read (as we all did) *The Four Just Men*, and probably others. Wallace is most warmly remembered for his work on that classic of cinema *King Kong*. He died in Hollywood before the film went into production. And although he made enormous amounts of money, he left enormous debts behind.

Present at the reception were a number of acquaintances from the past, such as Dr Oliver Impey, Barry Juniper and Robert Nelson, to name but three men who were, like me, of The Cobra generation. The Cobra was the Indian restaurant George owned – so called, one always assumed, because the food was poison. Eric Korn was also present, together with Molly, his ex-wife: both of them clever and untidy, she now acting, Eric an antiquarian bookseller and reviewer for the *TLS* and elsewhere, often heard on radio in the BBC's 'Round Britain Quiz'.

We talked of George – and with some affection. I was surprised to find Oliver and Barry did not know that George had worked for the gas company, employed rather humbly as the man who went round emptying people's gas meters. One day, he happened on Penny Wallace, and something we must assume was romance blossomed.

George acquired several properties in Oxford: among them 24 St Giles, a place in Summertown, and two restaurants, the (Chinese) Golden Dragon on the corner of Keble Road and the Cobra in St Ebbe's. George never maintained his properties: all were magnificently tumbledown.

It was Derek Grigs, a reporter on the *Oxford Mail*, who introduced me to George when my first marriage collapsed, and George who found me a room when my wife took the children off to the Isle of Wight. By that time, Clive had a small sister, Caroline Wendy. I rented from George the front ground-floor room of Priory House, No. 12 Paradise Square, moving in there in the late summer of 1959 – or rather breaking in through the window, since George absent-mindedly forgot to give me a key. Later, that same room was occupied by Barry Juniper.

Priory House has become something of a legend to its erstwhile denizens. Before we moved in, it had housed the Indians and Chinese who worked in George's restaurants. They had walked out in indignation at the bad conditions. The cellar, beneath my room, served still as a laundry for the soiled linen of the restaurants; curry-coloured steam sometimes squirmed upwards through my floorboards. Living there was rather like being cast back in time to a thirties slum in Wolverhampton.

Also in the house were three other people, each tucked into a shabby room. Two of those remarkable characters have been dead for some while. Derek Grigs died of a heart condition in the sixties, aged forty-four; everyone liked Griggy and wondered if he had any sex life. Above him, on the top-floor back, lodged a sports editor on the *Oxford Times*, Len Aitken, a Derby-born alcoholic of whom I grew fond – a harmless, tragic man. In the room next to Griggy was an undergraduate of Christ Church, by name Nicholas Tanburn, who was determined to go into oil and become rich; Tanburn lived on black coffee and introduced me to William Burroughs' *The Naked Lunch*.

Instability ruled at that time. On the one hand, I was happy to be free of an irksome domesticity and the ban on swearing; on the other hand, I bitterly missed my children and grieved that all I had built up until that time, when I had levered myself out of a stupefying indigency, had been destroyed. Or if not destroyed, then given away. Given with a gesture of self-disgust. Everything I owned now belonged to my wife, except for some books. The money from the sale of the Victoria Road house went to buy a house in the Isle of Wight.

I had the clothes I stood up in, a knife, fork and spoon bought in Woolworth's, and George Halcrow's picturesque rented room. My mood veered between elation and deep misery.

All present at his funeral agreed on George Halcrow's kindness. He charged me 7/6d per week for my room, a sum I was often hard put to find. George would shamble in, nod and chat, and say, 'Um mm, well, we'll forget it for this week, Brian, mm mm.' He was a champion mumbler.

The Cobra played a vital part in my life. The first time I ever took Margaret out for a meal, I escorted her down seedy St Ebbe's to the Cobra for lunch. It was in the nature of a test run, to see whether she would or could eat curry. She could. Her fate was sealed. If you could eat Cobra curry you could eat any curry.

At night, the Cobra came into its own. It was housed in another of George's dumps. The food was cheap. The *tarka dal* soup was good. Ali was George's right-hand man, a cheerful little Dravidian and, according to Barry, a thumping crook.

I could afford only brunch, sometimes at Crawford's in Queen Street, a biscuit or a slice of malt loaf at tea time, and then usually a meal at the Cobra late at night. If I was eating in the Cobra when George came in, he would, as often as not, sign my bill, so that I did not have to pay. In one way and another, he was of the greatest assistance to me.

The Cobra used to shut about midnight – this in the days when all of Oxford was dead by ten-thirty. George, usually the mildest of men, could be very tough with intruders, or with those who tried to escape out of the back of his premises without paying. Often he had trouble, and met it half-way.

Once the restaurant closed, and the door was locked, George would settle down with his favourites for a good chat. Ali served beer and *dal* soup. Many good talkers were there. Eric I especially remember, but there were experts in all subjects, including senior University men. Often the talk was ribald. There was much laughter. It was an informal club for the promising and the sleepless.

I recall seeing Penny in the Cobra once only. She had not her husband's gregarious habit. The shock of debt when her father died was considerable. In the late fifties, however, the Wallace estate revived.

Along came a German film company who bought and made into B-features I know not how many of Edgar's thrillers. The estate went from red to dramatic black. Four million pounds was a figure I heard mentioned.

The film series had a trade mark: a large, ominous black bust of Edgar Wallace, slowly revolving, which later stood in Penny's front window in Bradmore Road.

Often, I would stagger away from the Cobra at three in the morning, back to the square near by. Oxford was black, tomb-like, all its living and defunct scholars in their respective beds. At the town entrance to the square, where the road from what is now Bonn Square dipped downhill, stood the Salvation Army Citadel. This grim brick building was the sentinel of the square, constructed so as vaguely to imitate some Scottish variant of a Spanish castle: beyond it lay only blackness, in which the severely underprivileged lived, Morlock-like.

A sense of destitution was somewhat to my taste. I pushed my way into No. 12, with its reek of damp, to collapse on my Army bed. Later, I bought a cheap new bed in Webber's for £9; much more comfortable. At this time, I was scarcely able to write – nor had I a typewriter at first. That essential tool of my trade had, I discovered when the home broke up, never belonged to me.

Yet my reputation was growing in the States. One day, a Hugo Award for *Hothouse* arrived, wrapped in a Dublin tabloid newspaper. A kindly SF fan brought it across the Atlantic as far as Margaret's doorstep in Leckford Road, depositing it beside the morning milk. I hadn't even heard of Hugos at that time; they are the premier award in the science-fiction field.

Some money filtered in, proceeds of *Non-Stop* and *Hothouse*. I scraped together enough money by 1962 or '63 to purchase a terrace house in Marston Street. I bought it from Anthony Harris, the *Oxford Mail* industrial and financial reporter. Meanwhile, the bulldozers moved in on Paradise Square in the mid- to late-sixties. Down came the modest Victorian houses. Up went a multi-storey car-park, a ziggurat-like temple constructed to the further glory of the automobile. A whole area, a whole lifestyle, was swept away.

All the little crooked streets behind Paradise Square have been destroyed, Gas Street and the rest, the residue of Victorian Oxford.

To walk in them was a grave pleasure at that time, so closely did they match my feeling that I had lost everything. Those streets were still lit by gas. Few cars ever passed that way; certainly the inhabitants of the little terraced houses did not own cars. Strolling through them at night, treading their broken pavements, was a melancholy hobby of mine.

I used to buy some food at an impoverished Co-op in Gas Street. It was the poorest of shops; you entered on to bare boards. The assistants, thin, stringy women of indeterminate age, would cut the traditional English quarter-pound pat of butter in two for you: an eighth of a pound was all some people could afford at one time. I also bought half-loaves of bread there. The Co-op understood poverty, and catered for it.

Mr Baines was the grocer in the square. His was a little palace in comparison with the Co-op. After his shop closed in the evening, Mr Baines made his own deliveries on a bike. He too struggled to make ends meet, like everyone else, as economic trends slowly wore him down.

Mr Baines gave me used cardboard boxes, Bovril, Oxo, Ambrosia Rice Pudding. Into these I packed the books I had reviewed for the *Oxford Mail*, and sent them off to Harrods. Thomas Joy, the manager of Harrods library, would pay half the published price if he received the books within a month of publication. For at least a year, I lived off my Harrods cheques for my *OM* review books. Plus the beggarly fee I received from the *OM* as literary editor. During my eleven years in that role, it never wavered from £5 a week.

At least I was living as a real writer, down-at-heel, often drunk, writing little. Able in a curious way to please or displease myself. Going always under the shadow of what I had done, my crime.

At night in my wanderings, I would return late to the square. Oxford was then ill lit. Its crime-rate was low. Bitter and sleepless, I faded into the lost world of Paradise Square, its cracked pavements, its lost hopes, its forlorn inhabitants.

I had a green electric kettle of antique design which Dot gave me. I could make myself tea and coffee. That kettle lasted many a year more. I used to toast slices of malt loaf in front of my little gas fire. My life was in slack water. The one sail in sight was that shy, pretty lady who had recently come down from Covent Garden Opera House, to walk on gazelle legs into Newspaper House, where she became secretary to the editor, Harford Thomas. ('Very fine ankles,' Dame Beryl Grey had observed of her at the Opera House, one day.)

Attached to the square, part of its parasitical life, were Warburton's scrap yard, and several little pubs, including the Gardener's Arms, where Griggy and I often downed a pint or two. Griggy knew a rich man he could sponge off; so frequently he would take me to meet this man in the Randolph Hotel. The man was pleasant, rather effeminate, and plied us with whisky. We sopped it up, while Griggy would scoff a whole plateful of chicken sandwiches.

Even our bouts of drinking and horseplay did not dispel my guilt at the failure of my marriage. Many a night, it was too much to bear. Sometimes I walked all through the night hours. A customary walk took me down the High, up Headington Hill to the roundabout, left on to what was then the Northern Bypass and is now part of the ring road. A long tramp there, with fields on either side of the road. Coming to the roundabout at the top of the Banbury Road, I turned south into town for the two-mile walk back to Paradise Square, where early workers were already stirring.

An obsessive trait in my thought, which served me well when writing a novel, kept me captive to my failure. It was there when I woke in the morning. It came with the slice of toast.

During the day, a kind of truce could prevail in my mind, as if inner battle was best fought at night. The sun shone through the dusty windows of my room. I could look out on the playground of the local school, to watch the children rush about, shrieking with delight at being alive. Long hours dragged by. Most days I spent alone, going out only to find a bite to eat. I read a great deal, mostly books I had to review. Sometimes my mind would drift away from the reading and I would sit, lost in reverie.

The room was simple. A bed covered with a red spread Dot gave me, a table in the window with a side lamp on it; an armchair. Little besides. Ideal as a silent, hidden room in which to be lost.

Then the sadness of dusk filled the air. Night once more. There were occasions before my wife took the children away when I walked, concealed by darkness, to stand outside my own house, looking up at a lighted window, where Clive was being bathed. Sometimes I could hear his squeals of pleasure. I hoped for an invitation to return. But matters had gone too far. I had walked out with a papier mâché suitcase and nothing else; she had watched me go, cold and dry of eye. Now the old theme of desertion was being replayed.

Though it mattered little to me at the time, I now had less than when I arrived in Oxford after my return from the East. I was thirteen years older.

Hundreds of men have gone through the same anguish – that isolating anguish. For five years, I had been Clive's constant companion, since for most of that time I had been working at home. We were the dearest friends; I was betraying his trust. His smiling face rose in my memory. The most painful thought was that if *I* suffered as much as I did, how much more must *he* be suffering at his vulnerable age?

Over the years, this thought has hardly become less painful.

Occasionally I sent him small presents: a toy car, a box of Lego bricks. Lego bricks came in small boxes, 2/4d in the old currency. I found myself stealing these boxes from shops – horrified at what I was doing, yet unable to control the impulse. Nothing else, just boxes of Lego for Clive. I have since learnt that this form of kleptomania, associated with separation, is not uncommon.

As we reminisced, we ate scrumptious little chocolate meringues. Penny Halcrow sat rather isolated on a low chair; it was difficult to know what to say to her. Some of us could remember the Cotswold Lodge when it was a private house, ample, Victorian, obsolete as far as domesticity was concerned. As a hotel, quite amiable. Alcohol available at Reception. Please Ring Twice.

Margaret grew tired of standing, so we had to leave. I shared a last word with John Veale as we went out. He had shed the large floral wife we used to see in Summertown, and was keeping company with a lady I took for a schoolmistress.

John looked much as ever he did, though his hair was white. His round florid face was improved by gold-rimmed glasses: a good-humoured face which as ever lit up when he smiled. He often smiles. We joked about Kingsley Amis who once stayed with the Veales, and stayed and stayed. Hilly was with Kingsley in those days.

John said his music was being performed again; he had just written an ambitious oratorio. I thought as we talked, Well, this is all something: how rich life is, while it lasts . . . Perhaps in John's eyes I read the same kind of reflection: though I am not ranked with Stravinsky, yet I have lived and survived . . . Something of the sort.

We said goodbye to Penny and family, and drove out into the busy traffic on the Banbury Road.

In twenty minutes Margaret and I were back home on Boars Hill. Safe for the time being.

XVIII

The Homeless

'Sir, I have quarrelled with my wife: and a man who has quarrelled with his wife is absolved from all duty to his country.'

Thomas Love Peacocks
Mr Cypress in *Nightmare Abbey*

W riting proved a saving miracle. At a time of maximum inner struggle, when everything about me was unacceptable, I was becoming accepted as a writer. It was as if a tree of which I knew nothing had taken root and flowered of a sudden overnight. Well, a small tree.

After leaving book shops behind, I had settled into the back bedroom of our North Oxford house to write my first science fiction novel, *Non-Stop*. Telling myself the story gave me great pleasure; I was absolutely sure of what I was doing. Faber published the book in 1958. Its publication brought in enough money to enable me to buy my own typewriter. That Swiss Hermes portable and I lived on intimate terms for many a year; I used it as a pillow on more than one occasion. Many words, letters, stories, novels ran through its metal veins.

Hothouse appeared from Faber in 1962. Between the two publication dates lay implications of great social changes to come: the Pill for women, and the trial for obscenity in the case of D. H. Lawrence's *Lady Chatterley's Lover*. The gates were open for greater freedom in sexual mores and sexual language. And for a higher divorce rate.

Thirty or so years later, despite all the change, *Non-Stop* and *Hothouse* remain in print in England. But their warmest initial reception was in the United States of America.

* * *

The two publication dates are used here as reference points, with the help of which I negotiate a difficult period. They were hardly milestones at the time. Between the two dates, came two new players, one aged, one about to sample life. Both to prove a blessing.

After Bill and Dot followed me to Oxford, Aunt Dorothy returned quietly to our lives.

After H. H.'s death, Aunt Dorothy vacated Whitehall and lived near by, in a modest house, 'The Pallant'. When Bill and Dot left Dereham, she found herself exposed to the hostility of Gordon and his family. She told me later how Joyce, Gordon's daughter, was sent to spy on her. At one point Dorothy caught Joyce reading some of her letters. The drama is not unfamiliar: small town, small minds, small sums of money.

Dorothy left Dereham. She went to live in Church Stretton, Shropshire with her mother, whom she nursed through a long terminal illness. So went her life through the war years, a placid, retired life, gardening, jam-making, embroidering and looking after mother: a lifestyle not greatly changed since Jane Austen's day. She and Dot kept in touch.

She bought a small house in North Oxford within easy reach of us. After Bill's death, she and Dot began to see more of each other. The ladies' characters differed in many ways. Where Dot was, at least on the surface, outgoing, Dorothy was reserved. Dot liked a splash; Dorothy liked the quiet life. But they got on well enough, though the vein of history ran between them like a treacherous little river.

Dot had been a faithful nurse to Bill. Once he was gone, she showed a new side to her character. She was a dodgy woman, was Dot, as I, too much her son, should know. She rented a flat in London, in a not unfashionable position between Kensington and Hammersmith. Betty, who was working in London, joined her. Dot developed the habit of visiting local pubs for lunch, drinking a sedate g and t, and chatting with all and sundry. No one from Peterborough or Dereham was there to see her.

She moved further afield, acquiring a taste for the pleasures of Italy; its palaces, its cemeteries, its *trattorias*. Sometimes Betty and Dorothy went with her, sometimes only Dorothy. Italian waiters were an attraction, even more than the sun. We all have lives we have not managed to live; Dot was belatedly enjoying one of hers. Her main complaint was that Dorothy was stingy and often would not pay for her round of drinks.

When Dot's lease on her Hammersmith flat ran out, she returned to Oxford, buying herself a little semi-detached house in Victoria Road. At that time, my first wife and I lived at the other end of the road. Clive was able to run a hundred yards on his own to visit his Nana. It was a congenial arrangement. She and he watched television companionably together. She was kindness itself to him, and to Clive's new baby sister, Wendy.

However, on one occasion, after some minor peccadillo of his, she said in my presence, 'If you do that again, Nana won't love you.'

There flew that old terrible threat which had made a misery of my childhood.

I found tongue. I warned her that if she ever used that threat again, I would take Clive away and she would not see him any more. A real tit-for-tat response.

'Oh, I didn't mean it. You know I didn't. You know how I love him.'

'Then why say it? It will make him insecure. I mean what I'm saying.'

A week later, she told me, 'You can't think how you hurt me by what you said.' And when I tried to commit suicide, when the marriage was going down the drain, she said, 'You can't do this to me.' Just as Kane in *Citizen Kane* did when his wife was about to leave him.

Dot was growing older. The years passed. They were sunny for her. But her legs developed trouble; she was diagnosed as having dropsy. In the mid-sixties, she came to a sensible decision with Dorothy. She sold her little house and moved into Salisbury Crescent. She lived downstairs, Dorothy upstairs. They tended their garden between them, pruning the Queen Elizabeth roses.

The arrangement suited them well. Margaret and I used to call regularly to see them.

In October 1978, Dot died, in circumstances to be related. By her own wish, she was cremated. My sister came down for the funeral service. May's ashes were scattered among the roses in Oxford Crematorium. There they blended with those of the man she had met before World War I. So both May and Stanley had left the road along which we all make our way.

The downstairs half of the house was let out. Dorothy lived on upstairs. I went once a week to see her, Margaret shopped for her. We loved that brave old lady, on medication, uncomplaining, in a cold house. Until the age of ninety, she caught buses into town. Then her legs failed her and she was stranded upstairs in her room.

We bought her a big comfortable armchair in which to sit. And there she sat, day in, day out.

She was not mean, as Dot had averred; she had next to no money. Wendy – adult by this time – was working in social services and knew how to negotiate a way through red tape to practical assistance. She came down from London and gained Dorothy proper financial support. We regarded it as a masterstroke – one of Wendy's many.

Even when we lived out at Begbroke, near Woodstock, we often drove in to town to tuck Dorothy into bed. She would cheerfully crunch up a Mogadon sleeping tablet and fall asleep. The draught from the front door rushed up the stairs and under her bedroom door like a feral cat, until Margaret made her an upholstery snake to block the gap. I regularly took her her favourite medication, a bottle of rough brandy called Beauregard. Beauregard had the fiery temperament of a coarse Greek Metaxa. I too became addicted to it, and would swig my tumblerful with her as we chatted.

Towards the end, Dorothy suffered many little strokes and cancer of the larynx. As happens when we become old, we begin to die from more than one disease. It's a toss-up which one delivers the *coup de grâce*.

Dorothy Frances Aldiss, née Royou, died in bed at the age of ninety-four, a look of terror on her face, as if, when Death came for her, she found him as frightening as legend has it.

We had her corpse taken to East Dereham. In her will, she requested that she be laid beside H. H.; I was determined to carry out her wishes. The family attended the service; that is to say, Betty and Antony, Wendy and Mark, Tim, and Charlotte; Clive was working in Athens.

I gave a eulogy before earth was thrown on the coffin. Dorothy was a grand Victorian lady, outliving her husband and both my parents. As we walked back through that long cemetery, housing so many decaying Norfolk bodies, we felt more glad than sad – glad we had known such a kind and decent woman.

But to the second of my new players. One generation left the stage, but another had already entered from the wings.

A babe was born. The baby was my daughter Caroline Wendy. Some children are remarkable in possessing at birth the characteristics they will display in later life. Wendy was such a child. Born into a household where fierce contention was the order of the day, she bubbled with fun and good humour. Soon she was to show good sense too. She was a pretty, darling child, one day to become an illumination in our lives.

The sight of that pretty infant provoked an unexpected response from the past. I was not wanted and must go. A serpent lay at the heart of the marital disaster, the deserted become the deserter. I had a psychodrama to act out and had yet to understand its ramifications.

The children of bad parents are most likely to make bad parents themselves. My strong fatherly instincts were overwhelmed by a learned response.

As the jaws of separation closed, my dead thoughts were that I must not become too attached to her, or she to me – to spare her hurt, if that were possible.

So I kissed her rosy cheek and left. I write down the words in disbelief. I must have been desperate.

If it was a sin to leave my children, it is one from which I have never entirely exculpated myself. I left home again. My wife held her little girl tightly to her breast to watch me go. Yes, there was some comfort: she had her baby as consolation, as well as Clive.

Again – as when Bill left me at Grandmother's house in Peterborough – some great thing had ended, the consequences of which could not be foreseen. Perhaps it would have been less terrible if I had totally willed it.

Simply to think over that time again, again self-hatred fills me.

It is an emotion of long familiarity.

I returned for the Christmas of 1959, fearfully, thinking that it might be possible to patch up the marriage. Clive was as lively and bright as ever. Wendy bounced and thrived. Otherwise, my reception was chilly. Whatever had once been between my wife and me was now stricken by winter frost.

We contemplated each other across a chasm that was, after all, at least to some extent, of our own choosing.

Visits to the Marriage Guidance Council did nothing to heal matters, while providing some comfort.

'Can you convince me I am not going mad?' I asked.

My consultant was a Mrs Boniksen, a Scandinavian whose name remains fragrant in memory. Describing our troubled relationship, I sought to draw a sketch of my wife and of myself, of our attitudes to life, our psychological make-up. What I needed was to know which was more valid: her nervous certainty or my questioning. Mrs Boniksen would judge whether the portraits bore any resemblance to the living realities, and whether, as I suspected, my wife *had no image of me.*

After she had talked to my wife in a couple of sessions, she agreed: *No image . . .*

An echo from the past came in. Here was the stolen shadow motif again, the small boy forced to wander the earth to reclaim it. Such echoes were a plague, a tinnitus of the mind. I wished to forget childhood, but all the old moth-eaten mummies and trophies came back, rattling out of their hidey-holes to reinforce the pains of the present.

Another discomfort situated in the present day lay in the fact that the country was experiencing a continuous demolition of traditional values, which stemmed in part from the years of war. To give an example, we had been married in church in Wolvercote because my wife wished it; yet I had no belief, beyond believing I should please her. I myself was merely a symptom of nationwide change, less an individual than a fragment of social history. The large churchgoing congregations of East Dereham did not survive the cessation of hostilities.

If I felt sorry for myself, I felt as much for my wife. I knew that happiness had been withdrawn from her childhood; more than her shadow had been devoured by an oppressive mother. She needed more than sympathy. The child who is unloved not infrequently grows into the adult who cannot accept love, who elects to be unloved. If only she would speak of her sorrows, some light might shine in. But she never confided. Not to me. Not to Mrs Boniksen. Coldness and silence became increasingly our lot.

In those awful days and years, I saw all the fault as being hers. Now I'm less sure. My belief in marriage is unshaken. Partners should not fly apart at the first quarrel. They should command understanding, and understanding takes time and needs a contract sworn to by both parties.

So to another spell of homelessness. My wife had a lodestar in her life: the Isle of Wight. She had desired to be there since a brief happy spell in her oppressed childhood, when she had enjoyed a holiday in Totland Bay, alone with her father – without that mother of hers. Handed the money from our North Oxford house, she bought a house on the island, in Totland. She took with her our possessions, the furniture, the gramophone records. I gave everything away.

I went down and laid flooring for her in the Totland Bay house, and kissed Clive and the infant Wendy goodbye.

Then a wandering time, directionless. A stay in London with my first literary agent and editor, Ted Carnell. Kindly Ted, who took me to meet such SF writers as Bertram 'Jack' Chandler, John Christopher and John Wyndham.

Wyndham was a mild, Home Counties sort of chap. A moderate drinker, educated at Bedales. He said he had gone into a bar one day for a dry sherry (sic), and overheard two working men discussing gardening. One told the other, 'I've got a bloomin' great weed growing up behind the shed on my allotment. I reckon as it's a triffid.' Wyndham knew he had coined a word which had passed into the language.

After the shelter of Ted's home in Plumstead, a lodging in a Henley inn. The Old Row Barge has since been pulled down. There in my Spartan attic room I could throw myself into despair. It was a nineteenth-century building which creaked like a galleon, osteo-arthritis in every plank. My window looked out on untended gardens. The landlord and landlady never asked questions and charged little rent. There I remained as summer days were borne away on the river.

I walked every day along the towpath by the River Thames, was driven to walk, like the victims of Walking Sickness in H. G. Wells' film *Things to Come*, sometimes getting as far as the outskirts of Reading. Rest was impossible. The grave hushed beauty of the Thames valley stood in judgement of transitory human woes.

High summer prevailed, yet rarely was there another soul to be seen. I walked, walked from early morning till evening, in great pain of mind. Occasionally, I stripped naked under sheltering trees and dived into the river. There I swam, separate from the rest of humanity. I never spoke to anyone. I never ate during the day.

Divorce has become a more common and easier thing since the early sixties; many more people must know the pain of being separated from one's children, and children of being separated from a parent. Most agonising was to think that the separation must be worse for the children – for *Clive, for Clive* – than for me. Reinforcing the pain was a traitorous knowledge that this compulsive walking, this obsessional chewing at the rags of thought, was in some way truer than the emptiness of the previous years.

From a phone box on a dusty Henley road, I phoned that young lady with the gazelle legs in Oxford, asking her to come and see me. She was affronted at the suggestion, and refused. Such were the mores of the time.

I confided in no one. The Buddhists say that guilt is a form of self-indulgence. This was not apparent to me at the time.

Still I walked and walked, caught in a maze of frozen reveries, not unlike Raskolnikov in *Crime and Punishment*, 'Scraps and fragments of thoughts swarmed in his head; but he could not fix his mind on a single one of them, he could not concentrate on a single one of them even for a short time, much as he tried to . . .'

Summer was fading, the light growing frailer, when I left the Row Barge to return to Oxford. Trees were beginning to discard their worn leaves into the dark waters of the Thames. For some while, I stayed with my friends Tony and Ann Price, until I could rent a room from George Halcrow. It was then I lived in 12 Paradise Square. It was Ann Price who had asked me, 'Are you in love with Margaret Manson?' – and a flash of lightning filled the mental skies.

Then came all the drinking with Len Aitken and Griggy, long night walks through the streets of Oxford, up to Headington, round the stretch of the northern bypass. Oxford was now a hostile place, stonier than ever before.

During those painful days, my wife once returned alone from the Isle of Wight to Oxford to see me. I took her to an Indian restaurant for a meal. Her manner was strictly reserved. She talked formally, as if we were strangers.

While we picked at our *biryanis*, she told me how she hated Oxford. I understood her code. She had returned only because her mother had died. She wished me to accompany her to the funeral, so as to be able to confront Alice's grim Cheltenham friends. I went with her. We stood together at the formidable old woman's graveside. Not a tear was shed.

Then we went our separate ways. For my gesture, she gave me a travelling clock, which I still have.

When I could manage it, besides paying a weekly allowance to my children, I had sent some money, a paltry sum, down to Totland. It had been returned. I admired my wife's rectitude; on reflection, I felt convinced it had been conscience money. In times of trouble, we credit ourselves with base motives. If only I had had courage enough when a boy to toss Bill's ten-pound cheque in his face.

Matters took a turn for the better for Olive. She inherited her mother's estate. At least the old girl had not left it all to the cats' home . . . Now her daughter could afford to buy another horse for her paddock.

As I wrestled with myself, walking the night-sunk streets afforded some relief. There was another salve at hand – writing. Even when writing my first science fiction novels, I had been aware of a

BWA

The Guv'ner, H. H. Aldiss

e Aldiss shop, East Dereham, 1920

Bill and Dot, with children,
Betty and Brian,
Peterborough, 1931

Return from Burma.
Aldiss and 'Chota'
Morris with engine
driver, 1945

The Mu River, Burma. S Relief
(Aldiss right), 1945

Aldiss and Harrison in discussion,
Newbridge, Oxfordshire, 1973

Margaret and
her mother,
Bathie Manson,
Southmoor, 1972

Aldiss and Kingsley
Amis, Groucho
Club, London, 1990

Margaret, Tim, Charlotte,
with BWA, Heath House,
Southmoor, 1974

'Welcome to China, Mr
Deng!' With Deng Xiaoping,
Beijing, 1979

Whitehall, East Dereham, 1931

Woodlands under snow,
Boars Hill, 1988

Clive and
Youla on their
wedding day,
Isle of Wight,
1993

On set of *Frankenstein
Unbound* with John Hurt,
Italy, 1989

The family in Bellagio: Wendy, BWA, Charlotte, Margaret and Tim, 1989

First International Symposium: (left to right) Eremi Parnov, Arthur C. Clarke, Julius Kagarlitski, Vasili Zacharchenko, BWA, ?, Sakyo Komatsu, Vasili ?, Frederik Pohl. Tokyo, 1970

With Bridget Fonda as Mary Shelley, *Frankenstein Unbound*, 1989

Society of
Authors evening:
(left to right)
Michael Holroyd,
Margaret Drabble,
William Golding,
Ann Golding,
BWA and
Margaret.
London, 1984

World SF Convention:
(left to right) BWA,
Sam Lundwall and,
Guests of Honour, the
Strugatsky brothers.
Brighton Metropole
Hotel, 1987

Margaret, Wendy,
Mark with Thomas,
Youla, Clive,
Charlotte. Paros,
Greece, 1995

Some British SF writers: (left to right) Robert Holdstock, Chris Evans, Jim Burn[s?]
David Langford, Graham Charnock, David Garnett, Lisa Tuttle, Garry Kilworth[?]
Tanith Lee, BWA, M. John Harrison. Forbidden Planet, London, 198[?]

Margaret and Brian,
Woodlands, Boars Hill, 1990

BRIAN ALDISS
WITH
DAVID WINGROVE

TRILLION·YEAR·SPREE

THE HISTORY
OF SCIENCE FICTION

'METICULOUSLY
RESEARCHED...
IT IS A PERCEPTIVE,
SENSIBLE STUDY,
STUDDED WITH WIT'
THE TIMES

PALADIN

Symbolic cover
by Chris Moore,
Paladin, 1988

metaphorical element in that mode of writing. To give a familiar example, the intensity of Mary Shelley's *Frankenstein or, The Modern Prometheus* owes much to Mary's identification with the poor motherless creature whom Victor Frankenstein brings to life; in this symbolic way, she was able to deal with her own situation as the daughter of a mother who died giving birth to her.

Non-Stop is more than a tale of interstellar flight: it is a story of people caught within a confinement of circumstance not of their own devising. *Hothouse*, the dark concluding parts of which were written in Paradise Square, is basically a story of flight by a fugitive, set at the end of the world.

The novel on which I now embarked was *Greybeard*, the story of an England without children.

No children have been born for many years. An ageing population falls into decay. England, becoming untended, is an entanglement. Ceasing to be a nation, it is merely a wild country, without name. The central character, Algy Timberlane, known as Greybeard, and his faithful wife Martha, a childless couple in their fifties, move amid the ruinous villages bordering the Thames at Oxford. It is my intensely felt novel mourning the loss of my children, and dedicated to them.

Although *Greybeard* is a different kind of novel from the earlier ones, and far more a novel of character, it shares with them the theme of nature taking over. The jungle has become anglicised. At this distance in time, it can be seen that, if the style owes something to Thomas Hardy, the atmosphere owes more to Richard Jefferies's haunting 1885 tale *After London*.

Science fiction is a plot-dominated mode; the blind alleys of our lives are not allowed to intrude. Wishing to escape from that convention – for I saw my book as being only marginally SF – I divided the story into seven compartments. The four odd-numbered compartments take my ragged company slowly down the River Thames, from source towards mouth, in a consecutive story. Compartments two, four and six are set each in an earlier date, from near-present to distant past, when Timberlane is a child in London (near the place where, in fact, we conclude). It's one thing to have a story to tell; how best to tell it is one of the problems a writer must resolve. The plan I arrived at seemed the most effective one.

Timberlane is intended to be a sympathetic character. Yet when we first meet him, and when we leave him, he has just been shooting; he is not the most pacific of men.

Faber published the novel in 1964 in their customary smooth way.

In the States, it was published by Harcourt Brace. My editor there had written an acclaimed novel himself – *Tobias Brandywine*. Yet he deleted from his edition of *Greybeard* the vital sixth section, in which we learn something of Timberlane's boyhood. This impertinence rankled greatly at the time.

The grief at being apart from my children was slow to abate. I was able to go by train and ferry to the Isle of Wight and be with them as frequently as possible, to play with them and see them grow. And to find that Wendy loved her father.

It was a telling discovery. My experience had been, on the whole, that one had to work very hard, to practise self-denial, to earn a woman's love; here was this sweet child whom I felt I had wronged, who desired to be with me, to be cuddled, to please me, to smile at me. To love me.

As small children, Clive and Wendy enjoyed life on the island. The beaches were good. Both became excellent swimmers. West Wight was a beautiful unspoilt place, more comfortably prosperous in the sixties than in the nineties. Dot also went down to see her grandchildren, staying in a grand Edwardian hotel, the Totland Bay Hotel, too soon to be demolished.

My remorse stays with me; and yet I found a new source of life, even before *Greybeard* was completed. Thirty years later, that novel is still in print. Who reads such a book of mourning? Are they comforted by it? One never knows.

The company at the *Oxford Mail* was agreeable and somewhat raffish.

One of the men on the *Oxford Mail* was Anthony Harris, a specialist in financial affairs. He became interested in Alison Brittain, on the grounds that he and she had spent all one evening on a reporting job and she had not bored him once. Alison was secretary to Mr Hudson, the editor of the *Oxford Times*.

Before he married Allison, Anthony Harris had lived a roistering existence, in a house in Cranham Street, Jericho, which he shared with my friend Kyril Bonfiglio – Bon. At one time Griggy was their lodger. On the night before Bon's marriage to his Margaret, he swore he would not turn up at the register office. They forced him to go. That Margaret, a stalwart bluestocking lady, reported her mother as saying, when she announced her engagement, 'You always were waiting for Mr Wrong to come along . . .'. Or perhaps Bon himself coined this apposite remark . . .

Bon and his Margaret moved into the house in Norham Gardens. He was a great humorist and much else besides. His knowledge of art was extensive. The cunning by which he detected and bought an unidentified Giorgione in a Reading junk shop was as widely admired as the two million he got for it was widely envied. His was the only Rolls-Royce I ever rode in which had a compartment wherein a record player with a sapphire needle played EPs.

Bon inherited an SF magazine. When Ted Carnell retired, Michael Moorcock took over *New Worlds*; Bon took over the sister magazine, *Science Fantasy*, strangely enough. He was not attentive, his habits were dilatory. We would invite him to dinner at eight; at two in the morning, he would turn up, producing a bottle of Glenfiddich – not untouched – by way of peace offering. Bon was learned and amusing company, though we became less friendly when he pinked me in my throat with my own swordstick during one of our evening sessions. It was a question of jealousy, not entirely unfounded – and he had been an Army sabre champion.

When the trio in Cranham Street broke up, Griggy went to Paradise Square. Anthony bought a small terraced house in Marston Street, between the Iffley and Cowley roads.

When Anthony secured a job on the *Guardian*, in London, he put the little house up for sale. I bought it from him. There it was, in No 24, that I finished *Greybeard* – and, eventually, several other books.

I worked with a one-bar electric heater at my feet and Ram Gopal playing his ragas on the record player. My main sustenance consisted of Saxby's pork pies, whisky and coffee. It was a pleasant walk over Magdalen Bridge and up the High to the *Oxford Mail*. Whenever I returned to Marston Street, my little cat, Nickie, would be awaiting me. Nickie had strolled in one day, dapper as you please, and came to stay.

Here I was able to collect Clive and Wendy from the Isle of Wight, and have them to stay with me. How fond I was of that little Marston Street house! I was coming back to life again. It was two-up, two-down. It had been modernised by Harris, and boasted under-carpet heating. A small garden at the rear backed on to the Church of the Cowley Fathers.

Dot and Betty came round to inspect and were enthusiastic. Dot bought me a good sturdy table on which I could work. A more regular visitor was Margaret Manson, she of the gazelle legs.

The world – or England at least – suddenly became a livelier place in the early sixties. Ram Gopal would have had the door slammed in his face had he tried one of his ragas in the early fifties. As if the nation had been traumatised by its long war, it now awoke. In 1963, Harold Wilson became Leader of the Labour Party and, in the succeeding year, Prime Minister.

Wilson was a brilliant academic and a good-hearted man. After Churchill, Harold is the one Prime Minister one can think of with affection. When he resigned in 1976, he had been elected as PM three times, and presided over a Britain enjoying some of its balmier and more optimistic days. Perhaps some of our economic happiness was illusory, but without comforting illusions people find it hard to live.

That period of the sixties, in which, eventually, I was divorced, and Margaret and I were married, and our two children were born, had a kind of social generosity that failed to survive once the seventies ended. The seventies, indeed, with strikes and major economic problems, became gradually more difficult. Although there is a fashion now to deride the sixties, at least the Gradgrind philosophy of Market Forces of later Toryism did not prevail.

Harold was no ideologist. If he was a man of few beliefs, he did believe in fair shares for all: which is a simple position to hold, and a good deal better than ideology.

For me too, everything became livelier. I was caught up in events. Like light into deep water, a new existence filtered into my days.

Much of this was due to my beautiful and elegant new wife. Margaret is a self-effacing person, deeply feeling, emotionally on an even keel. I passionately adored her and her sweet self and body.

She loved me. She loved my children – loved Clive and Wendy unaffectedly because they were mine. She never tried to be a surrogate mother, but simply to enjoy their company when they were around. To which they responded with the unfeignedness of children.

I looked round. I couldn't believe it. Happiness was back.

At some time or other, I had written a piece on science fiction cinema for an Italian newspaper. It had to be short, since there were few SF movies worth talking about at that time. As an indirect result, I received an invitation from a Signora Flavia Paulon in Venice to attend the first Festival of Science Fiction Films in Trieste, in July 1963.

Here was a brilliant idea, not too brilliantly carried out. The festival lasted for a week every year. It was designed to show SF or near-SF films from all over the world, East as well as West.

Overseas guests to the film festival were given rooms in the Grand Hotel de la Ville, a fine building on the seafront. It had once served as the British Consulate, in the days when Sir Richard Burton was consul there. From the bedroom windows, you could watch ships glide in from Venice, or move slowly off in the direction of Piraeus – 'the Piraeus', as the British liked to say.

In the nights, lubricious youth belted about on Vespas or Lambrettas, seeking out sex. Long, sad goods trains whistled thin and high like Latin ghosts, as they negotiated their way along the front towards Rijeka and distant Dalmatian stations, Trogir, beautiful Zadar.

The time will come when this period will be seen as halcyon, as some regard the Edwardian age. It must have dawned for the many who once called themselves Jugoslavs.

We arrived with our suitcases at the Grand Hotel. Sitting on the verandah outside, enjoying a Buton brandy, were Harry Harrison and Kingsley Amis. I had met them both before. Harry was already an old friend; we had stayed with Harry and his wife Joan the previous year, in their home in Denmark – our first experience of Scandinavia.

Kingsley I had met in Oxford. He gave a lecture in Jesus College, under the auspices of W. W. Robson. We had had a drink – well, several – afterwards.

Harry, Kingsley and I fell to talking. After dinner, washed down with plenty of Asti Spumante, we fell to talking again. We sat in the hotel's comfortable foyer and drank and talked, talked until, with some dismay, we saw through the open doors that a graceful white ship like a gull, mooring up in the harbour, was touched by the glimmer from a new day's sun.

Kingsley was one of the festival jury, together with Pierre Kast, Umberto Eco and Jacques Bergier. Politics came into the judging, as I found in a later year when I was a member of the jury. If an American film won an award, then a Soviet film had to have an award; art took second place to the stability of Trieste.

Other signs of the struggle between East and West were plain to see. Built on a high promontory overlooking the bay was a grand new church, surmounted by a huge cross. The church was illuminated by night. It was visible far down the coast – down that dark, threatening, atheist coast, which we were later to visit. Yet the two rival camps could not exist without each other. A taxi through the city was liable to make a detour over the frontier to a conveniently situated Jugoslav filling station, where Jugopetrol was cheaper than Shell.

A Jugoslav – we would call him a Slovene nowadays – turned up at the festival, Joe Dolnicar, always known affectionately as Joe the Jug. Joe was to play a role in our later life. In Trieste, he played the role of taking us to the best pizza places, the cheapest grappa dives. Much grappa was consumed. It's a villainous and destructive drink, smelling, even at its most refined, of gasoline, and certainly habit-forming. Kingsley took to grappa like a hangman to rope.

The sun, the heat, the new lifestyle held immense appeal. For some years, Margaret and I were in and out of Trieste. I returned to the Trieste Festival by invitation on two later occasions. Large cars from the Circulo della Stampa would carry us through the choking traffic to exhibitions of early German Expressionist cinema, or to exquisite restaurants in the hills for gigantic repasts, or to villas mysteriously presided over by ageing ladies with titles dating from pre-war days and countries.

We met dashing Hungarians with witty wives, Polish would-be film producers with polished manners and bad breath, French musicians with too-faultless English ('Whence have you come, Monsieur Brian?'), and tanned Italian dignitaries in sharp suits. Altogether, the company represented a more sophisticated world than the one from which I had recently emerged; a wish I had once made with Betty to be less provincial was assuaged. This was foreign territory, this was fun!

We wined and dined with the engaging Hungarians, sometimes talking in coded language. In the old quarter of Trieste we ate fresh fish, rinsed down with a strong white draught wine. On the beach at Miramare, beside the toy castle, we swam. On the Lido we talked with film directors who knew Edward G. Robinson. On the mole called Audacity, protruding far into the harbour waters, we danced into the early hours of the morning with the wives of prolific German authors.

Disinterring the past for the construction of this book entails checking in old boxes and cupboards and books. The past hides there, perhaps more reliably than in the memory, which is more fluid. I have just come upon a notebook which conveys a less favourable impression than above of the festival. My notes describe the award-giving and banquet in the castle on the final night.

Brief speeches for once. The toadying to the Italian judge, the quick cringe of shoulders, the polished Italian bad manners. At the cold buffet, vultures descending, necks extended, with many a soft '*Scusi*'. Smudging their over-charged plates on the back of your dinner jacket, gobbling every last remnant of food.

The women *soignée*, lean, bejewelled, hungry, sharp of breast; the men plump in trim suits, eyes flickering, already drinking to next year's bonanza of booze and scampi.

But perhaps I was merely practising to write an Aldous Huxley-type novel. It had been a hard war for the Italians. They were eager to catch up, dress up, eat up. We ate with them.

'We are all the centrepieces of our own dreams,' an Italian journalist told me. I made a note of the remark.

Films were shown in the castle courtyard, under a clear starry sky. Kingsley discovered we could see them quite well from a little bar at the back of the courtyard. There we viewed Roger Corman's *The Man with X-ray Eyes*, starring the fading matinée idol, Ray Milland. Corman and Milland were in the audience. I was not to meet Corman again until the eighties, when he filmed one of my novels.

Among the better movies were some never seen in the West. Particularly pleasing was *Icarus XB-1*, a Czech film about the discovery of a derelict spaceship containing a mummified captain and crew. This film later appeared in mutilated form as *Voyage to the End of the Universe*. On the whole, however, we were often subjected to Japanese monsters such as *Gappa*, making the well-known monster noises as it destroyed a one-foot high Tokyo. There were Balkan updates of Edgar Allan Poe; ponderous Soviet attempts at SF (but we'll come to that later); ugly Polish houses where *something* may have come back from the dead; von Daniken asking, with a friendly word from Werner von Braun, if God was an Astronaut; a ravenous British baby born with teeth. And so on. The sleep of reason produces monster movies . . .

It was said of Kingsley Amis that one of his many famous dislikes was Abroad. He showed no signs of this pathological condition in Trieste. His first wife, Hilly, was with him – the evenings were often made more interesting by their breaking-up rows – and both were more or less looked after by the go-getting Harrisons. Joan and Harry seemed at home in Italy; but I have seen Harry at home in many countries. The man is peripatetic to a fault. He also speaks a kind of demotic Italian. He and Joan energetically shopped for sustenance over and above the call of duty. So did Ted Carnell, attending with his wife, Irene. Ted's main complaint was that you could not buy Cheddar cheese in the local market. Fancy that, fifty varieties of cheese, but all foreign!

We tracked down more than cheeses in the backstreets. There was the old Roman amphitheatre, permanently being restored. In a market by the Grand Canal we discovered Italian editions of my early novels – pirated editions with attractive covers. Only four years previously, Richard Ellman's magisterial biography of James Joyce had been published. I reviewed it for the *Oxford Mail*. With its cumbersome assistance, we tracked down the Berlitz school in the via San Nicolo, where Joyce had taught. Joyce spent some impoverished years in Trieste, falling drunk into every Austrian gutter – and every gutter noted by the genial Ellman.

Joyce drank heavily in Trieste. It must be something in the air.

When the 1963 festival ended, the Harrisons had a few days of holiday to spare. They had driven down from Denmark with their children, Todd and Moira, in their Volkswagen camper. After one final Harrisonian shop in the congested markets of Trieste, Margaret and I piled into his van and were driven up the winding dusty roads into Jugland. We crossed the frontier and were in Istra, wonderful Istra!

The Istran peninsula is itself like some enormous castle, built on a greater scale than Earth can accommodate. It was dotted with a progeny of smaller castles and villages which, in partial ruin, resemble old Gormenghasts. The fact that these starveling villages are built on top of uncomfortable eminences, instead of in sheltered valleys where a ration of fertility remains, tells you much about the history of the area. Invasion and Plague are poor husbandmen. The result is a capriccio of decay.

From the latest round of devastation, many people had fled. We wound up yet another hill to find yet another village occupied only by cockerels and some pensionable goats. Elsewhere, such houses as were inhabited bore huge patriotic slogans painted across their stoney façades: *MI SMO HRVATI*, or *HOCEMO TITO I SAMO TITO* – 'We Are Croats', or 'We Want Tito and Only Tito': life insurance in a troubled time.

Old Labin crowns this tumbled Istran territory, indolent, grand, with its soiled Commie cuffs. From Labin's ramparts you can gaze out to the Kvarner Bay and its islands with fragmentary names, Cres, Krk, Losinj and beyond, headlands, islands, beckoning the viewer south.

We halted a few kilometres from Labin where, at the steep bend of a road, stood a farm acting as *gostilna*. Food was being served after the conventional East European wait. We sat on benches in the shade of a tree. The heat sizzled, the cicadas sang away at their *guzlas*. I caught a cicada in a glass tumbler for Todd; the table vibrated with its discomfort.

Gradually the planking of the table was loaded with flagons of dark Istran wine – wine in Jugoslavia is termed, in Homeric fashion, *crno vino*, black wine – with plates full of ill-fated chicken, with the immense local tomatoes called *paradisi*, with oily potato, with huge chunks of bread, and with a great bowl of black olives.

Happiness! Both Harry and I were making our names as writers. We were with women who loved us. Margaret looked wonderful in her floppy sunhat. For the first time in our lives, we had money to spend. And the glorious sun shone upon us as we laughed and ate.

What a feast! Never was a meal more enjoyed. Something in our freedom, in the sense of being in alien territory, in the heat – something about that plate of black olives, big as your thumb and shining with oil – carried a strong reminiscence of the East. There and then, as I threw down another tumbler of the wine, I resolved to see and know more of Jugland.

Before the shadows grew long, before we turned the nose of Harry's old van in the direction of Italy, a plan was forming in my mind.

XIX

The Jugs

At Semlin I was still encompassed by the scenes and the sounds
of familiar life; the din of a busy world still vexed and cheered
me; the unveiled faces of women still shone in the light of day.
Yet, whenever I chose to look southward, I saw the Ottoman's
fortress – austere, and darkly impending high over the vale of
the Danube – historic Belgrade. I had come, as it were, to the
end of this wheel-going Europe, and now my eyes would see
the splendour and havoc of the East.

Alexander William Kinglake
Eothen

Margaret was in her room in Leckford Road, Oxford. I went to
see her to tell her I had passed my driving test.

'How'd you like to come for a long drive with me?'

'Where were you thinking of going?'

'I thought perhaps round Jugland.'

She laughed. 'Then we'd better start learning Serbo-Croat.'

Thirty-eight was rather an advanced age at which to pass the
driving test. By present-day standards, it was rather an advanced
age at which to buy one's first car. But you do what you can when
you can.

Although my life was still at an impasse, a more sunny side of
my Multiple Personality Disorder had taken control. A permanent
state of remorse, however it might be said to assuage my conscience,
was of no use to my children. Writing success had come fast; I was
famous in a limited way. My books were already translated round
the world, including the country of the old enemy, Japan.

All this, of course, I took for granted, just as I had taken the barren
years for granted. It was what happened.

Television was creeping up on us. Bill lived to watch the 1954 version of Orwell's *Nineteen Eighty-Four* on BBC TV (there was only BBC at that date). It was adapted by Nigel Kneale, with Peter Cushing playing Winston Smith. Kneale featured largely in early British TV. He was the author of the Quatermass series.

Bill saw the first of these, *The Quatermass Experiment*, which ran in the summer of 1953. These two SF plays, both performed live, were responsible for selling many hundreds of thousands of television sets. Kneale later wrote a television script based on *Non-Stop*, which never got filmed.

For a few years, the BBC understood how popular SF was, and how it was of interest to adults as well as adolescents. In 1961 and 1962, the corporation screened two series which were greatly popular. These were scripted by John Elliot from a storyline by the eminent astronomer Fred Hoyle. This input from a scientist (and author of *The Black Cloud* and other SF novels) gave to *A for Andromeda* and *The Andromeda Breakthrough* a welcome seriousness.

In the early sixties, written SF was also being taken more seriously. Robert Heinlein's *Stranger in a Strange Land*, a tremendous campus best seller, was published in 1961. The next year brought Anthony Burgess's *A Clockwork Orange*, Philip K. Dick's *The Man in the High Castle*, and J. G. Ballard's first novel, *The Drowned World*, a brilliant re-creation of sunlight and heat.

Jimmy and his pretty wife, Mary, often drove down to see Margaret and me in our early days, while I was still living in Paradise Square. Another visitor was Michael Moorcock. Jimmy, Mike and I were slender then. Mike affected a sort of *fin de siècle* air, being elegant, fair-haired and beardless. Much as we argued, we had a basic point of agreement: we thought most of British SF boring, and determined to change it.

Both Jimmy and I found England flat; our yearnings for Shanghai and Singapore had much in common. We missed the heat, the vitality. With the royalties from his revolutionary collection of short stories, *The Terminal Beach*, Jimmy could afford to take Mary to the south of Spain.

He sent us two exultant postcards from Alicante. The second card ended with the news that Mary had a cold. By a grotesque turn of fate, she died there of pneumonia. We certainly felt the shock; it unhinged Jimmy for some while.

The world, as is notoriously the case, ground on.

Ballard published 'The Burning World' in Moorcock's *New*

Worlds. William Burroughs published *Nova Express*, and Dick appeared with another masterpiece, *Martian Time-Slip*.

Life had never ceased to be a continuous upheaval. I had little ambition but to survive. My dear Uncle Bert, Herbert Wilson, the good man in my childhood, died. I went to Peterborough, to the Methodist Church, to attend his funeral. Truth to tell, he had fallen from the context of my days; there seemed hardly time to mourn him. I mourn him now, and trust that clear fenland water still courses through those veins in the marshes he once helped to harness.

So Margaret and I thought of a nice long drive round Jugland. First I went to the seaside in my unreliable Renault Dauphine to see Clive and Wendy.

I could never give up on my children. In my previous little Standard convertible, bought for £95, I had made regular trips down to the Isle of Wight to be with them. They never turned against me. And now my little girl, Wendy, was growing up, full of life, fun and affection. Without my having to work for it – far from it – without my even deserving it – Wendy loved me. There was a new force in the universe, like seeing clearly with the pineal eye. She clung to me. As soon as she was able, she accompanied Clive on the long slow journey to Marston Street.

My first wife never interfered with my access to the children. What we felt for each other is hard to say. Long association counts for much. Emotions easily war with each other. Divorce, as the law operated then, was no easy matter; besides, we always ended up in bed whenever I was in Totland – to fall apart afterwards in spitting hatred, at least on one side.

'If I can't have you, no other woman shall!' Where did the line originate, if not in some Victorian drama? Poor jade! Two-hour monologues late into the night, while Clive and Wendy slept innocently upstairs, were the style, self-reproach and self-justification being the yin and yang of it.

It was all long ago. Two people in confrontation: one now dead, one much changed. A scene perhaps from a Hardy poem. 'When you shall see me in the toils of time . . .'

On 4 March, 1964, a Land Rover drove down to Folkestone and boarded a ferry for Calais. On the driver's door was painted the legend 'Oxford–Ohrid' in Latin and Cyrillic characters. To its roof was lashed an inflatable ex-RAF dinghy, destined for Joe the Jug in

Slovenia. Inside were Margaret and I, in quest of heat, wilderness and black olives. We dressed like the vehicle in sombre green; mine was an ex-Nato service jacket. Jugland was well accustomed to uniforms; often we were saluted as we passed Jug soldiery.

Armed with an advance of £150 from Faber, a few reference books, and a foothold in the language, we drove across a wintery Europe. How hospitable the Continent was, Luxembourg with thriving markets; Germany with welcoming *gasthofs*; Vienna, where we parked in a side street while we went to the opera, to *Don Giovanni* – and returned to find no one had stolen Joe the Jug's dinghy. We negotiated the Semmering Pass, crossed a bleak frontier, and arrived in Maribor in a howling snowstorm. So began our six months of Jug gypsy life.

We delivered the dinghy to Joe, and stayed in Ljubliana with him and his wife, Rosa. Then we were off on our own. Half the time we slept in a tent; for the other half, we stayed in small hotels – and were generally glad to leave them.

All about us lay the remains of vanished peoples, the Celts, Romans, Byzants, Bogomils, Vlachs, and particularly the Ottomans. We stood on the field of Kosovo where, in 1389, the Serbs were defeated by the Turks, and a new era in European history began. We stood on the bridge in Sarajevo where the shot that heralded the start of the Great War was fired. Finally we reached Lake Ohrid in Macedonia, and stood on the frontier – then closely guarded – between Jugland and Albania.

Some account of our travels forms the bulk of my only travel book, *Cities and Stones: A Traveller's Jugoslavia*. That beautiful country has broken into its component parts and all but destroyed itself in the process. But in 1964, under Tito, all the disruptive antagonisms, of history, race and religion, had been swept under a red carpet. Jugland was a safe place for travellers. If we ever ran into danger we did not know it.

Margaret and I lived simply, losing many pounds in weight in the process. Not liking the look of grey milk, we drank only camomile tea with our bread-and-jam breakfasts. For the rest, we ate salami, local cheese, *baklava* and massive doses of bread, washed down with plenty of the divine *slivovica* and *crno vino* – as did the majority of the population. The diet seemed to agree with us. We were never ill.

But we never found any more black olives.

Margaret was unused to hardship; she never complained, was always eager for the next new day. It says a great deal for her courage that she accompanied me on this long outing; but, after all, the Mansons were descended from Vikings. Her father had already forbidden us to take off for a winter in a boarding-house on the island of St Lucia, together with my old pal Charles Parr. Perhaps he felt that we could be more easily retrieved from the Balkans than the Caribbean.

Margaret had stood by me – through thin rather than thick. But I also stood by her. We owed each other affection. The Jug tour was the seal on that affection. I thought of her when she was showering as in that line of Fulke Greville's, 'Washing the water with her beauties white'.

Those months in the fresh air were a learning period – learning about each other as well as the country we travelled. Bosnia in particular held a charm beyond the confines of contemporary Europe. On the old Turkish roads between Prijedor, Banja Luka, Jajce and Travnik, we met with shepherds driving their sheep to new pastures; walking with tall staves, whistling up their hounds, cheerful and stalwart, the men with their rubicund faces powdered with dust from their travels, preparatory to being painted by some romantic nineteenth-century artist. They slept in hedges. They wore crude sheepskin jackets. Their boys played wooden flutes. Their dogs cohabited with wolves.

Not unlike the shepherds, I imagine, our concerns were practical. Where to sleep, how to procure bread and petrol, how to add to our Serbo-Croat vocabulary, how to tune the Land Rover engine with a razor blade between the tappets, how to keep warm or – more generally – cool.

At one point, we left our vehicle behind, stranded on gravel in a dried river bed. We had indeed come to the end of wheel-going Europe, to use Kinglake's phrase. We ascended a mountain on horseback to arrive at Galicnik – but this was in Macedonia, that largely conjectural country. Galicnik is a village hunched to itself high in the Bistra Planina. No wheel travels its vertiginous streets. The inhabitants – 500 in number when we visited, 5,000 a generation earlier – are isolated. Once a year, in July, a priest used to venture up from the valley to marry any couples so inclined; then there were three days of celebration.

But the percentage of population of marriageable age was shrinking. The young had left to find work in Thessaloniki or Trieste or even further afield. Margaret and I paid the equivalent of nine shillings for a night's board in a dormitory. The price included lumps of cold mutton, a *rakija* and *turska kava* – Turkish coffee.

As in some ancient story, the people of Galicnik depended for their livelihood on one animal, the sheep. The men tended their flocks, guarding them from the still-prevalent wolf. The women sat in small stone barns, weaving carpets from wool on crude looms weighted with boulders. The milk of the sheep was made into a cheese called *kackavalj*, to be eaten hot or cold.

As in that same old story, two factors ruled the harsh life of Galicnik, weather and politics. The climate is such that winter conditions prevail for almost nine months of the year; during the other three months, people talk about the terrors of the last winter, the pains of the one to come. After the Balkan Wars and the Great War, territorial treaties told against Galicnik. Since time immemorial – and time scales the heights of immemoriability in Macedonia – the herds were always driven southwards by those dusty shepherds, to more clement winter pastures. That was in Ottoman days. Now a frontier existed with Greece, a land of lost content beyond which man and animal might not go again.

So the herds had dwindled, the men had weathered and aged, their houses had fallen into decay. Only the cruel winds of winter had remained unaffected by new frontiers.

All over Jugland, what may be called the Galicnikisation of country and people was taking place on a deep psychic level. The bafflements of Istra, with its corrosions and chthonian upheavals, its shattered villages and cockerel-crowned castle ruins, its underground waters – those rivers which ran in one direction to the Adriatic and in the other to the Danube and the Black Sea – its violations by many races and religions and diseases, its confusion of frontiers like lines drawn in the dirt of a playground – these elements could stand as a model for the whole. They were present, masked, all over that strange country, where houses were scooped from rock, so that ferns grew in the walls of rooms. The curse of tongues brought Slav vowels with Italian endings; the civil war when it came in the 1990s would hinge on whether the word for bread was *hleb* or *kruh*. Men in deepest Serbia sat in a butcher's shop, eating meat at a tree bole with a dagger for utensil; here were the Dark Ages, next to a new steel plant. The disruptions of time mirrored the convulsions of a land which had defeated even the Nazi divisions Hitler sent to subdue its occupants.

Throughout our travels, I was making notes for my book. I did no other writing. When published, *Cities and Stones* was banned in Jugland, I'm not ashamed to say. But the influence of Jugland remains. Perhaps because we were in love, and rather in love with the country, that time has stayed vivid. The pain is that, as with Burma, the country we knew has disappeared in a cloud of folly and hatred. I wrote a story, 'The Day of the Doomed King', based on the old Serbian dynasty of the Nemanijas and, much later, 'The Other Side of the Lake', based on Ohrid, and 'Igur and the Mountain', about a village much like Galicnik. But the spirit of those times, that country, has pervaded our lives. All the family, alone or together, visited Jugland and holidayed there – until it disintegrated, in another striking example of Berg's Madkind theory.

One incident on our Jugland tour illustrates well the nature of the East-West divide at that time. Towards the end of May, we gained the southernmost point of our endeavours, and camped on the shores of Lake Ohrid. The shore was mild and meadowy. Only a short distance away, in the low hills between Ohrid and Prespa, were small villages of a bygone age, where the people were all in costume and their houses all in ruins.

The town of Ohrid is beautiful, full of tall old Turkish houses with heavy brows, leaning across the street to each other, conferring on archaic architectural formulae.

Ohrid was a township in the dim epoch of Illyria; later, it lay on the Roman Via Ignatia, which runs from Thessaloniki in Greece northwards to Durres, on the Albanian coast. These days, cut off by the civil war to the north and Greek hostility to the south, Ohrid must be more remote than ever, vegetating on its little inland sea.

Looking across the lake from our tent, we saw the mountainous western shore, dark, withdrawn, snow-crowned: the land of the Shiptar. The frontier between the two hostile countries lay in the middle of the lake, patrolled by an occasional speedboat.

In that tranquil place, we lounged outside our bivouac, and read or cooked, relaxing from our travels. I was reading Dostoevsky's *The House of the Dead*, a perfect book for that time and place, brimming with human suffering and hope.

One morning, we peered out of our tent to find we had neighbours. Some distance from us along the lake shore stood a camel-coloured bus, parked under a tree. Camel-coloured people climbed from it. They erected little camel-coloured bivouacs all round the coach. They never strayed far from this coach. They never ventured into town. Their very movements about their chosen site seemed guarded.

Darkness fell. Margaret and I lit a small fire at the entrance to our tent to ward off mosquitoes. As we sat there enjoying the evening and the plopping silences of the lake, we became aware of a figure prowling beyond the range of light. There flashed through my mind the image of Neanderthal's first encounter with Cro-Magnon, most likely prompted by William Golding's novel *The Inheritors*.

Our communication was not by word of mouth, at least at first. Our wary interloper began to whistle. It was code. He whistled – for this was 1964 – a Beatles' number, 'Love Me Do'.

We responded in kind.

Now he came quickly to the tent. He took bread and *crno vino* with us. We sat talking long into the night. He was Bulgarian. The Bulgarians had been allowed this coach trip to a foreign country, a country outside the Warsaw Pact. A week away! They carried their own food in the coach. They had been warned not to talk to foreigners. But he had discovered we were English; he had heard our voices and longed to talk to us. He had listened to the Fab Four's music in Sofia. He did not like the rulers of his country. What he wanted was to get to Liverpool and meet the Beatles.

In those days, everyone wanted to get to Liverpool. The West was in reasonably good fettle and had contempt for the countries behind the Iron Curtain. Nothing creative or amusing emerged from those regions: all was silence and drabness. After the defeat of the American Forces in Vietnam in 1975, the mood became darker; general confidence was lost. Not only did many of us fear we would all blow each other to bits, but it seemed that the Soviets would win. We knew how decadent the West was. We were decadent ourselves, watched too much television, and spent too much on health care. In 1964, however, the West had a secret weapon: pop music!

That glorious summer wore on. We almost surfeited on little Orthodox monastic churches – never ever to be revisited – Zica, Ljubostina, Studenica, Decani and Patriarchal Pec, that huddle of lost ancient churches, their gardens full of flowers, their walls full of rigid Byzantine saints, their chambers full of ancient nuns, their prayers candles in remote anti-religious landscapes.

We stayed in some curious places. Pulling open drawers in various pieces of furniture, I saw how empty they were.

In England, drawers are crammed with all manner of things – spare pairs of scissors, erasers, penknives, non-functioning fountain pens, cotton reels from long ago, engagement diaries, little metal toys, postcards of Menton and Le Touquet, empty UHU tubes, copper rheumatism bracelets, abandoned wristwatches, magnifying glasses, peacock feathers, the odd cigarette card, notebooks, hair-pins, old banknotes, missing typewriter keys, souvenirs of various royal events, combs, theatre programmes, marbles, blown sparrows' eggs the odd crayon, lost padlock keys, newspaper cuttings, orna-ments, paperclips, folders of matches, toothpicks, air-gun pellets, boxes of shagreen containing eyebrow tweezers, sticks of agabatti, loose playing cards, nail files, signet rings, pencil sharpeners, sou-venirs of Paris and Prague, badges, medals, love-letters, string and other objects.

In Jugland, the drawers were empty. Such is the fate of countries long invaded and fought over. Personal possessions are few.

What did Henry James say of Europe? 'Centuries of blood and bric-à-brac.'

In Makarska, on the coast, we met up with the Harrisons. It was a marvel. Harry and Joan were then living in Denmark. We dropped them a card in April from Belgrade, to say we could meet them in the camp in Makarska, if there was one, at twelve noon on such and such a date in July. Harry could not respond; we had no address.

Our Land Rover, crippled by adverse interior roads, made its slow way northwards from Sveti Stefan, all the way to Makarska, simmer-ing under its great cliffs of *karst*, grey as Halibutt's Plasticine. At five minutes past noon on the appointed day, it rolled into Makarska's crowded seashore camp. Not five minutes later, the familiar old green Volkswagen bus with its Dansk sign rolled in behind us. Joan and Harry, plus Todd and Moira, tumbled out, cheering.

How grand is the Adriatic coast, the masculine equivalent of the supine Rimini beaches on the western side of the sea. We swam from the Makarska camp. Near by, beached on the rocks, lay survivors of Tito's Partisans, all missing at least one limb, heroes of the Patriotic War being cared for by the State. How fare those heroes now that the State has withered away?

Joan and Harry brought us provisions from the West – *flode pulver*! – and books to read, including Oscar Lewis's *Children of Sanchez*. Much celebratory drinking went on in Makarska – so much so that Harry and I swam in a muddy bay which proved later to be the city sewage outlet. Margaret became fed up with my beastly behaviour. Over supper, she hurled a cup of good filter coffee at me. Next morning, there she was, patiently washing the shirt concerned.

By August, temperatures even on the long Dalmatian coast began to fall. By August, Margaret and I had become certifiable gypsies.

So this expedition came to an end. We rolled back through Western Europe, dazzled by its prosperity.

Several years later, talking over the trip with Harry, I said, 'But we never again found those delectable black olives we enjoyed that day in the depths of Istra.'

Harry laughed. He and Joan had bought the olives in Trieste market, in order to bring them along for the picnic. 'Only the Italians know how to grow olives like that,' he said. Illusion had prompted our months on Jugland's dusty roads and in her green valleys.

As soon as we returned from our Jug trip, I went to see my children. In the perilous and rusty Renault Dauphine, I made my way back to the Isle of Wight to take them on a holiday to the West Country, and to be together again. They appeared happy enough, enjoying the seaside and its freedom. Clive was becoming a star cricketer. Wendy introduced me to her pony, Toby, as innocent, as plump, as amiable as she. Everything had changed in the rest of the world, but not there.

On the way south I stopped for a coffee at a restaurant in Brockenhurst, where I heard the Supremes on the radio singing, 'What did I do wrong, To make you stay away so long?' The words struck home, as simple words sometimes will, penetrating the hell of being in two minds. Was it possible, came the treacherous thought, that *she* might ask herself Diana Ross's question? And that, if only for the children's sake, we might . . .

But it was not possible. Decisions had been made. Perhaps I had even made mine. The grinding preparations for mid-sixties divorce began. My solicitor engaged John Mortimer as my QC. One day in July 1965, a marriage that had existed since the late forties was annulled. Once more, everything was changed.

That afternoon, Margaret and I went with our friend Eddie Cooney to a pub on the Fulham Road. There we met up with Kingsley Amis, a drink or two ahead of us, to celebrate. When Margaret's father, Jack Manson, hosted our wedding reception at the Randolph Hotel in Oxford, in December of the same year, Kingsley was among the guests, as were Joan and Harry. Kingsley had with him his new wife, Elizabeth Jane Howard.

As my new wife and I left the hotel to fly to Paris, champagne corks were still popping. A most encouraging sound. A cheerful omen for the future.

XX

The Sixties

Being reasonable has nothing to do with being a writer.
Doris Lessing in an interview

'Nothing could change you, you dull bastard,' Roger said.
Kingsley Amis
One Fat Englishman

Whenever my Margaret entered a room, she carried with her her own cache of serenity. There was a radiance about her she has never lost: or perhaps one should say an inner calm, a kind of desert island calm, very different from the typhoons raging inside me. She called me a shaggy bear. I likened her to a gazelle, because of her grace and her pretty slender legs. These animal metaphors come in useful. Fortunately, there is no record of a bear preying on a gazelle. Or of a gazelle running from a bear.

I cannot talk of Margaret without embarrassing her, and will say only that from the day she walked into the newspaper offices I admired this slender, tall, elegant and self-effacing lady.

In the great gale of the English language, we have only the one word for love. The Inuit living within the Arctic Circle possess, we are told, thirty-six words for different kinds of snow. We lack so many words for different kinds of love, for the whole spectrum of love. But love goes so far beyond language – the language of body as well as speech – that I can only say I adored Margaret without being able to state how much, or in how many ways. And in uttering that commonplace one feels one's uniqueness. And hers.

*   *   *

We had much to teach each other. Margaret was then a silent person, especially in company, not given to conversation. She changed. What she taught me was that I might turn to her for help. She made me realise how deeply early training penetrates the psyche. For if ever I complained or looked for help as a boy, there would be Bill, singing in his anti-clerical sarcasm, 'The noble army of martyrs . . .', turning me away.

'Don't turn away,' she urged, gently. And soon I didn't.

So continued the process of growing together. This is why old couples are often described as being like each other.

The little Marston Street house had to be sold; it had insufficient accommodation for her clothes and my books. We lived at first in a Tudor cottage, 'Jasmine', near Wheatley. It began its existence as four small cottages for farm labourers. Three of them had been somewhat casually knocked into one house. The fourth, Field Cottage, served as my study. They were marvellously ancient buildings, hiding shoulder to shoulder at the end of a lane. We were four miles from Oxford city centre, yet could have been in the middle of nowhere.

Jack Manson helped me lay slabs for a terrace on the sunny side of the house. My cousin Shirley sent us a dozen rose bushes. Dot and Aunt Dorothy came and admired. Kenneth Allsop visited. Many people visited.

When Clive and Wendy came to stay, they loved Jasmine. It was built on such a scale that, small though they were, they could easily look out of the windows. The original sixteenth-century structure had been designed for men and women who lived off mangelwurzels, with the odd rabbit or squirrel thrown into the cauldron at weekends. In consequence, they rarely grew more than five feet tall. It helped survival if you had a small frame to nourish.

For the children, as for us, it was a magical place. There were four wooden staircases leading to five bedrooms. The door from the living room to the kitchen was so low that you might bang not just your head but your shoulders too. Our cat, Nickie, patrolled the thatch, chasing off birds.

That first autumn of our marriage was phenomenally calm and mild. Leaves remained on the tall trees until well past their October bedtime. We bought a Ford Anglia. I still did my literary editing, Margaret still worked for the editor of the *Oxford Mail*. We grew Shirley's roses.

Meanwhile, the great narrative of the outside world was roaring on. This was the time at once of the rock and roll concerts with their untidy encampments and of couples (or trios) embracing in barely furnished rooms. A time when we thought poverty did not matter, or would go away. When people marched on Aldermaston and gave flowers to soldiers. Joan Baez, Marlene Dietrich, Bob Dylan, the Beach Boys, and, of course, the Beatles. And, in the other corner, LBJ, Ho Chi Minh, Khrushchev, Mao Zedong.

So much for the stratosphere. But public events mean little compared with one's interest in the girl next door (and whether she read SF).

My novels were successful, to be found in airports in Fiji, Ibiza and Helsinki, as well as more renowned places. Translations abounded, bringing forth invitations to visit hitherto unknown lands. I was famous to a limited degree. Mine was a household name in scandalously few households.

In her autobiography, *Under My Skin*, Doris Lessing relates how she submitted her first novel to a London publisher, had it accepted, had it acclaimed, and, in her naivety, *thought that that was what happened to everyone*. My response was much the same. In Pope's words, 'Whatever is, is right'. One also feels, contrapuntally, that one is 'getting away with it'. And that in due time one will be found out. Or, if one has not yet been found out, one writes an autobiography.

Writing short stories remained as much a pleasure as it had been at school. Often a report of something new would start an involuntary line of thought. Discussions of VM, or vibratory motion, conjured ideas which went into a story called 'Dumb Show'. The hypothesis advanced by Fred Hoyle of a universe of continuous creation, fuelled by hydrogen atoms popping into existence, was poetically ingenious. That interest resulted in a story called 'Visiting Amoeba'. It was told in the second person singular: a fresh way of telling a story as far as I was concerned.

The future was a magical realm, subject to conjuration. Not so much a continuity as a series of disparities which could not be anticipated. When telephones came in, no one foresaw that they would enter every house in the land, or that workmen would one day converse with each other over mobile phones. When the military installed their first computers, no one foresaw that PCs would invade every home; still less that the Internet would connect the globe with a fine invisible web. When the Pill came in, no one foresaw the rise of feminism or the appearance of AIDS.

One way in which the sixties were brighter than the previous decade was the sudden proliferation of LPs, banishing the old shellac 78 rpm records for ever. I recall how, in the late fifties, Tottenham

Court Road in London – always consumer-technology sensitive – blossomed with those square bright LP covers. Post-surreal artists like Roger Dean infiltrated every home. No one then imagined how, two decades later, the LPs would themselves follow shellac into extinction as CDs came in.

A standard defence of SF used to be that it was a predictive literature. Non-readers are still eager to believe as much. Chaos Theory alone denies such linear foresight. If we arrive now at something that may happen in fifty years, it's almost pure accident. Something unexpected will emerge.

When Margaret and I returned from Jugland, we found the miniskirt in vogue. The miniskirt had not been predicted. Womenkind had changed their minds and their clothes. Betty and I had been eager readers of naughty postcards by Donald McGill when we lived at Gorleston. In the McGill world, women had either been sprightly young things showing a lot of leg or blowsy middle-aged matrons. London and other cities had become a McGill world in that respect. But no one accuses McGill of having been a prophet.

Writing a novel is hard work, though anyone can think of harder occupations. The incentives would be fewer if the process were not also enthralling and a sense of revelation strong. In the need to experiment with my new-found abilities, I produced during this period two novels of contrasting kind.

Despite the achievements of my immediate seniors in the writing field, Amis, Wain, Osborne and Murdoch, Britain was in the grip of no great literary movement. In France, however, the *nouveau roman* was attracting an intellectual public, and even causing a faint ripple of excitement on our no-nonsense shores. Alain Robbe-Grillet's *Jealousy* was published here in translation in 1959. His objective descriptions of personal events was disturbingly original, a Mondrian in prose. Even more interesting was *L'emploi du temps*, by Michel Butor, published in English translation as *Passing Time* in 1961. In Butor's novel, two sorts of time meet and coalesce, as diary time catches up with real time. A foreigner in Liverpool seeks to hold his personality together. Both Butor's and Robbe-Grillet's novels introduced strange states of mind to which I readily responded.

Also in those early sixties years Margaret and I went several times to the cinema to see a film that ranks among the most original ever made, *L'Année Dernière à Marienbad*. Robbe-Grillet's screenplay for *Marienbad* was directed by Alain Resnais. The gorgeous Delphine Seyrig plays – often in feathers – the lady who may or may not have had an affair with an importuning man, in Marienbad, the previous year. The isolation of the novel is here personified by a large lugubrious hotel, its grounds filled with painted shadows, almost immobile guests, and a funereal play which guests watch, or fail to watch. All elements conspire to reinforce the enigma of the relationship between the two lead characters.

At that date, the short-lived Space Age had been born. It was so much less grand, so much more entangled in global politics than SF writers had cared to imagine. Leaving Earth is hard enough to achieve, hard and expensive. Leaving Earth entirely has not yet been achieved.

Those brave astronauts and cosmonauts – those first heroes to enter a new realm – arrived there floating about on their backs in the metal wombs of primitive spaceships! A curious position for explorers . . .

The phenomenon of spiritual isolation was more effectively, because more strikingly couched in common experience, embodied in Robbe-Grillet's lugubrious hotel, than in the giant firework of a Saturn rocket.

Fifties SF magazines had been filled with speculation about space travel and interstellar flight, in a rather curiously premonitory way. Although the fear of nuclear war ran as a sort of counter-point, anxious, apotropaic, the acceptable attitude was optimistic, 'upwards and outwards'. Futurity was seen as being synonymous with enormous speeds. But what of stillness – as much worth investigating, as terrifying, surely?

I conceived of an anti-novel called *Garden with Figures*. Part of the fortifying inspiration came from science, from Heisenberg's Uncertainty Principle, since my life at the time, like an elementary particle, was apparently operating under some such physical law. This work I submitted to Faber in 1962, as my attempt at a *nouveau roman*. Charles Monteith rejected it. One's first rejection is always a surprise of a fairly major order, comparable with one's first punch on the nose at school.

When we were about to head for Jugland, Ted Carnell retired from his editorship of two magazines to which I was contributing. *Science Fantasy* was taken over by Bon while *New Worlds* was taken over by Michael Moorcock. Mike proved himself a revolutionary, dynamic and daring editor. Nailing Ballard to his masthead, he set out to prove to the world that we had arrived in the future. It was alive and well, and living a rather shifty existence in Notting Hill.

Mike wrote asking for a contribution that was not merely the old Carnell tat. Making a few revisions, I retitled my novel *Report on*

Probability A and sent it to him. Mike published it. It occupied almost all of *New Worlds* No. 171, March 1967.

I resubmitted the manuscript to Charles. He accepted it this time. Faber published it the following year. We used as jacket illustration a print of Holman Hunt's 'The Hireling Shepherd', altered only by a little doctoring I gave it. The painting features in the novel as an example of suspended time. Whether Charles remembered he had previously rejected the novel under its earlier title was something I never cared to enquire about. There are secrets in publishing with which man should not meddle.

Much notice, often unfavourable, was taken of *Probability A* within the SF field. I had hoped, as far as I hoped anything for it, that it would be enjoyed by those who enjoyed *Hothouse*, as something entirely new (as far as anything is ever entirely new). Yet people still talk about it now and again. I met a nuclear physicist who was obsessed by it. 'I've read it eight times,' he said. 'Now you can tell me what it's all about.'

Probability A was often reprinted. Published by Doubleday in the States, it later appeared there in paperback under the misleading banner 'Astounding Science Fiction'. Beyond the SF field – an enthusiastic review by Jill Tweedie in the *Guardian*. Nothing else! Silence. The usual comatose philistine response. Later, Rayner Heppenstall mentioned *Probability A* in his work on the *nouveau roman*. When I met him personally, his praise was nothing short of ingenious. But Heppenstall was regarded as somewhat eccentric. *He liked foreign things . . .*

However, foreign things were soon to come into vogue. Delicatessens began to appear in Britain, together with foreign fruits and translations of Primo Levi. We were able to hear new foreign composers like Penderecki and Lutoslawski. Travel became cheaper and easier, at least to those countries not under Soviet rule.

The second novel produced by my delight in experimentation was *Barefoot in the Head*. *Barefoot* is not, as critics have claimed, inspired by James Joyce. The line of thought leading to it was more directly linked to world events. In 1956, the Hungarian revolution erupted. The gigantic statue of Stalin in Budapest was thrown down, the courageous Cardinal Mindszenty was freed from prison. When Imre Nagy announced that Hungary wished to leave the Warsaw Pact and become a neutral state, Russian tanks rolled into the capital. Radio hams began calling on the West for help.

And how did we respond? What was happening in the West? Under Prime Minister Anthony Eden, and the connivance of some members of the Tory Party, British armed forces were invading Egypt and the Suez Canal zone. A secret plan had been hatched with the French and Israelis. It was a disastrous idea, a strategy of dying imperialism. People talked of nothing else. For once, the USA and USSR united in condemning Britain. Our forces withdrew ignominiously.

By November of that year, our humiliated forces were back in their barracks, and Hungary had been beaten into submission by its Soviet overlords.

Behind the operation lay the same high-handed manner in which many British had for so long treated Arabs, Indians, and almost any race they came across. In the sixties, anyone sympathetic to the 'tune in, drop out' mood of the time could make a bucketful of LSD for twopence. It seemed not beyond the bounds of possibility that Arabs could cheaply and easily be revenged on Britain. It needed only a few gallons of LSD in Staines reservoir and the country would be out of the competition.

What would follow would make an interesting story. I proceeded to write it.

Bits and pieces of the novel were written in bits and pieces of Western Europe. My main influence was not Joyce but the great turmoil of Europe itself, as we had encountered it, from Metz in France, through Stockholm, London, Germany, Belgium, Holland – Holland in particular. There in the dark of a scruffy Maastricht backstreet a broken neon light gleamed with an announcement: STELLA ART . . . Maastricht later became famous in the history of the EU. Mine was the first novel to mention it.

Maastricht, where Wendy had a stomach upset and we stayed in a hotel without hot water . . .

In what language do you write of a post-LSD catastrophe world? My solution was the one to be adopted later by Russell Hoban in *Riddley Walker*. You use the freak-speak of a survivor. I wrote the story in parts, which Moorcock published in his *New Worlds* as 'The Acid War Stories'. Then I rewrote them entirely to make a coherent novel. Ever since its publication, *Barefoot* has received nods of approval from critics who probably have not read it. To my mind it is one of the fake milestones of science fiction. Perhaps the storyline of the would-be messiah is good enough. And perhaps, for all my labours, it would have been better told in plain language. One has to try these things.

If filmed today, *Barefoot* would probably be called *Hippieworld*. The writer B. S. Johnson became interested. He launched into a screenplay prompted by finance from FarThing Films. What happened to the screenplay I do not know. In 1973, Johnson committed suicide. Another writer going against the grain!

Barefoot drew angry comment. I suppose the objections from older readers were no more irrelevant than the praise of younger readers. Well calculated to alarm was a letter signed God, threatening to strike down me and my family. I noticed from the postmark on His envelope that He was living in Reigate at the time.

We must invent what does not exist, and stage confrontations unlikely to happen. There is a paradox, not unknown to modern philosophy, involved in thinking of things that we cannot conceive – conceiving the inconceivable. Is it meaningless to imagine a world like Earth where a year fills the equivalent of three thousand Earth-years? Clearly it is not meaningless if it has significance for those who entertain such thoughts. That fascinating work of Ludwig Wittgenstein *Tractatus Logico-Philosophicus* concludes with a statement that for me has all the aspects of challenge: 'What we cannot speak about we must pass over in silence'.

Sorrow can be unspoken, yet speak. Writers write to defy Wittgenstein, and to conceive the inconceivable. The latter is also the occupation of scientists. Long live imagination!

Moorcock's *New Worlds* was in financial trouble. On one occasion when he rang me, he wanted to know if I could see any hope of saving the magazine.

'We'll go and ask the Arts Council for some money.'

He laughed. 'For science fiction?'

'They're throwing money away, Mike. It's worth a try.'

I launched a campaign, persuading people such as Amis, Robert Conquest and Kathleen Tillotson to write in to the Council. After which, Mike and I went to see Lord Goodman. Goodman was one of the figures of the sixties, glad to see the social life of the country become less stultifying. The interview was less taxing than we had anticipated. Mike got a subsidy for his magazine.

Even the subsidy was not enough for the grand, slick magazine into which Mike transformed *New Worlds*. His wife, Hilary Bailey, would lock him in a room for forty-eight hours with nothing but a bottle of whisky and a flask of coffee, or so Mike claimed, and Mike would write a fantasy 'novel'. This he could sell to an American paperback company for a sum which was then ploughed into *New Worlds*. I was in London once when I came across Charles Platt, barefoot, selling *New Worlds* on a street corner. I have never heard that Cyril Connolly did the same with his *Horizon*. God, how we've lived – often desperately!

Moorcock gave SF a voice to match the times. We were discovering the ferment of the present in Ladbroke Grove, in the backstreets of Holland, in hash or Stella Artois. The Moorcockian revolution, soon dubbed the 'New Wave', gained a more intelligent audience for science fiction, much more in tune with everyday life. It also brought in some good new writers who have weathered the storms of the years. Christopher Priest is one such. Priest has put difficulties in the way of his own career by not wishing whole-heartedly to write SF – or, for that matter, non-SF. He has developed an arid mindscape of his own.

The creative atmosphere of sixties London lured a number of writers, editors and general hopefuls from abroad – not only from the United States and Australia, but also from Scandinavia. Those friends from Scandinavia, Jon Bing from Norway, Jannick Storm from Denmark, and, in particular, Sam Lundwall and Goran Bengtson from Sweden, remain friends, thirty years on.

The new freedom blew about the streets and thoroughfares of the West's great cities. Youth travelled cheap and fast. Cities were growing at a great rate – one of the factors that made the sixties exciting. Things were being made new. It took more intelligence than before to either work or avoid work. Altering the profile of society more dramatically than the space race was the tide of men and women retreating from the fields, not just in Britain but in the USA, Europe and the East, before more efficient agricultural methods; to swell the myriad city-dwellers and speed the divorce from nature.

Although most of us did not realise it, the USSR was beginning to lag behind the West. Their agriculture was in ruins. When Nikita Khrushchev fell from power in 1964, he was kicked out mainly because he had failed to raise agricultural production. He had his problems. When he sent seed potatoes to the peasants to plant for the next year's crop, the hungry peasants simply ate them.

Shortly after Margaret's and my marriage, I acquired a new literary agent. It is more painful to change agents than publishers. Although I left Ted Carnell with reluctance, I was not alone; everyone was making their bows. Ted had never intended to be an agent. He had filled the role to oblige his authors because no literary agency in the UK handled science fiction properly. Ted was kindly, efficient and totally honest. It could be said of him that everyone loved him; but he had a flaw that spells trouble for any agent's clients: he accepted with gratitude any offer any publisher made.

Hilary Rubinstein was a man of different mettle. He and his partner, Michael Horniman, heir to a myriad tea leaves, had just taken over A. P. Watt, the longest established literary agency in town, if not in the world. Hilary and I rapidly became friends. He was the nephew of Victor Gollancz. I first met him in his office, the size of a fairly capacious wardrobe, in his famous uncle's offices in Henrietta Street. I was trying to sell him a book, which he gracefully turned down.

Hilary had his own claims to fame. He had met Kingsley Amis while they were both up at Oxford. Hearing that Kingsley was writing something longish, Hilary wrote to him and secured for Gollancz that delectably funny first novel of Kingsley's, *Lucky Jim* – a feather the size of a palm leaf in anyone's cap. One of the many advantages of a university education.

It was always a pleasure to visit A. P. Watt's offices. Hilary and I would smoke cigars in those days, and chat about literature in general. Or I would go and see members of his staff. Jeremy Lewis (later to become a famous literary-man-about-town) sat amiably in an outer office. I could never make out what he did. Only when I read his amusing memoir *Kindred Spirits* did I learn Jeremy was just waiting for lunch. Carol Smith (later an agent in her own right) was present, calming her clients. In particular, there lived and breathed the vivacious young Maggie Noach, whom Hilary had engaged as foreign agent. The marvellous Maggie immediately began selling my books all over the world. She too later set up her own agency.

The sun shone on life. Everyone's fortunes were changing, often for the better. It was all a part of the awakening many experienced in those days.

How extraordinary it was to have unexpected cheques rolling in from everywhere. From Japan, for instance! It is amazing to reflect on what a difference a good agency can make to a writer's career. Hilary remained my agent for over twenty-five years, until his retirement. I miss his company.

The possibility to travel further afield arose. It was eagerly seized upon. In March of 1966, Margaret and I flew to New York. We travelled by the cheapest means possible. That entailed a train journey to Glasgow, where we caught a turboprop airliner belonging to Icelandair.

Before we were deposited in Reykjavik, we flew over Sertsey, an island being formed by volcanic action. The plane dipped low over the sea to give us a good view. As we approached, we could see a chunk of the planet being created, chthonic fires blazing under the ocean, the long plume of ash and smoke trailing eastwards above the waters.

Two years later, vegetation was beginning to grow on the still-warm soil, the seeds carried by winds and birds from both Scandinavia and Canada. New possibilities were being born. Without mankind, the entire globe would regenerate itself in a season.

We arrived in New York in time for lunch and the deep Martinis all American publishers drank at that time, as though Prohibition had ended only at dinner the previous day. A decade later, and the smart set were reduced to a glass of white wine. Nowadays, the hardcover contingent at least confine themselves to Perrier. And people tell you publishing has improved . . .

Visiting one's New York publisher became a sort of annual ritual. It was a baptism, permitting one at last – not without reservations – to think of oneself as a real writer. New York for a while seemed old fashioned. No miniskirts! London at that time had a lustre since departed: it became a European city. The beehive of Centre Point was in course of construction, new flyovers were going up. Europeans were flocking to join in the Happenings and general feelings of artistic liberation; Antonioni was filming *Blow-Up* – London as brittle art form. Chaps were wearing their hair long, and adopting the American habit of wearing jeans. Flights of young ladies, such as had never been seen before, brightened the capital. New York was sober by comparison; over the Empire State hung the thirties shadow of King Kong.

New coffee shops, new pubs, new art galleries, new music, new opportunities, sprang up like mushrooms overnight.

Following the Suez disgrace, Britain was able to perceive through the fog of nosthedony a faint reality. She was no longer a world power. We laid aside our colonies with commendable grace. Prime Minister Edward Heath was a staunch European, while Harold Wilson was at least a lukewarm one. In Europe lay a more modest role for the British. So the Romans became Italians.

We too, caught in the general excitement, wished to be known by new names – Margaret as Chris (adaptation of her middle name, Christie), I as Wilson, my middle name.

With all the joys and freedoms of the Swinging Sixties went that

Shadow side which seems inseparable from human affairs. The world of LSD was foreshadowed in R. L. Stevenson's *Dr Jekyll and Mr Hyde*. Stevenson's fable concerns the shattering of the fortress of personality. Hyde is the personality's destructive side. The drug Jekyll takes is not the instrument of Hyde's appearance, merely a neutral means of transmission from one state to the other. In Jekyll's words, 'The drug had no discriminating action; it was neither diabolical nor divine; but it shook the doors of the prisonhouse of my disposition'.

The Jekyll/Hyde tragedy was to be acted out in the USA. Under the love-ins of the Flower People, the trashcans of Haight Ashbury began to fill with dead foetuses.

Another new world, another Sertsey, was springing up nearer home. My clever and industrious wife became pregnant. She spent the later weeks in our cottage garden with her pretty feet up. When her time came, in August of 1967, she underwent a long and painful labour. I remained with her at the hospital. In those days, to have husbands present was a new thing, a token of the liberalising times. It means something to witness the courage of women, and to see another human life emerge – the biological version of Sertsey.

Timothy was born on the 5th, a sizable infant, a little ruffled from his long journey. If one was from another planet, it would not be easy to recognise the relationship between the adult and that little red withered symbiote, a new-born child. But everyone was pleased by Tim's arrival, including Clive, then twelve years old, and including Tim himself.

Margaret's dear dad, Jack Manson, died in 1968, a true Scot, generous and humorous. He had been at first reluctant to accept me as a potential son-in-law with, it seemed, scant prospects, but we were soon on good terms. He had asked me only to keep his daughter's name out of the mess of the separation and the hotly contested divorce proceedings. That I had tried to do. Jack was tremendously kind to my children, and at least lived to admire his grandson.

Those happy years had a spring to their step. We made a lot of friends and excitements. A shelf full of photographic albums holds a visual record of those days. Like memory itself, some of our photographs are fading. But the album pages show why we left Jasmine. That delightful home proved too complicated a place in which to bring up children; there were too many stairs down which to take a tumble.

'Heath House' was different, upright as a grenadier, with a Regency air of rectitude. It stood aloof from the village of Southmoor, behind its field, at the end of a long drive of limes. Its pencil-box lines had been mitigated by a porch with Corinthian pillars and a huge bay window, round which honeysuckle romped. Its appearance in consequence was half-severe, half-jocund. Perfect to suit my divided nature.

On the whole, we lived a rewarding life, unlike half of the rest of the planet. Before coming to the *Oxford Mail*, Margaret had been secretary in the office of Sir David Webster, General Administrator of Covent Garden Opera House. It sounded like an exciting life yet, after some years, she had left it without regret. She took up painting – we both dabbled – and went to evening class. The woman who acted as the class life model then came to work for us. She was German and seemed, as far as Margaret could make out, to have arrived in England more or less by accident after the war.

It was not the first rather serious accident to afflict Mrs Thomas. She had walked barefoot from Moscow to Munich, only to discover she had left her handbag behind; so she had walked back to Moscow to collect it – as far as I could understand from her still-fractured English.

Charlotte was born in March 1969, eighteen months after her brother. Unlike Tim, she slipped into the world in the twinkling of an eye. When the maternity ward phoned me, I dashed to the hospital. Margaret was already walking down the ward, smiling her dear smile. Our new baby slept peacefully after her endeavours.

How fortunate I was, how blessed! Clive and Wendy stayed with us for part of every school holiday. The alchemy of our relationships is something to wonder at. Margaret never tried to play mother to them; she simply loved them and looked after them. They, for their part, never took against her. Gradually the bond between us all grew firmer.

Nor were Clive and Wendy jealous when Tim was born. Clive seemed interested to have a half-brother. When Margaret was expecting again, Wendy told her that this time it must be a girl for her; Margaret said she would try to oblige. Her time grew nearer . . . Lo and behold, she delivered Charlotte punctually on Wendy's tenth birthday. Everyone – rightly! – regarded it as a miracle.

In no time, we were carting all four of them off to the Continent for holidays. And in no time, it seemed, they were growing up. The four children have always been close, as adolescents, as adults.

Heath House was marked on the One Inch Ordnance Survey maps. When Tim was old enough to run about, Concorde was making its preliminary sub-sonic flights from Fairford, Gloucestershire. We were sure it always used our chimneys as a landmark by which to make its turn. There the great metal bird was, only a half-mile up, and Tim would rush into the garden calling 'Concorde, Concorde!'.

'Concorde' was among the first words he spoke.

In our living room in Heath House, we viewed the Moon through binoculars, low above the trees as the sun was setting. At the same time, we watched the Moon-landing on the television. It was July 1969. We shared this strange double vision with the children. Billions of people all round the world were following this event, wondering what to make of it.

The astronauts involved with the space programme knew what to make of it. They were at the cutting edge of technology, but their view of Earth from space turned several of them towards mysticism. For the Russian cosmonauts, it was no different. One of them, Aleksei Leonov, became a celebrated space artist. Leonov spoke of seeing the Earth from space 'so touchingly alone'. He referred to it as 'our home that must be defended like a holy relic'. Or so the translation goes; one wonders if he did not speak of that view of Earth as 'a holy ikon'.

During that period, there was some expectation that that ikon, far removed from the old school globe of Earth with all its political divisions, would make us all better animals, more able to conserve our precious resources. The ecological movement gathered strength, but most of us went on in our old unregenerate ways.

Distinguished science fiction writers, such as Kim Stanley Robinson, write of terraforming Mars so that mankind can live there. I find myself surprisingly green on the Red Planet question. Are we really to turn it into a poor imitation of Earth, and build our shoddy cities under its shrivelled sun? No doubt the military will keep a powerful custody over it. Who will live there? Indentured labour? Tibetans? Perhaps we are as yet not at an advanced enough state of consciousness to take over another planet – there merely to repeat the mistakes we have made on this one.

Mars could be kept as a sort of Everest or Ayers Rock in the sky. One will go there to wander, to watch, to meditate, to be alone, and to turn into a person with wider horizons, oriented on Mars and the mysterious universe rather than on our present god, Mammon.

It's a puzzle to see why understanding of the wholeness of terrestrial life, and its uniqueness – the wonder of it all – has not gripped our populations like a fever, in the way they are gripped by football and the question of which side gets a ball in a net. An ever larger percentage of Earth's population lives in cities, blind to the world of nature. Concrete does not grow on trees.

In James Lovelock's 1979 book on Gaia, he remarks on the effects of citification, and how it makes it difficult for information to flow from explorer to academic – and thence to the general public. He says, 'Those of us who go forth in ships or travel to remote places . . . are few in number compared with those who choose to work in city-based institutions and universities.'

The same applies to literature. One might speculate whether it is not living close together in cities that has greatly encouraged human concentration on sex and sexuality. A concatenation of pheromones? Dramatically increased urbanisation has led to overemphasis on human relationships; whereas, in so-called primitive cultures the emphasis is generally on human relationships with natural things, with the habitat.

One example among many of how the habitat became fouled up by commerce took place in the sixties. Timber imports from Canada, bringing in fatal bugs, changed the English landscape greatly for the worse.

Dutch Elm Disease struck while we were in Southmoor. We had to have dozens of trees felled. Much of my time was spent in our field with an axe, hacking up great trunks, or splitting them with metal chocks and a sledgehammer. We had a large fireplace. Two cylinders of the slow-burning elm would stay alight all night, gently smouldering.

Many long conversations unscrolled by that hearth.

Margaret and I found that we were regarded in Southmoor as 'pillars of local society', who lived in 'the big house'. This was not at all our image of ourselves; it spoke rather of the longings of Southmoor's inhabitants for a clear social structure that had collapsed.

Few people had been born in the village. Southmoor is one of those semi-rural aggregations which spring up outside towns. Ten miles beyond Oxford, new housing estates had been built; houses and rates were cheaper than in town. Southmoor was pleasanter than many such villages, since it retained an old core, although the old order had faded away. Along the main road to Faringdon were strung a post office, a shop, a fruit stall and a bakery, as well as two pubs. But it did not function as a unit, as villages once did, if only because most people had cars and worked elsewhere. The dull remained on the estates, the upwardly mobile moved on to better things in town.

There was no religious core to Southmoor. Local people were not religious; nor did we bring our children up religiously – a fact I have regretted since. The social centre of the village was the primary school, an excellent institution, run by Graham Platt. Dances, fêtes and similar lay occasions were held at the school.

At this period in our lives I was invited to open garden fêtes in neighbouring villages, Longworth and Hinton Waldrist. Let's hope it did no harm. I wore a Panama hat for such occasions, amused to think of myself as a parody of my grandfather, old H. H. Respectability was thrust on an unlikely candidate.

About the time Charlotte was born, I received an invitation from Brazil to attend a science fiction conference in Rio de Janeiro, in connection with the Third Annual International Film Festival. These festivals received rather a hostile press, the government of Brazil being then in bad odour; but the organisers of the SF branch were of a different ilk. It happened that various members of the festival's treasury discovered they were SF fans. They secretly sent out invitations to their favourite writers, syphoning off the odd million *cruzeiros* to pay for it, waiting until later to announce the conference locally.

Margaret insisted I should attend. It was a rare opportunity. This showed her generosity of spirit; perhaps, too, she was content to be left alone with her lovely baby girl, to dream and exude milk. She had a mother's help and cleaner to assist her.

Ahead of the plane was a new day in all its glory. A panorama of vast ecstatic mountains unfolded, into whose ravines, upon whose peaks, one peered eagerly for sight of men or cities. But these great pinnacles lit by an awakened sun, the blue rift valleys, the enormous cliffs – all were built from vapour. Nature's fevered imagination had conceived, far above the Earth, another world, more grandiose and more transient, concealing the continent of South America below.

As rococo as the most Catholic of Brazilian churches, the clouds parted as we descended, to reveal a landscape of sea and city spread beneath.

Rio was as bizarre as could be wished. Ballard and I stepped off the

Aerolineas Argentinas plane, to be hit by the heat as by a sweaty sock in the face.

'Ah!' said we, and breathed deep. The tropics once more, in all their diversity . . .

We were established in a hotel overlooking Copacobana Beach. Harry was there, enjoying the heat and excitement, and numerous amusing Americans. On the more naive end of the spectrum was one Sam Moskowitz, a man who wrote about science fiction. He was observed in the searing heat wearing a long serge overcoat, reaching almost to his ankles.

'Sam, why are you wearing that thing?'

'I don't want it stolen, do I?'

We were too courteous to enquire what such a garment was doing so close to Capricorn.

My friend Colin Steele in Canberra has just sent me an extract from the John Wyndham Archive catalogue. Wyndham, then at the height of his fame, was invited to Rio. The report says, 'He has declined to attend for fear of staying up drinking at all hours – which he remarks is more suited to the likes of Brian Aldiss and Kingsley Amis.'

It's true John was a one sherry man. Rio is not a one sherry town.

While aged SF films were shown in the centre of Rio, and distinguished writers such as A. E. van Vogt and Robert Bloch trotted diligently to see Whale's *Frankenstein* for the umpteenth time (but here dubbed into Portuguese with English subtitles), a crowd of us stayed with the beach and its passing show. Frederik Pohl, Robert Sheckley, Harry, Jimmy and I used the Bar Bolero as a base, overlooking those long beaches.

At night, when the ice-cream sellers had shed their wares, the humped beaches were given over to the delights of miscegenation.

All along the front were posters reproducing the face, pale, tranquil, free of lust, northern hemispheric, of Neda Arneric, Jugoslav starlet, toast of the festival. Every lamp standard bore that ikon of purity and innocence, a reminder of something beyond Rio's reality.

The Bar Bolero became a brothel at night, like most of the rest of Rio. During the day, it served *cachasa* in tall glasses, and an excellent *fejoada*, cousin to the *pasulj* we ate in Jugland, relation by marriage to the noble French *cassoulet*. We drank, we ate, we smoked Mexican Saddle with Bob Sheckley. Sheckley had a reason to celebrate. The movie *La Decima Vittima* (*The Tenth Victim*) was being shown as part of the festival. This stylish but empty film is based on Sheckley's clever story, 'The Seventh Victim', and stars Marcello Mastroianni and Ursula Andress.

Once I persuaded someone to drive me through the sprawling, roaring suburbs and *favelas*, up into the hills to the jungle beyond. Hardly virgin jungle, but jungle nevertheless. I took a turn within the majesty of that organism, rejoicing to have the great trees overhead. Returning to the car, I saw Jesus Christ in concrete, his arms outstretched on Corcovado, overlooking the city and the sea.

We were taken every evening to a party at one of the foreign embassies. Here was great splendour. A surplus of exotic fruit, food, drink of every variety, and women the same. The entertainment was lavish; we could have been caught in a time warp, back to ancient Egypt. Up the walls of those putative castles climbed, cascaded, plants that Margaret nursed at home in small pots. Amid all the chatter, dancing and music, one tune was the hit of the festival – Mary Hopkin singing 'Those Were the Days'. Even there, where eudemonism reigned, and the Present riotously prevailed, the serpent of nostalgia entered.

On the closing night of the festival, we were invited to a grand banquet. It was to seat one thousand people in a grand hall. After the feast, the most spectacular costumes from the Mardi Gras were to be displayed, with music. Black limousines carried us through the sweltering traffic-choked gasoline-sweet lanes to this great event. We arrived at the hall. Two thousand people had turned up, all bearing tickets. Some artful dodger had been forging them and making extra pocket-money.

Eventually, a typically generous Rio arrangement was arrived at. All two thousand people were let in and all two thousand were fed. It was a triumph of disorganisation.

Fred Pohl and I decided that there should be more international festivals. Sitting at the Bar Bolero, discussing the matter, I recalled that in the following year Expo 70 would be held in Kyoto, Japan. We agreed that when we returned to our respective homes in New York and Oxford, we would try to arrange something.

Fred returned to various problems, some involving *Galaxy*, the magazine of which he was editor. The matter rested with me. Although I had begun to correspond with people all over the world, I knew the name of only one person in Japan. He was Endo Hiroya, an avid reader of science fiction. So I wrote to him.

Endo achieved everything. How he managed it I never understood, but in no time invitations were issued to the First International Symposium of Science Fiction. The symposium was to be held in Tokyo, Toyota Motor City, Kyoto and elsewhere.

This was a more serious event than the Rio splurge. Here for the first time, writers from Capitalist and Communist blocs faced each other. Not least, we all had to face the same exacting Japanese timetable:

1.00 Arrive Toyota Motor City
1.05 Checking into hotel
1.15 Free time
1.25 Lunch in hotel
1.45 Assemble at coach
1.55 Arrive at conference hall
2.00 Conference begins

The conference held particular significance for me. Here for the first time, I was facing the old enemy, the Japanese, on their home ground. They knew something of my history.

'Did you shoot any of us?'

'No, and you did not shoot any of me.' So the peace treaty was signed, with good humour on either side . . .

Our forums were arranged with two long tables. At one table sat the Westerners, Fred Pohl, Arthur C. Clarke, who had taken up residence in Sri Lanka, Judy Merril, who had recently taken on Canadian nationality, and I. We sat around in jeans and casual gear. Facing us at the other table were Russians in formal double-breasted suits, among them their leader, Vasili Zakharchenko, his secretary, Irina, Eremi Parnov, and Julius Kagarlitsky, a man of learning and wit with whom I became very friendly; we met later on numerous occasions. Vasili was the editor of a popular sci-ence/science fiction magazine that sold two million copies every month – a figure which made his Western counterparts groan with envy.

In the middle of the two opposing teams sat or stood a number of Japanese writers and translators, led by Sakyo Komatsu, whose novel, *Japan Sinks*, had sold as many copies as an issue of Vasili's magazine.

One notable evening in Toyota Motor City, I was ushered into a room with two of the Russian team where, over several bottles of vodka, I was treated to a lecture/confessional on how bad every-thing was in Moscow (and worse elsewhere in Russia), and how anti-Semitism was rife. The terrible stories went on into the night, injustice piling on injustice, villainy on villainy.

Western Europe and the USA held conflicting views of the nature of the Soviet system. Although I had read Robert Conquest's en-lightening work *The Great Terror* (1968) and similar books, I was well aware of the propaganda war being waged on both sides of the Iron Curtain. Like millions of other people, I inclined to the view that Capitalist and Communist systems in some respects were mirror images of each other. This notion was encouraged by the development of the Space Race; in Prague, we bought our first packet of Apollo/Soyuz cigarettes, the packaging of which played on the mirror image idea.

Besides – well, in the words of Chesterton's poem, 'We knew no harm of Bonaparte and plenty of the Squire'. We exercised the healthy habit of doubting what our own governments told us.

After that grim, vodka-riddled night of confession in Toyota Motor City, there was never again room for doubt that the government of the Soviet Union indeed operated like a large-scale criminal organisation. Later, in the early seventies, a British publisher began publishing the translation of Alexander Solzhenitsyn's heroic work *The Gulag Archipelago*, in three volumes. It confirmed all one's beliefs – and Conquest's researches – in a striking way.

Solzhenitsyn's is the finest book to be published this century. What can stand beside it in its record of human suffering and endur-ance? Solzhenitsyn occasionally rounds on the reader in the West, saying, If you think I am condemning Russians or the Communist system, remember that I am also speaking of the human race, and of *you*. It is a great-hearted work; thinking of it, I am ashamed to continue this story of one individual.

It happened I had met Julius Kagarlitsky some years before the Japanese symposium. Margaret and I were invited to a dinner in London to celebrate the centenary of the birth of H. G. Wells. J. B. Priestley and his wife Jacquetta Hawkes were present, and spoke. Everyone knew Priestley, while his wife, an archaeologist of distinction, had written a prose tone poem, *A Land*, of impressive strength and learning.

Priestley had said to me earlier, in his ripe Yorkshire voice, 'Better write the sort of stuff you write well than dilute any further the already thin stew of English Letters.'

After the speeches and homages to Wells, I wandered about the place trying to find a drink of some sort. Down a dim side-passage, I spied a light. I came on a butler's pantry. There stood the celebrated Russian author of a book on Wells, bottle to his lips, elbow resting on a convenient shelf, the more easily to get the wine down his throat. Julius and I shared that bottle of Jugoslav wine – as later we were to share other bottles. He was an amusing man, with a wonderful downbeat Jewish humour.

Some years on, when I visited the Soviet Union, Kagarlitsky was the only one of my Russian friends courageous enough to visit me at my hotel. I admired and valued him, and portrayed him as Rugorsky in *Life in the West*.

XXI

The Writer

We generally pause and then begin to laugh, at the ridiculous figures human beings cut in struggling all their might and main against a destiny which forces millions and millions of enormous planets on their way and against which all struggling is useless.

Claire Clairmont, in a letter

T he year was 1965. I was Guest of Honour at the 23rd World Science Fiction Convention, held in London. The hall was full of people listening to my speech. At the far end of the hall were tall double doors. They opened while I was talking and a little stocky man entered. Above his head he held a piece of paper I recognised as a telegram. It promised him, and by proxy me, thirty million dollars.

The changes in my life were exhilarating. The decade whose opening saw me pretty well down and out, saw me Guest of Honour at this major event in the SF calendar, and as an established writer, comfortably married, by its end. Hardly a meteoric rise, but certainly a turn for the better. The dreadful anhedonia that had pursued me all my life was now held at arm's length.

A restlessness which was part of my nature still showed, but I had now become incontrovertibly English. Despite which I continued to persevere in that peculiar American-dominated form of literature, SF.

As I had always done, I was writing short stories. Short stories are toys (as long as we regard toys as serious objects). Grandma Wilson did better than she knew when she presented me with the short stories of Saki (H. H. Munro) for my twelfth birthday. Betty and I were addicted to Saki.

I have always had a taste for the labyrinthine glooms of the Danish story-teller, Isak Dinesen. There were Maupassant, John O'Hara, the slices of life of Katherine Mansfield, also V. S. Pritchett and William Trevor, and many splendid story-tellers in the SF mode, such as Pohl, Sheckley and William Tenn. Tenn in particular, with his acerbic fables, makes one regret that the barrier which cordons off SF prevents many people from enjoying such writing; but we all suffer for our prejudices.

A phenomenological view of life suits me. My stories are fragments of a fragmentary life. To make one's fortune, to become really popular, one does not write short stories. But I never sought such goals, or not ardently. My ambition was to write well – which is much harder than becoming popular.

A Cambridge paper praised one of my early collections, *The Canopy of Time*, saying the stories showed 'Classical perfection'. It would never do. That was not quite what I wanted, so my stories began to grow wilder, less dependent on the tread of logic, more amenable to the flight of fancy.

Popularity in the sixties changed my perception of the world to some extent. I appeared on television shows, judged fashion contests with Barbara Attenborough, contributed to fashionable magazines. Our friend Dr Chris Evans edited a special number of *Harper's Bazaar* in 1969; for him I wrote a short story entitled, 'Super-Toys Last All Summer Long'.

Like the chap in James Joyce's poem, who heard an army charging across the land, my ears detected the thunder of many changes – which is not to say that they were shaking 'their long green hair'. The romantic stance of exile, misfit, had suited me. Now I was a family man, with a few bob to jingle in my pocket. I was a taxpayer, a man with a wife who knew the names of garden plants.

I had gained a place in society, if not in the garden. Whether I wanted that position was another matter, but the suspicion remains that position is something worth having. It affords some protection if mankind is an aberrant species, mad nor'nor'west like Hamlet, as Charles Berg suspected. It is hard to see how the history of the twentieth century can be explained in any other way than by supposing we have only an insecure hold on the branch; or – to be less abstract about it – how the behaviour of almost everyone at Framlingham College when I knew it, from senior master, 'Rupe', downwards, could be otherwise accounted for.

The madness of that telegram, held aloft during my speech at the

World Convention, was of a more benevolent kind. The telegram brought an early brush with the film industry, an industry – because of its inescapable mingling of many arts with money-making – famous for creative insanity.

The holder of the telegram, Cy Endfield, came up to me after my speech, as I was autographing copies of my books.

'Now will you work with me?'

Cy was an admirer of *Hothouse*. More importantly, he was the man who had recently directed *Zulu*, one of the great successes of British cinema, a film that can be watched over and over again. Cy was an American who had taken up residence in England after falling foul of Joe McCarthy and the Un-American Activities brigade. He mainly made B features, shot cheaply in Spain. At one time, he offered Harry and me a job; we were to live in one of his houses over the winter, writing scripts under his direction. We never went. I might have lost Margaret by so doing.

Cy formed a production company with Stanley Baker, who plays the lead in *Zulu*, triumphing over Michael Caine as well as Chief Butalezi. Baker was rather a gloomy old thing. I enjoyed several rides round London with Baker and Cy in their Rolls-Royce, and cannot recall Baker ever saying a word. Cy talked all the time.

The impetus of *Zulu* enabled Cy to think about his great love, SF. He had learnt that Stanley Kubrick was filming *2001* from an Arthur C. Clarke story at Kubrick's usual leisurely pace, and hoped to make a space epic to forestall or ride along with the anticipated success of the Kubrick movie. I was to be his down-market Arthur Clarke. Thus what Cy had in mind for us, and what I was refusing to get involved with, was a thing called *Only Tomorrow*, set in part on the Moon.

Cy's scheme was for one of those conspiracy stories, choked with big sinister organisations that are out to take over the world; his future was to be little more than window-dressing for a sixties-type plot. Whereas Kubrick, that warped genius, was planning something infinitely more imaginative: the future as mysterious in itself, unknowable, inscrutable to those of us stuck down here in next century's past.

But there was that telegram! It came from the film mogul, Joseph E. Levine, promising Cy a thirty-million-dollar floor for his next movie, *Only Tomorrow*. I had resisted Cy's idea so far; Levine's was harder to withstand.

'Let's go,' I told Cy.

We went.

It was then I began to wish I was still writing short stories. I took orders willingly enough in the Army, seeing the necessity for it. Taking orders for writing was another matter. Cy was great fun. I used to go round to his flat in Thurloe Square, only to find he had chänged his mind from last time we met. In any case, the plot of *Only Tomorrow* being fairly silly was the more easily changed. Where there is no fundamental logic, the illogical passes muster.

'We don't want to have the secret agent find this alien organisation by going out back of this Chinese laundry. Why not have the organisation right out front, with big and glamorous offices smack on Fifth Avenue?'

'Look, let's scrub New York entirely, okay? It all takes place in San Francisco instead. I can rent the Golden Gate Bridge by the hour. I want to have a Rolls-Royce die on it.'

'This bit on the Moon – it's never going to work. I've been thinking. Let's move the whole damn thing to Mars.'

In the middle of all the rewriting these second thoughts entailed, another script swam like a new planet into Cy's ken. He was not one to stand still for long, silent upon a peak in Darien or anywhere else. He pressed upon me a tattered carbon copy, dog-eared from its passage through many despairing hands. It was the story of the building of the Taj Mahal. Cy became excited.

'This is crap, Brian. But you've been to India. We'll rewrite this fast and make it an epic, something big. A passionate love affair, a nation being born. How d'you feel about six months back in India?'

The answer to that was *Not Much*. However, one is never adverse to hearing a film producer talking big; it is their role in life. But at that point, another Endfield epic emerged from post-production, again starring Stanley Baker. Margaret and I were invited to a private theatre, all velvet and plush, in Kensington.

Ameliorating drinks, with those seaweed-flavoured crackers then briefly, but not briefly enough, in fashion, were followed by an early first viewing. The theatre, like a little porn cinema, seated no more than thirty people. Among those thirty were big names in the movie world, none of which I knew; but Cy made sure I was introduced to Joseph E. Levine's personal representative.

The name of the new movie was *Sands of the Kalahari*. Stanley Baker wrestled with one of those baboons with which the Kalahari is infested. By the time the baboon was laid out for the count, Levine's money carpet for *Only Tomorrow* had been whisked from under Cy's feet. You could hear it go, tinkling icicles on its way to the door.

This was neither the first nor the last of my marginal affrays with the film world. They're hard to resist. It's something new and – in my case – always desperate to attempt. The thing is to keep working hopefully, without at all hoping overmuch, while understanding that one is involved in the modern equivalent of a great play by John Webster or Cyril Tourneur, bound to end in tragedy and death by stabbing in a velvet-hung room. I admired Cy. He never had another success like *Zulu*. But then, how many people could have achieved the sheer organisation and artistry that went into the film?

The sixties set me free. Not only was there my new marriage, and the knowledge that Margaret was as kind and loving to my two older children as to her own babes: water was irrigating the gardens of the Alhambra, money was filtering through the system at last. I loved her; she was an untroubled ocean, so I took her for granted.

We contracted the habit of travelling, from Italy and Switzerland to Scandinavia. Wherever we went, we found friends whose friendship has in many cases continued to the present. Through the clarity of Margaret's character and the formal arrangements of Heath House, it was possible to feel that life itself had clarity and joy.

And we went up to Scotland, that admirable place, the home of Margaret's parents and forebears. I had often thought of marrying a Scottish lady. Now I had my wish granted. While our children were small, we rented a gaunt manse on the shores of Loch Awe. Wendy came with us, Clive visited us. A bleak place it was, raining most of the time, and the loch as deep and dark as a parson's bedsock. But Tim had his new computer, so we were fine, and played many games of Chucky Egg.

While I was at work on *Barefoot in the Head*, the psychedelic factor had a strange effect on me. I began to see the New Animal in our peaceful garden. Margaret suggested I took a break and wrote something else.

Acting on her advice, I began a long novel rather paralleling my schooldays and Army life, about an obstreperous youth called Horatio Stubbs. 'Horatio' after Bill's brother, Nelson, who had died at school, and Stubbs because it is an impertinent-sounding English name, as in the painter, George Stubbs, and the William Stubbs, who wrote a constitutional history of England. Despite these connections, Stubbs, with its suggestion of smoked cigarette butts, is a heartily working-class name.

When I was half-way through this story, I saw how the prolegomenon, the story of Stubbs' sexual awakening, had an appealing configuration, a boomerang shape, an aesthetic curve of its own.

Though brief, this part of the story would stand alone. We called it *The Hand-Reared Boy* and despatched the manuscript to Hilary. After which, I continued with *Barefoot*.

Hilary Rubinstein now showed his mettle. He persisted with my manuscript. Because of its strong language and frankness in dealing with sex and masturbation, it was turned down by many publishers. By nineties' standards, it is a mild book; by fifties' standards it would have been unpublishable, except in Denmark.

Finally, at Hilary's twelfth attempt, Hutchinson accepted the novel. A contract was signed, the due processes of publication began. Eventually I received proofs of the Hutchinson edition, and a pull of their five-colour jacket. It was then I went to Rio.

When I returned home, Hilary's face was more than usually rubicund. Trouble waited. The managing director of Hutchinson, Robert Lusty, a well-known name in the book trade, had read the Stubbs proofs. Staggering out of his office, red-faced, he had said, 'We can't publish this filth. How could I defend this in court? It's pornography!'

Lusty was a big ungainly sort of chap with a large face of a sort of heraldic red – gules. Perhaps he had once been floridly handsome. Now he was a big ungainly Deaf Person. He wished to reject *Hand-Reared Boy*. One of Hutchinson's young editors, Michael Dempsey, who died an awful death while still young, rang me, to say they were fighting my corner. He sounded very brave – until he asked a fatal question. 'Volume Two won't be as bad, will it?'

'Stubbs will be in the Army. It will get much worse.'

I knew it was time to take the novel elsewhere.

Hilary accompanied me to see his brother Michael, a lawyer in Lincoln's Inn Fields. 'We shall sue,' said Michael firmly.

Lusty had a great rival in Tony Godwin, one of publishing's so-called 'whizz kids', then working at Weidenfeld & Nicolson, a thriving and independent company. Somehow, news of Lusty's decision reached the pages of *The Times*. The story also carried my photo, with word that I was suing Hutchinson for breach of contract. Within twenty-four hours Tony Godwin had bought the novel.

In his autobiography, *Bound to be Read*, Bob Lusty – he was by then Sir Robert – has an apocryphal version on this little drama.

When Weidenfeld published *Hand-Reared Boy* in January of 1970, the book was already well known. Never before had so many people read a book before publication. John Osborne declared it the first contemporary novel he had been interested in buying; from which I noted he did not say he had actually bought it. But he did go to

the extent of trying to film it, with his wife, Jill Bennett, playing
the school matron, and Lindsay Anderson as director.

Hand-Reared Boy sailed immediately to the top of the best-seller
list. I have no compulsive interest in such lists, but you become more
interested when you are on it and upwardly inclined. Slowly, week by
week, another book with a boring title began to climb to the top spot.
Eventually, it knocked Stubbs off his perch and Stubbs disappeared.
But *The Godfather* remained, sunning itself on its lonely peak.

The next portion of the Stubbs saga was *A Soldier Erect*. Here was
Stubbs in India and Burma, randy as ever. This novel too went to the
top of the best-seller list. I account it one of my better novels – and not
only because of the sex. As far as I know, it is the only novel dealing
with life in the ranks during the war against the Japs in Burma.

While these books were current, I saw people reading them on
buses in hardcover, a rare sight. Once I sat next to a young woman
on the tube who was avidly turning the pages of *Hand-Reared Boy*.

Among other amusements at this time was my stint as a film
critic and an occasional reviewer of art exhibitions and such like
for the *Guardian*. The *Guardian* was hospitable at this period, since
many reporters and sub-editors on the *Oxford Mail* had graduated
to the London paper, including a good friend of ours, Mike McNay.
From my enthusiastic column I wrote for the *Guardian*, much was
to follow.

Looking into a small engagement diary for 1971, I find it choked
with events. And over one page, writ large, the comment, 'Fool's
Paradise'. If it was so, this fool was lucky to have lived in it. We had
remained friendly with a few Brazilians. The Brazilian Ambassador
to Britain was a debonair and cultivated man. I lunched with him
on several occasions and Margaret and I attended a splendid party
aboard a Brazilian battleship which moored on the Port of London.
We dined in Oxford colleges. I appeared on television to comment
on the Apollo moonwalk; it may have been one small step for Neil
Armstrong, but it was a leg-up for me.

I opened Kidlington Branch Library and Karel Thole's art exhibition in Amsterdam. Hoping to awaken in Clive and Wendy an
enjoyment of opera, we took them to a performance of Offenbach's
gorgeous *Tales of Hoffmann*. We thought that the fantasy elements,
the mechanical doll, for instance, and the tuneful music, would
delight them. They hated it.

Richard II at Stratford fared better: Clive was studying it for O
Levels, which he sat that year with six passes. The week he was
actually sitting his exams in Carisbrooke, Isle of Wight was the

week of a London event, long remembered, the Bedford Square Book Bang, the inspiration of Tom Maschler. It rained all through the day I was there.

We went to see some first proofs of G. B. Tiepolo's *Capriccii* at Agnew's, but could not afford one. James and Judy Blish were newly over from the States. Jim, a learned crusty character, is best remembered for his 'Cities in Flight' series and the novel *A Case of Conscience*. We took them to see Brecht's *Galileo* enacted in the gardens of St John's College, and other similar events. He was a devout anglophile.

That summer of '71, Margaret and I took all four children to Denmark for a holiday. Just before we left England, John W. Campbell died. From 1939 until after the publication of Harry Harrison's *Deathworld* series in the early sixties, Campbell's magazine provided the most deeply enjoyable reading I ever came across. *Analog* (formerly *Astounding*) had become formulaic and more empty of psychological content. But Campbell had still presided there, the editor longest in the chair of any pulp magazine, a lonely stone face on Easter Island, gazing towards the future, the future he wanted.

Yet that brilliant holiday in the north of Denmark was enough to dispel gloom. All the children were in fine fettle. We took them round Hamlet's castle, Helsingor. We went on the ferry to Sweden, on an excursion we all remember. We drove to a remote house owned by the Swedish academic and writer, Sven Christer Swahn, on a peninsula near Karlskrona.

The house was called Swan's House and had been built in 1901 by an elder Swahn and a woodman. The two men had cleared the headland and constructed the house, together with most of the furniture in it, from the timber they had felled. To sleep in it was to sleep in a beached galleon, creaking comfortably as it sailed through the years. But Jannick Storm, Sven, and a visiting friend, the media culture-vulture, Goran Bengtson, and I slept little. We sat by an oil lamp through the dawdling shades of twilight, talking and drinking, eating bread and cheese and olives. Mainly we drank Goran's Calvados, of which he had brought an unending supply. On the night Goran arrived, he played us a two-hour interview he had recently taped with Philip K. Dick in California, the writer we greatly admired.

Ah, happy nights, with the lukewarm Swedish dark beyond the wide windows! Occasionally, one of the ladies would appear in her nightdress, and bring us coffee in pewter mugs, or simply place a hand on our shoulders to tell us we were crazy, as if giving us a blessing. Outside, not a light showed. There was no Moon. Tall reeds rustled at the water margin.

In the morning, to cure our hangovers, we would strip naked to swim. We ran along Sven's little wooden quay, Clive with us, and dived yelling into the Baltic. Even in summer, that post-glacial sea froze the gonads. We were out of the water as soon as in, to towel ourselves down, laughing and hearty, before sitting down to join the ladies at a generous breakfast.

Charlotte Mew has a poem, 'In the Fields', which ends

> Can I believe there is a heavenlier world than this?
> And if there is
> Will the strange heart of any everlasting thing
> Bring me these dreams that take my breath away?

The Danish house in Zeeland in which we lived for a fortnight was Jannick Storm's romantic wooden house in Hornbaek. As Sven had translated *Hothouse*, so Jannick had the more formidable task of translating *Barefoot*. The weather in Zeeland that season was irreproachable, and the beach was Topless, to Clive's delight. In Jannick's garden, Wendy and I and the others had a splendid water fight, soaking ourselves and everyone else, who ran screaming from the scene.

We enjoyed the pleasantness of Denmark, its good plain food, its amiable people. Later, Clive, looking for work, slaved in a restaurant kitchen in Århus, and formed a less favourable impression. But that holiday was the happiest of times. We strolled on the stony beach of Gilleleje, near Hornbaek, where Soren Kierkegaard had walked, to gaze across the Kattegat, thinking his sombre thoughts. As far as I understand Kierkegaard's thought – moving a mere pace along his extensive metaphysical beach – he suffered from a depression of spirit which he mistook for God's voice. In 1840, Kierkegaard broke off his engagement to a lady called Regine Olsen, presumably the queen of his heart. He had decided that God had elected him to be a writer, and to be a writer was incompatible with the married state. So much for Kierkegaard. At Gilleleje, where he had walked wifeless, I bought my wife a pretty shirt which she wore for many a year.

By this date, I had met many writers. Few qualified as 'real writers'. Few took writing as seriously as did Kierkegaard! They wanted only to be rich, or to be famous, or preferably both.

One week, among my collection of novels for review, I received a novel of a rare kind, published by Peter Owen. It was foreign in flavour, sparse in wordage. Its title was *Ice*, by Anna Kavan. *Ice* qualifies marginally as SF, of the kind Kafka wrote and I desired to do. I voted it my best SF novel of 1967. Peter Owen, was pleased. I got drinking with him and his wife and through Peter I went to meet Anna.

Anna Kavan was lame, tired, in her late sixties or so. She lived in a house she had designed herself, just off the Bayswater Road in West London. One ascended to her living quarters up a stair encased in glass, outside which greenery raged within the smallest of stone-walled gardens, a small slice of an imprisoned Botswana, or maybe Gondwana.

We talked and talked. Like most authors, Anna had fallen in her old age on hard times, and was delighted to be regarded as a science fiction writer. She said it made her feel modern again: she was of that generation for whom 'modern', 'fast' and 'pneumatic' were key words of praise. Imagine, in the late sixties, it was a fashionable thing to be a science fiction writer! She admired *Probability A*, praising 'the way the people in the book remained always apart'. An unamiable person was making herself amiable.

Seated on her brown sofa, surrounded by plants and paintings, she held forth to please me. She had found a new audience.

And I was better at listening then than I am now.

Of course I read her books. *Asylum Piece* speaks of mental instability. The theme, along with that of addiction, drifts below the surface of her writings, a medusa waiting to sting. Sometimes there are metaphors: *My Soul in China*, the title of a novella, is a way of speaking of personal isolation.

Anna was a dedicated writer. She never enjoyed any great success; her books contain a strangeness and coldness which guarantee her status as a cult figure, but are caviar to the general. She worked with Cyril Connolly on *Horizon*, and had a grudge against him because he would not help her in some way or other.

What I did not know when we met was that she had a heroin habit of many years standing – thirty and more; she is a successor to the great Thomas De Quincey. I was so taken up with *Ice* that I tried to persuade my publisher at Doubleday to interest himself in the novel.

Margaret and I had a plan to induce Anna away from her painting-lined nest, to stay with us at Heath House for the weekend. She wrote me a little note to say that she was feeling too inhuman to move. Forty-eight hours later, she was dead.

After a week or two, I received a letter from Larry – Lawrence P. Ashmead – the benevolent editor at Doubleday, to say he would publish *Ice* if I wrote an introduction to it. It was a piece of good news that never reached Anna's ear.

Good as his word, Larry published *Ice* in hardcover with my introduction. Later, a paperback edition appeared in the States. In 1985, Norton reprinted it in hardcover. *Ice* has happily not disappeared from view.

Anna had a good friend in the novelist Rhys Davis. He wrote a novel about her, *Honeysuckle Girl*. As her executor, he had much to sort out. He seemed to live a life as complex as Anna's, being, I was given to understand, bisexual. He was then living in a hotel room near Russell Square, and from under his bed in the cramped room, he dragged a trunk full of paintings, gouache and watercolour. All were Anna's work. He presented me with three pictures. They hang framed in my study. One shows two naked bodies, conjoined but without a head, another a similar scene, where the bodies float in space, and the third a woman slumped naked in a chair, having masturbated or given herself a shot. They are uncompromising gouaches. Too bad that an exhibition was not arranged. The public never knew what a good minor painter Anna was.

Margaret became tired of my obsession with Anna Kavan. What I admired about her was the fact that she was so individual and non-commercial. With success, I felt I was becoming too commercial; it ran against a basic socialist instinct. Failure – we know it – is a bitch, success a bitch goddess.

Certainly my imagination was captured by that hard little crippled woman. Her ghost appears in several stories I wrote in the early seventies. In 1990, I edited and introduced a selection of Anna's writings, *My Madness*, for Picador Classics. It quickly sold out.

Supposing she had taken not to the ice, the heroin, but to something less self-indulgent, prayer? Would she have been a happier woman, a better writer? The questions are unanswerable.

To learn more of Anna and of Rhys seemed to me important, but a lassitude was overtaking me. It was perplexing. I tried to escape it by travel.

In 1971, Margaret and I took Tim and Charlotte on a trip to the States, eventually arriving in San Diego, California, where Harry and Joan Harrison were then living – 'up to our necks in a knee-high culture', as either Harry or I put it. We used to drink in his local bar, the Saddle Bar. One window was smashed; jealousy had caused the shattered pane. The previous week, a Naval man had shot another guy, snatching a Beretta with which to do it out of his girlfriend's bra.

Harry got the LA science fiction crowd down to meet us, Van Vogt, Forry Ackerman, Bob Bloch, Poul Anderson and others. Todd Harrison launched a rocket to celebrate the event. Up, up it went, in the general direction of Jupiter, to land on the roof of the Saddle Bar.

We drove into Mexico in Harry's camper, complete with Harrison and Aldiss kids, across chemical deserts, to arrive in San Felipe. San Felipe is the end of the line, the end of time, sagging into the Gulf of California. You're back in the Permian, at oven temperatures. Old men who once worked for the US postal services now prop themselves up at the counter of Bernie's Bar to get pissed by nine in the morning, quietly, regularly. They rest up in trailers that will never move again. The desert is punctuated by imported wooden ranch houses lying at odd angles, like ships beached when the Aral Sea dried. They have been trucked from the US and set down at random. No plumbing, no electricity, no fences. Just the surreal sorrow of displacement.

The waters of the Gulf are chill. Harry and I threw ourselves into the waves yelling, threw ourselves out screaming. The women laughed.

Aged pelicans with rusty feathers took off, low across the sea from the reef, wings creaking like wicker chairs. Thanks to all the chemicals pouring down the Colorado River, emptying into the Gulf, their eggs scrambled when they sat them. The long good-night was coming. We rode mules into the hills, ate turtle, drank tequila, sang long into the night. The desert sky was wide and high, like the prairie sky in Texas.

The desert was a quilt comprising sands and chemicals of varying malignance. Ornate crosses by the roadside marked accident sites; those who died there were buried there.

Harry and I drove up to Los Angeles and drank in the London Brasserie with Ray Bradbury. Ray was a generous host but, knowing the waitress, he managed to get many more glasses of a little green drink – absinthe? – than we, to Harry's envy.

We were somewhere driving on a sideroad. A young woman in T-shirt and shorts was running along the road, trying to stop vehicles, and clearly a danger to everyone involved. She looked frantic.

'Hang on,' I told Harry. 'See what the fuck she wants. Looks as if she's in a lot of trouble.'

Harry slowed. The girl clutched at his door handle. On her face, youth and debilitation fought in every furrow.

'Let me in, fuck you,' she said. 'The CIA are after me!'

Harry accelerated.

'Let's hope the fuck they get her,' he said.

For the first time, I seemed at a loss in my writing, without direction. I put together a space opera with songs in it, called *The Eighty-Minute Hour*. It was written in spasms as we moved about North America, talking, drinking, flying, driving, although much of it takes place in Middle Europe and Jugoslavia, where I reinstated the old Pannonian Sea. Names of seas are always more evocative than the names of the continents they abut: Timor, Euxine, Aegean, Red, Dead, Caspian, Tyrrhenian, Baltic and the grand Pacific . . .

This may be as bad a time as any to mention a conundrum which, trivial-seeming in itself, leads to mental confusion. There are many well-authenticated cases of the importance of one's position in the family to which one is born. It was annoying that even at this stage in life, established with a second family of my own, I was uncertain whether I ranked as my parents' first-born or whether I was merely their middle child; and of course for five years – those long, embalmed five years – I had been their only child, *more or less* (since the steel-engraving angel had always been a hovering presence). *No established position!* – the story of my life!

A ridiculous matter for an adult to worry about, but worry I did.

My general puzzlement with life increased at this period, and I embarked on a series of triptychs I called Enigmas. The idea of this label was to signal to readers that I was not playing the game strictly by the regulations.

I had always seen in SF a strong vein of symbolism: merely to write about a future time is to indulge, not necessarily in prediction, but in an idiolect removed from realism, however extensively the methods of realism are used to create a needful degree of plausibility. It has often occurred to me that, just as M. Jourdain in Molière's play exclaims that for more than forty years he has been speaking prose without knowing it, so some SF writers have been symbolists without knowing it.

My two early novels, *Non-Stop* and *Hothouse*, the latter especially, are symbolist novels, but, rather in the manner of M. Jourdain, I was unaware of it at the time . . .

At the time of Anna Kavan's death, I had become more aware as a writer, more conscious of the themes that pave the way for narrative, more conscious of the manner in which meaning lay beyond the words, more conscious that the most self-aware artist may articulate something that perhaps a reader alone will hear. Anna's vision in *Ice* of a disrupted world with the glittering cold closing in, and events becoming sliding panels with hidden continuities, is a transfiguration of her personal world to paper. In the Enigmas, I sought to do something similar. I used word association. In the middle of some other composition, I would stop and write down six or more phrases.

> cloud shaped like a piano
> living without consciousness
> the kapok tree
> Beringia
> waiters whistling as the last bar closes
> light minutes – how far?

These would then form the basis for associative material, shaped into three short related stories. The impulse was particularly strong in the seventies. My last story collection to be published by Faber was *The Moment of Eclipse*, in 1970. When Jonathan Cape published the next collection, *Last Orders and Other Stories*, in 1977, the emphasis was very different, the stories stranger, the Enigmas denser. Reviewing the collection, Angela Carter said that the author was 'singing the science fiction blues with wit and panache'. Thereby, she used a phrase we later employed as a title.

My low mood continued, not at all alleviated by whisky.

Sometimes, driving back home from the *Oxford Mail*, I would stop for a bite to eat at a pub. One day in 1971, I was sitting in a pub in Cothill; an unfriendly pub it was – I chose it for that very reason. I ate alone. There I decided that two jobs were too much – that everything was too much – that I would be a writer only. I would no longer be a literary editor. I had filled that post for twelve years; it sufficed. I resigned. Farewell, conviviality!

When the black mood was finally lifting, I had to go to the doctor for some minor ailment for which he needed a blood sample; he revealed I had contracted hepatitis, undiagnosed until then.

An awful sadness possessed me, a sadness beyond my self. I understood illness as metaphor; indeed, I have a book by Susan Sontag with that very title. Sontag speaks of how much harder it is in advanced industrial societies to come to terms with death. I would say it is much harder to come to terms with life. We understand, as those before us did not, how much existence has gone by, a torrent of existences, in which we are nothing but a speck. Our knowledge of time is like a disease, a TB of the mind?

And once more I felt a sorrow for the human race. The grounds of Heath House still contained, seeded on that original heath before buildings came, one or two tall pines. Ragged and isolated, they stood aloof, like flyblown firs in Tiepolo's etchings. The solid beams of our house, pocked by woodworm, had come from Nelson's Navy when the old wooden walls were broken up after Trafalgar. Beneath our foundations lay deep pure sand without a fossil, sand bequeathed us by a Jurassic ocean, bereft of its primeval shores. The great Berkshire wind blew like a scavenger across our plot, coming down from the White Horse Hills and continuing on, on. The skies toiled towards Wessex, crushing all beneath them, reducing in time whatever time had engendered. We were but an interval, nothing. That well-known verse of Fulke Greville's came to mind:

> Oh wearisome Condition of Humanity!
> Borne under one Law, to another, bound:
> Vainely begot, and yet forbidden vanity,
> Created sicke, commanded to be sound.
> What meaneth Nature by these diverse laws?
> Passion and reason self-division cause . . .

Written early in the seventeenth century, the poem cries out about dilemmas still keeping us company today. How do we differ from Greville, sitting in his wooden room by candle-light, striving to resolve the conundrum of intelligent life by day and bad dreams by night?

Once it had been detected, the hepatitis slunk off like a villain in a melodrama. But *Weltschmertz* is no uncommon thing. As at this chapter's heading, Claire Clairmont, abroad in Pisa in 1832, complains of it in a letter to her half-sister, Mary Shelley: 'Destiny which forces millions and millions of enormous planets on their way and against which all struggling is useless'.

XXII

The Future

'Oughtn't the word "serious" to have an embargo slapped on it? "Serious" ought to mean simply the opposite of "comic", whereas now it means "good", or Literature with a capital L.'
C. S. Lewis in conversation (in *SF Horizons*)

If, as a boy, I had a hero apart from my father, it was Captain Justice. My early forays into oral story-telling in the school dormitory were largely based on the adventures of Captain Justice, whose adventures appeared weekly in the boys' magazine *Modern Boy*. As far as I was concerned, they lit up the 1930s.

Captain Justice and his faithful band lived on an artificial island, Station A, in mid-Atlantic. Justice was called in to solve any global problem too big for the governments of America and Britain to handle. For their time, the Justice stories were fairly high tech. Justice had at his elbow the redoubtable Professor Flaznagel, eccentric but ever inventive. Flaznagel's greatest invention was the Flying Cloud, the mighty airship that became invisible when a certain lever was pulled.

Justice's finest adventure, to my mind, was 'The World in Darkness', when Earth encountered a vast belt of black gas.

The Justice adventures were written by Murray Roberts, the penname of Robert Murray Graydon.

In the eighties, a publisher friend was vaguely interested in producing a Captain Justice Omnibus, containing three of his best adventures, provided I would write an introduction to it. I returned to the tattered little paper volumes, once so much loved. They were ridiculous, lurid in style. They had served their purpose in their time, but that time was over.

The lesson is one critics should remember. Most books are of their time. Only a particular cast of an author's mind, which finds expression in style and subject matter, guarantees a shelf-life beyond one generation.

A novel that has leaped over generations to find new favour and understanding in our time is Mary Shelley's *Frankenstein or, The Modern Prometheus*.

This astonishing novel, published in 1818, was written when Mary Shelley was still in her teens. Mary Shelley's reputation has remarkably revived in the last two decades, but for many years, the novel was regarded merely as horror material and treated as such by Hollywood and Hammer Films. Certainly the theme of composite parts of corpses, brought together and animated to make a new life, is horrific enough; but Mary, in her introduction to the 1831 edition, declares she wished to think of a story 'which would speak to the mysterious fears of our nature'.

She has put her finger on one of the functions of science fiction. The reasons for regarding *Frankenstein* as the first real example of science fiction are argued in the early chapters of *Billion Year Spree* and, more acutely, in David Wingrove's and my revision, *Trillion Year Spree*.

Of course, *Frankenstein* is other things besides SF. As, incidentally, is much good SF, being omnivorous. Much can be done in SF that cannot be done in ordinary novels, though seldom is it done.

One reading of the novel suggests it concerns sensuality and the lack of it: the Alpine setting alone indicates as much. An acute critic – perhaps because he harbours a weird sense of humour – Nicholas Ruddick, of the University of Regina, has spoken in an authoritative paper of 'a special relationship between Aldiss and Mary Shelley'. (His paper is included as an Appendix in *Bury My Heart at W. H. Smith's*. It is as perceptive on me as on *Frankenstein*.)

Of course, Mary's is a dark book, following the example of the novels of her father, William Godwin, *St Leon* (1799) and *Caleb Williams* (1794) in particular. I fancy that both Godwin and his illustrious daughter would have approved the words of Pushkin when he set out to 'lay waste the hearts of men' in his writing.

I have nourished a similar ambition. But because of my divided nature, I have hovered between the darkness of that experiment in Geneva and the improbabilities of Station A.

That division can frequently be detected in SF in general.

However science fiction began, from whatever English roots, it was cautionary by nature. But popular science fiction, achieving escape velocity from pulp magazines, was by contrast American, and rested on the assumption that the future was better than the present, and could be purchased. Although SF is such an integral part of life, involving much thought about the future, I have never been able to persuade myself that what is expensive is necessarily desirable.

I was sitting in a lounge in JFK airport, awaiting a plane that would take me back to England. An American woman sat opposite me, with a daughter, perhaps three years old.

'Look what I can do!' exclaimed the child. She gave a twirl round, almost falling over in the process.

'Why, that's wonderful, Janine!' exclaimed the mother, as though movement itself was news to her. 'When we get home, you must show Daddy what you can do.'

An English mother would have said, 'Come and sit down and don't show off.'

So national characteristics are born.

American SF was always a heartening mixture of disaster and accomplishment. Disaster made exciting reading, but the good guys generally won through and overcame the alien threat.

From the start, the wild element in American SF held great appeal. This was much in evidence in such writers as A. E. Van Vogt, whose *The Weapon Shops of Isher* and *The World of Nul-A* suggested the old magician had had a quick read of Gurdjieff's *All and Anything*, as well as Alfred Korzybski's General Semantics book, *Science and Sanity*, before rushing to his typewriter. Van Vogt's successors included Alfred Bester and Philip K. Dick, who freely admitted Van Vogt's influence.

I knew Bester and I knew Dick. Dick was a wonderful and various man. He had a true humility I found attractive; he teemed with ideas and with humour – which in itself is a kind of idea. Bester was witty, but had no humility. He and I were strolling along Fifth Avenue – he was directing me towards Sardi's, where we would meet the Tin Man of *The Wizard of Oz*, Jack Haley Jr., and the striking Penny Singleton, who played Blondie in the Dagwood radio series – when Alfie said, 'You realise we are the two best SF writers in the world!'

It was a ghastly moment.

Nevertheless, American writers were more fun than their British counterparts, and more ready to be friendly. Frederik Pohl was another writer with whom I became immediately on good terms. The great James Blish was another such.

My first encounters with the British mob were not inspiring.

London fans contacted me after *Non-Stop* was published; or rather, I was approached by a woman who worked in Hanging Sword Passage. She took me to meet a group of people in a pub in Hatton Garden. They were weirdly lowbrow, with the exception of a writer called Sam Youd. One or two were missing a finger. Some of them played pool in a basement.

Sam Youd was bright and spiky. He wrote books under many names for several publishers. As Hilary Sharp he wrote an amusing novel of London literary life, *Felix Walking*. Under another pseudonym he had a detective called Dust; I believe one of the titles was *Dust and the Dear Girls*.

Youd was best known to the SF world and beyond as John Christopher. As John Christopher he wrote the successful *Death of Grass*. This alarming novel was renamed by its New York publisher. It is known in the USA as *No Blade of Grass*, because Janine and her doting mother at JFK think Death is just nasty and silly; and although neither of them reads books, *certainly not science fiction*, they have great influence over cultural mores. Whereas in England there is still a fair chance they would be told to get lost.

English SF conventions at first tended to be drunken routs. 'Humorous lowbrow' would describe the mood of the company. It seemed to me, to my disappointment, to be much of a sub-culture. I would not have cared to escort Mary Shelley to such an affair.

The same description applied to a great extent to the two (British) Nova SF magazines, *New Worlds* and *Science Fantasy*, which did good work and also published some dismal stories of a purely generic nature. Which is to say that they imitated what had gone before. It is noticeable that some writers prefer to be one of a group, rather than to become an individual writer (or, it follows, an individual); they are the enemies of the individual. Small wonder Editor Carnell found first-rate material hard to come by.

Only J. G. Ballard, in those early days, seemed to realise that the future was nothing, nothing but words on paper, a hieroglyph that had to be the best hieroglyph in order to exist at all.

With the coming of the New Wave, IQs rose noticeably. A new age, a new audience. Asa Briggs chaired a conference on the new literature. At conventions, literary questions arose, with panels on 'Oral Traditions in Story-telling' or 'Is Heinlein More than Just Wishful Thinking?' Publishers and literary agents leavened the mass of fans and authors. The smart money moved in with the snappy dressers –

ultimately to destroy that in which they invested. But for a few years – say between 1968 and 1975 – British SF enjoyed an Indian summer, and was condemned in the Houses of Parliament.

In both the United States and the Soviet Union, SF authors could, if they wished, occupy more prominent positions. The Americans became involved with NASA, where almost everyone had grown up reading SF. Soviet SF writers, too, were taken to Baikonur to witness rocket launches, and shown the more exotic engineering feats of their nation.

In England, SF remained stubbonly literary – or maybe sub-literary; an older generation always hopes new things won't catch on. When I was one of the panel of judges for the Booker Prize in 1982, the year that the laurels went to Salman Rushdie's verbose *Midnight's Children*, I saw how things were. Our chairman was Malcolm Bradbury, who admitted to having read some Ballard and the writings of his SF namesake, Ray Bradbury.

One of the most powerful and renowned authors to enter the science fiction field – more committed even than Kingsley Amis and Anthony Burgess – was Doris Lessing. Her *Canopus in Argos: Archives* series opened in 1979 with the brilliant and disturbing *Shikasta*. In 1981, *The Sirian Experiments* appeared. Its wide perspectives, its strategy of having the female protagonist reporting approvingly on what she later perceives to be wrong, made it a strong candidate for the prize (not that Lessing cared about the Booker).

Or so I thought. The other judges had different ideas. But this was *science fiction*, wasn't it? Even if it was by Doris Lessing, it was still SF. I mean, people travelling between planets . . . ?!

I read the judges passages of beauty, argued the metaphorical content of the novel. On the jury panel was a literary lady from the University of York, Hermione Lee. I liked Hermione, liked her spirit, was not particularly put out when she called me a shit. Such is the nature of loftier literary debate. Hermione was the great Rushdie protagonist, enchanted by his pretentiousness. She raised the objection that Doris's book contained no characterisation.

But *The Sirian Experiments* hinges on the chief protagonist's immature judgement; her character is integral to the account, the novel. Nor do I believe that interaction of character can remain the fixed critical mark by which the worth of a novel is decided. Pleasing though it is, Jane Austen's is not the only kind of novel worth writing, as the sonnet is not the only verse form. I held forth to the other jurors. Horse trading was done. So, in the end, *The Sirian Experiments* was grudgingly accorded a place on the short list of six novels.

Midnight's Children won the Booker. I felt it was the kind of book readers would not read – buy but not read. Of course, the Booker has its own lofty aims, which do not necessarily include kowtowing to intelligent popular taste.

Salman Rushdie began his novelist's career with *Grimus*, in 1975. It's a curious mythological performance. The *Sunday Times* held a competition for an unpublished science fiction novel. Arthur C. Clarke, Kingsley and I were the judges. Typescripts flooded in, most of them pretty dire. Among them was *Grimus*, in typescript, submitted by Gollancz, who were intending to publish it. Although its mixture of fantasy and allegory was to neither Kingsley's nor my taste (Arthur was in Colombo and so unable to argue), it did and does contain the forceful Rushdie dynamic. We considered handing it the laurels when Liz Calder (then at Gollancz) withdrew the manuscript from the competition.

What forethought on Liz's part! Supposing *Grimus* had won the competition . . . For then onwards, poor Rushdie would have been branded an SF writer, and nobody – including, presumably, the Ayatollah and Hermione Lee – would ever have heard of him again!

There were several novels on our reading list that I greatly enjoyed and felt should have some kind of acknowledgement. Off my own bat, I dropped a word to several authors, among them Brian Moore, Piers Paul Read and William Boyd. Boyd's *An Ice-Cream War* had been submitted to the Booker jury.

A response soon came from Boyd. He and his wife Susan were actually living in Moreton Road, only a few doors from the Aldisses. Sharing a relish for literary life and white wine, we immediately became friends.

In 1996, the University of Oxford, lagging behind the example of Harvard and Princeton and other places, awarded Doris an honorary degree. Margaret and I were there to witness the ceremony. The honour, of course, was for her lifetime's work. We told ourselves it was for *Shikasta* and *The Fifth Child*.

Her encomium, given in Latin, did not miss the chance to be snooty about SF: 'She even took on the immense task of inventing a whole world, a genre of writing in which we expect to find nothing serious, which hardly accedes to the truths of ordinary life.'

Bloody university! Bloody ordinary life! To the ordinary everything is ordinary.

In July 1988, in Houston Grand Opera, the première was held of *The Making of the Representative for Planet 8*, based on Doris's *Canopus* series novel of the same name. The music was by Philip Glass, with libretto by Lessing. Margaret and I went to see the opera when it came to the London Coliseum in the same year.

From where we sat, we noticed Doris sitting in the stalls, some rows back, quiet, unannounced . . . And this was her splendid opera from her splendid novel!

(This is not quite the first SF opera. If Janacek's *The Makropoulos Case*, with its three-hundred-year-old heroine, taken from Karel Capek's play, *The Makropoulos Secret*, does not qualify as SF, there is also Karl-Birger Blomdahl's opera, *Aniara*, based on Harry Martinson's epic poem of the same name, featuring a voyage to the planet Mars.)

Publisher led, the SF fashion has grown for trilogies and related series set on post-Tolkienian planets. I satirised this kind of dreamworld-building in the opening chapters of *Forgotten Life*. The dreamworlds have become so commercialised that they are sometimes farmed out to additional writers, in the manner of *Star Trek* novels.

As to having a true vision of the future, that is hard work. Kubrick's film *2001* rests on the reasonable assumption that the future is inscrutable to us. But we have to assume knowledge to gain knowledge. Conjuring the future is at least as sane an activity as conjuring up the past – and to my mind more exciting.

'The future' is predominantly a state of mind, much as Italy and Spain served as states of mind to Jacobean dramatists like Webster and Tourneur. Not all SF writers see it this way: but I hope yet to persuade them.

Aided and abetted by Isaac Asimov, American writers at one time tended to justify their writing, mainly of a Campbellian sort, by claiming that it predicted the future. Then came Chaos Theory. As soon as I heard of it, I thought of a Ray Bradbury story 'The Sound of Thunder'. A tourist time-traveller steps from the pre-scribed path in a long bygone jungle. In so doing, he treads on a butterfly. Returning to his present, he finds the USA he knew utterly changed. The story – by a writer regarded as being non-scientific – is a wonderful prodromic dream of the function of Chaos.

If, indeed, Chaos functions as billed, then it is clearly impossible to make any rational prediction of the future. Of course, you may have a lucky shot if you write enough. If two out of a hundred bullets you fire at a barn door should hit the target, you still do not earn the title of marksman.

The use of the future is as a metaphor for today, a mirror in which we see an abstract of our present hopes and woes. Maybe life itself is a metaphor. Who knows?

I speak as a writer of a generation later than Asimov. I do not mean to denigrate him. A dottiness typical of ageing science fiction writers descended on him, in that he wished to wrench all his novels into one unified conceptual universe. They were forced into a Procrustean bedlam. In a more metaphysical way, Moorcock shows a similar tendency. But Asimov's early 'Foundation' stories stimulated my intellect when I read them serially in Campbell's *Astounding*.

Asimov's popularity towered above Heinlein's and even Arthur Clarke's. According to the reliable *Pocket World in Figures* published every year by the *Economist*, Asimov, in the 1993 edition, was the tenth most translated author in the world. By 1995, he had moved up to eighth position. Transitory figures above him in the listing, such as Gorbachev, have slipped into obscurity.

Incidentally, Shakespeare slides from fourteenth to nineteenth in the same period. Secure in fourth position in both instances is Jules Verne. Such figures testify to the enduring worldwide popularity of SF – which may be why the literary critics of the stratosphere are so scornful of the mode. Others abide the question; Shakespeare is free . . .

Perhaps the pseudo-science of futurology owed something to Asimov's concept of 'psycho-history', a way of predicting the future in large chunks.

The Hudson Institute, under the aegis of Hermann Kahn, was set up to give futurology a cutting edge. Many of its predictions soon became suspect. For instance, the idea of clearing the Amazon basin and creating a series of Great Lakes, with fishing villages on their shores, as if South America could become a sort of mirror image of North, was greeted with derision by growing green movements in the seventies.

American writers have always been ingenious at depicting varied futures. Now, with the advancement of the sciences related to space, they are forced to move farther and farther out into the galaxy, and hence more remote from human affairs. America has never shared the British upper-crust suspicion of technology – think of it, all those railways and motorways rushing through our great estates! William Morris has had more influence in England than in the States; perhaps they don't even go for his wallpaper.

Recent evidence of these prejudices emerged when P. D. James, ordinarily a bestselling middle-class thriller writer, set *The Children of Men* in the future. The novel was published in 1992. I began to worry about her novel when readers wrote to me, pointing out many similarities between James' novel and my own *Greybeard*. *Greybeard* was published by the same publisher, edited by the same editor as James', thirty years earlier; it was still in print, easily accessible. Indeed, the points of similarity between the novels are astonishing. Both centre around Oxford and are set in a world, dominated by a tinpot dictator, where there are no more children.

I wrote *Greybeard* in distress, when I was bereft of my children. It is an example of a personal dilemma dramatised as a universal woe. But, in the case of Baroness James (as she has become), I felt that ideas were free, and did nothing about the matter. That is, until the Baroness's article appeared in Waterstone's New Books, a sort of trade paper in which the retail chain puffed the books their shops were pushing. Dump-bins everywhere were full of *The Children of Men*. And in Waterstone's columns the Baroness was 'at pains to point out that she does not think of the novel as sci-fi' (note opprobrious term).

'I didn't want any technology intruding. Science fiction to me is about alien worlds full of robots and machines. This isn't an alien world; it's England. They have computers, and drugs to prolong life, but these things are not shown.'

As once the legs of the grand piano were decently concealed . . . ?

At that I had to write in protest against such a condescending, misrepresentation of facts. Well . . . I had a civil enough letter back. But the close similarities – and the misrepresentations – remain unexplained.

But how much more open and intellectual is the attitude of Doris Lessing. She might have lost some of her older audience by launching into the space fiction series which began with *Shikasta*, but she certainly won an enthusiastic new readership.

Because a knowledge of rejection has always beset the SF field, its members closed ranks. The state of play was likened to being in Israel, with hostile nations all around about, perhaps because so many SF writers are Jewish. We were confined to the SF ghetto.

An enterprising Luxembourgeois, Hugo Gernsback, emigrated to the States early this century and set up shop as an inventor – of batteries, wireless sets and hearing aids (the 'Osophone') among other things. He published SF stories in his technical magazines and in April of 1926 launched *Amazing Stories*, the first magazine to be devoted entirely to SF. This daring innovation was a great success. Later he published such magazines as *Science Wonder Stories*.

Perhaps his smartest move was to institute the bunch of support-ers of the genre known as fans. Fandom has influenced the course of SF in a way quite out of proportion to its numbers.

Gernsback certainly generated a trend. Gradually, more provoca-tive, less parochial lights began to shine. Magazines of science fiction and its kissing kin, fantasy, appeared, among them the respected *Astounding*. When the so-called paperback revolution came in the fifties, a death knell sounded for the pulp empire. Not for SF. Magazine SF continued, and still continues, a haven for the short story, even when other pulp magazines had disappeared. The authoritative history of the magazines, edited by Marshall Tymn, lists 279 English-language magazines. Of this thriving sub-culture, regular literary critics know nothing.

An SF magazine typically carried long stories and short, with perhaps a serialised novel. It would have an editorial and several departments, such as a science fact article and letters from readers. The whole SF culture at one time revolved about such magazines, in particular around those of greatest excellence. Fan groups sprang up everywhere.

Although I was never a fan, I responded to the landscape of the magazines, the stories arbitrarily placed cheek-by-jowl rep-resenting a jumble of opinions, together making a cryptic state-ment of doubt and subversion. Things were going to change, for better or worse. The wild writings of A. E. Van Vogt, innocu-ous seeming in retrospect, were subversive messages at the time – holding every meaning alien to the received opinions of East Dereham.

Fans ran conventions and conferences, to which they invited the stars, the writers themselves.

There was and is an immense reservoir of humour and good humour in fandom. The magisterial Clute/Nicholls encyclopaedia estimates that currently some 500 fanzines are in production. Fanzines are fans' own (non-professional) magazines, the publica-tion of which entails much labour and no profit (one of the sources of pride within the field has been the way in which all of us have worked simply for love, not money, at various times).

The isolation of the field, and in particular of early fans in the States, found its voice in the title of one long-running fanzine, *The Cry of the Nameless*. The historian of fanzines, Rob Hanson, tells me that *Cry of the Nameless* was first issued by an SF group in Seattle in

1950. It ran to 187 issues – by which time the fans involved were no longer nameless.

Bruce Gillespie in Australia has been producing elegant fanzines for many years, such as *SF Commentary* and *Metaphysical Review*. Many SF writers have contributed to Bruce's magazines, including Ursula le Guin, Stanislav Lem, Philip K. Dick and me, as well as such natives as Damien Broderick and Peter Nicholls.

Fans were the ones who established such early publishing enterprises as Arkham House in 1939 and Gnome Press in 1948, which reprinted magazine fiction within the more durable dignity of hardcovers.

As Harold Wilson used to say of the Labour Party, when covering up internal disagreements, SF is a 'broad church'. Anyone interested can contribute something, a joke, a fanzine, a cartoon, a fancy dress, a splinter of knowledge or speculation, or just a LOC (letter of comment) in a gestalt of creativity.

So it was that this culture brought itself up by its own bootstraps, against opposition and indifference. Some of the fans, shedding their spots, went into research or technology or, later, into computing. Others went into agenting, editing and publishing, rather in the way that secret agents used to be smuggled into Berlin. In one way or another, SF shaped our futures.

An example would be Malcolm Edwards. Onc Monday morning after a heavy weekend with Kingsley Amis, when Kingsley was living in Cambridge, I staggered on to Cambridge railway station. There, on the platform, was someone I would have to talk to, a young anthropology student, M. Edwards, whom I had met as a member of the Cambridge University SF Club. The Club had been founded two years earlier by Charles Platt, who was later to become part of the *New Worlds* movement.

We climbed aboard the train together – to keep ourselves much amused throughout the whole journey, hangovers forgotten.

Malcolm read manuscripts for Gollancz as I had once done for Faber and other publishers. Later, he joined Gollancz as an editor, and while there saved my bacon.

Billion Year Spree, despite a fancy title which enshrines what I feel about generic SF, can be seen as a precursor of a new development in the SF world: the study of it as a contemporary form of literature. Such was its success that its publishers, Weidenfeld & Nicolson, asked me in 1985 to update it.

The previous years had seen such expansion in the field that one could no longer read everything. (Between 1973 and 1986, the two publication dates, over half the science fiction ever written had been published.) I enlisted the aid of a feisty friend, David Wingrove, and between us we accumulated an enormous manuscript, wonderfully full of discovery and disclosures.

But our editor at Weidenfeld had changed. No longer was Faith Evans there, with her discerning eye. Instead, a young lady sat in the editor's chair, wielding a new literary theory. She wrote to say that my sentences were too short for such a long book; or perhaps, for I forget, it was that my book was too short for such long sentences. Precisely the kind of handicap from which Henry James and Marcel Proust suffered throughout their writing careers.

There came a more valid objection from the lady. David and I had written more words than the contract stipulated. A third of the book must be cut.

This pronouncement arrived on a Thursday. I immediately phoned Malcolm at Gollancz; he knew about our book, having given us helpful advice. He went round to David's house, borrowed a copy of the manuscript, read it – and rang on the Saturday morning to say he would publish it as it stood at Gollancz, if we withdrew the book from Weidenfeld.

As good as done.

On Monday, I received the Gollancz contract and rang Weidenfeld to say goodbye. There was much cheering in the Wingrovian and Aldissian households, and at Gollancz's offices.

Probably over at Weidenfeld's, too.

The length of the sentences proved not too great a problem. *Trillion Year Spree* won a Hugo Award at the 1986 World Convention in Brighton.

Malcolm was to prove a searching, sensitive editor on *Forgotten Life* and *Remembrance Day* in particular. He ascended to the heights in HarperCollins UK, where he controlled much of the fiction list. In 1997, he moved on to Orion.

Most readers of SF never go near conferences and conventions. The fans who attend such affairs – a small percentage of the readership – tend to conform to the manners of the ghetto. T-shirts and sweatshirts bear cryptic messages understood only by the faithful: '42 or maybe 42.02'. They may cover their chests with badges from past conventions, like old soldiers' campaign medals. Similar adornments are popular, the now-vanished 'beanie' being an example. At large American conventions, some fans may go about dressed in costume for days on end, toting swords or space-blasters.

It's *fun*. They're *having fun* . . .

I have been to many conventions and enjoyed most of them. Harry and I were regular stars during the sixties and seventies, and have become co-Presidents of the Birmingham SF Group, the most hospitable and long-established group in Britain. Following my 1965 stint, I was Guest of Honour a second time (a rare honour) at the 37th SF World Convention in Brighton in 1979. By then, Margaret's and my children were either growing up or grown. They too were able to enjoy that amazing, amusing event.

Writers who refuse to tread the conformist path, like David Wingrove with his *Chung Kuo* series, meet with the same hostility I did, almost a generation ago. Others, like the brilliant and convivial Iain M. Banks, are of a new cast, popular as both SF and contemporary novelist. Which is as it should be.

As for the critics and scholars, from whom one hoped so much, among them are voices still exhorting us to read or reread the lamentable effusions of Hugo Gernsback and the early juvenile stories of the twenties. Being unable to learn the Captain Justice lesson, they do science fiction itself damage. They cause both the nonconformist and the creative to despise the field.

Short stories are a valuable part of SF. They have a music quite apart from the novel, never mind the pachydermous trilogy. Whereas the backbone of a novel is theory, whatever its flesh, a short story can be made from no more than a glance, a sound, the effect of light on water, an encounter, a kiss or lack of it. (The author of *The Story of an African Farm*, Olive Schreiner, wrote in a letter to a friend, 'One would barter all one's knowledge for one kiss.' There's a short story! – Henry James constructed a whole novel on less.)

Critics pay little attention to such small-seeming matters as stories. The more reason to be grateful to those who have made any extended comment, such as K. V. Bailey and the American scholars, Gary K. Wolfe and Philip E. Smith II. But these men have read widely beyond the margins of science fiction.

There is, in SF's thrust towards the future, inevitably something of – it was Wells' great word – a conspiracy. We need each other. It is a new thing in common culture, the art not of the masses but the like-minded, the poor man's intellectualism, the shifting metaphor, the cryptic. I saw it as a new kind of art form or maybe anti-art form (in Duchamps' sense), breaking with tradition, yet strengthened by its own traditions. SF had to be the only way of saying certain things.

Well, I'm older now. Maybe. Maybe not.

Perceptions change.

SF today flounders like an old whale in a miry sea of commercial fantasy. Which is about as subversive as an Eton collar.

By the time *Trillion* was published, literary studies of the field abounded. Such useful books as Neil Barron's *Anatomy of Wonder* provided an excellent overview of the matter, unrivalled until the Nicholls/Clute *Encyclopedia of Science Fiction* appeared in 1979, revised and enlarged in 1993.

Another treasure trove of a book is *Science Fiction, Fantasy, and Weird Fiction Magazines* (1985), edited by Marshall B. Tymn and Mike Ashley.

Marshall became a great friend. He was a dominant personality in the early years of the IAFA, the International Association for the Fantastic in the Arts. This organisation made me welcome. Dr Robert Collins invited me to their third annual conference in Florida in 1982, when I was in pretty low water. Recognition from American scholars came as a tonic.

The conference has taken place in March every year since then. It is now situated in Fort Lauderdale, and has accorded me the unique position of Permanent Special Guest (that 'permanent' is relative is hardly worth mentioning on a T-shirt). I have been able to invite several Guests of Honour over the years – Roger Corman for one, who came with his wife and was a winning presence. The modest Robert Holdstock also shone. Tom Shippey, long overdue, made a triumphal appearance in 1996. But perhaps the greatest success was Doris Lessing. Her sharp good humour pleased everyone. The feminists came to celebrate her, but Doris belongs in nobody's camp.

The IAFA meetings are well planned. Papers are intensive, and feature a wide variety of subjects. Unfortunately, scholars are generally rather bad at presenting their papers, so that close attention is required. But I like all that. The scholars go deep on a subject but are not widely read – which is where those of us such as John Clute, Charlie Brown, David Hartwell, Tom Shippey and others come in.

Occasionally, a paper is delivered on an aspect of my writing. That's a challenge for both subject and scholar. People like Nicholas Ruddick, Charles Platt and Dede Weil have been perceptive – a quality in short supply everywhere.

Dede, Gary Wolfe, Charlie Brown, Ursula Kiausch, and the current president, William Senior, have become particularly close friends. Just for a few days of one week every year, we live in an intense high-pressure world that excludes outsiders.

Of course one takes SF seriously. But the SF fraternity enjoys itself more, and is more sociable, than any other type of writing fraternity. Along with the proletarian beers go discussions of who owns the sea bed, whether there is water locked under the surface of Europa, and whether nanotechnology will improve medicine and the human lot. Dooms and Utopias jostle with gossip about others in the field.

In England too, academia did not entirely turn its back on the future. Even in the University of Oxford, with its long traditions of learning, signs of renewal were present. Professor Tom Shippey, at St John's College, tutored the first ever student in SF. The student was Colin Greenland, I was the external examiner for his PhD.

While Colin was at Oxford, I was of some assistance to the SF Foundation. The Foundation was a first tentative step towards bringing SF into the British educational system, the brainchild of George Hay. I was always at odds with George. He wanted SF to be an educational tool, whereas I wanted it to be poetry, literature; but the SF Foundation is one of his successes.

I was the prime mover in getting the Arts Council to give the Foundation a grant, to fund a writer in residence. The Arts Council, in the person of Charles Osborne, persuaded me to be one of the interviewers of the four or five interviewees for the post. I dreaded the task, since it entailed having to decide between candidates, all of whom I knew and liked.

In the event, there was no competition. The least egotistical man got the job; by common consent, it was Greenland. I suffered much from this decision, from the enmity of the envious and egotistical chap who failed, and who, with his pet hornet wife, attacked my good name. But Greenland proved an excellent choice. He worked hard, and produced a fine piece of research, a scholarly book based on his PhD, *The Entropy Exhibition: Michael Moorcock and the UK 'New Wave'*. Colin has since become a successful and idiosyncratic writer of space opera.

The SF Foundation is now housed within Liverpool University where, under Andy Sawyer, it has taken on new life.

Supposing you write about the future, then you can't be serious, can you? That's an attitude often met with. It can lead to feelings of persecution.

Paranoid this may be, but proof continually shows up, not least in the coverage the media gives conventions and the silence the *haute cuisine* literary world maintains. To give an instance. We held a Philip K. Dick conference in Epping Forest some years ago, some of which later transferred to the Arts Council. There were lectures, discussions, forums and two plays, Geoff Ryman's and mine. It was a stimulating weekend.

Towards its conclusion, a young man came to me with a question. He had been sent by the Features editor of the *Independent* to cover the event and write a mocking piece about it. However, he had become interested in what he heard and saw, had found those attending were not loonies, and had bought a Dick novel from the bookstall which he thought brilliant. What was he to do?

There seemed to be only one piece of advice to give. He had to report events as he found them. Would that put his job at risk? He did not know.

His piece appeared in the *Independent*. It made the whole weekend sound childish and silly, of course referring to SF as 'scifi'.

The reporter phoned me that evening. He was miserable. He had risen to the challenge and written an honest piece, reporting the conference fairly. However, the Features editor had changed his copy without consulting him, to make fun of the event.

I said, 'Do me a favour. Write me a report of this editorial interference, giving the facts. Withhold your own name if you like. I want to use this piece of evidence.'

He failed to do so, and I did not hear from him again. But I have not forgotten that piece of journalistic dishonesty of which he and SF were victims.

Living in Oxford, I came to know C. S. Lewis, a charismatic man and renowned figure. He was kind and tolerant where I was concerned, commenting on my early stories and recommending *Hothouse* to his friend J. R. R. Tolkien. Tolkien was also pleasant, and wrote twice to me about my novel in eulogistic terms. It was unusual for any member of the University to know of, never mind read, science fiction; but Lewis and Tolkien were distinguished and learned men. Lewis and I founded the Oxford University Speculative Fiction group, which met regularly, often at my house in Marston Street.

Always at my elbow, as it were, was the great old University, the enemy of the frivolous. It could not be by accident that, of all England's cities, I had come from North Devon to this unforgiving place, among whose living monuments I walked every day.

Through Oxford have passed several distinguished writers of fantasy, not merely those I have mentioned, such as Lewis and Tolkien and Lancelyn Green, but also Charles Williams, Oscar Wilde, Max Beerbohm, Aldous Huxley and others.

*   *   *

For many years I had the good fortune to be in the hands of three of the best editors and publishers of their day. Firstly, Charles Monteith of Faber & Faber, who so lavishly and eruditely entertained his authors at All Souls. Then the enthusiastic Tom Maschler at Jonathan Cape, who supported such enterprises as the Helliconia novels, and, almost concurrently, the 'whizz kid', Tony Godwin at Weidenfeld & Nicolson, who published the sexy Horatio Stubbs novels and *Billion Year Spree* with such flair. When the air in the book world was growing chillier, another publisher cast in the Monteith mould, Christopher Sinclair-Stevenson, published my selection of poems, *At the Caligula Hotel*. These were formidable men, who worked with brio and relished merit. They did not omnivorously like or dislike SF novels and stories: they simply enjoyed whatever they found good.

As with my publishers, so with my literary agents. I avoided those who dealt primarily with SF, although after I joined Hilary Rubinstein at A. P. Watt, other SF writers followed me.

As for my American agent, I was at a loss after having to buy my way out of Scott Meredith's Agency. I got on a train for Paddington one day, and there was Giles Gordon, formidable literary agent, sometime publisher, author of at least one excellent book. I told him my problem.

'There's just the agent for you in my office at present,' Giles said. 'It's a she – Robin Straus.'

In London, I was ushered into the presence of a scrubbed and pretty young woman (5ft. 3in.) who had never heard of me. She did not greatly want to take me on her list of clients. If I would send her a book or two of mine, she would see how she felt about it. Maybe yes, maybe no. All this and more was said as demurely as such dreadful things can be said.

An excellent start, I thought, marginally amused.

Robin liked the books, and from thence forward we have got on like the proverbial house on fire.

Through Robin, I have now found an American publisher who cares about my work, Gordon van Gelder of St Martin's Press. A writer should seek to publish, of course; he should not necessarily expect to prosper.

Science fiction may meet with many numb responses, but it has flourished and inspired people. The long-running television series, *Star Trek*, survived only through the concerted efforts of fans. It was no coincidence that in 1976 the first experimental NASA space shuttle to lift off was christened *Enterprise*, after Captain Kirk's ship. Since then, *Star Trek* has gone into movies, spawned an industry, become a legend – providing the same excitement for a media-wise generation as the space opera of 'Doc' E. E. Smith did for readers in their grandfathers' day.

Within the span of a generation, SF has developed from a minor cult to be an integral part of the future. It is splendid to have played a part it.

XXIII

At Large and Leisure

He murmured with a smile, 'Time is forever dividing itself towards innumerable futures and in one of them I am your enemy.'

Jorge Luis Borges:
The Garden of Forking Paths

The confrontation between East and West continued. Nuclear weapons stockpiled until there were enough of them to blow up the entire solar system.

All Charles Berg's theories of human insanity seemed to be confirmed. We were several apples short of the Tree of Knowledge.

Yet ordinary life continued. Our children grew and rejoiced in their youth. Having to start again from scratch at the age of forty, I was intent on building security for my precious new wife and family. I wanted a reputation, if only because that now seemed possible. And, after the lost years, I thirsted – my various personae thirsted – for experience, hepatitis or no hepatitis. Opportunities seemed to present themselves like magic.

I was always up in London, broadcasting, doing something with the Arts Council, hobnobbing with friends, agents and publishers. I wrote a book about Margaret's and my daily life against a background of world events, *The Shape of Further Things*. So life is: the pleasant details of ordinary family existence set against the abrasive motion of historical processes.

When Arthur C. Clarke wrote from Sri Lanka to tell me of all the important events in which he was taking part, I wrote back telling him that Margaret and I had just bought a pound of sausages in Abingdon. I'm sure Arthur appreciated that only by some miraculous dispensation had Margaret, Abingdon and the sausages been spared from destruction.

Further Things was a book that brought a great number of letters from readers (strange that *Hand-Reared Boy* had produced no correspondence). It included speculations about computers and human dreaming which are now dated. However, if computers were still fairly novel, so was the discovery of REM sleep. Every new invention or discovery provokes a new line of thought which time will deflect into more truthful channels. Besides, I had been to the National Computer Laboratory with Dr Chris Evans. Chris was a charismatic character, very much a sixties type, ideas shooting off him like seeds from a gorse bush.

Among his friends, and tangentially mine, was Kit Pedler, a scientist and powerful artist, who also wrote SF. Kit's best-known novel was *Mutant 59: The Plastic Eater*. I used to dine with Chris, Kit, Kit's wife, Kit's pal, Gerry David, and Arthur Bourne, who has something to do with *Dr Who*. Kit also associated with several scientists who appeared regularly on television, as Kit and I did. It was a high-tide kind of time, when we were free to move.

Kit worried about the hazards inseparably involved in technological progress. Gerry and Kit enjoyed success with their BBC TV series *Doomwatch*, which ran for three seasons in the early seventies. *Doomwatch* was SF that dealt with serious subjects of contemporary interest. Among the excellent actors was a new face – Robert Powell's, later to be seen as Christ. He got himself killed at the end of the first series, to everyone's amazement and distress. On the third day he rose to act again.

Both Kit Pedler and Chris Evans died in the eighties.

I had been drawn into other literary circles, and came to know writers of various kinds. I gave talks and readings here and there – once at Harrow with an under-confident Margaret Drabble (very pleasant and human) and an over-confident Ted Hughes (now Poet Laureate).

On another occasion, Margaret and I were guests at a literary convention at Thornbury, near Bristol. We stayed in a house with the other guest speaker, Roald Dahl and his wife, the husky-voiced American actress Patricia Neal (excellent when playing opposite Paul Newman in Martin Ritt's film, *Hud*).

Dahl was an irritating man. When we were on stage together, a woman in the audience asked us what was the most boring book we had ever read – such was the level of debate . . . Dahl jumped to his feet and began raving against Solzhenitsyn's *Gulag Archipelago*.

I was angry, and, in my turn, said that Solzhenitsyn's work was probably the greatest book of our century, though intended for adults. Dahl and I were not on speaking terms after that.

Harry and I collaborated on various anthologies, as well as producing some of our own. Gradually, I was drawn into the writing of criticism. With a publisher friend, Tom Boardman, Harry and I ran a short-lived magazine of criticism, *SF Horizons*, to which such people as James Blish, C. S. Lewis, Robert Conquest and William Burroughs contributed. In my mind was always the thought that enthusiasm far outpaced critical attention in the science fiction field.

In that journal, I published the first article in defence of J. G. Ballard, 'The Wounded Land'. SF was just beginning to be taught in American universities and colleges. An academic friend in Fullerton, California, Willis McNelly, reprinted my article in his book *SF: The Other Side of Realism* (1971).

If I am to be remembered at all within the science fiction field, I suppose it will not be for my fiction, but for my history, *Billion Year Spree*, received with such hostility at first, and some indulgence since.

The troops opposing my history were unclear about what kind of battle they were fighting. Some of the so-called historians of the field were quite capable of claiming, on the one hand, that Homer was an SF/fantasy writer – not to mention chaps like Dante and the author of the *Epic of Gilgamesh* – and, on the other hand, that Hugo Gernsback was The Father of Science Fiction. (With more legitimacy, H. G. Wells has also been hailed as The Father of Science Fiction.) Gernsback was merely the Young Pretender.

In fact, magazine science fiction had a much longer and, it must be said, less ignoble tradition in Europe than in Britain and America. The Swiss-Austrian-German magazine *Der Orchideengarten* published fifty-four issues between 1919 and 1921. It published stories by such as Villiers de l'Isle Adam, Poe, Capek, Kipling and Wells. *Hugin* was Swedish, and published eighty-six issues before dying in 1920. It published Verne and Kurd Lasswitz, and glorified the wonders of the future.

Gernsback's magazines, which flourished to a modest degree, paid no attention to literary aspects, and laid emphasis on the importance of prophesy. European science fiction inclined more towards satire and surrealism, *à la* de l'Isle Adam. These differences of emphasis have remained.

It happened that while I was writing *Billion Year Spree*, chapter by slow chapter, another book appeared in which Isaac Asimov annointed John W. Campbell with the title Father of Science Fiction. All this absurdity had to be cleared away. If I was to go on writing SF – and after the ill-natured reception of *Probability A* and *Barefoot*, I was in some doubt about that – I felt the whole tangled matter should be cleared up. To pretend one was in some way a direct descendant of mighty Homer was too pretentious for words; nor did I wish to be identified with the jejune outpourings of Gernsback's magazines.

Happily, as I soldiered on, a naughty and fruitful thought came to me.

Verne, Wells, Gernsback, Campbell . . . what was this obsessive Freudian quest for a father figure? I considered Gernsback, who dominated the little SF world for so long, a disaster; the other three men I venerated. But . . . how about a mother figure?

The question to ask was – and in the early seventies, no one had fruitfully confronted the question – what was SF's central concern? The answer now seems fairly clear. It is about power, power in several guises, and mankind's usurpation of powers that previously belonged to Nature or to God. Ever since the days of classical Greece, there had been tales of men (always men, never women) being taken to the Moon by one means or another, by angels or migratory geese. While such tales clearly bore a relationship to the fantastic side of SF, it is idle to claim them as SF, since they do not concern 'the conquest of space'. Such is the argument of *ante hoc, ergo propter hoc*.

So if we understand that SF is a literature of mankind taking, or trying to take, power unto himself, it is obvious we should look not to Ancient Greece or depression America but to the period of the Industrial Revolution. We come by logical steps to the Napoleonic Wars, the Romantics, and to Mary Wollstonecraft Shelley. She wrote two novels which qualify as science fiction, even under narrow definition, *Frankenstein or, The Modern Prometheus* to which reference has already been made, and *The Last Man*.

In *Frankenstein* (1818) we have a man looking for the secret of creating life. Mary Shelley was perfectly clear she was writing a revolutionary novel. The old is rejected, the new embraced. And life is bestowed by science, not by religion or magic. There is no Golem in her book, no god. Power over life and death is now in man's hands. Nor is this any accident. Victor Frankenstein is shown to be capable of repeating his experiment.

Of course, *Frankenstein*, a complex work, is about many things other than science. Mary's orphaned feelings give force and eloquence to the poor rejected creature. But, in this young writer, ha!

– I had found Science Fiction's Mother Figure! My *Spree* is predicated on that belief.

Sportingly offering myself as a target, I concluded *Billion Year Spree* with a prediction. 'Academia and the middle class are moving in on SF and will create order out of chaos.'

The prediction has largely come to pass. Certainly academia grew exponentially. Hard-pressed scholars thankfully accepted *Frankenstein* as the cut-off date for their studies. No longer need they vex students with Homer and Gilgamesh and sundry eighteenth-century bishops who long to get on with Joe Haldeman and Frank Herbert.

As for women scholars and writers, I believe they were encouraged too by a slight dissipation of the fug of male chauvinism in the classroom.

It was Gernsbacking who created the bad odour which still hovers about the name of science fiction, turning a literature of the unknown future into gimmick tales. In England, H. G. Wells' scientific romances were not disbarred from society or literary consideration.

A new order of American writers came along and have righted old wrongs, to give us wonder and delight. In some cases, a reading of Mary Shelley's complex and haunting novel encouraged them.

Billion Year Spree was important for me in other than literary ways. Bill never wished to listen to what I said. As the CO, he had merely to look pained when I spoke, and RSM Dot would pass on an order to the troops: 'Don't argue with your father.' If one's opinions are always silenced, the fruit never ripens on the bush. I became unable to see things in black and white; for me the intellectual world has always been predominantly grey. But I was able to be entirely definite when it came to the question of the function of SF and which of the idols had feet and heads of clay.

The book brought me good friends – and some enemies. Some who have never managed to outgrow their amazement at *Amazing* cannot forgive my demotion of the inventor of the Osophone. But we have to grow up if possible.

We learn to be ourselves by watching others. Perhaps Kingsley's example fortified me. Kingsley was always definite; he liked things or hated them. It is a useful characteristic for a comic writer.

Looking over the page proofs of *Billion Year Spree*, I realised that, of all the novels and stories I had surveyed, the one that held the firmest place in my imagination was Mary Shelley's novel. Not only does it mark a turning point in literature, but it is a prime example of a writer able to mythologise her feelings.

Mary's mother, the splendid Mary Wollstonecraft, died in childbirth. Victor Frankenstein's attempt to create life without the normal pains of childbirth, together with his creature's wounded orphan feelings, spring directly from Mary's own psychodrama. And there is something more, for the sinews of the book are Mary's understanding and intuitions of science as it stood at the beginning of the nineteenth century. The best exposition of this particular umwelt is in Marilyn Butler's introduction to her 1993 edition of *Frankenstein*.

The power of Mary Shelley's emotions, so forcefully expressed, has produced a new legend, the legend of the artificial construct, Frankenstein's monster, which cannot be controlled.

Small wonder Mary says of invention that it springs not from the void but from chaos. 'It can give form,' she says, 'to dark, shapeless substances, but cannot bring into being the substance itself.'

In any artistic field, creation – the *giving of form* – is a positive way of dealing with negative and destructive emotions (though not those alone, for invention by itself delights the inventor). Creative fields present the chance to explore oneself, increasing self-knowledge thereby. By this inward alchemy, writers and other artists may find themselves freed from the psychological miseries of their past; they become, in a sense, born anew. Which is why writers of autobiography may sometimes define their harried lives most clearly by not adhering to what the outside world sees as chronological order.

But novels and stories should transcend a mere recitation of personal woes; they become transformed by memory and art. Every woe is common human stock, and a foundation for narrative. Not all of us suffer Oedipus's troubles, but we empathise with his being 'up against it'. A problem is set: it is to be resolved, or to fail to achieve resolution, in a dramatic and aesthetic manner. Anthony Storr, in his book on the subject, *The Dynamics of Creation*, has this to say: 'It is because the great creative artists can do this for us in their works that we gain so much more than mere pleasure from art. By identifying ourselves, however fleetingly, with the creator, we can participate in the integrating process which he has carried out for himself.' Storr adds that strength and skill enable the artist 'to rise above the merely personal, and to relate his personal deprivations to *the discontents implicit in being human*.'

How smartly that last phrase (my italics) strikes home. It is natural enough to complain about our lot, as the soldiery did at Milestone 81. Such complaint has a choric quality.

* * *

The Weidenfeld jacket for *Billion Year Spree* had a small inset picture of New York being blown to pieces by terrible flying machines. The city is going up in flames. I chose it from the cover of a pulp magazine whose monthly issues bore the splendid legend, *Read It Today – Live It Tomorrow*. Doubtless New Yorkers took this in their stride. In 1973, a rather different catastrophe befell Britain. The lights went out.

Under Edward Heath's premiership, the country was hit by strikes in the coal, power and transport industries. Our little village became dark at sunset, as villages had done throughout past ages. In the house, we enjoyed roaring log fires, and Tim and Charlotte walked about the house with lighted candles and saw their way upstairs to bed with oil lamps in their hands, making their faces glow like children in a Georges de la Tour painting. Heath House became a little pageant of shadows and transitory glimmers, as it had been in the nights of Richard Church, its architect.

After an abrupt increase in oil prices, a fifty-miles-per-hour limit was imposed on all road vehicles as an economy measure. We rather enjoyed it. Fifty seemed a reasonable speed. With the rise of the Arab states, this seemed the end of the West's cheap oil bonanza.

One positive turn of events at least emerged from the Heath government. Heath was a confirmed European. Once he had negotiated his way round de Gaulle, Britain joined the European Union – the 'Common Market', as it was – on 1 January, 1973.

In 1974, Harold Wilson returned as PM. Even Harold's conjuring tricks failed to revive the economy, and inflation rose alarmingly.

Although inflation rose, it did not alarm me. I failed to notice it. All that caught my attention was that a bottle of Glenfiddich increased in price every time I bought one. I was so busy. Everything seemed to be happening at once. There were four trips abroad that year, the best being a family holiday in Austria and then over the remarkably named Karawanken Mountains into Jugland. We took Wendy with us, then in her early David Essex mode; Clive was at the City of London Poly, and had other fish to fry.

Those precious progeny of my first marriage were rapidly growing up. Clive was embracing Marxism. To enter university in those early seventies days was to be dipped in a red political vat; but over and above that, Clive had an inborn sense of the injustices existing within society. Since his rather frugal childhood, Clive has remained ungrasping, a vital element in our extended family.

I could only hope that in their childhood by the sea Clive and Wendy had missed me less than I missed them. The years of their childhood had seemed endless. While I longed for them to become adult, I longed more for them to stay for ever children, that I might still have their company in those dear impressionable years.

Margaret and I invariably went on holiday abroad with Clive and Wendy, and with Tim and Charlotte, too, when they arrived on the scene. However, in 1972, we did a European tour, just the two of us, in a BMW lent us by the *Daily Telegraph*. This tour took us through Wurzburg again and, at our southernmost points, to Trieste and a town in Jugland, on the south of the Istran peninsula, near Opatia. There we found a little modern hotel, the Hotel Medved, named after a nearby mountain, but on the coast.

It seemed the Jugs had really got it together. It was a slick, smart hotel in shades of white and grey. We sunned ourselves, swam, and retired to the bedroom to make love all one afternoon. The sun shone in little slices through the jalousies, glittering and swimming on the polished marble of the floor.

Some years later, again in Jugland, we rented a villa on the outskirts of the pocket-sized city of Rovinj, which we shared with our friends the Stricks. Rovinj perches on the edge of the Istran peninsula, overlooking the placid Adriatic, the *Jadransko More*. Boats moor at its quaysides, while the dazzle of sea filters along the town's alleyways to those unexpected theatrical spaces beloved of architects of the Serene Republic, who fashioned them even in the most cramped cities. At that time, Rovinj burst with inhabitants and tourists, strolling the cobbled streets night and day. You could get lost in Rovinj, were it not that, winding your way uphill, you would unfailingly come to the church that crowned the hill on which Rovinj was built.

The tourist trade flourished in Rovinj in those days. We found agreeable little restaurants in which to eat when Margaret was not cooking in the villa. Most evenings, we sat round a table with the children and compiled a Travel Book. This institution began in 1961, when I took Clive up to London. I made him a little book noting all the places where we had been and the things we did, so that we would have a record. As they grew older, all four children had to work on the current Book.

At first they thought this was too much like school. But their enthusiasm grew. So did the Books. All kinds of things were stuck into their pages: wrappings of foreign chocolate bars, wrappings of sugar cubes, train tickets, *seilbahn* vouchers, menus, postcards, the labels off wine and beer bottles. The text, written in various coloured pens, straggled round these exotic obstacles. Now we have an entire shelf full of our Books, recording various tours together round Europe, from Scandinavia to Italy, from Spain to Poland.

One could scarcely imagine a happier holiday in a more pleasant place than Rovinj. Jugland was peaceful and moderately prosperous in the seventies: how the Jugs let it all slip away beggars belief. Was there at no stage a statesman wise enough, farseeing enough, to cry Stop!, before the avalanche of destruction began? The break-up of Jugoslavia, and the ruination of the lives of millions, is a personal tragedy for many beyond, as well as inside, its frontiers.

The Aldisses lived on the ground floor of the villa, with the Stricks above. Owing to the steepness of the land, we had a garage below our floor. The agent explained that this garage was kept locked, since it contained the owner of the villa's possessions. Beyond the front garden with its few spindly trees was a path leading down through thick bushes of fennel to the rocks and the sea. The scent of fennel always conjures up Rovinj, with swims in pale apricot dawns.

The sea was scattered with rocky islets, some with their own protective fringes of sea urchins. Wendy said we had to avoid them in case they had rabies. Margaret rowed our dinghy with Tim and Charlotte beside her, while Wendy and I swam behind, to explore new desert islands where we could picnic and play.

One of the great happinesses has been to see Margaret and Wendy so loving together, the one so considerate and unpossessive, the other so warm and helpful.

Margaret inflated a small paddling pool in the villa garden for Tim and Charlotte to play in. We noticed how, by morning, the water in the pool was clouded as if by strange algae.

After a day or two, I heard a noise in the garage. Finding it to be unlocked, I flung up the folding door. Four Shiptars (Albanians) stood there, looking apprehensive. They lived a secret life under our floorboards, much like Morlocks, washing during the night in our children's paddling pool. The poor fellows were the lowest paid of all Jugoslavia's ill-paid workers.

Jugs always represented Shiptars as an enemy to be feared; so strong was this prevailing attitude that we came to share it. Years later, in May 1990, Wendy and I were in Albania, doing an article for *Marie Claire*. We met great-hearted people, marvellous at making the best of things. One afternoon, a coachload of Albanians from Jugland, from the Kosmet, arrived in Skanderbeg Square in Tirana. People rushed from bars and houses to applaud and welcome them.

It was Wendy's second visit to Albania. She was busily photographing, leading me into places I would hardly have gone on my own.

How exuberant the Albanians were! We attended a wedding feast, were favoured guests. Meat and drink prevailed in medieval quantities. We danced the night away in a hotel overflowing with indescribable urinals.

XXIV

The Global Dance

(it) gets danced, gets jumped (medio-passive) otherwise, differently Here we dance differently. ('here it gets danced differently')

Spoken Albanian. (Spoken Language Services, Inc.)

Much time became taken up with doing some of the things
writers do when they are not writing. The Society of Authors,
to which I had belonged for some while, asked me to serve on the
Council of Management. The Society was then run by a, or rather *the*,
Triumvirate. I liked going round to the offices in Drayton Gardens;
the members of the Triumvirate were always amiable. They were,
in the late seventies, oppressed by a more recent association, the
Writers' Guild.

Certainly, the Guild, to which I also belonged for a while, was
the more militant of the two organisations. It seemed to be run by
two ladies particularly feared in Drayton Gardens, Brigid Brophy
and Maureen Duffy. The dedicated Duffy has achieved as much
for writers as anyone, and remains insufficiently acknowledged.
Brigid Brophy was a different matter. Whether deliberately or inadvertently, she never recognised you. You were forced to introduce
yourself over and over again. She had never heard of you.

Phillipa MacLeish, the female third of the Triumvirate, and I flew
to Strasbourg to speak for British authors' rights in the European
Parliament. With us went representatives of the Guild, including
Maureen Duffy and Lord Willis, Lord Ted.

Ted Willis was an engaging, bibulous man, famous chiefly for
stories of crime and lowlife, in particular for a long-lived television
series about the decency of an ordinary copper on an ordinary beat,

as portrayed by Jack Warner in *Dixon of Dock Green*. I suppose it is something to have spoken in the grand chamber of the Council of Europe. Chiefly remembered is how we laughed to see that it is not so much the English but the Europeans who love a lord. How they deferred, how they fawned, when Ted spoke! 'Perhaps if we might assure Milord Willis . . .' Ted's every utterance was worth a bag of gold.

On my committee in those years I had several writers I admired. They included Michael Scammell, later to write a life of Solzhenitsyn, Alethea Hayter, author of *Opium and the Romantic Imagination* and other works, the irrepressible Giles Gordon, Michael Holroyd, then working on his Shaw biography, and William Trevor, one of today's best short story writers. It was a pleasure to work with them, even when we disagreed.

With Maureen Duffy and others, I campaigned for Public Lending Right, that principle whereby authors should be paid a pittance whenever one of their books was borrowed from a public library. We often trooped in and out of the Houses of Parliament, addressing various bodies. There, courtesy of Ted Willis, we met another lord, George Brown. George Brown had been Foreign Secretary in the first Wilson government, known for his *faux pas* when suitably over-refreshed. He lent a glow to the bar of the House of Lords, a little portly man, full of kindness, good will, and good brandy.

A writer I got to know slightly during these campaigns was the elusive J. G. Farrell. He won the Booker Prize in 1973 for his novel *The Siege of Krishnapur*, which deals with the Indian Mutiny. His *The Singapore Grip* in 1978 is about the surrender of Singapore to the Japanese. The year after this latter novel was published, J. G. was swept out to sea while fishing in Ireland, and drowned.

Once when in the House of Commons, I walked into the wrong chamber, where a delegation of miners was gathering to meet. They were curious and said, 'Tell us about free books for libraries.' I told them. They were indignant to think that writers had to give their work for nothing. 'It's same as us having to give our coal away.'

The lobbying succeeded. PLR became established. Writers currently receive two pence per loan, estimated across the country. Unfortunately, libraries in the nineties are not the fortresses of contemporary fiction they were in the seventies.

When I became chairman of the Society's Committee of Management, the Triumvirate was preparing to retire. We interviewed a number of people for the post of General Secretary. Unlucky the first time, we then found Mark Le Fanu, who happily still remains in the pilot's seat.

During my term in office, I turned the Society into a union. Lady Antonia Fraser, that firebird among authors, resigned as a result – in the most diplomatic way possible. It was difficult to do one's own work while giving proper attention to the Society's affairs. One thing seemed to lead to another, and I then became a member of the Arts Council Literature Panel. We met in the smart surroundings of 105 Piccadilly. I was astounded at the amount of money being given away to various chaps who had to yield up no account of their activities. One good thing the Council did was to establish a market for writers by founding the *New Review*, editor Ian Hamilton, to which I used to contribute.

The literary panel was then run by Melvyn Bragg and Charles Osborne. After our meetings, they would disappear like demons down a trap door in a pantomime, rather than face informal questions.

With that same genial Charles Osborne, and other writers such as the poets, Jon Stallworthy and Elaine Feinstein, I went on a tour of the Soviet Union in 1977. Such tours were treated very seriously in those days. Not only were we briefed and debriefed before and after the tour, but we had to swear to say nothing against the USSR until at least six months following our return.

By 1976, the Harrison family had moved to Ireland and were living in Dublin. Harry called a grand convention. Sam Lundwall, Tom Shippey, Maggie Noach, Bonfiglioli, Wolfgang Jeschke, Frederik Pohl, Forrest J. Ackerman, Gianfranco Viviani, Peter Kuscka, Eremi Parnov and many other celebrities from the world of science fiction attended. There and then, World SF was founded at Harry's instigation.

This laudable institution maintained contact between professional people, whether Communist, Capitalist, or anything in between. Our annual meetings were held at first in semi-neutral countries, Ireland, Sweden, Jugland, and so on. Later in Hungary, Poland, Brighton, Italy and – perhaps our most formidable meeting, when Malcolm Edwards was WSF President – in Chengdu, China.

Harry is an internationally minded man. The decades of WSF mark his finest hours. Harry was the WSF's first President. We did not always know whom we were dealing with. We found how much power resided in a sheet of stationery with an imposing heading and a listing of our officers; it often sufficed to extract someone from, say, the depths of Bulgaria to the West. When I was President in the eighties, I managed to move an important Chinese writer from San Francisco, where he was visiting, to our house in Oxford, and then on to Zagreb in Croatia (then a part of Jugland).

I also instituted a series of awards. The award by which I set most store was The President's Award for Independence of Thought in the Field of Science Fiction. Perhaps ten were awarded all told. One was presented to the Russian writers, the Strugatsky brothers, at the World Science Fiction Convention in Brighton in 1987. It was well merited.

Some WSF delegates were more genuine than others. Our long-standing Soviet delegate never produced any other WSF members. We found later that he had kept the whole matter secret, telling no one below him in the hierarchy of WSF's existence.

On the other hand, the Chinese wholeheartedly joined in. They surprised us by sending a delegate to our meeting in San Marino. She proved to be the beautiful and colourful Yang Xiao, who arrived at our conference with a video extolling the beauties of China, and in particular of her province, Sichuan. With her was a self-effacing man with whom I became very friendly, the witty Mr Shen Zaiwang, later posted to Hong Kong. Yang Xiao also attended the meeting in The Hague, where all arrangements were settled. Chengdu received more votes than Kraków – for which the Polish delegates never forgave us. Next year, 1991, off we flew to Chengdu.

Our reception in Chengdu was elaborate. Bands played. Children sang. Hot-air balloons floated above the city, bearing the WSF logo. Banquets were given. Toasts were drunk. We discovered we had at least 200 members, if only temporarily. Sessions were attended by delegates from every province bar one. During these sessions, the Chinese writers (having Western witnesses present) bravely spoke out for more freedom to write and comment on society. And we gained an inkling of how much power Yang Xiao wielded.

After speeches, national reports, and final summing up, the occasion was concluded by a visit to the Woolong Panda Reserve. This was no small matter. The Woolong Reserve lies many miles west of Chengdu, almost at the foothills of Tibet. The country near the Reserve is one of grandeur, verging on the savage. There we took walks by fast-flowing rivers and waterfalls, where shoulders of gorges heave themselves up on every side. Rhododendrons and potatoes grew. Landscape painters visited here, no distance from where yaks graze.

'Whatever excites emotion has charms for me,' says Mary Wollstonecraft.

'My soul in China'! – the phrase meant one thing to Anna Kavan, quite another to me.

The Pitiao River was so cold that no fish lived in it. Near by, peasants were close to starvation. There was never an answer to my question as to why cold-tolerant fish could not be introduced from chillier climates, say Manchuria. Possibly the consensus of opinion was that peasants were accustomed to living on the breadline.

Various persons, some with mystery wrapped about them like cloaks, joined me on our walks among the titanic scenery. Their confidences, like our surroundings, were romantic in the highest degree. It was as if the wild grandeur, above which blue sky was only rarely seen amid cloud, inspired solemnity of speech, and confession. Some men had been rusticated under Mao and still hated the brutish peasants among whom they had been forced to live; another was grateful for the insights rustication had brought. One pleasant man, younger than I, said he had heard I fought in the British Army against the Japanese Imperial Army in Burma. When I agreed it was so, he told me his father had fought there too.

We were strolling casually, apart from others, our voices submerged by the sound of the river as it battled over its rocks.

'So then, he fought with Chiang Kai Shek's army?'

'That is the case. He was a colonel. After later events, the Kuomintang is forbidden even to be mentioned.'

I remembered an embittered member of the DDR I once met who told me he had been imprisoned for simply mentioning the Berlin Wall.

My Chinese confidant was silent as we walked along. Then he said, 'My father had courage. He fought for China. And yet . . .' a pause, 'my family history has always been an impediment to me.'

'And is still?'

'You see that although I have managed to enter the Foreign Service by reason of merit, by reason of history I am only in the catering branch. Where I can do no harm . . .'

Chiang Kai-shek (Jiang Jiehi) was President of pre-Communist China for many years. He had great influence in the West, in part because of his remarkable wife, Soong Mei-ling, a woman of power, courage and beauty. It is strange how much influence such a woman can exert, by personality alone. Dollars in plenty flowed in to prop up Chiang's regime. He was eventually driven out of China by the Communists, and took refuge in Formosa – later Taiwan.

Anyone who served in Chiang's armies, like my friend's father, automatically became an enemy of the people when the Communists gained power.

The Woolong Reserve was marvellously remote. Few ordinary people were permitted to visit it. Many checkpoints stood on the bumpy road between Chengdu and Woolong; after all, this was one route to Tibet, Chinese-occupied Tibet. To visit the Reserve was a treat, for the Chinese members of WSF as for us. Here it was possible to tickle panda tummies while keepers distracted them with twigs of bamboo. The amiable-looking animals have sharp claws. Mostly, they trundled about their cells or snoozed. Gazing on them, I wondered if they did not suffer from some inner knowledge that they were almost the last of their line. The feeling got through that there remained little room for them in the twentieth century.

While we were at Woolong village, a violent storm brought down eight kilometres of avalanche across the road back to Chengdu. We were trapped. The word was that we might have to stay in the village for a week. We had with us a BBC unit, covering the WSF event, who transmitted the news to the outside world. Incidentally, they also transmitted greetings to Margaret, whose birthday it was the next day.

The European members of WSF were, in the main, elated by this adventure. The Chinese, responsible for our safety, took the matter more seriously. We spent some while in debate, which Shen Zaiwang led. It emerged there was an alternative way back to Chengdu; it involved a 600-mile detour across the high yak pastures of Tibet. We were keen to make such a journey. But twenty vehicles and 200 people were stranded, and a gasoline shortage prevailed in Woolong village. We would have to wait and hope. Waiting and hoping sounded like a traditional Chinese occupation.

That crisis proved to be a gift. People sat and talked with one another, while smoking Great Wall cigarettes. In particular, I talked with the personal guide I had been given, Liu Xiaoyian. She was a bonny woman of good understanding and wit, approaching middle age. We sat on a bank thick with sinewy herbs and conversed for a long while, about character being shaped by circumstance, and many other things, and we laughed.

Xiaoyian knew a great deal about the West – enough to make her account of recent intricate Chinese history more comprehensible. She was curious about many English matters. I sang to her, the song Stanley Holloway sings in the movie, *My Fair Lady*, 'With a

Little Bit of Luck'. Xiaoyian loved it. She said the Chinese had too few comic songs.

'What did we have in common except our century?' The question comes from a poem by Jon Stallworthy.

Like everyone else, Xiaoyian had suffered during the Cultural Revolution. She told me of the time she had been sent to labour in the country. Although she had later come to appreciate this broadening of her experience and understanding, it was no sinecure. The women were starving. She and three others somehow caught a hare. They loved the beauty of the creature but they needed to eat. They wept as they killed it.

As we sat talking on the sweet-scented bank, there came to my mind the story I had read in East Dereham, about the small boy who lost his shadow, only to find it a while later in China.

In Xiaoyian's presence I wrote a short poem, based on a gesture seen during our walks in the gorge.

> The girl by the fast grey Pitiao River
> Looking up to see us standing on the bank
> Opens her hand to show us stone and shell
> Collected just for fun defying cold
> Opens then closes her palm
> In that moment
> Organic and inorganic are one

Our WSF guides staged an entertainment for us that evening in Woolong village. After dark, we thronged to a wide cleared space. Here three great stacks of timber had been piled. Malcolm gave a speech of appreciation for the hospitality we were receiving, and then he, Fred Pohl and I were handed burning brands. We seized them up and thrust them each into one of the timber piles.

As the three fires sprang up, sending their sparks to join the stars overhead, music sounded, music from unidentifiable instruments. Women in antique costumes, coats, trousers, boots, emerged from the shadows and began to dance, circling the flames. In their merry round red faces, sloe eyes reflected firelight. The music was meticulous, almost menacing, a menace assuaged by their gleaming smiles. Intricate steps marked the dance. The women linked arms in a circle, looking inwards towards the flame. We could have been a million light years from Earth.

Many years later, a knowing friend from Eastern Europe told me that these dancers were all in the police force.

The shuffling circle was broken. We guests were invited to join the dance. The music became faster, wilder, bronze notes predominating. Round and round we went. We sang wordlessly. Some kilometres distant, pandas snored in their dens. We danced till the fires were mere glowing cones, volcanoes of a prehistoric epoch.

What did we experience that night? The real China? Hardly – but certainly a China far from the concrete offices and prejudices of Beijing.

Overnight, 700 peasants and soldiers cleared the landslide – under what pressure from authority we never discovered. We climbed into our Toyota 'Coaster' vans at dawn. Twenty vans formed a slow convoy. At first we travelled by the verges of the grey-and-white Pitiao. Women in black turbans rested on their hoes, unsmiling by the roadside to let us pass. We bumped over the remains of broken trees and piled stones. The road was only just negotiable. Sometimes we climbed out and walked, to spare the springs of the vehicles. By dusk, we were safely back in our Chengdu hotel, and the luxury of its baths.

Years later, Margaret and I met Jung Chang, celebrated author of *Wild Swans* – a book almost to stand beside Solzhenitsyn's *Gulag Archipelago* in its frank testimony to human folly and courage. We found she knew Yang Xiao and Liu Xiaoyian! It was amazing. She had attended the same school, and later was sent to the same work camp in the country.

Being president of WSF was no sinecure. Since dues were almost impossible to collect, or at least to pass on from country to country, the president paid for many of the functions from his own pocket. While Harry, Fred, Sam, Gianfranco Viviani and I ran affairs, all went smoothly. Later, we became snared in problems. We selected poor presidents who in some cases simply did not function, or disrupted the organisation.

During his term as president, Frederik Pohl instituted the Karel Awards for Excellence in Translation. The Karel is a cute glass robot representing Karel Capek sitting on a globe. During my term as president, I instituted annual awards, the Harrison Award for Improving the Status of SF Internationally and, as mentioned, the President's Award for Independence of Thought. These were solid monoliths of acrylic in shamrock green and deep blue respectively. We also published a newsletter, a journal and anthologies. Sam Lundwall and I edited the *Penguin World Omnibus of Science*

Fiction, which vehicle contained stories from twenty-six different countries.

WSF consumed a great deal of time and energy. After the Soviet Union dissolved itself, our organisation became less necessary, the visit to China being exceptional. It was certainly true for Harry and Sam and me, and probably for others, that we gained much information about the workings of sinister systems. Was it true that so-and-so's wife was related to Elena, wife of President Ceauşescu of Romania? Our language was often coded, when we were unsure with whom we were actually dealing.

Sometimes the going got rough. Poznan is a large industrial city lost somewhere in the wastes of Poland. A large convention, EuroCon III was held there, mainly with delegates from Warsaw Pact countries, dominated by the Soviet Union, with several writers from the West, such as Jon Bing from Norway, Sam Lundwall from Sweden, and me from Britain. This would be in the summer of 1976. Margaret and I drove to Poznan across Europe in a motor caravan, with the children. The whole trip was a great event in our lives. We were away for a month. When we returned home, Mao Zedong died.

But the official proceedings, grandly opened by Soviet cosmonauts, were rather a challenge. The party line was that the West endured the same restrictions as the East. Specifically, although a speaker admitted that no SF novel could ever be published in Moscow in which Capitalism was permitted to triumph over Communism, equally, he claimed, no novel could be published in the West showing the triumph of Communism over Capitalism.

Although I rose and denied this, I could recall no examples.

Back in England, my life as an Englishman insisted I write such a novel. It was entitled *Enemies of the System*. In it, the Russians have long ago overrun the solar system, and a small group of the privileged is about to enjoy a vacation on a distant planet, Lysenka II. There they come across the degenerate remains of Capitalist humanity. *Enemies* was published without fuss by Jonathan Cape in England and Harper & Row in the United States, both editions in 1978.

Our system was less repressive than theirs. QED.

Not only was there an exquisite tension in being in Lenin's lair, so to speak, but Communism honed a fine sense of irony. Wit and sarcasm were the barriers built against futility. It was soothing to be invited into homes into which the concept of repainting and redecorating had never entered. In those houses, those brown rooms, were carpets and furniture that spoke of earlier regimes, and of a Europe that had once been less divided, with Vienna and Paris as its twin capitals.

Sometimes the world seemed topsy-turvy, a mirror-image of what we called common sense. In Poland, for instance, I was almost a zloty-millionaire. Margaret and I arrived late at the branch of the *Narodna Banka*. They let us in the back door – something Barclay's would never allow. I produced a receipt. The cashier unlocked a safe, bringing out a suitcase full of currency – mainly royalties from *Non-Stop*. These he spilt on the counter before us.

When we exclaimed, he stuffed the pile of money into a carrier bag. We thanked him and tiptoed away to the hotel with our fortune.

The zloty was useless outside the national frontiers. Even Bulgarians could not use it. We had to spend it all there and then.

I would meet Margaret and Wendy in the evening for a drink, after a long day in the conference hall. They had been out shopping.

'How much did you manage to spend?'

'Ten thousand zlotys.'

'It's not enough. Out, out, spend more!'

So the ladies acquired spurious rings, the children large grotesque cuddly toys, and I a surreal painting by a local artist. We drank some excellent vodka with the artist.

At the end of our trip, we gave the remaining bundles of money to him.

He had a smart little wife and a dog on a lead. He was trying, despite everything, to live a neat bourgeois life. Again, a mirror-reversal of life in the West as far as painters were concerned.

Despite its frustrations, there is this to be said about being abroad: that you can, as the expression has it, 'knock about', and keep irregular hours and eat a hot dog from a market stall and drink obscure liquors and smoke evil cigarillos and go to bed late and have bizarre conversations and sit around in hotel lobbies of strange aspect and be driven here and there to odd destinations in taxis for which others in some unknown ministry pay.

But did we achieve anything? We certainly did. We met with people for whom SF was no mere entertainment. It was a serious medium for smuggling subversive ideas into print. I correct this page, I hope for the last time, on an afternoon in the autumn of 1996, when horse chestnut leaves are falling solemnly to the ground. This morning I received a letter from an East European who played a major role in WSF in his time. He has this to say:

Though I have not mentioned it to you, my foreign friends, originally I am a poet. Then I turned against the Communist system. I participated in the revolution. I was blacklisted and could no longer be published, not even my name. All my family lived in hunger and need.

Then came SF. I became acquainted with Ray Bradbury's writings and had them published. Later I had published an anthology of eminent short SF stories, yours included. Thereafter, in the seventies, I had the possibility to edit that magazine you know well. My name was not blazoned on it. I sought after international contacts, in the so-called Socialist countries, later in the West. I was kept under surveillance, censored, my letters opened. Orwell wrote about it. I however went through it.

There is a lot I can thank you for, and Harry and Sam and Fred. I always remember you, your friendship and encouragement provided me with warm regards.

Nevertheless, SF had an additional meaning with us. With you, it was considered as interesting, exciting reading, while here it was a literature awakening ideas and encouragement. Even Soviet SF undermined the ideology of the State and the Party. SF contributed to the breakdown of Communism.

I withold my friend's name in order to protect him, not from the past, but the present, which still has its problems.

In 1995, I assisted Harriet Harvey Wood, who was organising an event for the Cheltenham Literary Festival, 'In Search of an Enemy'. We brought over a number of writers from ex-Communist countries to speak of their experiences and read some of their fiction. Paul Bailey and I held one session at which we introduced WSF members from Romania (Ion Hobana) and the former East Germany (Angela and Karlheinz Steinmuller). Among other attendees was Piro Misha whom I had met in Albania. An excellent week concluded with a reception in the Master's Lodgings of Magdalen College, Oxford, a look at some of the treasures of the library, and an organ recital by candlelight in the glorious college chapel.

This could be said to be the conclusion of one chapter of WSF. The presidency has now passed to Italy. Unpretentiously, without publicity, at our own expense, we defied the ethos of the Cold War and made what common ground we could, where we could, with those whose governments were enemies of ours. We took a look at other cultures and enjoyed each others' hospitality. We did not visit Poznan or elsewhere to promote sales of our own books.

'And how well did all these people write?' a curious person might ask, a century hence. Well, nobody scts out to write badly. Some wrote to please their masters, some wrote to please their public, some wrote to please themselves. Their achievements must be judged to be very various. All sang the song of the *Zeitgeist*.

The WSF visit to Sechuan was my second trip to China. The first trip was much more tightly bound to the *Zeitgeist*. President Richard Nixon generally received a better press in Europe than on his home territory, mainly because the Europeans approved of much of his foreign policy, while having merely to look on at the Watergate drama. Early in 1972 came one of those television pictures you never forget, not for its beauty, but merely because you know it marks one more turn of samsara, the inscrutable wheel of history.

We watched as Nixon, attended by Zhou Enlai and other senior Chinese officials, walked upon the Great Wall. China had become even more frightened of its old Communist ally, the USSR, than it was of the Capitalist running dogs in the West. As Confucius put it, 'Best to love neighbour, however naughty; but when naughty neighbour not looking, ram bayonet up bottom.'

The Wall is steep near Beijing. Nixon had hardly ceased breathing heavily when hopes arose that we might all live more peaceably than before. Other less official Westerners began almost immediately to visit China. In 1976, Zhou Enlai, one of the world's few wise leaders, died, as did his mad boss, Chairman Mao. A power struggle ensued.

Chairman Mao was succeeded for a brief while by Chairman Hua, a name already fading from the pages of history. However, it caused a sensation when this new leader of the People's Republic of China came to England in 1979 for a visit. He visited Oxford.

I was then in Beijing, and could not receive him . . .

Like his future successor, Deng Xiaoping, Hua claimed to be a countryman; scorning the Bodleian, he went to visit the premises of the Pig Improvement Company at Fyfield Wick, outside Oxford.

In that year, while I was in China, Clive was in Marakesh and Morocco, backpacking in the Atlas Mountains. Having taken his degree, he discovered there was no demand for Earth Sciences. Like many young Englishmen, he was finding it difficult to get a decent job. At this juncture, he was travelling instead.

The job this led to makes a later story.

* * *

The managing director of Jonathan Cape, then an independent publishing house, was Graham C. Greene, benevolent member of the Greene family, whose cousin was the novelist Graham Greene. Another cousin was Felix Greene. Graham C. invited me to go on a China tour with Felix.

There was about Felix a sweetness and an other-worldly sagacity which sometimes led him to make mistakes. He had moved into that rare and suspect category, Friend of China, whose motto might have been 'Your country, right or wrong', always a surrender of conscience. When Felix's book on China, *The Wall Has Two Sides*, was published, I was one of its enthusiastic reviewers. Felix had been head of the BBC offices in New York. His book *Vietnam! Vietnam!* was published in the States in 1966. It is mainly a photographic record of American brutality and Vietnamese suffering in the war. It forced Felix to leave the States.

In that book, Felix quotes Ho Chi Minh's mild recommendations to his fighting force. They include this, as one of Ho's 'Six Permissibles': '3. In spare time to tell amusing, simple, and short stories useful to the resistance, but not to betray secrets'.

Perhaps it was this reference to simple short stories that decided Graham and Felix to include me as a member of his expedition. The other members – the 'Distinguished Persons', as we were designated – were David Attenborough, Iris Murdoch, Maisic Webb (Deputy Director of the British Museum), Michael Young (one of the founders of the Open University, later Lord Young of Dartington), and a black Rhodesian journalist, Chen Chimutengwende, engaged to Felix's daughter.

With us also were Derek Bryan, Chairman of SACU, The Society for Anglo-Chinese Understanding, and a secretary from the same organisation, Janet St John-Austen.

One main objective of our visit was to have a filmed audience with Deng Xiaoping. Deng was busily entrenching himself in power while Hua was away measuring the girth of Oxfordshire pigs. We settled into the comfortable old part of the Peking Palace Hotel, to wait until we were summoned to attend, as Western visitors to the emperors' courts had waited over the centuries.

During this stagnant period, I took a trip to Shanghai on my own, at my own expense, to deliver a lecture at the university. Two Americans were working there, Philip Smith II and his wife, Susan. It was enlightening to hear them talk about conditions in China at that transitional period. Peasants had only recently been permitted to enter city limits. I took as a gift to their class twenty-four copies of my *Penguin Science Fiction Omnibus*, kindly donated by Penguin Books, to assist as a teaching aid. They had much to say about the poverty and dedication of their students. In the evenings, these students sat together to talk and drink 'white tea', their sardonic euphemism for hot water without tea leaves.

Looking out of the window of my room one pre-dawn morning, I watched the students walking between buildings, straining to read their textbooks, enjoying a little solitude.

Back in Beijing, I rejoined the other Distinguished Persons. Continuing our wait, we witnessed the closure of the famous Freedom Wall, where ordinary people could voice their complaints. Out on the streets in the evening, we had people walking behind us, speaking a little English, perhaps asking where we came from, before vanishing into the dark. Contact with long-nose foreigner! *Ah, something same as forbidden sex!*

We all enjoyed conversation. David asked Felix when he had become socialist. Felix told us how a word long ago had awoken him to the injustices under which people live.

The Greene family was wealthy. Early one Christmas morning, when Felix was eight, he came downstairs in his dressing gown to look at the Christmas tree, below which presents were piled. The room was brightly decorated. A maid of whom he was fond was kneeling at the grate, clearing away ashes, preparatory to lighting a log fire.

Felix went up to her, put an arm round her and said, 'Happy Christmas, Matilda!'

The maid said, without bitterness, 'Oh, Christmas isn't for the likes of us, Master Felix.'

Iris Murdoch and I were invited to speak at the Beijing Writers' Union. Many serious men and some women were gathered about a long table covered with green baize. Iris spoke about philosophy and the meaning of freedom. I spoke about the Industrial Revolution, the Romantic poets, Byron, Shelley and Mary Shelley's *Frankenstein*. We were courteously questioned, and conversation ensued. For both sides, this was felt to be a momentous occasion.

Sitting opposite me at the table was a man of bonny and individual appearance. Towards the end of our meeting, he leaned forward and said, 'I am startled to find you sitting opposite me, since I am at present translating one of your stories for my journal.'

His journal was entitled *Oceans of Fiction*, and his name is Wang Fengzhen. We became friends. We have met several times. Once he stayed with Margaret and me in Oxford; he later entertained Margaret when she made her own trip to China and Tibet.

The dreary capital city was brightened by large exhortatory posters, each individually painted, in socialist realism mode. Well-built men and women stood in triumph among gigantic harvests, Red tractors gleamed. Children smiled, skies were blue. Everyone was handsome. I was reminded of the paintings you see outside Indian cinemas, where the faces of the stars are dashed in boldly with reds, blues and violent greens.

At last, our call came to enter the Forbidden City. Deng Xiaoping was prepared to see us.

We had each prepared a question to ask Deng, together with a backup question. These we had had to submit to the Chinese Embassy back in London. We were warned that we could not deviate from the set plan.

But the Chinese in Beijing deviated. Instead of asking our prepared questions, we would be allowed merely to ask Deng questions the Chinese supplied. Consternation in the British camp.

I was able to save the day.

'I gave my questions to the English press before we left England,' I said. 'There will be unfavourable publicity if these are now changed. People will want to know why.'

Our original questions were reinstated.

In fact, I had given my questions to a science fiction fanzine, circulation possibly 200 copies; it sufficed. Acting in character, I merely sought to ask Deng what future he saw for China in space.

So we were driven to our audience.

Felix had fallen out of favour (which may explain the difficulty with our questions). He had not been able to persuade the BBC to televise our travels or this audience, as had been originally anticipated. By October 1979, the BBC had overdosed on television coverage of post-Maoist China, and turned Felix down.

Deng was not pleased by this change of plan. Felix was forced to pay, out of his own pocket, for a television crew of six to fly in from Hong Kong to film us. Otherwise – no audience.

We entered an improvised studio. When we were seated, enter Deng Xiaoping, smoking the first of several cigarettes. He resembled a fungus, perhaps a French *cèpe*, masquerading as a hobbit. Under his chair he kept an enamel spittoon: it was there, unused, to testify to his assertion that he was a simple countryman.

His expression was amiable. His manner was informal. He gave full answers to our questions and the answers were what might be expected. Of course China hoped for success in space. In that sphere, as in others, China would take its place alongside other nations of the world. Mistakes had perhaps been made in the past, but now everyone looked forward optimistically to the future.

There was no flavour to him – as there surely must have been to Zhou Enlai, and, one must suppose, to Mao himself.

As we filed out, Deng came forward in a pleasant way, shaking hands with each of us in turn. Someone took a photograph of me, looming over the small figure, seeming to say, 'Welcome to China, Mr Deng.'

We caught a glimpse of Mao Zedong, or of what had been Mao, or of what was claimed to have been Mao. He lay in state in the Great Hall of the People. The queue to pay him homage straggled over half-way across Tiananmen Square. Embarrassingly, we Distinguished Persons were ushered right to the doors of the Hall, jumping at least a quarter of a mile of queue.

The Hall was impressive in an obvious fashion. It consisted mainly of a vast outer and a vaster inner chamber. Solemn music played, as if composed for the dead who do not hear. The queue was a blue-clad snake, never diminishing. Silent and orderly, it wound through one side of the outer chamber, into the inner chamber where, slow-moving, it filed past the raised catafalque, and then out by the far side of the outer hall, back into the open air. One splendour graced the bleak outer chamber, an enormous woven tapestry depicting landscape, pines, mountains, snow, a temple, no human figure in all its fifty-metre length.

All through the Hall, we trod on scarlet carpet. Our route was fringed with uniform pine trees in red tubs, five feet high.

A strange frisson came when we discovered that the pines were *artificial!* So what about that figure we craned our necks to see, raised up in his open coffin? Was Mao real? From what we could glimpse, the Great Helmsman was in good health. Extinct but in good health.

The question of reality was one we asked ourselves many times on our travels. Were the villages to which we were taken Potemkin villages? Exactly how much of what we saw was staged for our benefit could not be determined. Nor was it humanly possible, however long you stayed, to 'see China' in any meaningful sense of the term. Roads were in general made only for village traffic – hooves and feet and bicycle tyres, not vehicular modes. Air transport was sketchy.

Railroads were good, but ran only between centres. Planes decanted one here and there across the map, at selected spots where there was a cadre to receive foreign visitors.

Our indoctrination before we left London had made us hostile to endless figures of agricultural yields and so forth. Yet, on the ground, we became CIA – China Information Addicts. We had at first resented the way in which our days, once we were away from Beijing, were so crowded with visits. That changed at once.

We wished for no time wasted. We begged for more visits, more bicycle factories, more schools, more agricultural brigades. We demanded people to come and lecture us in our hotels in the evenings. We became obsessed with everything Chinese. Every remark made was to be scrutinised later.

'You notice she spoke of her school's achievements with a particular smile, as if . . .'

'Do you think that when he spoke of *voluntary social work* he really meant . . .'

'He was very intelligent. Do you think he was possibly criticising us when he spoke of public transport being . . .'

'Haven't we heard that phrase "self-defensive counter-attack" before, when we were in . . .'

'Disconcerting how that woman used the very same turns of phrase as the manager used yesterday in . . .'

It was as if we had but to collect a hundred, maybe five hundred, maybe a couple of thousand, pieces of information and we could fit together the whole jigsaw of modern China . . .

We went among the minority peoples – for instance the Eis in the south, only some 200 miles from the frontier with Burma. Our Han hosts told us that there had been a great deal of 'big nation chauvinism' in the past, which had now ceased. We bumped along country tracks to visit Ei production brigades. There, women in costume thrashed corn.

The farmers had set out tables and trestles in the open. We sat about, enjoying the sun and the peace. Fruit and tea were piled up before us. The scene was an interpretation in visual terms of the Beijing posters.

Our interpreter, tall, smooth, humorous, translated back and forth. We adored him. It was not only the women of the party who wept when time came to part from him on Guangzhou station.

It must have been the same for other visiting parties. We all got on extremely well together; all contributed to a general Gestalt. We knew no other world than the one through which we moved. Every morning, we were eager to get together again.

Everything was new. Yet there was ancient China, dented but immarcescible. The most banal thing had about it an aura. An old broken fence – and we saw many of those – was not just any old broken fence. No, it was a *Chinese* old broken fence . . . Great was the difference that made. And of course this was the land to which the boy in that boyhood story had come, to find his shadow again.

We witnessed some Chinese economies that the West would do well to introduce. They were then experimenting with biogas, methane heating for cooking generated from pits containing human excrement and vegetable waste. In one remote village in particular – those villages, simply built of mud, so much a part of nature you wished you were of sufficient fortitude, certitude, to stay in one for a year – we saw a structure so basic it stormed the imagination.

When Chairman Mao spoke of the pig as 'the shit factory', he was speaking in no metaphorical terms.

A large rural family lived about three sides of a courtyard. In the centre of the courtyard was a circular enclosure, within which the family pig was confined by a low wall. In the middle of the enclosure stood a concrete umbrella, or probably one should say mushroom, perhaps nine feet high. Round the thick stem of the mushroom wound a series of steps, leading up to a circular platform, sheltered by the roof above. In the platform was a round hole.

The family climbed the steps each morning and crapped through the round hole. Their droppings fell into the sty below, to help feed the sow. An example of good husbandry.

The pigs at the Pig Improvement Company premises in Fyfield Wick enjoy a different diet. It must be remembered that rural Chinese are mainly vegetarian, and that Chinese, at least at that time, ate perhaps a fifth as much as the average European.

Energy consumption in the countryside was minimal. Driving after dark proved a novel experience. A vehicle used no lights, flashing its headlights only when another vehicle came along, or a brave cyclist. Caution and patience saved batteries. We sometimes passed large villages where not a single light glowed all night. An ancient tradition was observed, long forgotten in extravagant Europe, of going to bed at nightfall and rising with the sun.

Once I had a room in a VIP hotel situated within a walled garden. Rising early, I looked over the wall at an endless still countryside. Heavy with dawn mist, it resembled an undersea landscape, drowned by the Tethys Sea long ago. If all humanity had remained at the stage of husbandry represented by the Ei peasant farmers, the planet might have supported about one billion people.

There need have been no want. Nor would intellect have been missing. All the great names in early history, Akhenaton, Socrates, Lucretius, Aristarchus, Jesus, and countless others, came from village communities. But there is something in human nature (it is what makes us human) which compels us to leave our villages and discover other ways of life, some of which lead on to greatness. Mao Zedong was a peasant from a village. He came to exercise more power – political, psychological and mental – over more people than any man or woman before him.

We loved rural China. It was like being lost in another time. Paradoxically, it was also like being home at last. We saw so many kind faces. Whatever damage had been inflicted on the Chinese psyche by the depredations of Mao's Cultural Revolution, with the consequent famines, in the villages at least the relationship between human culture and the natural environment remained unbroken.

On one occasion our vehicle broke down on a country road. Near by was a small town swarming with people. It was market day. Here for once was an unscheduled stop! Despite protests from our guides, the DPs vanished into the village, to be surrounded by the curious. To them we were visitors from some distant star.

Even there, remote from any large town, the damage caused by the Cultural Revolution was apparent. A fine Buddhist temple had been in part destroyed by the Red Guards. Small trees grew on what remained of its green-tiled roofs.

I walked through the weed-choked courtyards of the temple. How was it that something in us permits us to follow one man into whole areas of desecration? Again, that pressing question regarding the sanity of mankind.

A crowd of onlookers, who had never seen a foreign devil before, followed me, no more threateningly than a herd of deer, prepared to retreat at any moment. I mounted some ruinous steps in an inner courtyard. They stood waiting, so I addressed them. I told them to be brave and kind. I quoted St Juliana of Norwich to them: 'All shall be well and all manner of things shall be well.' They did not understand a word. But something seemed demanded of me. I waved my arms a bit.

We all felt that prompting to communicate. In one beautifully maintained show temple elsewhere, Michael Young suddenly burst into song. All stood silent and listened, wondering.

More was demanded of Iris Murdoch. Each of us had a tale to tell of that village, but it was brave Iris who had the tale for which we honoured her. The Chinese women who surrounded her were as curious about divergences in East–West female genitalia as our troops had been in Singapore. How remarkable that they too asked the legendary question, whether the vital slit ran North–South or East–West. Iris had herself taken into a room, and there and then demonstrated to her audience that all women are sisters under the skirt.

Desmond Morris, an expert on such matters, believes this legend of genitalic compass bearings must have arisen because at one period the three main groupings of humankind were distinct and apart; had a few more centuries of division ensued, three separate sub-species of humanity would have developed. Sexual intercourse between the sub-species would have been possible, but not conception. The genitalic legend which still persists is a thought-fossil of those times.

What further upheavals that development would have caused on our small crowded planet!

The Distinguished Persons took long walks through the countryside. Sometimes we set each other competitions. Praise be that we were not followed by BBC television cameras, as originally planned. But how would the *National Geographic* describe us? We visualised a photograph of ourselves above a caption in Geographicese: 'Curious Westerners Tramping Through Hong Kong's Giant Neighbour.'

Wherever we went, men and women were in the fields, looking somewhat immemorial, leaning on hoes, taking it easy.

We visited a factory where they were producing parts for lorries. In one room stood a huge new machine, scarlet finish, smooth as a sword blade, made in Italy. Once an ingot of steel was pushed into the slot at one end, it looked capable of turning out an entire lorry in ten minutes.

It was not working. It had never worked. It would never work. It was not IT.

As soon as we entered the tool shop, all the workers knocked off, lit up cigarettes – Great Walls, or smokes even more poisonous – and watched our progress, taking it easy. A pretty young woman in overalls had a small photo of Zhou Enlai stuck to her lathe. She was turning a brass something which could have been a hubcap. Chen asked her what it was. She did not know.

'It's obviously part of an atom bomb,' Chen told her.

At the factory entrance was a 'Shame' poster with blackboard, pillorying those workers who arrived late or drunk. Yet there seemed no particular pressure on anyone to get on with it. Western propaganda at the time suggested that the People's Republic was a kind of anthill, with the workers as worker ants. We were surprised by the way in which people everywhere, possibly excluding Beijing, *took it easy*.

On my later visit to Chengdu, Liu Xiaoyian and I made a joke about 'taking it easy'. The phrase appealed to her. In the new cities which now line the Pacific coast of China, the rush for wealth has produced a new breed who do not take it easy. As they mutter prices into their mobile phones, their motivation is more Capitalist than Communist.

Even in 1979, a new spirit was awakening.

In Kunming, we stayed in a magnificently beautiful house, delicately designed and full of mirrors, polished glass and mahogany screens, indicative in its fine detail of a cultivated taste. It had probably belonged to a brigand chief. Our rooms overlooked a park – rather a sad, scruffy park, it must be said. Early in the morning, old ladies arrived there, hoping by callisthenics to ward off the worst excesses of old age; in their worn blue dungarees they went through the ghostly gestures of t'ai chi.

In the evening, different postures were enacted by a different generation. David and I took a stroll in the park after nightfall. Once upon a time, the park had been illuminated by lights hanging from cables strung overhead. Very few bulbs remained, and they mainly of seven-and-a-half watt power, as far as we could tell. Seven-and-a-half passed for light in those days; doubtless, the illuminations had only recently been switched on.

Under one patch of bulbs, a crowd of youths, male and female, gathered. Someone had brought along an old wind-up gramophone, of the kind we kept in our air-raid shelter in Bickington, over thirty years earlier. As well as music, fizzy lemonade was available. Here on a wide path the youths danced. A whole suppressed aspect of the Chinese character was reviving.

We heard much in those days of how records and sheet music of Western composers, mainly Mozart and Beethoven, had been hidden away from the ravages of the Cultural Revolution, to re-emerge once Mao was dead. This was different. These youths were dancing the tango.

How well they danced, how lithe they were, how radiant their faces, how quick their movements! In the dim light, men and women danced together to South American music. It was funny, sad, erotic, all in one powerful bundle. They were remembering the tango! Not only Mozart and Beethoven had survived the rages of the years. Edmundo Ross and Guy Lombardo were also among the saved.

XXV

The Sicilian Yacht

However unconsciously, we all seek for signs and wonders, as Cinema encourages us to do. Omens become comprehensible only after some fatality, such as the defeat of an army. Thus, a sail at sea may later be interpreted to signify the departure of a living soul. Such foregoing events might have forewarned us, had we the skill to read all the mysteries of Time and Chance.

C. C. Shackleton:
'From Beowulf to Dog Star'

All the family have contracted the love of travel. This is clearly a case of nurture rather than nature. Betty and I, when still nestlings, used to beg to go abroad. Bill's response was invariable: 'Why go abroad when you haven't seen all of England yet?' Generations have changed in that respect.

As mentioned, Clive went backpacking in North Africa. The quest for work took him to Denmark, where he worked in a restaurant in Åarhus, in Jutland. He then took a job in the Geological Museum in London. For a while he did what many young people were doing, and worked on a kibbutz in Israel, having rather a hard time of it. These adventures brought him eventually to live abroad.

Clive always kept in touch. Postcards arrived from exotic places. We wrote to each other regularly, and still do. We are a close and loving family – that fortunate thing – and stay always in touch with each other, wherever we happen to be.

When I got this far in writing my book, there came a reason to hesitate. It happened that my publicity officer, Beth Macdougall, volunteered to read the manuscript. The next day, I received a letter from David Wingrove, making the same kind offer.

Never ever have I let anyone but Margaret read a book before it was finished. But this book, my computer tells me, was started in 1994, and now it is September of 1997. Progress is slow. So I dump 150,000 words on Beth's desk. We share a bottle of wine in her office.

We talk. I say, 'The most difficult thing is to write about Margaret. I love her greatly, but if you set it down cold on paper it may simply look mawkish.'

'You could set down what her best qualities are,' Beth says.

Off I go, rattling on about them. Beth chuckles and interposes. 'It's no good just saying she changed your life, darling. You have to explain how.'

Ideas are generated in conversation, much as heat is generated in running.

'Yes,' I say, growing excited. Early on in our relationship, Margaret and I had a falling out about something or other. Feeling hopeless, I turned my back and was going to leave. She said, in her calm, dear voice, 'Don't turn away from me.'

Don't turn away! I did not recall anyone ever saying that to me before. I turned back to her and took her in my arms.

Margaret's words showed me how I had learnt to behave. Always, the sense of being unwanted . . . A harsh word confirmed that underlying feeling. A harsh word and I was off. What Margaret said showed me how Bill and Dot had never called me back. Bill would have speeded me on my way with a parting jibe. I would have retreated to my room, to solitude and a book.

In one of my notebooks, I have a quote from Mary Wollstonecraft's *Letters Written During a Short Residence in Sweden, Norway, and Denmark*. She remarks, 'What a long time it requires to know ourselves; and yet almost everyone has more of this knowledge than he is willing to own, even to himself.' Indeed, I would say that once you set out on this journey of inner discovery, it proves to be a long lane. Possibly with an old church at the end of it.

We went about the business of rearing a family and of integration. Who did the integration? Well, we all did. Margaret's quiet affection opened a door for Clive and Wendy. They were able to visit us frequently. Tim and Charlotte were always delighted when they came.

In 1978, we were living in North Oxford, in Charlbury Road. This peaceful road has the Dragon School at one end and the Oxford High School at the other. Tim went to one, Charlotte to the other. We took Tim on a tour of the Dragon before term began. It happened that we had just bought an inflatable dinghy. On that particular day, it was in the sitting room, where the children had been playing with it. When we returned from the school inspection, Tom jumped into his boat, seized the paddle, pretending to row, and announced, 'I'm off to Treasure Island.'

Poor boy! The words conjured up the hours of incarceration in dusty classrooms which lay before him. He was not one who took kindly to school. Treasure Island was much more in his line.

At the back of Charlbury Road was St Luke's, a private nursing home into which Dot had moved of her own volition. At the beginning of that year, 1978, Dot was eighty-six. Her room was quite snug, though when one went to visit early in the morning, the establishment smelt like the bottom of a ferret's cage. Dot still had many of her faculties. Walking was difficult for her, but her eyesight remained keen, as did her wits. She had comic tales to tell of the other denizens of the building. She read a lot and played patience.

One day, she said she would like to read more Dickens. What had she not read? We ran through the titles. No, she had never read *Hard Times*. I bought her the Penguin edition, light for an old lady to carry. She died before she could finish it. I wished that the last book she read had been more cheerful, but like me she had a taste for literary misery.

We still have her copy of the novel. In it, I found a clever little palindromic game, drawn in pencil on paper, with which she had been amusing herself.

But before Dot leaves the earthly scene, another story must be told.

During 1978, I travelled a great deal. My restless nature was well satisfied, but in fact most of the travel resulted from those random events with which the universe is filled. During the summer, we took all four children up to Blakeney on the North Norfolk coast, to a spacious apartment called 'The Granary Flat'. The Granary Flat overlooked marshes and sea, those wild marshes, choked with bird life, and that wild cold sea whose very name suggests the proximity of icebergs and such ports as Murmansk. To Murmansk little Elizabethan ships once set sail from Blakeney, loaded with wheat, to return with furs and caviar.

So began our love affair with that fairly unfrequented region of England, the land of wide open skies and broad undiscovered beaches. Margaret was later to buy a flat in Blakeney, after her mother died.

Travels abroad were to Iowa, to receive a Pilgrim Award from the

SFRA (Science Fiction Research Association), in Cedar Rapids, set in territory far wider and flatter than Norfolk; to Australia, that relic of Gondwanaland, where I walked in the Dandenong Hills with Lee Harding one fine morning, and saw two lyre birds in a forest straight out of the Carboniferous; to Dublin, to support Harry in his founding of World SF; to Palermo, to a conference of critics; and to Sumatra.

Sumatra must have its own chapter. Palermo requires immediate attention.

The Pilgrim Award was one indication that, beside my creative writing, another reputation was growing – as a critic. During my first plunge into that sepia world of 'neutral-tinted haps and such', created by Thomas Hardy, I came across a study of his works by Henry Charles Duffin (Third edition, 1937), which showed me that there was much a casual reader might miss in any book, towards which a critic might direct him.

When I started writing criticism of science fiction, this became my own approach. I sought to address both those who were already enjoying science fiction, with those individual tropes which distinguish it from other types of fiction (for instance, the conviction that, however we begin, we may never return to that base again), and those who might be spirited enough to try it.

This attitude informed my history of SF although, it must be admitted, I hoped also to create perhaps a more favourable climate in which my own writing might flourish.

Since my *Billion Year Spree* had welcomed the increasing academic interest in science fiction, I was *persona grata* among scholars around the world. When invited to a meeting of critics in Palermo, I accepted, curious to hear what might be said about SF's diversity by someone who had seen only a few indifferent films. Rather more eagerly, I wished to see something of Sicily, that meeting place of cultures from all quarters of the Mediterranean.

Palermo, the Sicilian capital, was a great roaring place, crumbling, aspiring upwards, choked with poverty and smart cars. It was a hot city, yet I felt no warmth towards it.

Most of the critics at the conference were Marxists, and talked in Marxist jargon, jargon rendered more impenetrable by instantaneous translation. These translations formed a new idiolect, florid, nonsensical, comic, a *lingua blanca* of scholarship. Russian guests were present at the conference. Much kowtowing went on in their presence. When they spoke, they were obsequiously permitted to speak beyond anyone else's allotted time. The prevailing assumption was that the democratic West was finished and the sanity of Soviet Communism was about to take its place.

There was a small minority who felt about all this as I did, an Italian, a marvellously depressed German from Kessel, and a Russian. We ate together – food in Palermo was irresistible – and discussed the problems of life in the West. The Russian was my old friend, Kagarlitsky.

Since he was arriving a day later, following the usual Russian difficulties over passports, I made the effort to drive out to the distant airport to meet him. 'Never speak ill of Mussolini to taxi drivers,' I was warned. 'He's remembered here as Local Boy Makes Good.'

The taxi caught fire once or twice *en route*. The driver would stop, open up the bonnet of his old car and beat out the flames with his hat. I pointed out this phenomenon to Kagarlitsky on the journey back into Palermo.

'It is more easy for the man to buy a new hat than a new taxi,' he told me.

He wearied of the oratory of the conference even more quickly than I.

'You see, Brian, tomorrow will be much the same as today. Slogans have not much variety. We can miss tomorrow and remain saner for it.' He gave me that sly grin of his. 'We can take a bus trip to Monreale and see the frescos there. You as a rich Westerner will be delighted to pay for my little journey . . .'

The two of us took the day off and caught a coach heading inland. As we passed through the grim and crooked outskirts of Palermo, I remarked on their unrelenting filth to Kagarlitsky.

He shook his head. 'Merely a little untidy . . .'

He lingered a long time in the cathedral of Monreale, drinking in the mosaics, claimed to rival those in Ravenna. Afterwards, we drank beer in the market square. How civilised was his mixture of sadness and wit: the ideal perception, it seemed, of a spoilt world. When he spoke of the fate of his country, I asked him how Britain might evade a similar one.

'First, it's a good idea not to shoot your royal family.'

On the last morning in Palermo, I found my way alone to a quayside where I could look northwards across the Tyrrhenian Sea. A yacht with a white sail was setting out from a nearby anchorage for unknown regions. I watched it go, white against blue, with its freight of inevitable symbolism, life, freedom; also death, the soul departing.

And suddenly into my mind flooded a whole novel, a cascade of circumstance, characters, narrative. In those overwhelming moments, it was as if a life was born. Once before, when I was less equipped as a novelist, a similar opportunity had opened up. Then I had not embraced it, pleading to myself that there was much else to be done. This time, standing on the lip of the Mediterranean, about to fly home to Margaret, I resolved that whatever happened, I would write the novel that had presented itself to me so unexpectedly.

When I returned to Oxford, just after the midnight of Sunday, 22 October, Margaret told me that Dot was ill. The St Luke's doctor had given all the occupants of the Home an anti-flu injection. Dot had protested to him that she was allergic to such injections, having suffered badly from one some years previously. He had insisted: the home must be kept flu-free during the winter. She had suffered an immediate adverse reaction.

I stood by her bedside on Monday morning. Her face and her poor little hands were badly swollen. She could not open her eyes. But she was *compos mentis*, and asked me about Palermo and the conference, showing her usual interest in foreign places. We talked for a while. I gave her a rosebud from our garden, from which I had removed the thorns. She clutched it.

Obligations awaited fulfilment. On the following morning, Tuesday 24th, I had to go to London to present the Society of Authors' annual report at the AGM, to be held in the Arts Club in Dover Street. On the Wednesday, I had to attend the Arts Council.

On the Tuesday morning, I was hustling about, shoving papers into my briefcase, preparing to leave. Margaret told me I should go round to St Luke's to visit my mother.

'I haven't got time. I'll go this evening.'

'I think you ought to go now. She didn't look at all well when I went round at teatime yesterday.' Her gentle persistence won the day.

I phoned the doctor. He was casual. 'Oh, these old ladies are as tough as old boots. She'll be running round the garden in another few days.'

When I got to Dot's room, I could see she was weaker. She could scarcely speak. By her bedside lay a postcard I had sent her from Palermo; she had been unable to read it. She had wanted nothing to eat. My rosebud remained clutched in her hand. She was able to murmur a few words, not of complaint. After a while, I kissed her cheek and left, to drive up to London.

Margaret went to see her before noon. As she climbed the stairs, she met a nurse coming down, weeping. Dot had just died, still clutching the rosebud.

Margaret phoned the news to one of the Society of Authors officials, with strict orders not to inform me until after the AGM. As I was ascending the platform to deliver the report, the official came up and broke the news.

'Your mother's passed away.'

Of course there was nothing for it but to deliver my report and continue with the proceedings.

Back home that evening, I phoned Betty in London with the news. Margaret and I had been looking after Dot for some years, doing her shopping and other chores. Dot was always delighted when Betty put in her rare appearances, and left her most of the family belongings and her estate.

I went to the mortuary to say goodbye to her. Elizabeth May Aldiss my dear mother . . . Looking down on her with choked regret, I thought again of her life, of the lost daughter, which had brought her so much sadness, her hatred of winter, her loyalty to Bill, her love of laughter, indeed of the whole mystery of existence. Inevitably, too, of the sorrow and happiness of my own existence and those dear to me. Her cheek was firm, cold.

According to May's wishes, she was cremated. Clive and Wendy came up to Oxford to stand with Tim and Charlotte for the ceremony, as did Betty. Afterwards, Dot's ashes were cast to the winds.

The boat with the white sail, white against blue, the symbolism of a soul departing . . . had I been more sensitive, that moment on the Palermo quayside could have been premonitory.

But life had to be lived. The day after the cremation, Margaret and I received two old friends, Michael Moorcock and the Czech writer Josef Nesvadba, as prearranged, and showed them something of Oxford. Nesvadba was charmed to find boxes of fireworks in the shops, and bought one to take home. We feared that they would be confiscated at Prague airport.

I sat down to write *Life in the West*. One aspect of the ground plan that had been given me in Palermo needed alteration. Included in the novel is a scene where Tom Squire and his sister Deirdre grieve over their dead mother, lying in her coffin over a cold Christmas. It was a way of saying in fiction what cannot be spoken in fact.

A whole wearisome landscape stretched out, abraded by thin layers of snow like leprosy on skin. There was brown in it too, speckled, extending from my mother's dead face. The world was in winter – this time the final winter. We were alone in the room, I as motionless as she. Electricity fell like dandruff from the walls.

Sorry, so sorry it hadn't been better . . .

The fact that it hadn't been too bad was hardly a consolation, hardly checked the breath of the north wind . . . How imperfect that my mourning had to be done on paper. How typical.

Life in the West was published by Weidenfeld & Nicolson in 1980. Anthony Burgess, a generous man, named it as one of his ninety-nine best novels published since the conclusion of the war in 1945. The novel ends with almost the last question Dot ever asked: 'How was Palermo?' – although in the book Palermo is disguised under the near-anagram of Ermalpa.

Margaret, like me, was also busy at this time. During one week in November 1979, for instance, she had a choir practice, a choir evening, was off to her pottery class, and to a lunch, attended an embroidery course, and then was involved in choir rehearsals for a Christmas *Messiah*. I was always singing about the house: hers was a voice more fitted for public performance. We were also looking after Aunt Dorothy and the children.

And while the congested flow of family event continued, the larger world was busy transforming itself into something our fathers would hardly have recognised. Manual typewriters had succumbed to electric typewriters – which, with their resounding golfball technology, were with us less than a decade – to be followed by electronic typewriters. Now typewriters are themselves obsolescent ('Goodbye, carbon copies!' cried Margaret delightedly), fading before the onslaught of word processors, those foot soldiers of the computer cavalry.

In 1975, there was not a single PC in the world; by 1980, one person in ten in the West had one. Now everyone has a PC or its equivalent. And now the PCs communicate with others, all around the world.

In 1970, we sold our Ford Anglia and bought our first Volvo Estate. Automobiles were improving as rapidly as the roads: superior design, more power, better brakes, lights, steering, comfort. Radios in cars . . . CB band radio. Seat belts.

Driving back from London (as we did last night), drizzle and light mist closed in at midnight. The road sizzled before us, well laid, well lit, mile after mile, the dual lights high overhead stretching their illuminated spine into the distance. Then we were swallowed in a whale of starless night. The superb dead quality of the dark was punctuated by an occasional car, diamond bright in the opposing lane, red-eyed ahead of us. The beauty of the technological sublime, the pleasure of speed . . .

London to Oxford? Little more than an hour. A snip.

Seen from the viewpoint of our childhood, this was the future: slick, heavy, brutal, surreal, rich, parentless . . .

XXVI

The Wilderness

What censors cut out of films is never the shooting, the burglary, the profitable swindling and gambling; it is the kisses. What justifies [this] right-thinking attitude is the fact (in my opinion enormously creditable to human nature) that the deadly sin of concupiscence is, for most people, much more attractive than the deadly sins of anger and even avarice.

Aldous Huxley
Ethics in Andalusia

There was never reason to doubt that it is impossible to return, after some years have passed, to a place once loved. As Proust says, we are really seeking a time – *temps perdu* – as well as a place. Sagacity apart, we must take a chance when it offers itself. And in 1978 I had the chance to return to Sumatra – and grabbed it.

My novel set in Sumatra, *A Rude Awakening*, had been written. The act of writing, as so often, seemed to release new possibilities – the possibility of revisiting that distant land, which I had thought never to see again. In the tangled way of time, publication of the novel by Weidenfeld & Nicolson coincided with my return home. I found that there was a bitterness in its pages I did not intend.

Before the Singapore plane touched down at Medan airport, I had made friends with a Singaporean couple, Tan Teck Meng and Rosie Ong. Rosie was the prettiest lady you could rest your eyes on. We trudged from the plane across to the airport building. By Customs, an engineer was kneeling, prising up white floor tiling with a screwdriver. A flash of memory struck me. Good God, a similar man had been prising up that same tile back in 1946, when I was leaving Sumatra!

Nothing else was the same as before.

In the intervening thirty-two years, the capital city of Medan had crawled outwards to encompass the airport, which had previously stood in wild country. The urban sprawl resembled the slums of Jakarta or Manila, an unplanned eructation of people and attap roofs. It was but a symbol of what was to come.

Once again, the story twists back to the war, the damned war, the time when everything changed. To the days when I was all feeling and no expression, a gaunt young man of good will, who accepted whatever happened to him as fate.

The Japanese surrender in August 1945 left thousands of their forces scattered throughout the East. It was the task of the Allies to release all Allied prisoners of war, and disarm the Japanese and return them to their rightful homes.

This was more easily said than done. The Japanese 25th Army was in control, and keeping a fragile peace in a country that had recently declared itself an independent republic.

In October of 1945, a convoy sailed from Madras to Sumatra, some ships going to the port of the capital, Medan, on the north-east coast, some to the port of Padang, across the equator, on the south-west coast.

A large detachment of 26th Indian Division embarked on a small crowded ship, the *Dilwara*, from Madras. We sailed for Emmahaven, the port of Padang (since rechristened Teluk Bayur).

We carried in our kitbags a booklet issued by the Army which made reference to Sumatra in not very encouraging terms. After warning of dangerous diseases, insects and snakes, it said, in patronising Army style, 'But don't worry – you are unlikely to be posted there.'

Sumatra is pierced by the equator like a sausage on a spit. When we crossed the line, the usual coarsely comic ceremonies went on, and King Neptune came aboard. We passed the Nias Islands, where reputedly King Kong was captured. It was on 13 October that we landed at the deep-water port of Emmahaven. The excitement involved in entering a strange tropical land was intense. Paul Gauguin could have felt no more moved when he sailed from Marseilles in 1891 and caught his first sight of Tahiti. Oh, that I had had Gauguin's genius for expressionist colour and symbolic content while on the great island!

In a letter home, I reported our arrival.

* * *

Sumatra looked dull, wet and miserable from the ship; clouds wreathed it about and we could make out no details. We entered into much gloomy discussion, wanting to know why we, the interfering British, should occupy a Dutch island. It did not make sense. The 25th Japanese Imperial Army was waiting to surrender to us, and if they did not cause trouble there were always the head-hunters and cannibals [to contend with]. So the discussion went on until a cold, slanting rain drove us off deck.

Next day, the weather was fine. The little islands looked green in the blue waters; the land looked definitely 'tropical', as you read of it in books; the surf was white where it beat against the strip of yellow sand; up to the edge of the beach grew palm trees and, behind them, steaming jungle . . .

That day, a lot of troops went ashore in LCAs (Landing Craft, Assault). We, the Signals, were standing by with kit packed, but nothing happened. We were told to be ready at eight o'clock next morning; we spent that night on the ship; I slept on the mess table.

We were ready to move at eight next morning, but it was ten before we got going. The docks were quite large, fairly well equipped, with moorings for several large ships. We didn't like it much because we had to carry a lot of heavy stores off the ship, and were hot and fed up by the time it was finished. We sat by the stores and waited for a train. The sun was hot and strong.

At least we had something to look at. A party of Japs was moved up under an Indian guard. Their uniforms were smart, if varied. Some looked like the typical Jap you see pictures of – all goggles and grin, big teeth.

The train came up. It was a train but only just! We stowed all the kit aboard and crammed on. The engine gave an almost human cry of anguish, the coaches bucked, and we set off at a furious pace, inland towards Padang. I stood on the platform at one end of the coach to get a good look at the scenery, our first exciting view of the island. There were so many fleeting impressions it is hard to record them all.

First and foremost, we were interested in the people, the population we would have to live among. They presented distinctly Oriental features – flat faces, hooded eyes, high cheekbones, resembling slightly the Burmese. Their skins are a pleasant colour, a light golden tint, as if they had lived their lives at a warm English seaside. They seem more Westernised than the Indians.

The variety of clothes is interesting. For the most part, the men wear shorts, but there are a lot of flannels and pyjamas and silk sarongs, most of them gay with flower patterns. They wear slouch hats, which look most odd, no turbans, but occasionally the big coolie hat, two feet across, a wonderful effort. The first day, we hardly saw any females, but now they have found we are different from the Japanese they are bustling out and about. The ladies, like the men, are part-Westernised, skirts being much in evidence; Indian saris are not worn, but long sarongs, with well-filled blouses. There are many Chinese woman, most of whom wear the traditional dress – either a kimono or pyjamas. The kids are all plump and healthy-looking, and everyone is clean and decent.

The women wear pigtails, or dress their hair Western style, while the men will have nothing of the Indian custom of shaving their heads or wearing their hair long, but have honest-to-goodness partings!

Most of the houses are rather like the better Burmese ones, made of timber and raised off the ground for fear of snakes. Some are the usual shack type . . . Most Sumatran homes have decent shutters to their windows, and verandahs. We could see solid tables with cloths spread, and beautiful carpets on the floor: all opposed to the same class of Indian dwelling, where the inhabitants eat off a mud floor.

Outside a few houses were dovecotes, or cages with pretty birds inside. In the rooms, one could see mirrors and coloured prints. All such details impressed us very much. I should have been glad to be invited into these houses.

Everyone was friendly, waving and smiling. How delightful it seemed, after the squalor of India! We judged everything in comparison with India as, I suppose, is only natural; and everything seemed superior to its Indian equivalent. The reason is fairly obvious: Sumatra is a hot, fertile island, abounding with every necessity of life, and a lot of its luxuries. India for the most part is desert, or artificially irrigated; the people slave to earn a bare living. Here, nothing can stop the fruit and vegetation growing; the climate is ideal. Rainfall is 170 inches a year – Norfolk gets 35 inches.

The short railway journey ended far too soon for our liking, and we came to a sudden stop at Padang station, five miles inland. Here we had the job of unloading our stores from the train on to lorries, while a highly interested and respectful crowd looked on.

It was baking hot now, and our bush shirts were wet rags on our backs. I kept thinking of Noël Coward's 'Mad dogs and Englishmen go out in the midday sun . . .' And we asked each other why the defeated enemy couldn't have done our work, to save us having to work like coolies.

Nevertheless, we fell in smartly when we had loaded up the lorries. We turned to the left, and started marching off to our new billet. It was an hour's march away.

We moved into a barracks only lately vacated by the Japanese Army. We had no beds. Two shelves seven feet in width stretched from one end of the barn-like structure to the other. On these we slept, cheek by jowl, under our mosquito nets. No doubt official thinking was, If it's good enough for the Japs, it's good enough for our troops.

Almost at once, we were put to our duties, working long shifts with continuous R/T and W/T traffic. I was on exchange duty in the town hall, the HQ of Allied Forces in Sumatra, announcing, when I wrote home that I operated a new machine which I described as 'smashing': an American model made by Western Electric. It had sixty lines out. 'There are 27 plugs, 60 jacks, and 70 lights on the thing. Also 16 switches.' I liked working it, complaining at the same time of the arrogance of officers who treated operators like dirt. That sort, I explained, always had to wait; their calls were always unaccountably delayed.

Sumatra had formed the westernmost unit of the Netherlands East Indies (NEI). During the three years of Japanese occupation, matters changed there as elsewhere. On 17 August, 1945, Dr A. Soekarno proclaimed the old NEI to be the new independent Indonesian Republic. This left the British Force Commander in a dilemma. He had a commitment to reinstate the Dutch, who were – at least in their own eyes – the rightful owners. Shipping the Japs back to Japan was a move approved by the local population; the shooting began only after we started to move in Dutch contingents.

In Java, where Indonesian politics are born, matters were always worse than in Sumatra. In Sumatra, our difficulties were low-key but continuous.

We were short of men, which heightened the ambiguity of the situation. During our early days in Padang, no official surrender ceremony had been enacted. The Japs were still at large; indeed, the British used them as police, almost as Allies. It was irregular, but British Forces numbered only 5,000, Japanese 50,000.

Some friends and I were sitting in a small comfortable café near the harbour. We were all armed with Sten guns slung over one shoulder. At another table sat a quartet of Indian troops, rifles slung. At a third table sat a body of Dutch, armed with American carbines, and at a fourth, armed and jackbooted Japanese soldiers. It was hard to imagine a more delicate situation. But the Chinese waiters served us all, calmly and efficiently . . .

Other powers took an interest in the situation. At a meeting in Moscow in December 1945, Ernest Bevin, then British Foreign Secretary, was discussing the matter with Molotov and Vyshinsky. Bevin said, 'The duty of taking the surrender of the Japanese and restoring civil government fell on Great Britain. Trouble had not been expected. Our duty was to remove hundreds of thousands of Japanese and between three hundred and four hundred thousand internees, Dutch, European and Eurasian. But we were attacked. We sent Brigadier A. W. F. Mallaby to meet the Indonesians and he was murdered.'

Later, Bevin continued: 'When we have completed the task allotted to us, we will clear out and leave the rest to the Dutch and Indonesians.' He said he did not know how it would work out, and he didn't much care.

The British could hardly be expected to fight for Dutch possessions when they were planning their withdrawal from India. In this the British were wise. They did not become embroiled in costly colonial struggles, as did the Dutch, French and Americans. At the same time, the indifference shown by those in high places, exemplified by Bevin's remarks, explains why we lingered for a year in Sumatra, doing very little, effecting very little.

No doubt there was American pressure in the background of Britain's decision to venture so far towards the Pacific. The United States was at that time more suspicious of the British Empire than of Soviet intentions. Already the Empire was falling apart. The will had expired, along with the economic strength. So a period of uncertainty prevailed of which we were among its early victims.

My intention is to get to the subject of Medan as quickly as possible; but if I do not say something about the British occupation of Padang, *perhaps no one else ever will.*

As in the early days of the occupation of defeated Germany, we were at first forbidden to fraternise with the natives. Such bans cannot be enforced, and a barter system was soon established.

The political situation affected the financial one. Our Army pay was in Dutch guilders, but we were kept on half-pay, the other half being banked for us. However, the guilder was no longer acceptable local currency; it could be used only in the NAAFI. At that time, no form of Indonesian currency had been established. Instead, the worthless Jap occupation currency, an imitation guilder, remained in circulation. Everyone knew the Jap guilder had no value but, since everyone was forced to use it, it had a chimerical worth. It was just an obsidional paper token. There was not, and never had been, any bank to back it. We were in a besieged city.

A city with the word MERDEKA! scribbled on its walls.

The Army had to accept the situation. In no time, along with our meagre ration of guilders, we were issued with a stack of the Jap notes.

We behaved like any other occupying army. When off duty, our relief took the S Section truck and bucketed about town and nearby countryside, looting furniture, being kind to kids, and getting drunk or laid. It was a way of life.

We found a swimming pool near Emmahaven, gloriously neglected and full of bright green water. The jungle had closed in about it. Roots of trees crawled towards the deep end. Highly picturesque, we thought, as we plunged in. Despite the fact that both undergrowth and trees crawled with snakes, we bathed there frequently.

One night, a brigade major and his lady friend, a nurse, drove to this pool after dark, to swim naked in the glare of their Jeep headlights. The Indonesians came and shot them up. Their bodies were found next day, floating in green and red water. From then on, the pool was out of bounds.

By saying 'Indonesians' here, I mean the 'extremists'. We never used the words *terrorists* or *nationalists* or *republicans*; they were always, mild word, as of a differing political party, *extremists* . . . In the same way, the later vicious Communist infiltrations of Malaya were dubbed The Emergency. How calming, the British use of litotes . . .

As the Jap Army HQ in Brastagi was investigated by the incoming British Forces, it was discovered how much booty they had accumulated during their three-year tenure of the island. Some of this booty was released to the troops, including drink. The most precious Dutch liquors had been stored away, now to be liberated. To our mess every

Saturday morning, a large wooden crate was delivered. We opened it with crowbars and drank its contents that evening. The drinks varied, week by week.

I remember the riotous kümmel evening. At the end of it, a mate and I carried or dragged the RSM to his room, slinging him comatose on his bed. My friend ripped the electricity cable off the wall on our way out, and half the camp was plunged into darkness.

The crème de menthe evening is also etched in memory. There I sat, beaming among friends, with a one-pint beer glass full of the green liqueur in my fist. It all went down. To the best of my memory, it stayed down.

It is hard to say how character-forming such experiences were.

A favourite venue was the RAPWI Camp. This acronym stood for Repatriation of Allied Prisoners of War and Civilian Internees. Acronyms were much in use. Our unit became part of ALFSEA, Allied Land Forces South East Asia. IFTUS stood for Inhabitants Friendly To Us. Many of the inhabitants of the RAPWI Camp were friendly to us, we being their liberators. These included a number of Dutch ladies who, after three years behind barbed wire, were eager for a little fun before they returned to the Netherlands.

I struck up a friendship with a pretty blonde girl who was half an inch taller than I. We were tender with each other. How strange it was to be tender. Unfortunately, a mate of mine, Paddy, regarded the lady as his property. On one of our drunken Saturday evenings, he was rushing about our compound in the dark, yelling in fury for my blood, firing off his Sten into the air. This encouraged others to fire away at random too. Which encouraged me to make myself scarce. Some wild nights we used to have, and all!

Paddy and I patched up our differences. He was an interesting case. An Irishman, a good-looking man, he had signed up in the British Army in order to fight the Germans, whom he hated even more than the English. His hatred of the English was deep and ineradicable. Many men would not listen to him, but he found I would sit tight to hear of Irish suffering.

'The bastarding English,' he would say. 'They'd have the shirt off of your fucking back. They ruined Ireland, stole everything we had – except our pride. I'd kill every fucking manjack of them, given half a chance.'

Then he'd pat my arm and grin. 'Nothing personal, mate, nothing personal.'

The knowledge that I had made it to the southern hemisphere filled me with delight. I loved Medan. I wandered about the bazaar and talked to whoever would talk to me. When I had accumulated Jap guilders enough, I bought carvings, some of which I still possess. I sat and drank excellent Sumatran coffee in roadside hovels where my friends would not tread. 'Aldiss – *pukka jungley wallah!*' they said.

When a posting came from Padang to Medan, we went by ship, the *San Sovrino*. The shorter route, across the mountainous interior, where ancient volcanoes smouldered, was considered too dangerous. One morning before dawn, I skipped breakfast to get up on deck and wedge myself into the bows. The ship was a speck on the calm bowl of the Pacific. The very name of the Pacific acted like an elixir.

Straight ahead of us, out of the horizon, came the flame of equatorial sun, ripening red as it climbed into a faultless sky. The ocean changed colour to greet it. The world rejoiced in its generous lord, giver of all life and beauty.

A lesser light failed that month, February 1946. Grandma Wilson died in Peterborough. She had seen out the war; it was time to be finished. My Uncle Bert, himself now old and impoverished, sold Brinkdale and went to live in digs. He still continued faithfully to send me books and cylindrical tins of Player's cigarettes.

The sense that the Sumatran venture was getting nowhere, and was being sidetracked by Bevin and the War Office, reinforced the feeling that one's youth was passing, wasting, being brustalised. If happiness could be snatched in a glass, even a glass of crème de menthe – well, there it was.

When returning to Medan in 1978, I was again in a cloudy mood, for at home Margaret and I were unprecedentedly at odds with each other.

Of course everything had changed. The NEI for which we reluctantly fought in 1946 had faded away like a shadow. The Indonesian Republic was firmly implanted in the tropical present tense. Here was a great encompassing Muslim world in which hardly anyone spoke English. I was to find no one who recalled that the English had once been here, that English graves lay in the tropical earth.

Progress had burst upon Medan. The population explosion had hit, poisoning existence. The streets thronged with people. Vendors and passers-by spilled over from the pavements, where there were pavements, into the roadways, endangering their lives. Traffic choked every thoroughfare. It consisted mainly of motor bikes, mopeds and scooters, all spewing forth rank emissions. Accelerators were cunningly linked to hooters, so that fumes accompanied a babel of noise. The poor little city lay open to flies like a broken egg.

There were places I wanted to revisit. My memory was of a quiet place, shaded by grand trees, shabby-comfortable streets down which an occasional bullock cart would trundle. Signs saying *Merdeka!*, certainly, but interesting shop signs in Sanskrit and Chinese characters, courteous people, and good ten-cent cigars.

Well, *Merdeka* – the Freedom they wanted so badly – had certainly come, but at horrendous expense for much of the population. The Japs had been booted out, the British had been booted out, and finally the Dutch had been booted out. Soekarno then set about booting out others. As his regime became more extreme (less extreme than his successor, Suharto, who booted Soekarno out!), many citizens were killed – according to Bertrand Russell, that old man unafraid to speak his mind, the number could have been as high as ten million. Perhaps he was unafraid to exaggerate too.

As at home, so here: I was adrift.

As I pressed through the crowds, I saw few foreign signs. Talking to one old Chinese who had some English, I learned that Chinese traders were now forced to take on Muslim names. I wandered the streets with an inadequate map. The Dutch names with which I remained familiar – the Kesawan had been the main street – were swept away, replaced by names of generals or the dates of dire events, all in Malay; the language which seemed so friendly in Malaya suddenly became foreign, baffling.

I had often been shot at in Medan in 'the old days'; still I had loved the city. Now I felt alienated and lost.

Yet – there was a friendly landmark! A cinema I knew. Its name had been changed. Its curving walls needed painting and repair. But it was unmistakably the old Dutch cinema I had occasionally visited to watch a fantasy of one kind or another. Years and regimes had gone by. It was still showing fantasies; *Sharkmen of the Pacific*, *The Doom of the Cobra God*. At least that had survived.

With the cinema as a landmark, I could navigate somewhat. So I found my way to a nearby street I had once known well. It possessed arcaded shop-houses of an old Singaporean style which had served as dwellings in the time of disruption. There I had spent a great deal of time, wholly pleasant, with an educated Chinese family recently released from a Jap prison camp.

We used to sit outside of an evening, under the arcade.

In a distant street, a click-clack, click-clack could be heard. It grew louder. Eventually down our street would come a little leathery-faced man pushing an elaborate wooden barrow-stall on two wheels. We would hail him. He would stop and detach high wooden stools from his stall. On these we sat at the stall and were served delicious bowls of soup and noodles, followed with juicy skewered satay, all by the glow of his gas lamp. How happy those evenings were, and I half in love with the night and the Chinese lady.

Now, sacks were stored where she had lived, men bustled about with trolleys, raw-faced, hurried, as if they switched themselves on and off and had no time for anything else.

Now that I thought I could get the hang of the town, I returned to the hotel, to report to Teck Meng and Rosie, and prepare for a more serious expedition. We had with us a helpful guide, a Christian Batak named Michael. With him in tow, I caught a taxi to go to see where I had once lived.

Our signals section, fresh from Padang, had moved into comfortable Dutch houses in occupied Medan. No longer did we sleep on stone, wood, earth or concrete; we had looted beds. The balcony of my room looked out over the *maidan*, with a vista of a quiet unhedged road and several large trees. It was a corner house, with two doors, one on to one street, one on to another, a sidestreet on which stood a lesser house adapted as our mess.

My disillusion with the Army pecking order was such that at this stage I declared myself a Communist, as did most of my friends. We depended on every word written by Captain Gallagher in the *Daily Mirror*. When the first general election came after war's end (the election that swept Churchill away and brought in Clement Attlee), I was under twenty-one, and so disbarred from voting. Had I voted, it would have been for the British Communist Party, which polled two million votes. After having, as the saying went, fought in Burma for king and country, being denied the vote brought further bitterness.

While in Medan, I managed to extract myself from the signals routine of night duty and other rituals. When I launched a modest O Section magazine, I found few contributors. It's no unusual experience. I wrote most of the magazine myself, while a nice Dutch lady in the Company office, Ady, typed every issue out for me. I also drew a few sketches.

The idea was to drain a little of the Army out of my veins. An amateur talent contest was staged in the De Witte Club. I entered. I sang a comic song, accompanied on the piano by a friend, Tony

Mercer, himself a beautiful singer, who later starred on television in George Mitchell's *Black and White Minstrel Show*. Reader, I bombed.

I was awful. At the end of my act, I walked off the stage to dead silence. None of my friends, merciful friends, ever mentioned the incident again.

It did not stop me circulating poems, stories and parodies.

Our officer was a Captain Shamboo Singh. He summoned me to his office one day.

'Aldiss, I understand you can paint and draw?'

Oh God, what had I done? He had found one of those scurrilous poems about the RSM . . . The vision arose of Sammy Howells at school, discovering some of my more subversive writing.

'A bit, sir. Just for fun.'

'You are an artist?' His expression was benevolent enough.

'Very amateur, sir.'

'Some good news. We are taking over a theatre. Morale must be maintained. We will have films and perhaps a social event once a week. Also other events.'

'Yessir.'

'We might have dances and invite some local people, to show we are friendly.' He paused, regarding me thoughtfully, wondering perhaps if he had chosen the wrong man. 'If you are prepared to decorate the theatre and take charge of it, I can release you from all signal office duties. You understand?'

'Where is this theatre, sir?'

Things were looking up.

True, the theatre could be described simply as a barn, with rattan sides and attap thatch. But it was large and substantial. It had a stage with dressing rooms to the rear. It was now my domain.

I set to energetically. Two sepoys were seconded to assist me; despite their limited English, they were helpful and enjoyed the work. With Shamboo's assistance, seats arrived, and a bar. The Army Cinematography Unit donated a screen and promised to obtain recent films from Singapore. Everything had to come from Singapore.

A series of large boards arrived. I procured a selection of oil paints, retrieved from a Japanese cache. With the confidence of an amateur, I primed the boards, painted them, had the sepoys secure them round the walls of the theatre, my theatre. By the time the first film was shown, the audience could gaze upon a surrounding array of tropical scenes in my best artistic manner – palm trees and sunsets, of course, rafflesia, tigers and other animals, funny British soldiers, slinky brown dancing girls, a row of heavier Dutch dancing girls.

I installed a looted bed in one of the dressing rooms, on which I might take a siesta in privacy. The theatre was never used during the day. It was a haven of silence.

The Saturday binges were a success. We had waiters in white uniforms, looking smart, and a scratch band. Tony Mercer sang. Some Dutch and Chinese turned up to dance, but no Sumatrans; they were probably ordered to stay away. The political situation was deteriorating. A lot of random sniping took place and in Batavia British troops were involved in heavy fighting against *Merdeka* armies.

On one occasion, when we were watching a live act, a random shot was fired from outside our perimeter. It came through the thatch and landed on my foot. It was spent, and my shoe stopped most of its force. Not much of an event, but still the first time a bullet had struck me. I have kept it, as parents keep their first child's first tooth.

Our beer came in cans from places like Milwaukee. Large numbers of empty beer cans remained after the bar closed. My sepoys collected them up in sackfuls when doing the cleaning.

At the end of our sideroad stood a high wire netting barrier, the perimeter, set up to stop extremists infiltrating our lines. But somehow a hole had conveniently opened in it. One could easily climb through into a kampong where women and children, and possible extremists lived. I liked the kampong and always greeted people as I passed through it.

Generally speaking, I was heading for a little café on the edge of the kampong.

The café was run by two Chinese and a Sumatran. They seemed to have little trade. I liked sitting there chatting with them. We drank coffee. Sumatran coffee is excellent. At the end of our conversation, I handed over my sack of empty beer cans, for which they paid in Jap guilders. It was not quite a racket, more a valuable extra source of income.

It took me a while to realise that my cans served as cases for Molotov cocktails. Primed as bombs, they were thrown at British troops – not necessarily at Signals, a very non-combatant kind of troops, but rather at the 'Swobs', the South Wales Borderers, who patrolled the Medan area. My career as an arms dealer was brief. Reluctantly, I gave up this source of worthless guilders.

Attempts to get myself remustered as a draughtsman were in vain. But my responsibilities permitted use of a Jeep, complete with Indian driver. I could go more or less where I liked by day; there was a curfew at night, after darkness had fallen. In fact, the British held little but the major towns. The extremists held the countryside. We were confined within Medan.

There I met the friendly Chinese family of whose traces I came in search in 1978. My fear was that they had been eliminated by Soekarno's purges before they had managed to leave the country. I had had no news of them for twenty-five years or more.

As we crawled through 1978 Medan, which had acquired one way streets and strange new roads, Michael and the taxi driver were encouraging. 'Was it here?' 'Is this it?', as I scrutinised yet another street, another house, searching for *my* house.

The road system was baffling. The city had spread so much. The Malay names conveyed nothing to me. I was growing desperate. It had been a good house, that house in which I had once lived. Surely no one would have pulled it down.

We came to the next street. I asked the driver to stop. I got out and stared. We had been driving about for over an hour. I was losing hope, as well as straining Michael's patience. The house on the corner could have been the house where I had lived, where an upper room had been mine. It now had railings round it, and an attempt at a garden.

And even if it was not the right house ... well, I couldn't let Michael down.

'This is it,' I told Michael cheerfully.

He entered the shady garden with me, and rang the bell. The house was white-painted, like every other house in the road. It did look a little older. Of course, the friendly neighbouring kampong had been swept away. But it would be too much to ask if—

The door opened. By luck the family living here were of the Batak tribe to which Michael belonged. We were shown in with great courtesy. The family seated me in a neat living room, plying me with coffee and the local Garuda cigarettes, flavoured with nutmeg. Four adults and as many children starred curiously at me as I explained my quest through Michael.

They shook their heads. No, they never heard that British troops had been in Sumatra. Only Dutch.

They were curious. Yes, I could look at other rooms. *Tidak apa.*

We had had a sort of washroom under the back stairs in our day. Only these were the front stairs. That is, the front stairs now. Suddenly, I was confused about the layout of the house I thought

I had remembered so clearly. But, yes, there was a modern little bathroom under the stairs, with a door opening in the same way. And the window on the stairs – surely that was the same . . . The family clustered round, trying to read the Rosetta stone of my face.

Conviction overwhelmed me. Yes! By luck I had stumbled on the very house in which I had experienced such happiness as a young man!

They all smiled in response to my smiles. They led me upstairs. Which had been my room? Again, I felt unsure. I had forgotten how many rooms there had been on the upper level.

No, wait. You came up, you turned left . . .

'This one,' I said, pointing.

It was Grandpa's room. No, no trouble, they would wake him and I could enter. Grandpa would not mind. He was very old.

Grandpa must have been ten years my junior. He was withered and bent, short alike of teeth and breath. He bowed and grinned and made coaxing noises. The rest of the family stayed on the landing.

I looked about the room. Again I was sure. It looked right, it felt right. Here I had brought her. Here the miracle had happened.

Dora was one of the Chinese family with whom I sat in the cool evening and ate satay. We had exchanged glances. All three of the sisters were attractive; and we never saw each other alone. Besides, Dora was married to Lin, and had a small child by him.

One of my pleasures had been to call on the sisters in my Jeep and take them shopping. They liked to try on hats and shoes in shops while I stood by, admiring them, enjoying the company of women, and their pleasure in being free again. What a pretty peaceful picture they made! And Dora always the most impulsive. The one who actually bought a hat.

On one occasion, some of us had our photograph taken under the arcade where they lived. Dora stands between her husband and me, almost touching me, but not quite.

I called round there one afternoon. Only Dora was in. She would be delighted to come for a spin with me. She wore a sleeveless print dress, shoes and a little white round hat which showed off her mischievous face, framed in dark curly hair. She wore make-up. I was proud to drive her round town.

She talked about Rita Hayworth. She would like to live in London and be like Rita Hayworth. I thought she was just as beautiful as Rita Hayworth, and told her so.

'I am curious to see where you live,' she said. 'Show me.'

It was forbidden, naturally. When we were up in my room – *this* room – she said, 'I love you so much.' She came towards me from the balcony and kissed me on the lips.

How bold, how wonderful of her!

I clasped her, kissed her in return . . . nothing more – but that was far from nothing! Later, of course, there was my secluded bed in the theatre, and secret meetings, which I concealed even from my closest friends. I was redeemed by her love. She was to me what dew is to grass.

For once someone loved me without my sweating to deserve it. In that room, the days of wine and roses came back to me.

But hang on! The balcony! I remembered (didn't I?) her walking in from the balcony towards me. This room, Grandpa's room, had no balcony. There was a window. I looked out. Of course, balconies generally fell off in the tropics. It was natural, the way coconuts fell off trees. This *had* to be the room, the very room, where we fell in love, where I found my soul in China.

Sometimes when I returned in the night after curfew, a random shot would be fired in my direction. I grew used to flinging myself down to the ground. Danger meant nothing. If anything, it gave keener flavour to love.

Leaving Dora, going back in the dark, I could sneak across the kampong and through the perimeter wire to gain my room. That way, you avoided the MPs . . .

I stood rooted in the room as long as I dared, remembering Dora. She had longed to see London. I had wanted to see Singapore.

But even as I shook Grandpa's hand, even as I was escorted downstairs by the family, doubt entered my mind again. How could I have found the place? Why did it mean so much? Although I had once hoped to marry Dora, I had no wish to see her again, aged like me, except to know that she had escaped Soekarno and Suharto's purges.

We had only a few months together, meeting in secrecy, sleeping in secrecy, locked together so that our flesh plopped with sweat when we came apart. Like so many romances made by war, this one was broken by war – and of course by racial prejudice, for in 1946 Dora would have had a hard time of it in chilly England. I was prepared for us to live in Singapore – greatly to be preferred to Gorleston on Sea.

But my intentions proved as worthless as a Jap guilder: I had the backing of no possible bank. The Army was strong, I was weak, and besides . . . well, military convention fell back on a moral code to which it did not subscribe: adultery was a more popular word of condemnation then than now . . .

As Captain Shamboo Singh reminded me when I approached him on the subject.

Now I think of what Mary Shelley said in a letter to a friend, 'The eight years I passed with [Shelley] was spun out beyond the usual length of a man's life.'

I bowed to the Batak family, shook all their hands, smiled, thanked them. *Tidak apa . . .*

Yes, yes, I was happy to have seen my old home so well looked after by such a nice family. Thank you, thank you again. *Terimah kaseh . . .*

As Michael and I climbed back into the taxi, the driver asked, 'So was it your old place?'

'It was.' I tried to sound convincing.

But who was I deceiving, him or myself, or yesterday's ghosts?

The civilians from the RAPWI were sent to Holland, the Japs were shipped back to Japan. It was as Ernie Bevin had said, the task allotted to us was completed. We cleared out and left the rest to the Dutch and Indonesians to sort out.

I was despatched to Nee Soon Camp in Singapore, disillusioned, silenced. And the usual aftermath of love, when we are suddenly cast from that bliss of sex, fulfilment and tenderness, from which those three elements concoct a greater thing: I questioned whether I believed what I had felt, whether she had meant what she said. And so on. I had another drink.

In Singapore I volunteered again for service in China. Instead I was sent to Hong Kong. Like Singapore, Hong Kong was another post-war slag heap. It was less grey than Singapore and was picking up an enormous vitality which lasts to this day. Whores abounded. They descended like a pack of pretty wolves, screaming, on any vessel pulling into harbour.

My first job was to run the Hong Kong telephone exchange. For a few days, the whole city's communication system was under my control. Then a quieter job, looking after the signal office. Some nights, we had excursions into the hills, armed with pick helves. We belted through the night in Jeeps, to deal with thieves who were cutting our cable, our land line to Stanley, the copper of which was valuable.

Whores rode around Wanchai, Hong Kong's entertainment district, in trishaws. While the driver pedalled along, they let their skirts drift up in the breeze, showing their legs and a tantalising strip of white pantie in the crotch.

They were not really whores; rather, young women whose familes had become dispersed in the upheavals of war, whose men had been killed, who had made their way to Hong Kong and safety. While there, they had somehow to make a living. That nest of spicery, to use Shakespeare's phrase, between their legs, half concealed by a neat little wilderness of hair, had cash value. Demand for it was brisk among young men far from home. Those enjoyable nests, those beautiful faces – and perhaps a beautiful Chinese woman is the loveliest in the world.

Sometimes, when trade was slack, one heard a little of their histories. Always horrific, perhaps not always truthful.

I was led one night by an attractive whore through the out of bounds district, up towards the Peak. Curiosity sharpened the point of lust. She had only the standard phrases of whore's English. 'Hello, Johnny. Why you no come my flat? You likee jig-jig? You come my flat with me, Johnny. Plenty good jig-jig.'

When we eventually arrived, her 'flat' was a marquee tent, pitched on a stretch of waste ground, near an inland cliff. Inside, it was lit by bright paraffin lamps. It held about forty Indian charpoys, all jammed close together. On every bed, men and women were entangled, copulating vigorously. I had never seen anything like it before. It was bedlam. It made your hair, and much else, stand on end. Before long a bed was free. Contact in such circumstances was brief. Then back to the nearest bar.

I read that there is an old imperial Roman tombstone somewhere, on which were incised the words, 'Baths, wine, and sex corrupt our bodies; but baths, wine, and sex keep us alive'.

The jig-jig winter of '46–'47 in Hong Kong was a severe one for Europe and Britain, where cold and deep snow combined with rationing to bring months of misery. Div Sigs was still swimming in Big Wave Bay every day, and eating five fried eggs and chips in the NAAFI for supper every evening.

By this time, I had been three years abroad. The men I was working with now had come straight from England, peacetime soldiers. Those of us still remaining who had served in Burma found it hard to communicate with them, as the old soldiers of Milestone 81 had had no communication with me when a new recruit. They regarded me as old. So I was, old, decayed and depraved.

Discipline was in fashion again, eagerly wielded by young officers fresh out of OCTU. Correctness in dress. Drill. Marching about to no effect. Haircuts. I flatly refused to exchange my bush hat, symbol of the old Forgotten Army, for a history-free beret. Since I was now sporting a bar of four medal ribbons, the commanding officer permitted me to continue wearing a bush hat; but he too, having been On Active Service, perhaps had a secret sympathy for my argument.

I was given leave, and went to stay at a hotel in Portuguese Macau, forty-four sea miles from Hong Kong. Macau was then known as 'The Wickedest City in the World'. The title has been snatched away by a thousand other cities since then.

The Portuguese, less racially conscious than the English – a not incredible feat – intermarried and interbred with the Chinese, to produce some of the most elegant women in the world.

A rickshaw took me on my first night to a whorehouse of huge proportions, a flesh factory, feebly lit, steaming, odorous. Because of the heat, the girls wore only vest-like garments, which reached down to, but failed to cover, their little wildernesses of pubic hair. Some sported thick bushes, some merely a few saucy eyelashes: the effect of long privation, one supposed.

Dozens of girls stood about on each floor. One was welcome to touch, to feel, before making a decision. Young Paris's problems of choice on Mount Ida were nothing . . . It was a bizarre dream. While the customers were engaged in the horizontal position, whores stood sympathetically about the bed, little goddesses chattering in Cantonese.

I had a proper respect for those small furry entrances into pleasure; in that whorehouse, they hung like so many fruits on a gigantic Christmas tree.

In less crowded houses, the girls had a preliminary ceremony, washing their customer's sexual organs, and sometimes also his feet, with potassium permanganate. This preventive medicine was designed to ward off syphilis, that scourge which made the act of intercourse dreadful in the literal sense of that word. What it actually did was what all delay does – increase randiness.

British troops also had their prophylaxis: never kiss a whore on the mouth, however tempting it may be. In this apothegm, fear and shame were conjoined. Many of those troops, left in the tropics without promise of return home, were on the same downward path as I. Inevitably, in a way. Men wake in the morning with erections. Where to put them is a problem of global dimension.

The solution offered, by COs and sergeants alike, was always the same: 'Stick to the old five-fingered widow'. But the widow's clasp was dry and shadowy, and ultimately degrading. The widow held much of that sense of youth wasting which lends urgency to real sexual acts.

Mine is the underdog's story, the BOR's tale. We were down on our spiritual uppers, surrounded by cultures for which we had no tuition, and few bonds other than the primitive sexual level. That rush of little whores in scanty dresses down to the docks, where newly berthed ships were mooring, was as driven by instinct as it was by economics.

In Macau I met a girl with whom I spent a memorable night. We took to each other. We were both skin and bone. She led me off to a sidestreet, down an alleyway, through a meagre grey room in a dilapidated building, where six men in dirty vests were drinking, smoking and playing cards. You had to climb a ladder to get up to her wretched attic. But how lovely and sweet-spirited this unknown girl was, how like a flower was her little wilderness, which men secretly crave all their lives. We hardly slept. When we slept, we slept entwined.

I have never forgotten her. The sordid attic was a refuge from the world. In Orwell's *Nineteen Eighty-Four*, all Winston Smith wants is a quiet room somewhere, with his girl; perhaps it was Orwell's modest dream of Utopia. Came the dawn, my girl made us some herb tea and then dressed for church and the confessional.

It happened at that time that the Portuguese were celebrating the four-hundredth anniversary or so of the birth of Luis de Camões, the great Portuguese Renaissance poet, author of *The Lusiads*.

In Cascais, in Portugal last year, Margaret and I drank coffee with other tourists in the Praça named after Camões. In the centre of the square stands a statue to the poet. But Camões died of poverty, drink and neglect. It is the death all writers must fear, as Bill once feared the workhouse. One biographer claims *Os Lusidas* is to be considered 'the supreme Renaissance epic'. Its author was given a pauper's funeral.

In Macau, when I stayed there, the adventurous poet was being celebrated with a vengeance. Everyone was drinking for the anniversary. It was an extraordinary occasion. The streets, normally deserted in daylight hours, burst open after dark with people and song. This was before the days of neon. The night was held at bay by lights and flares. The perspectives of streets, stretching towards the ocean, were theatrical. I marched along with platoons of unsteady Portuguese soldiers, and drank hooch with them in their barracks, which were thrown open for the occasion.

How impossibly jolly the world became. At one point, I was in a gentleman's club, where they solemnly toasted the British as liberators, to the extent of giving me money – possibly to go away.

A widowed banker with three daughters took me to dine in his mansion. The daughters and I consumed mounds of delectably oily paella, a dish which a second British guest, a mannerless oaf, dismissed as disgusting.

After the meal, the banker took the oaf and me on a stroll to his favourite whorehouse. Cockroaches scuttled everywhere but, as a special courtesy, a plump young lady was brought for me from a nearby convent. So I was told. Despite the cockroaches, she was most encouraging. Immediately after the act, she peed into a pewter chamberpot in my presence, which delighted me. Prophylaxis again. But I was not allowed a second helping.

Perhaps it was evensong time at the convent.

I gave myself over to booze and debauchery, of which I had intended to yield salacious details here, bottled up over a lifetime, as if they were of some archaeological interest. But sorrow and reticence overcome me. Thank goodness tastes change. As Dr Johnson remarked, a lad does not care for a child's rattle, or an old man for a young man's whore.

It was all long ago, and in a foreign country. Besides, most of the wenches are dead . . .

That summer, I was one of many men to board the SS *Arundel Castle* in Hong Kong for the journey back to Britain – leaving the East, if not for good, for my own good.

On that long voyage home, I was reading Homer's *Odyssey* on deck, in the sweet sea air, putting myself in touch with what E. V. Rieu, Homer's prose translator, calls 'the first expression of the Western mind in literary form'. I was well aware that I too had undergone an odyssey with its own magics and travails.

Within a couple of months, I had found myself a job of work in Oxford, and was attempting to become a different kind of being.

BOOK THREE

Ascent

XXVII

The Fog

I have made a mess of my private life – I have not lived up to
my ideals, and I have failed to get or give happiness.

Bertrand Russell, in a letter

S o to another chapter of my long-protracted life.
When my Sumatra novel, *A Rude Awakening*, was published,
it did not repeat the success of its two earlier siblings, *The Hand-
Reared Boy* and *A Soldier Erect*. I had already lost interest in Horatio
Stubbs; he was proving too limited a mouthpiece for his fictions.

I had had to be coaxed to write this third volume of what became,
in later paperback format, *The Horatio Stubbs Saga*. Weidenfeld &
Nicolson had invited me to lunch in order to inject a little encouragement. Over that lunch, my editor said an extraordinary thing.

'You should carry Horatio's life further. We received more letters
from readers about *The Hand-Reared Boy* than about any other
novel we ever published.'

'What? I had no letters!'

'Oh, there were two sacks full – two, or was it three?'

'Where are they?'

'Oh, we burnt them. We didn't want you to be bothered by
them.'

'But they were my letters!'

I still find this impertinence hard to credit. But so it was. They
burnt my letters.

The anecdote illustrates the presumption of some publishers.
Of course, one can change publishers, but this may be in itself a
disastrous move if not undertaken with caution (and probably in
anguished consultation with one's wife, agent and lawyer – not
necessarily in that order . . .).

I remained on speaking terms with Weidenfeld, not least because I was friendly with their publicity department. In the palmy days of the early seventies, they lived in Winsley Street, over Bourne & Hollingsworth, the department store which had a frontage on Oxford Street. Publicity was presided over by Jeremy Hadfield, a spruce man and a remarkable drinker. His father, John Hadfield, author of *Love on a Branch Line*, had accepted some of my early essays for his glamorous annual anthology, *The Saturday Book*.

I never sought a quarrel with any publisher or, indeed, with anyone else. If there was ever a quarrel, it was never of my seeking. Nor was I one to suck up to those in power; rather the reverse, in fact. I was not one, in Johnson's words, who cultivated those holding literary reputation in their hands.

After *A Rude Awakening*, I went on to other things. And, eventually, to other publishers.

Before leaving Weidenfeld, I edited a series of SF anthologies, of which *Galactic Empires* in two volumes, was the flagship. One does such things without much proof that anyone reads them or derives pleasure from them; in this case, however, I was to receive dramatic proof that someone at least took notice in what was said.

Anthologising is pleasurable work, selecting the stories, writing introductions and presenting them: it's a form of criticism. The stories were culled, in the main, from defunct magazines. In one of the volumes, entitled *Space Opera*, I described the function of space opera as a sub-genre.

> 'Analogously with opera itself, space opera has certain conventions which are essential to it, which are, in a way, its *raison d'être*. One may either like or dislike those conventions, but they cannot be altered except at expense to the whole. Ideally, the Earth must be in peril, there must be a quest and a man to match the mighty hour. That man must confront aliens and exotic creatures. Space must flow past the ports like wine from a pitcher. Blood must run down the palace steps, and ships launch out into the louring dark. There must be a woman fairer than the skies and a villain darker than a Black Hole. And all must come right at the end.'

In the year I went to China with Felix Greene and the Distinguished Persons, 1979, I was also invited to a conference in California.

I was taking the air one morning at the University of California, Riverside, when a smart young lawyer drove up. He represented a firm of lawyers, Youngman, Hungate and Leopold, in Los Angeles. They had been trying to get in touch with me in London and elsewhere, only to discover I was practically on their doorstep. They wanted to enlist me as witness in a court case.

George Lucas's highly successful Fox movie, *Star Wars* had appeared in 1977, to be followed a year later by Universal's *Battlestar Galactica* (originally entitled *Star Worlds*). Youngman & Co. were hired by Universal to defend them against a charge of plagiarism; they wanted me to be a prime witness.

Hollywood is surrounded by lawyers, like vultures round a dying water buffalo. That lawyers make money has never seemed to me a prima facie case for disliking them. These serious people worked hard all day, and drank only one icy glass of white wine with a tuna salad for lunch. In the evening, they played squash or swam a regulation number of lengths in their private pools. They installed me in the Hollywood Hilton, all expenses paid.

I breakfasted in my room every morning, looking out towards Century City, where the lawyers lived. At the same time every morning, an old black lady walked along the sidewalk to Century City; I never saw any other pedestrian. An hour later, I followed her, walking along the same path.

A serious meeting was convened in the lawyers' offices on the first day, eight of us sitting round an oak table.

What did I think of *Star Wars*?

My considered reply was, 'I experienced the pleasures of recognition.'

They thought about it. Then they smiled. We were in business.

The case would hinge on my definition of space opera, 1975.

Their argument would be that the two films (one of them much feebler than the other, but that was not the issue) both belonged to one genre, a genre already established. Of course both movies had spaceships, and so on. The maker of one cowboy film could not sue the maker of the next cowboy film just because men jumped on hosses in both instances. Jumping on hosses was part of an established genre. Belting through space in spaceships was part of another genre, established before *Star Wars* was made. So the argument ran.

Youngman & Co. liked me as a witness: English accent, touch of grey about the temples, military bearing. I would look well in the witness box. My life as an Englishman was about to pay off.

After a week I flew home, with a half-promise I would return to LA and testify if required, in return for a vast payment.

Eventually, the battling film companies settled the matter out of court. Meanwhile, Margaret and I had to face our own difficulties, of which I was the main cause.

Always susceptible to a pretty face, I had enjoyed more than one affair. A strange woman, sailing into one's orbit with her alluring mystery, always promised new avenues for exploration. With success, more promises appeared over the event horizon. Again came the attractions of the wilderness.

The havoc broke out between us in the kitchen, where quarrels start.

Women rarely take to heart the pronouncement of Anthony Burgess, 'Much can be forgiven a poet that is totally culpable in a dustman or journalist.' Nor, in the theatrical flash of discovery, do they consider how encouragingly imagination implies multiplicity in the romance arena. You incline to act out what you have written: and, of course, vice versa.

When Margaret discovered that I was in love elsewhere, great was her distress. It is not necessary to suffer from MPD to love more than one woman at once. It was my turn to discover the import of what I had been doing – hazarding what I knew was her true faithfulness and steadiness.

She stood in the sunshine, looking up at the façade of our house. She – no longer the innocent I had married.

'I am a prisoner here!' she cried. We were prisoners of each other at that time. At her very words, I was made captive.

Confronted by my failings, my buried self rose up, a boulder in my way. I at once relinquished that other cherished thing. But she too had someone else she cherished.

To quote Cowper, 'We perished, each alone.'

Women can wreak terrible vengeance and humiliation, perhaps without knowing how deeply they wound.

There followed mental breakdown, succeeded by illness. The kind of thing we call for convenience a midlife crisis.

Love hath ten thousand several mats for men to make their pratfalls . . . You have to hurt someone you love dearly, you have to leave someone else you love dearly. You can't say what you mean, you don't know what you mean. You are in a state of sin. My throat became perpetually dry; I could not swallow what happened.

I developed pains in the gut, later diagnosed as spastic bowel; I could not stomach what happened.

The succeeding illness was more insidious than the breakdown. The breakdown hit me – how shall I say? – like a blast of lewisite, in 1974. Within a week, I lost a stone and a half. There's no better dietetic than guilt and remorse.

We must forego the details. In the confusions of that period, I was not only guilty: another aspect of me was innocent, having been too trusting. It caused a war within me.

I tried to maintain a surface normality as clinical depression descended. Well, I was expert in hiding my feelings: one persona covered for another. In Chapter V of his autobiography, John Cowper Powys speaks of the same syndrome. He admits to '. . . a most formidable mental power of hiding up my real identity until I could get away alone, and then of pouring forth my whole soul . . . into such inanimate or such lowly animate things as I could encounter along the most desolate country road.' I travelled that same road.

Still I wrote, lectured, travelled, outwardly much as before. The career, such as it was, had taken on its own momentum.

What fortune in the middle of misfortune, that creativity at least never died! Forsaking my study, I wrote downstairs in the dining room, that tall shuttered room in Heath House, the novel, *The Malacia Tapestry*, dedicated to Margaret. Malacia is a city-state built, with thoughts of ancient Ragusa in mind, round a conundrum. Even Italian scholars seem puzzled by what the great Gianbattista Tiepolo intended by the delicate *Capricci* and *Scherzi* he etched towards the end of his life. They depict a world of magic played out in dusty sunshine, shaded by stricken pines, where serpents burn on altars dedicated to unknown gods. I tried to re-create Tiepolo's mysterious place in prose.

This was the second novel I had written round a pictorial theme. The first was *Probability A*, built about Holman Hunt's *The Hireling Shepherd*. That is what comes of frequenting art galleries. The melancholy artist, Fatember, in *Malacia*, expresses much of my feeling about the beauty of creation and the neglect of those who create.

When first looking up Tiepolo (1696–1770) in an encyclopaedia, many a year ago, I found him described as the last degenerate glimmer of the Renaissance. A few years on, and he is rated as the master of the rococo – that light and playful style which passed

England by. One of my newer encyclopaedias calls him arguably the greatest European painter of the eighteenth century.

A long road we travel . . .

Illness grows easily from melancholia, when inner defences are in ruins and seratonin is at a low ebb . . . I was unable at first to distinguish one stratum of misery from another. I communed with the dark soul of the night. Where to take refuge? Not, in my case, in drink or drugs, but in silence and books.

By shutting myself off from my self, I insulated others from my condition, as far as that was possible.

As the last few chapters show, ours was a busy life in the last half of the seventies. I was happy; the family remained intact; yet I was in misery. Happiness seemed a man of straw. I sank so far from wellbeing I did not want it. I wanted it for Margaret, but was not the best person to give it.

Waking in the morning was instantaneous. The whole scenario had been playing in the head all night. The obsessional side of me was on red alert. I went naked into the shower, as I had come naked into the world, with nothing. I wished I were dead. Everyone, I imagine, must know the feeling.

During the meeting in Dublin at which Harry instigated World SF, already referred to, I walked the streets with Tom Shippey early one morning. I was enjoying his discourse – all the while wondering how it would be if I cut my throat. (Tom later experienced similar pain.)

Stuart Sutherland wrote an excellent book on his own breakdown (called, simply, *Breakdown*). He explains that he spoke to a psychologist. 'When I expressed guilt over having had a number of casual affairs, he said, "There are always several ways of viewing things. Some people might say that anyone who does not have the odd affair is acting falsely and denying the animal side of his nature."'

Of course, I could not accept this of myself. Margaret certainly did not. Yet men have a philosophical problem; they tacitly approve, almost encourage, 'a bit on the side' (the euphemism generally employed).

Nor does one feel at all badly at getting what used to be called 'the glad eye'. One does not feel at all badly when one has approached – or has been approached by – an attractive woman, with some success. One does not feel at all badly when one is in bed with her, in a strange hotel or some hitherto unknown room. Covert social acceptance is on one's side, backed by millions of years of exogamy.

And, it must be said, in such pleasing affrays, the woman is an equal partner.

The whores of the East, though always approached with Congregationalist guilt, had afforded me no particular training in virtue.

Matters become even more complex when you fall in love. To flourish on a diet of fresh salmon and caviar is not to say you scorn the occasional Saxby's pork pie. I was of the susceptible kind. Then someone gets hurt: generally all parties concerned get hurt.

I try not to try to exonerate myself, but much cannot be said. Now as then I confront what Tolstoy, in *Anna Karenina*, calls 'the inexpressible complexity of everything that lives'.

Any self-regard I had acquired disappeared. I saw myself as a deeply flawed personality, unable to steer a clear course in the world's rough seas. For Margaret I cannot speak. She was not one to speak for herself; it was her body language that announced withdrawal.

In his perceptive book, *The Dynamics of Creation*, Anthony Storr has this to say of the manic-depressive temperament:

> 'Now, if a man fears the withdrawal of love, it follows that he must have experienced it . . . If self-esteem depends on receiving love from others, the recipient is at once put in the position of having to retain a good relation with the source of supply . . . Rejection and disapproval are a matter of life and death; for unless supplies of approval are forthcoming from outside, they relapse into a state of depression in which self-esteem sinks so low, and rage becomes so uncontrollable, that suicide becomes a real possibility.'

I know this to be true.

My trips abroad over this five-year period afforded a certain relief. These were the excursions to China, the Soviet Union, Sumatra, Australia and elsewhere, as mentioned. Among the heated bustle of other lives, there was little room for icy introspection.

The one person on whom I could rely at the start of this awful period turned out to be our old gardener, Mr Parsons. He took it on himself to tell me who was visiting the house while I was away.

Who would care to record those years, cut by cut? Not I.

*   *   *

Slowly I regained weight. There again, Stuart Sutherland held the understanding of personal experience. The emotional tone of life had faltered. I dwelt on the notion of suicide; the mere idea was a relief: not to be, to be finished. Once, there had been bright promise everywhere. Although I still pursued the old authorial activities, zest was gone. Pleasure was a pretence, kept up in the hope it would deceive myself as well as others. I wanted to protect Margaret and the family from myself and my contamination.

My mother died. My dear cat Nickie died. The Titanic slowly sank all over again.

I cut myself off from others. Isolation was at once the illness and the cure. Nor have I ever again been as sociable as once I was; and now age reduces, if not the inclination, the ability. At the time, I did not realise that one man in ten, according to recent figures, suffers from depression. There was one refuge to be had. Writing. Work.

Admittedly, writing now had a touch of Dr Manette, cobbling obsessively in his cell. I perceive this in retrospect.

In Kansas, I did a short spell of teaching and lecturing. When I returned to England, a 'For Sale' board was up at the bottom of Heath House drive.

After a short while in North Oxford, we went to live in 'Orchard House', a fine eighteenth-century stone building at the end of a quiet lane in Begbroke, between Oxford and Woodstock. The beauty of the place, qualifying it as candidate for the cover of a 'Beautiful Britain' calendar, seduced us into buying a property to which our purse would hardly stretch.

Orchard House gave an appearance of calm and refuge. Cowper could have sat under our great beech, patiently translating his Homer. Just as we tend to think of a part of the world with which we are unfamiliar, such as North Carolina in my case, as being flat, perhaps from studying political maps too frequently, so we are apt to think of other people's lives as being, like a political map, flat and coloured red or green; they give little sign of the mountainous country within their boundaries – the gorges, the traceless Gobis. In that pleasant house, I found myself mentally in a cold desert, strewn with fossil remains and without signposts.

Work, the patient addition of sentence on sentence, remained some kind of panacea. But every Wednesday, when the children were at school and Margaret away to her pottery class, I was compelled to rush out, to escape amid the clayey fields rising to Spring Hill

– that low eminence, named for water rather than season, which mustered its forces to flood Orchard House every winter.

My state of mind was such that when, one day, we received notice from our accountants that we were many thousands of pounds in arrears with our income tax, I almost welcomed the distraction. Anything, anything! This I could deal with; this was just a crisis.

Our accountant drove down to visit us in his white Rolls-Royce. He apologised for the misfortune. One of his minions, in charge of our three accounts, had had a secret drink problem, and was now discharged. We discharged the accountant.

It meant selling up the house to pay the demands.

Margaret was upset in her rather calm way. I said to her, 'Don't worry. It's only money. It isn't as though we had broken our legs.'

With these platitudes she seemed content. As always before, we worked together. So we sold up and went to live in a semi-detached house in Oxford.

We left one valued thing behind in Begbroke. The children were still young. In that last beautiful summer there, Tim and Charlotte – and Clive and Wendy when they were with us – spent much time in our heated open-air swimming pool. The pool was large and beautiful, lined with Portuguese tiles, sheltered by a stone wall. Private, serene. The water in it was almost as pure as drinking water. Since the family did not urinate in it, little or no chlorine was needed. We swam in it first thing in the morning, when we rose from sleep.

To meet the tax debt, I had to sell not only our house but my science fiction library. That library had been built up since my boyhood; it included thirties magazines, prophetic books on space travel, and all the novels I had reviewed for the *Oxford Mail* and *TLS*. Consisting of some three to four thousand items, it went to the public library in Dallas, where it is better maintained than I could manage. The books may be consulted but not read outside the library precincts. I have twice been to visit the library, an establishment whose funding and arrangements most British libraries would envy.

Dallas is a friendly city. Margaret advised me, 'You shouldn't buy me anything. But remember if you do I'm into chunky gold jewellery.' I went into Nieman Marcus, opened an account, and bought her a chunky gold bracelet designed in Paris. I was feeling pretty good in Dallas. They treated me well.

*   *   *

The four of us managed to fit into our new home in North Oxford. That was when we bought Tim his first computer, a Commodore. On which all played 'Chuckie Egg'.

Still the sick thing clung to my life. It differed in tone and feel from the depression; there was about it an impression of cellar dampness. While washing and shaving in the morning, I would attempt to establish in my brain what day of the week it was. After a long and laborious trail of deduction, I decided it was a Tuesday. But then – wait! – which day did I think it was? Did I just then think Wednesday? The sweet cheat had gone . . . the process had to restart.

I jogged round the nearby roads, Banbury, Lathbury, Woodstock . . . But as soon as I was out of sight of our house, I had to slow, to walk at a drab pace. The limbs had turned into wet socks filled with sand. The very winter of the mind had set in.

It was perplexing. We all carry maps of our home town and other cities in our brain. My maps vanished. I could not drive myself round Oxford with confidence. Left or right for Blackwell's? In London, I would emerge from the Underground at Tottenham Court Road and be unable to determine which was the road to Jonathan Cape. I was walking on the edge of a cliff in gathering snow.

As soon as my head touched the pillow at night, I became unconscious. It was cold and damp in there, like a small Thames-side cellar. If I woke at 3 a.m., I might then slump into a more normal sleep. Once, I dreamed my old recurrent dream. I was walking up that long road again. I was walking, yet I was not moving. The two antique figures were close, taking no notice of me.

With my vitality went my libido. Once I would have been glad to be free of it.

Of course, an answer soon occurred to me. *Alzheimer's!* Expecting no sympathy, I told no one. Every morning, as soon as I shut myself in the room I used as a study, I rested my head on the typewriter and fell into the same cold senselessness resembling sleep.

Somehow, I struggled through the writing of the three Helliconia novels. My spirits were at ground zero, but I had long been adept at feigning cheerfulness.

Margaret and the children liked the house in Moreton Road. Charlotte had a flatlet on the attic floor, with her own shower room. Tim was entering the terrible teens, and several wild parties went on, long into the night.

We took a holiday in Greece in the mid-eighties. Clive was getting on well there. The need to find work had driven him far afield. He taught English in private schools, living in a rather frugal way. At first he lived in Drama, in the north of the country. He started energetically to master the difficult Greek tongue. Drama he always described as a pleasant place. From there, he could easily cross to the island of Thassos – off the beaten track and therefore much to his taste.

Eventually, he had been lured to the capital. After some struggles, Clive became employed by the British Council. There, a good and conscientious man, he teaches and invigilates still. And whenever possible escapes to one of Greece's many islands – and the mild seas off those islands.

When we visited him, I was unable to retain a single Greek word in memory. That was passed off as a joke. Everything was fine, until the last day when, at three o'clock in the morning, Margaret and I became entangled in a terrible slanging match, she reproaching me, I defending myself.

There we stood, the ever-diverse pair, in the dark, lit by a distant harbour light. It must have occurred to her . . . well, I cannot say what occurred to her, for we were at odds, and that night by the water's edge on the Greek island, with no one else about, my whole nature was under assault. Margaret and the children remained in Greece for a few days while I returned home alone, ashen, to go to a prearranged event.

On a later and happier visit to Greece, Clive introduced us to the charming and ebullient Youla, whom he was later to marry.

'The stars shone at intervals, as the clouds passed over them; the dark pines rose before me, and every here and there a broken tree lay on the ground; it was a scene of wonderful solemnity, and stirred strange thoughts within me.' Thus thought Victor Frankenstein in Mary Shelley's *Frankenstein: or, The Modern Prometheus*, after he has met with his formidable creation, walking among desolation and shattered scenery.

'On the sea floated floes of ice, many carved into absurd forms. Some resembled stunted trees or monstrous fungi, as if the god of ice had taken it into his head to devise grotesque counterparts to living nature. These were the things that had come knocking at the heights of the storm, and it was a cause for gratitude that few bergs were half as big as the ship. These mysterious forms emerged from the mist, only to recede again into abstraction.' A first view of Persecution Bay, on the continent of Sibornal, in *Helliconia Summer*.

The captivity of melancholy can be translated into the freedoms of morbid landscapes. As Mary Shelley well understood.

I felt myself surrounded by falsehood, much of it of my own making. There's something to be said for suicide: its sincerity comes with a guarantee.

With the dreadful spectre of decline tightening its grip on me, I had to visit the doctor.

Diagnosis was uncertain. I was sent to have a brain scan. The machine resembled a giant bacon-slicer into which you inserted your head; cameras took the place of a blade. The doctor operating it happened to be one of my readers. Afterwards, he showed me the results of the scan on a monitor. There it was, that beautiful organ of mentation, growing like a coral in the dark of the head! I asked if there was anything unusual about it.

'It's just an ordinary brain,' he said.

Shucks.

It happened that at that time our Beaumont Street clinic had taken on a locum, a Dr Jackson. The lady had divinatory powers. She it was who diagnosed PVFS, Post-Viral Fatigue Syndrome. Nowadays a more general term, CFS, Chronic Fatigue Syndrome, is used.

Just to have a diagnosis was a relief. The immune system had been weakened (by sorrow?). It was not Alzheimer's after all.

In the early eighties, medical practice was reluctant to acknowledge that such a disorder as PVFS existed. Whenever I have mentioned PVFS in articles or interviews, I have received anxious letters from fellow-sufferers, sometimes as far away as Australia. Often enough, they claim their doctors and their spouses or partners have refused to recognise their ills as a medical condition.

Dr Jackson said that orthodox medicine could offer no palliative for PVFS.

'It's not uncommon in Oxford circles. It generally strikes men of about your age, intelligent men who feel they have never achieved their ambitions or received the recognition they believe they have earned.'

She recommended me to try a psychotherapist. I went.

The years had dragged on, those slow pale years, when the pulse of life outwardly ran as normal. With my writing I had paid off our tax debts. We could afford to move to a larger, more convenient house, with a garden to cultivate, outside Oxford.

Clive asked me why I wished to take on this added responsibility.

'To fight off old age,' I told him. The burden of something as grey as age lay on my shoulders. It could not be foreseen that this thing which enveloped me would lead to a new and better life.

XXVIII

The Secret Inscriptions

Jack can't tell Jill what he
wants Jill to tell him.
Jill can't tell him either
because although Jill knows X
Jill does not know
that Jack does not know X.

Jack can see
that Jill knows
he realises that she
does not know she knows X.
Jill can only discover
she knows it
by realising what Jack does not.
R. D. Laing:
Knots

Before we get to the beautiful and terrible things which this chapter must reveal, I must say how anguishing is memory loss. If, while suffering from PVFS, I met a friend in the street, I could not recall his name or exactly who he was; worse, I was unsure in what context we knew each other. My children seemed to notice no change in me; I am sure Margaret did. I was no longer any of my ordinary selves.

However memory is difficult to lose, easy though it may be to obscure. This chapter will show the truth of that, when things long forgotten seeped back among the things that are.

De Quincey agrees on this subject. In his grand prose poem of a book, *Confessions of an English Opium Eater*, he has this to say:

I feel assured that there is no such thing as *forgetting* possible to the mind; a thousand accidents may, and will interpose a veil between our present consciousness and the secret inscriptions on the mind; accidents of the same sort will also rend away this veil; but alike, whether veiled or unveiled, the inscription remains for ever; just as the stars seem to withdraw before the common light of day, whereas, in fact, we all know that it is the light which is drawn over them as a veil – and that they are waiting to be revealed, when the obscuring daylight shall have withdrawn.

Ah, those 'secret inscriptions' in the mind! Acting on Dr Jackson's advice, I prepared to visit Mrs Green, the psychotherapist recommended. I was in an optimistic frame of mind. Here was something new to try. Novelty was always welcome – even the dusty psychoanalytic trail.

In fiction, such matters are clear-cut. In life it is rarely so – hence the attraction of fiction. In fiction, matters are clear-cut for brevity; in life, which is long, it is rarely so. As in an Ibsen drama, the clarity of our lives is blurred by all that went before. Some storylines seem to have no beginning or end.

Should I go?

'Try it,' Margaret said. She had abandoned pottery and had taken up weaving. We bought a loom for her to work on.

So my mood was somewhat lighter as I crossed Mrs Green's threshold. Of my personae, my story-telling persona was most alert. He had a story to tell.

At the time I crossed that Green threshold, our dear Aunt Dorothy had died. By returning to East Dereham to bury her, in obedience to wishes expressed in her will, I had resolved one of the mysteries of my existence. The 'secret inscriptions' were to be deciphered and that small town, 'my home town', to prove a Rosetta stone. All because there was no stone . . .

Dereham in 1984 was changed from its pre-war state. Traces of the Aldiss family shop were disappearing. After my uncle Gordon died, the business passed to his son Tony. Its best days were past. I suppose he sold up; when I wrote to him I received no answer. The assistants, Betts & Co, have gone. The millinery department has vanished. The site where the business stood is now 'Aldiss Court'. One can buy odd plates there, and New Age toiletries for humans and pets, or be shampooed or tattooed cheaply.

The room where both Betty and I were born, under the ministrations of Nurse Webb, remains intact as part of someone's flat. You can stand and look up at its high window; as ever, it has no view; one would not much wish to be dropped from it on to the concrete below.

The elegant frontage of the old shop, designed by Uncle Bert Wilson, still survives, its large curved glass windows staring up Norwich Street, where once a woman with a baby in a pushchair had gone hurrying.

After Aunt Dorothy's funeral, the family retired to the Phoenix for lunch. I saw that everyone was comfortably seated with drinks, then, having a short while to spare, I went to investigate St Withburga and the ghost, with results already related. However, there was another ghost to lay, a ghost whose history stretched back to the beginnings of my existence.

At the back of my consciousness, the steel-engraving angel still fluttered. Her leaden wings had rarely ceased to beat at my shoulder. She was the ghost, the cause of my low self-esteem. Now came the time for another exorcism.

This idealised infant daughter, who had lived for only six months, had certainly haunted Dot. She had also been responsible for deserts of misery in my life. Throughout my boyhood, Dot had compared me unfavourably with this little angel – the perfect little girl, the bad little boy. The resultant sense of failure had remained, despite all my energetic gestures towards success.

Although for many years Dot and I had got on well, and Margaret and I had looked after her tenderly in her old age, I could never entirely overcome a sense of grievance against her treatment of me as an infant.

Here and now was my chance to find where this macabre child lay buried. While standing beside Auntie's fresh mound, I noted that this little phantom sister of mine was not in the family grave, under the white marble cross, with Grandfather. It was a small mystery.

How sure were my instincts then!

Togged up in mourning clothes, I went to the council offices in the market square. I stood before a lady sitting attentively at her desk.

'She would have died in 1920.' How macabre it all was – speaking as though I was under some antique spell . . .

A patient Miss Cross was willing to search in dusty folio volumes on my behalf. Her finger ran down columns of copperplate writing, tracing the names of the extinct.

'Mmm . . . Deaths in 1920 . . . mmm . . . April . . . Let's see . . . May . . . No . . .'

'The baby was born in March. She lived for six months. So she must have died in September of that year. Mother always celebrated the day in deepest gloom.' While speaking, I reflected on how long ago 1920 was, the year itself buried in the soil of all the years since then and, to Miss Cross, as inaccessible as Timbuktu.

'Mmm . . . here we are, September, 1920 . . . No, nothing here . . . Sorry.'

She looked up sympathetically and gave me a bright smile.

'Sorry,' she said again. 'Nothing registered.'

I admitted I was mystified. As I returned to the family at the Phoenix, I began to wonder if that morbid little angel had ever existed, enjoying even less reality than the shade of Bessie. Could this whole tale be another of Dot's disappointments? Another ruse to keep me depressed and docile?

I said nothing about my visit to the council offices to the family. We ate lunch, and were cheerful after our fashion.

Then we climbed into our cars and drove away from Dereham.

But the episode had a sequel.

Some weeks later, unexpectedly, I received a letter from Miss Cross. That excellent lady had searched in an old Burial Fees book. There she had made a discovery. She quoted the entry:

20th March 1920. Stillborn child of Mrs May Aldiss, wife of Stanley Aldiss. Entry No. 5115. Fees taken: Board Fee, 1 shilling, Grave Digger, 1 shilling.

Here was a veritable secret inscription! Blessed Miss Cross!

A certificate signed by a doctor indicated that a female child had been born dead on the 18th March.

I had been haunted by a being who had never lived.

Or, one might put it, had lived only in the womb. Dorothy had once said – the remark had been forgotten until I held Miss Cross's letter in my hand – that the child had been deformed.

Stillborn! That dreadful word.

Since the child was stillborn, it could not be christened. Since the child had not been christened, it could not be buried in the consecrated area of the churchyard. The consecrated area, like First Class seating on a Boeing, was reserved for those who might be expected to make it to the Heavenly Throne. But a resting place had been found for the tiny corpse, confined in its H. H. Aldiss box, under the chestnut trees fringing the cemetery.

There was no stone.

Poor Dot's fantasy had ruled Betty's and my small lives.

To salve her pain at bearing a dead child – perhaps that witty starch-fronted Nurse Webb had not permitted her even to hold the babe in her arms – she had bestowed on it an imaginary six months of life. That fantasy had been her comfort.

Six months – a life sentence! In those six months, how she could have nursed and loved it! How she could have given her heart to it.

'I wish I was as free as a bird,' she said. Though I clung to her, nothing I could do had comforted her.

And Bill? Bill never spoke of the child. He was not a communicative man.

What had happened between them in that bedroom with the patterned lino? Perhaps he had never comforted her properly. Perhaps he had grown tired of trying to comfort her.

One riddle was decoded. I could now be sure I was my parents' precious first-born (I think) . . .

Possibly more inscriptions awaited decoding.

Mrs Green was an unremarkable woman in her forties, married, given to wearing strange headgear, as if better prepared to read my palm than my mind. She worked from a small terraced house in Headington, one of Oxford's suburbs. She occupied rooms on the upper floor: a confessional, a toilet, a room where you could wait or blub. The waiting-room walls were hung with framed photographs of forests: whether by intentional symbolism or not one was unable to determine.

I strained to hear a thousand voices tell a thousand secrets in the confessional. English guilts, English woes.

But the Greens were American. They came from the home of the bared psychiatric breast.

Mr Green, the husband, in the same line of business as his wife, worked downstairs. Clients came and went secretively, as if to a brothel. Upstairs or downstairs, doors opened and closed softly. The house was hushed, the air dimmed by all the miseries brought to light within its faded wallpapered walls.

The room to which I was ushered for my weekly fifty-minute hour was small, overlooking a back garden in which an apple tree grew. The tree covered itself with a counterpane of pink and white blossom when I first arrived and shed apples on the lawn when I left, cured – or, if not cured, at least no madder than when I arrived.

Mrs Green and I sat regarding each other in armchairs. There was also the traditional couch in the room for those more completely overcome with the burden of their lives.

Here was given me – I could not have sought it – a chance to unravel a narrative: a cohesive, sometimes diffuse tale, such as I have told here. Its climax would be . . . well, a kind of deliverance such as one experiences when successfully completing a novel. At last I was ready to tell it, although I did not at first foresee, when facing the quaintly adorned Mrs G, that I would be able to jettison the entire sackful of fossil thought I carried rattling about on my back.

Psychotherapy, regarded as a mysterious process, is in essence simple: one speaks to someone who listens intelligently, taking on something of the function of a Wailing Wall. What is mysterious is how whatever is said, wherever you begin, the trail winds almost at once to the heart of the matter. All roads lead to home.

Everything had conspired to ready me for my narrative.

In session after session the catharsis unwound. The secret inscriptions – they were surely enough to keep Mrs Green enthralled! In session after session she sat there, occasionally uttering a prompt, a question, opening for me a thrilling subplot which later linked in a remarkable way with the main burden of my song.

So taken was I with this chance for exposition that I would drive back to Boars Hill and spill some of it out again to Margaret. She was far from being completely pleased, claiming to have heard it all many times before.

'How long is all this going on?'

'Don't you see, it's my *personal mythology*?'

I was proud of it, longed to get back to the next chapter. Perhaps Margaret felt the lack of an intense personal mythology.

Suddenly I felt rich. Over the years, Betty and I had laughed and told Margaret dreadful tales of our upbringing, of the Dereham shop, of Bessie, of things that happened abroad, of our parents, of picnics here and there, of wartime adventures; to all of which Margaret had launched few reciprocal anecdotes. She often regretted that she had no brother or sister; by contrast, Betty's and my life had seemed choked with incident.

Now the past was transformed. In the twinkling of an eye, it became something valuable to me, worth having. *My personal mythology*.

Perhaps what we perceive is determined by our perceptions, rather than by reality. Such was the approach to philosophy of Edmund Husserl, the phenomenologist. Husserl would presumably have made mincemeat of Bessie, while the steel-engraving angel was a clear example of perception standing in for reality. I had been inspired to become a writer of fiction – standing in for reality.

In those sessions with Mrs Green, in the house where people with averted faces went, up the narrow stair, in the unliving room, my narrative unwound. As the weeks wore on, she removed her toque. A sign!

The narrative seemed inexhaustible, just as I regard my creative side as inexhaustible. And during that period, I had a revelation. A visitation.

Let me call it a visitation. An amazing visitation.

Psychology had always been an interest. The library at West Buckland had its share of Freud's works, which I read with horror, fascination and disbelief. Later I reached out for mentors more in accord with my spirit. Carl Jung proved more to my taste. Jung shows good understanding of the creative impulse, which Freud regards as a kind of displacement activity.

While much might ail me, I also understood that a Nile of life, of thought, replenished me through my days. I saw too that the illness I had been enduring for almost ten years must fade like mist, leaving me whole. That the creative force which had never failed was still alive, and that I had within me the power to protect and love my family. That my sexuality was all a part of the delight I took in plunging into something new, to experience or write.

Yet how can we understand ourselves? As someone remarked, if we are self-taught, our teacher must be an ignorant man. Yet full understanding is necessary for a full life.

Seeking to mend my ignorance, I bought in 1982 a newly published book by Anthony Stevens, entitled, *Archetype: A Natural History of the Self*. Stevens makes clear some pathways through the labyrinths of mind. Particularly striking is his linking ontogeny with our basic phylogeny, clearly showing how the development of the individual self is subject to the evolutionary origins and development of the human species.

Archetypes are, in Steven's view, *active living dispositions*, leading something like a semi-autonomous existence within our psyches. Like the family face in Hardy's poem, an archetype is not subject to time or individual death.

> I am the family face;
> Flesh perishes, I live on

The sad poet of evolution speaks of that feature as 'the eternal thing in man'. So with the archetypes. They have a power to mediate and limit our behavioural characteristics and our typical experiences. It follows that our inner histories are determined not only by our personal histories but by the collective record of our species as a whole, stretching back in time to the days of things without fingerprints.

Jung says that 'ultimately, every individual life is the same as the eternal life of the species.' Hence it is no more than reasonable to perceive one's life history as run of the mill, a tale of childhood, adolescence, sexuality, marriage, procreation, maturity, eventual senescence and death. Such is the archetypal pattern of human life. Against which remains the remarkable fact that every life is unique, or contains aspects of the unique.

Hence the existence of biography and autobiography. If all lives were similar, all outlooks on life similar (as some imagine), such records would be unnecessary.

Through a reading of Stevens and others, I became more fully aware of that powerful and alluring archetype, my anima. Genetic inheritance ensures that we all contain components of the opposite sex which ameliorate our appointed sex, as an ocean ameliorates the climate of an adjacent land.

In my case, I identified my anima with the Moon. The Moon, long before I met with her in close-up in Burma, had always awoken intense emotions. In our generation, mankind has landed hardware on the Moon's face. Yet she remains a legendary creature, Diana, huntress chaste and fair, the mistress of the night.

In one of his essays, 'Meditation on the Moon', Aldous Huxley says, 'The moon ... is a highly numinous stone ... There is a cold and austere moonlight that tells the soul of its loneliness and desperate isolation, its insignificance or its uncleanness. There is an amorous moonlight prompting to love – to love not only for an individual but sometimes even for the whole universe.'

One night, on Boars Hill, I decided to address the Moon. She was full. It was November. The year was 1985. The sky was clear. The night was chill. I cast imprisoning reason aside and prayed to her.

This sounds eccentric? Such behaviour was old before the ice began to move southwards and swallow half of Europe.

In the small hours of the morning, before dawn, she spoke to me.

My anima answered my prayer. Well, something responded.

The dark was as bland and uniform as a tomb. There was no apparition, no imitation of Bessie. This was an experience of a visionary kind. Simply a benevolent voice, soft but undeniable in the darkness. What it said was of the kind of oracular wisdom one might expect from an archetype. A single sentence.

The gentle unspeaking voice simply assured me that my mother had loved me.

That was the message. Nothing more. It was as much an opening door as a voice.

I awoke, sat bolt upright in bed.

This certainly happened. Where exactly it happened is more conjectural. What we perceive is a veil of appearances, behind which is the world science has revealed, a flux of electromagnetic radiation and invisible particles. These revelations are at odds with our ordinary 'everyday' experience, much as was Bessie's apparition. My anima's Delphic utterance was similarly beyond – beautifully beyond – the currents of mundane life. And the conviction of that voice . . .

For a moment, I wondered if someone else was in the bedroom. Margaret slept sweetly beside me, undisturbed. The Moon, that silver stone, still shone. And again I was changed.

Much memory becomes buried as we go unrehearsed through life. Who, you might say, needs it? But as I sat in bed in the mild half-dark, filled with delectable Boars Hill silence, a shaft to the past opened up in my mind.

I returned in memory to that poky dormitory in St Peter's Court, Bacton. Once more the fugitive car, its headlights chasing across the room, double-declutching as it headed for Walcot and freedom. The agony of mind in that room returned freshly. Balancing the facts, I had decided for my peace of spirit that Dot did not love me. I had decided, because a decision was to be preferred to uncertainty; I would in future strive to match her indifference with mine.

In making exile from home bearable, mine had been the right decision for the time. It may have been factually incorrect, but it was necessary. I regard it still as courageous, the courage of a seven-year-old facing up to appearances. Over the years, the decision had become second nature, a mask grown by custom to fit the face so well I had forgotten I was wearing it: as Hamlet tells his mother, 'For use almost can change the stamp of nature'.

The words of the heavenly visitation alerted me to that fact . . .

Not for a moment did I question the truthfulness of the anima, or whatever revelation had visited me.

Now what was I to do or be?

She had loved me. Poor Dot had been an ordinary faulty creature, as I was. Those first five years before the Abyss had seen her soul in shadow, still grieving for her stillborn daughter.

Her feeble and mistaken attempts to control me had caused me grief; but I had been headstrong – 'going like a bull at a gate', she often said. Her talk of dying had been a wish she dare utter only to me. It had proved a burden too heavy for my frail shoulders. I had become an escapologist.

I was in a magical spell. Getting out of bed, I went and walked in the moonlight, in the chilly November peace of our garden. My life could be entirely reinterpreted.

Dot's behaviour had so wounded me that I had closed it off as best I could. A whole series of incidents unrolled in retrospect. There on the moonlit lawn, I saw how my decision had forced me to discount Dot's later affectionate care. This was the woman who had preserved every letter I had written from abroad, about four hundred in number, and had copied most of them into a folio book, word for word.

She had encouraged me to write.

She had awakened my love of the pictorial.

When Betty and I were unwell, she had burned eau-de-Cologne in a saucer to sweeten the sickroom.

She had moved the family from Devon to come and live in Oxford, where I was.

She had taken pride in my first book.

She had understood the agonies of the collapse of my first marriage, and accepted Margaret.

She had gone down to the Isle of Wight to see my children.

She had loved me and thought me worth loving.

All that I had shut away. My rebellious nature had grown from that seven-year-old's decision.

Now that decision folded up and was gone. I breathed a different air. I was at last truly in touch with my roots. It was from my roots that the anima had spoken.

This was early in the morning of 16 November, when the moon was full.

This extraordinary visitation was discussed with Margaret, who readily accepted what I told her, and later reported to Mrs Green. What she made of it no mortal can tell.

Perhaps I am wrong so to personalise my anima. That was how I saw it at the time.

The bitterness about Dot's early treatment of me was dissolved in compassion. I began to remember her better days, the laughter she, Betty and I had shared, her early encouragement of the small boy at her side to make books, binding the results in wallpaper. She had looked after us well during the war, in that poky little store in Bickington. Certainly she had always shown a preference for Betty, yet I was the offspring who had produced grandchildren, and she had loved them too. I remembered the spirit with which she cooked. And her vulgar dreams. How bravely she bore old age, when Margaret and I looked after her. And how we often rocked with laughter.

Recalling her trips to Italy as a widowed woman, I saw that Bill had probably been a repressive force on a naturally cheerful disposition.

And Bill . . .

One of the well-known effects of any form of psychotherapy is that a lesser memory may conceal behind it something graver, more terrible. It was so in my case.

Having rolled away the boulder of my early decision, I was confronted by a darker thing. It waited in a cave behind the boulder, an old mouldering corpse of cruelty which yet retained life enough to affect my life.

It was something to be approached with hope and trepidation.

So the record returns to that distant year of 1925. I, a mere babe in arms. I cried at night and could not be consoled.

Why does a healthy baby cry excessively when new-born? Research suggests that, utterly dependent as the child is upon its mother, it can sense friction between parents, perhaps sexual tension. Or, in my case, the infant may have sensed Dot's disappointment in discovering that she had engendered a boy.

And Bill? Was he still suffering from the trauma of war?

How traumatised was Bill? And what luck that I'm here to ask the question! One night, unable to sleep for the baby's cries, Bill had snatched up his helpless son and *held him – me! – suspended out of the bedroom window.*

That bedroom window, the window with no view, *the window with the concrete below.* He had threatened to drop me unless I stopped crying.

Bill seized hold of his sobbing child, flung up the lower half of the window, and thrust the child out over the drop. The child went rigid.

Crying? Ceased. Breathing? Heart?

Bill paralysed the infant.

It – I, *I* – remained silent, frozen, almost as dead as the stillborn sister who had preceded me into that bedroom.

I had been damaged. That brutish act had had its effect on my mental development, had created a little blister of misery somewhere by the amygdala that had caused me . . . well, who can say? – had caused me – and had shaped me—

It can hardly bear telling. Yet it is fortunate that I was able to drag this injury into the light where – much as textbooks reassure us it should – it dispersed, leaving behind, like Bessie after exorcism, only a foul stink.

I regard it as the ultimate secret inscription.

You may ask, as Mrs Green did, how I could possibly remember something, even something so violent, which took place before the boy was six months old. How could details be recalled with such clarity – being dangled out of that window, that window which still exists in East Dereham, above that concrete which still exists, the cold, the terror, the affront, the awful knowledge that I was powerless in the hands of someone who hated me? How did I recover from the injury?

The answer reveals another turn of the screw. I was told about it. As if it were a family joke.

Bill and Dot related the incidents – they occurred more than once – as we sat at a little table in that same bedroom.

The stillborn angel had been so quiet, and I so noisy.

When I was old enough to understand, they told me what Bill used to do with me and they laughed heartily. The Aldisses always had a wonderful sense of humour.

I laughed because they laughed.

I would do anything to please them, so that it did not happen to me again.

We all rocked with laughter, as we sat in that bedroom.

And then I buried the shame of it all away from anyone's memory.

The entire memory had been hidden, tucked away, locked in, among things too ghastly to face.

Now I knew, became utterly clear as the knowledge sank in, that that terrible act had caused the paralysis of feeling, the *Weltschmertz*, that had bedevilled my life, its lack of self-esteem, its identification with the underdog, its division into separate personalities . . .

And what had I said of my love of science fiction? That I wrote because I suspected the world was not as others saw it. Nor had it been as I saw it myself; there had been another probability world, the world of Probability A, where everything had remained frozen, without emotion, without future.

How truthful, how true to my inner self my fiction was! More than that, my salvation, most likely. My portable personal mythology.

No wonder mazes had held an attraction for me. They served as diagrams I drew of my consciousness. Well, I had behaved like a rat – but now I was out of the maze. Out at last!

The psychotherapy course petered out. The narrative had unfolded to reach its unexpected climax. The personal mythology had born its poisoned fruit. Mrs Green put on her bizarre headgear and set out for the United States of America.

My gratitude to Mrs Green is less than perhaps it should have been. For one thing, I could never have gone to her when my spirits were at their lowest, for then I could never have spoken – and, my problems were not of her resolving but of my own, for I had pushed against the invisible boulder, fought it, ever since adolescence. For another, I regretted she had not recorded our sessions as the narrative unfolded. Never again could I tell it as I told it then: once it was all out, it faded into thin air, like frost in sunshine.

Still, I owed her this: that she had listened.

Years earlier, the woman at Marriage Guidance had finally embraced and kissed me, and said, 'Together we did it!' Mrs Green was of cooler temperament. She left me with no impression that she thought my life had changed. But I knew what had happened.

I was coming up for sixty and my life had begun anew. My miraculous life!

When I mulled it all over, I thought: Poor old Bill . . .

After all, had he not been suffering still from the miseries of his war, as I was later to suffer from mine?

The whole concern withered and died.

The parents were laid to rest.

Oh, so it happened. So that's all it was, that shadow?

Fine. I was not going to let it spoil the rest of my life.

So strong was the thrust to recovery within me that I had no trouble, only joy, in forgiveness. More difficult than forgiving my father for almost dropping me to my death was forgiving him for never having amassed a library, however modest.

I had stepped out into the sunshine. I was changed. I had always prepared myself for change and now it had happened. There was reason for congratulation.

In his weird beautiful book, *Tractatus Logico-Philosophicus*, Wittgenstein says, 'The world of the happy man is a different one from that of the unhappy man'.

My resolution: 'Margaret shall feel the benefits of this.' She had withstood all the emotional upheaval. But – there she was! Once more, perception was all. I perceived her as the lovely woman she was, and is. What she had felt during these years of travail I do not know. She has never said, although she claims to have said plenty. Perhaps I was deaf. Perhaps wisely, she went about her own affairs.

The worst effects of the PVFS were receding.

In fact, I soon began to look upon my marvellous visitation as prelude to a spiritual drama – perhaps, if rightly considered, the first step towards a higher mental plateau, a clearer consciousness. Not an end but a beginning.

When I wrote articles on PVFS, I received anxious letters from fellow-sufferers. To them I said, by way of consolation, that PVFS is not just an illness, an infection of some kind; it is a signal that something in your life needs to change. Face the problem in that spirit and you may find much will be given you. I hope it has turned out that way for others.

Dr Jackson spoke truth when she said that many suffered because they felt they had not achieved the recognition they deserved. She could have added that that recognition had first to be achieved in their own eyes.

For me, with memory returning, and my sixtieth birthday approaching, the most serene decade of my life was about to dawn. I had transcended a testing midlife crisis. There was now nothing in the past I would have altered.

The wisdom and love that is almost everyone's birthright rose buoyant to the surface. It was a sunrise.

My writing was rooted in the soil of mistrust. It had grown into an abundant tree. In that, my experience echoed the experience of many writers, among them such favourites as Mary Shelley, Charles Dickens and Franz Kafka. Bertrand Russell is another startling example. Among fantasy writers, we note that J. R. R. Tolkein, Aldous Huxley and C. S. Lewis all lost their mothers when they were young. Pain moves one on.

Among my cuttings is a clip from a letter of Richard Wagner's, in which he discusses the intermingling of pain and pleasure. He says, in part, 'I want everyone who can take pleasure in my works, i.e. my *life* and what I do [to know] that what gives them pleasure is my *suffering*, my *extreme misfortune*! . . . if we had *life*, we should have no need of *art*. Art begins at precisely the point where life breaks off . . . I simply do not understand how a *truly happy* individual could ever hit upon the idea of producing "art".'

Things once enjoyed became even more enjoyable. The music of favourite composers, Sibelius, Smetana, Borodin, became clearer. Favourite painters, Gauguin, Kandinsky, Tiepolo, became more vivid. That precious resource of English men and women, BBC radio programmes, became better appreciated. The air of Boars Hill tasted even fresher. Everything was perceived anew.

The transformation has proved genuine and permanent. I had worked for it, had beaten my way through the glass forest and deciphered its secret inscriptions.

I refused to regret the past; it was my history, and that was that. Although no longer a Christian in any real sense, this post-Christian took to heart one of Jesus' sayings about forgiveness. 'Forgive' is a word that has acquired sloppy connotations. We learn from the movies, through many an immoral example, that hard men never forgive. Rubbish!

As often happens, a book arrived serendipitously: Leo Tolstoy's novel *Resurrection*. At the core of this great story of a man trying to remedy an injustice he inflicted on a woman some years earlier lies the message of forgiveness. Nekhlyudov has to work hard to achieve forgiveness. The unforced morality of the book, the drama of its setting as the chief characters move towards Siberia, make it for me one of the world's best books; but the books one finds great – that is, which touch and fortify one's deeper feelings – such books have to arrive at the time they are needed.

The principle of forgiveness appears also in *Anna Karenina* in Karenin's attempts to forgive his wife's adultery. There, it is a fire that warms a room. In *Resurrection*, it is a blaze embracing the whole house.

Forgiveness is a tough sinewy thing; it can open a heart the way an oystercatcher opens up an oyster on the wet seashore. The old protective shell in which I had encased myself at prep school fell away. I found I was able to forgive Bill and Dot. I was able to forgive Margaret. Loving flooded in without let or hindrance.

I say 'forgive Margaret'! That was only the first step towards recognising in her the pleasantest, most straightforward, most loving woman one might ever have the fortune to meet.

When I found I had also forgiven myself, I remembered what the Buddhists say, that guilt is a form of self-indulgence.

Forgiveness sets you free from all that.

One might assume a symmetry here: that a story-telling career which began with oral stories in a dormitory might end fifty years later with an oral narrative in a psychotherapist's little room.

But that is far from being the case.

XXIX

The Two Suns

Dawn, geese upbraid the awakened sun –
Shay Tal's bones lie deep under rajabarrels
They saw a thousand years of warring skies
White as bones, flowers in Oldorando's grass
               Homemade poem of the Late T'ang

While all the *Sturm und Drang* was taking place, roughly over the ten years from 1974 to 1984, one faculty seemed to remain unimpaired, and enabled us to hold together: the creative faculty.

The manner in which the creative act – a gift if ever there was one – functions remains obscure, but its workings can be shown by example.

Drama is age-old. On stage, on television, in books drama has not changed its essence since the days of Sophocles. It consists of a chain of events, or at least a situation, of high emotion, tragical, or at least liable to upset in some way the status of the characters involved.

The definition shows why drama is eternally popular. It mirrors our own lives, however distortedly, however distorted our lives, by war or any other kind of misery. We all go through the same hoops of high emotion, tragedy, and decisions as regard status, moral or financial, or whatever. Some of these mirrors attempt to reflect life directly, 'as it is', as the saying goes, and terms like Realism or Naturalism are evoked.

But there is another sort of drama where the mirror is held not up to Nature, as Shakespeare puts it, but up to a more abstract or symbolic thing. Oedipus sleeps with his mother and later puts out his eyes. Such extremes do not happen to all of us, yet we remain interested in the case of Oedipus.

Science fiction and the related field of fantasy are similar forms of drama. The mirror is held up to a more abstract or symbolic thing. Up to the future, for instance, or to another planet, as a transposition of our own. The device is somewhat similar to the way in which a Shakespeare play can be transposed from Tudor or Plantagenet times to a modern epoch, centuries ahead of Shakespeare's day. Richard Loncraine's film version of Shakespeare's *Richard III*, starring Ian McKellen, being an example.

In other words, science fiction differs little from other traditional forms of fiction. It must succeed or fail by criteria which apply equally to other dramas. That is to say, in judging any particular SF novel or drama, we consider such matters as style, characterisation, narrative pace, idea and *élan vital*. Yet many people, including devoted readers and writers of SF, regard it as a thing apart, subject to rather mystical laws of its own.

There is a received idea that prediction is one of SF's functions. This is also mistaken, to my mind. A supporter of this rather functional view (fiction does not *function*: it exists) was the late Isaac Asimov.

There are two attractive elements of SF that win my allegiance, although they are not unique to the field. The first of these is the imagery, whether the exoticism of another planet, the weirdness of cyberspace, or the mental landscapes of human or alien thought.

Special effects can make an SF movie unlike an SF novel; what we see on the screen may be melodramatic adventure with a gimmick, without anything new in the realm of ideas, or with plausibility deleted for the sake of melodrama. Director Paul Verhoeven's brutal and terrible *Total Recall* buried under its debris a quiet and disquieting Philip K. Dick short story, 'We Can Remember It for You Wholesale'.

Among many discomforts prevailing in the eighties, which in Britain included savage coal pit closures and the reign of 'market forces', I believe that spiritual life became a little more comfortable. Science – particularly the cosmological branch of science – drew nearer to religion. What we believe to be a new and better understanding of the universe leaves less room than previously for God, for any god. On the other hand, the universe itself is an object for wonder and reverence.

It has become part of our general understanding that space and time emerged with the Big Bang: that therefore before that moment there existed neither space nor time: so that nothing – according to the laws of our universe – existed or could have existed previously.

The physical laws are few and not too difficult to understand. What humbles us is to see the diversity that springs from them, including the diversity of life. Everything has developed from one egg of energy. In the beginning were only hydrogen and helium and ferocious velocities. All heavier elements were created in the heart of primal suns. We are ourselves composed of what was dead star material.

Science fiction writers often play games with what we might call the conditional condition of our world, our umwelt. The first word in an SF writer's vocabulary is *if*. An example comes from my *Helliconia Trilogy*.

Helliconia is a part of the aleatory nature of writing experience. Something comes to hand, and one takes it – whereupon it proves to be what one needs. The sketches of Victor Hugo were born in this way. Using the 'blotesque' method, spilling ink or cigar ash on his paper, Hugo produced figures of castles, men and landscapes out of what was accidental.

A publisher friend was seeking to persuade me to produce a book I did not greatly wish to write. I sent him a letter suggesting something slightly different and, from my point of view, more engaging. What I had in mind was an immense story, set on a planet much like Earth, but with a longer year. I wanted no truck with our puny 365 days.

There flies the first *if*. Despite recent claims by astronomers, we have no proof positive that other planets exist beyond the solar system – although admittedly it seems likely. There's never scientific proof from only one example, however. My planet was a speculative venture, unreal estate.

'Let's say for argument's sake this planet is called Helliconia', I wrote to my publisher, almost without premeditation. As I wrote, I saw a planet orbiting two suns.

The word was out. *Helliconia!* And from that word grew the book.

As I've said, the Helliconia novels were written during a period of emotional unheaval. And always over our shoulders the more threatening outside world was looking. In 1980, I was invited to be Writer Guest of Honour at the Singapore Book Fair. I could not but accept. My host was to be Kirpal Singh, with whom I had become friendly in Australia.

The family came to see me off at the start of my journey, at Oxford rail station. It was Wendy who asked, 'What shall we do, Daddy, if war breaks out while you're away?'

'I shall fly back immediately and take you all with me to live safe in Singapore.'

But what a question to hear one's child ask!

My publisher friend who had provoked the word *Helliconia* was under stress. Let's call him Jack.

Jack had been working for a well-known publisher with whom I had some contact. He approached me secretively to suggest that I should meet him at 2 p.m. on a certain day at a certain bench in Red Lion Square. Who could resist such an arrangement. Was he about to induce me into M5, the Masons, or the Rosicrucians?

Well, no . . . He was thinking of setting up his own publishing company and wanted me to write a book for him. That I did. The result was a novella which I – possibly I alone – hold to be almost on a par with Doris Lessing's *The Fifth Child*, her magical, terrifying novella. *Brothers of the Head* is based on a terrible dream I had in Hunstanton during our marriage crisis.

While my novels were still to be published by Jonathan Cape, Jack wanted to publish a 'Helliconia Encyclopaedia', which David Wingrove and I would edit together. Jack and I went to New York, together but apart. It was difficult to stay in touch with Jack; he was never there when I phoned: nor did I know in that vast metropolis whereabouts that phone of his was situated.

I spent some time with my American literary agent, Robin Straus; she was an enrichment in my life – enrichment sometimes even of a financial kind. She introduced me to my American publisher, Tom Stewart of Atheneum. Tom was an excellent publisher; I was fortunate to have the *Helliconia*s under his care.

The arrangement for those books was that Atheneum co-published with Cape. It was hands across the ocean, and while Atheneum would edit, they would not remove what Americans quaintly call 'Britishisms'. What brilliant editing it was too! It came as quite a shock to receive, on the manuscript of the *Spring* volume, a multi-page, carefully reasoned, line-by-line list of corrections and suggestions. Thereafter, aware of my dullness under PVFS, I relied on this loving care expended on my work by a person or persons unknown.

When all three volumes were out, I rang Tom and asked to speak to their copy-editor. He was vague, calling back after a while to say that the copy-editor was a woman who lived out in Queens. No, he had never met her.

I wired her some flowers via Interflora and then rang her number. I thanked her warmly for her scrutiny, which had improved my work. She was dumbfounded. After a while, she said that she had been copy-editing for twenty-eight years. No author had ever rung her before. She started to cry.

But to Jack. He and I returned separately to England. No luck with the encyclopaedia. Only years later, when the three Helliconia volumes were published, when my agent saw the chance to sell an encyclopaedia, did we find that Jack had in fact already obtained a reasonably large advance from a New York publisher. The money had gone to assist him in some of his financial difficulties.

Ingenious though Jack was at raising money, his small company collapsed beneath him. By then, I, ever the innocent, had invested £5,000 in the firm. Jack fled to Bombay (again showing considerable ingenuity, since Bombay is hardly the first place one thinks of as a refuge). He left his wife to pick up the pieces, which she bravely did. She even managed to return my investment. This excellent lady later had her portrait hung in the Royal Academy.

I liked the company of both Jack and his wife – the wife even more.

Dealing with strange landscapes and states of mind, I found it necessary to coin several new words, and to bring into use obsolete but valuable words, such as *candency* (meaning warmth or fervour) and *zafferine* (a splendid word meaning blue-coloured, which seems to have fallen from use in the thirteenth century).

A needed coinage was for that august moment when, for the inhabitants of Helliconia, their great sun, Freyr, sinks below the horizon of the Polar Circle. Some people know, some do not, that Freyr will not rise again for many generations. This is the onset of the long Helliconian winter.

Who on Earth, I asked myself, would have a word for the moment when our sun sank below the polar horizon, not to rise again for several months? Such a solemn moment must have a name in a terrestrial tongue. To my surprise, neither the Swedes nor the Norwegians possessed such a word in their vocabularies.

I phoned an astronomer in Iceland. Even the Icelanders have no such word, which seems odd. However, the astronomer gave me their word for darkness, which is *Myrkur*.

Even as it stands, *Myrkur* sounds rather Helliconian. Given a more Helliconian ending, it became Myrkwyr. So Myrkwyr is the death of the sun. We've all experienced it, to varying degrees.

Achieving a treatise was not my desire. So were introduced what for me is a fascinating element of life on my imagined planet, the gossies and fessups. Death is not quite the end for a Helliconian. His or her spirit survives like a guttering ember, sinking ever lower into null space towards complete extinction. The living may on occasion visit gossies to make with them what communication they can.

Yet a balance between such fantasy and reality must be held.

Helliconia's great sun, Freyr, can be located on star charts. In the constellation Ophiuchus is a dark dust cloud, the main portion of which lies close to the constellation Scorpius. The cloud is at a distance from our solar system of 700 light years. The cloud conceals a cluster of stars, one of which is Freyr. Location: Right Ascension 16th 25m. Declination – 24°30′.

The relationship between science fiction and science is incapable of precise definition, varying as it does from year to year. Science permeates our lives, and both scientists and writers are wayward people. What is clear is that science fiction can work in either quasi-predictive or digestive mode.

In *Helliconia*, the Digestive Tract method is employed. In 1979, while my novel was a mere building site, its foundations open to the alien sky, James Lovelock published a small book entitled, *Gaia: A New Look at Life on Earth*. A small book, but for me a large input of 'blotesque'.

The name Gaia was suggested by Lovelock's friend (I might even claim him as a friend of mine) William Golding, the novelist and Nobel Prize-winner. In Greek mythology, Gaia was the goddess of the Earth; Lovelock was outlining an impersonal updated version of that gubernatory personage. Lovelock pointed out that the continued survival of a living Earth is by way of being something of a miracle. Life flourishes within and despite an alarmingly narrow range of chemical and physical parameters – parameters subject to fluctuation.

How is it that Earth's temperature has not long ago increased, as has happened on 'our sister planet' Venus; that the salinity of the oceans has not grown more toxic than the Dead Sea; that atmospheric oxygen has not become tied down in oxides in the rocks, or that hydrogen has not escaped from the upper atmosphere? These are the kinds of question Lovelock's Gaia hypothesis addresses.

I would suppose them to be of interest even to literary men in universities. The hypothesis contends that every living thing on the Earth, the biomass, constitutes a single complex self-regulating entity – living, of course, but of course without conscious intention to maintain optimum conditions for existence or otherwise. Such maintenance has singularly failed to happen on Venus.

Gaia has no particular centre, no prime minister or parliament, no Führer, not even a Greek goddess; it functions through its unfocused complexity, built up over millions of years. The implication is that the work of bacterial and other forces has built, and maintains, the living world we know, best to suit themselves – a process in which humanity has played small part. Humanity is in fact almost irrelevant in the scheme of things.

Curiously, I had but recently encountered a progenitor of the Gaia hypothesis. ('Gaia' has recently been rechristened 'geophysiology', this term being considered less eccentric, and more likely to win general scientific acceptance.)

While I was immersed in the refreshing ideas of repentance and forgiveness – as one immerses oneself in a warm tropical sea – I was reading the novel perfectly suiting my mood, Tolstoy's *Resurrection*, that grand panorama of life and reform. Towards the end of the book, in Chapter Three of Part Three, the prisoner Simonson formulates a doctrine which is henceforth to regulate all his activity:

> According to this doctrine everything in the world is alive; there is no inert body, but everything hitherto termed lifeless, 'inorganic' matter, is simply part of an immense organic body which we cannot comprehend, and that the task of man, as a particle of that huge organism, is to preserve its life and that of all its living parts.

Interestingly, Lovelock is an independent biologist of a rather old-fashioned kind, unsupported by universities or other institutions. And his hypothesis relics on a method of close observation and enquiry which is such a marked feature of Charles Darwin's work. Darwin perceived where we merely see.

What Lovelock calls 'city wisdom' has become almost entirely centred on problems of human relationships; whereas, in a natural tribal group, wisdom means giving due weight to relationships with the rest of the animate and inanimate world. Indeed, the more intelligent science fiction often acknowledges this wider relationship; the interplay of character which forms a staple of received literature gives way to the interplay between human beings and something beyond themselves.

'City wisdom' is what we get from the majority of literary critics. On the other hand, I first read the word 'ecology' in a thirty-five-cent science fiction magazine.

Lovelock says, 'I speak from personal experience when I say that those of us who go forth in ships or travel to remote places . . . are few in number compared with those who choose to work in city-based institutions and universities.'

From travel, investigation and perception, Lovelock built up his integrative hypothesis. Whether it was *true* or not, I felt that it was just and could be proved by further research, and that here was a thesis which delivered to us helpful new understanding of our role in an all-embracing nature.

Or, to rephrase, whether this was just Lovelock's perception or an actual function of the external world, it became my perception too. I wanted to believe! And I wanted to proselytise.

Lovelock's seminal work appeared during the period of the Cold War, when we lived under the threat of nuclear destruction, possibly to be followed by nuclear winter. Had nuclear winter come about, it would have been the ultimate profaning of nature, the rape and slaughter of Gaia.

These intellectual and emotional ideas were in my mind when I sat down to the task – the adventure, I should say – of writing *Helliconia*. I hoped to dramatise on a generous scale, and on a planet where extremes of climate are more marked than on Earth, the workings out of Lovelock's hypothesis. But I did not wish to write a text. I intended to write a drama.

But behind that drama is a refinement of thought: the animist 'original boulder' of *Spring* becomes the religious 'Original Beholder' of *Summer*, which develops into a scientific Gaia concept by *Winter*.

Helliconia is a scientific romance of civilisations contained within a dominating nature. It talks about pretty ordinary fallible people living within fallible social systems, much like us – together with the alien who also has a share in us. The Helliconian aliens are called phagors. Deep hostility has long prevailed between humans and phagors. Yet one species is linked by phylogenetic law to the other. My phagors are not simply a threat to humanity; they function rather as what Carl Jung terms our Shadow side, sometimes threatening mankind, sometimes threatened by them, depending on season.

Humans and phagors form a sort of binary life form, reflecting the binary system within which they live. Incidentally, the Helliconia novels had an appreciative reader in the University of Oxford. After singing their praises, he said, 'But you couldn't really have two suns in the sky at once, could you?'

This struck me as amazing ignorance in a learned man. Here again, a matter of perception enters; for if 'two suns in the sky' are received as an impossibility, then my work is reduced to an idle fantasy. Perhaps herein lies one reason why SF is held in low esteem: ignorance. Ignorance of elementary science among cultivated men.

I had written a novel, *Life in the West*, some years before *Helliconia*. Being interested in the workings of the world of affairs, of economics and ideology and religion, in part as a natural result of travel, I filled *Life in the West* with such matters. Following that, I encouraged myself to do something similar on a larger scale. This ambition grew into *Helliconia*.

At first I thought of an allegory of a political kind, with the three major power blocs represented by three Helliconian continents. Happily, this scheme soon faded away – although three continents were left behind by the tide, Campannlat, Hespagorat and Sibornal. Only Sibornal carries a faint echo of Siberia and the Soviet power bloc.

For by then creative impulses flooded in, washing away more didactic ones. I fell in love with my planet. It was filling with life and diversity. It was a body orbiting diverse binary suns, Batalix and Freyr, and its year was three thousand Earth years long.

As I worked, all the conflicting impulses with which our minds are filled seemed to rise up and organise themselves in a remarkable way. Whole populations seemed to assemble themselves. With a great rustle of garments, men and women emerged from the dark. This astonishing creative process, with its seeming autonomy, is one of the major pleasures of writing.

Naturally, I had to find a strong story. Three stories, in fact. For the length of the seasons dictated that there should be a book for each season. Well, I wrote only three novels, *Spring, Summer* and *Winter*. I am no Vivaldi.

I already had general ideas, once I realised that a large cast of characters would have to assemble. For the seven years the research and writing took me, it was almost as though I was living on Helliconia, a thousand light years from Earth.

A problem with any novel is how to begin. What I lacked was a piece of key imagery: *I could not visualise the Helliconian vegetation.*

I was stuck. My three most able advisers, Tom Shippey, Iain Nicholson and Peter Cattermole, had done their best to drum philological and cosmological facts into my head. Still I could not clearly imagine a Helliconian tree. What would it look like? How would it function?

If I could not imagine a tree, I told myself, I was incapable of painting the whole new binary system I – we – had devised.

One fine evening in 1980, I was travelling from Oxford to London by train, to attend some function or other. Time was drawing towards sunset as the train passed by Didcot power station. My wife and I had often talked about the power station's six cooling towers; were they not, from a distance at least, beautiful? Wasn't the industrial landscape beautiful? Would John Keats have found such sights 'a joy for ever'?

The towers on this occasion stood with the sun low behind them. They were breathing forth immense clouds of steam into the still-bright sky. Towers and steam appeared to be a unity, black, solid, impenetrable, against the light background.

Of course. *They were Helliconian trees! I was looking at a clump of six great Helliconian trees . . .*

The cooling towers, those cyclinders with their corseted Victorian waists, were the trunks. The billowing ragged forms of steam were their foliage. The foliage would emerge from the trunk only at certain times of year.

I cannot describe my startlement at that moment. Nor can I explain the spark that leaped across from my perception to my imagination, transposing something I had passed hundreds of times into something no one had ever seen before.

That moment of revelation was what I needed. I started to write my scientific romance.

Among the many characters with whom I became involved, I felt most affection for Shay Tal, who stands her ground at Fish Lake; the lovely summer queen, Myrdemlnggala; young Luterin, due for a strange imprisonment; and especially Ice Captain Muntras, who plies a trade in Campannlat once fashionable on Earth in the years before refrigerators, selling what is sometimes prized, sometimes cursed – cold, in chunks.

As the whole matter had seemed to unfold from that one fecund word, Helliconia, so we believe the whole universe has unfolded from the primal atom.

So I encapsulated this principle in the second book, in *Helliconia Summer*. A defeated general walks alone through a Randonan forest, a great rainforest swarming with life, a seemingly permanent wilderness of growth. Yet, only a few generations earlier, the whole dominating congregation of flora burst out from a handful of nuts.

When the third and final volume, *Helliconia Winter*, was published, my enthusiastic publisher, Tom Maschler, asked me over a drink, 'What would you say *Helliconia*'s really all about?'

I gave him a very English answer. 'It's about a change in the weather . . .' I said.

Many so-called contemporary novels are freighted with nostalgia. Perhaps one reason for either enjoying or shunning science fiction is that it is relatively free of the poisons of forever glancing back – cosy teas with the vicar, Hovis, a warm Aga in the kitchen, a jolly innkeeper, servants, stables and an acquaintance with a title. SF looks to the future, to change, even when its eye fills with foreboding.

Science fiction has a remarkable and expanding history this century. It has diversified from cheap paperbacks and magazines to all forms of culture, whether acknowledged or otherwise. How strange that it is not better attended to by those deep in literary studies. The loss, the stimulation, is theirs. It is a curious fact that a large proportion of SF is staged off-Earth, sometimes very far off. Such scenarios, like the cosy room with the vicar, must relate back to some characteristic of the author. One day, a cunning critic will explicate these mysteries.

The volumes of *Helliconia* represent another drama taking place a thousand light years from Earth. But less distant from its everyday concerns.

Science fiction has been accused of many faults. No one would attempt to defend all of it. Does one attempt to defend all love stories, or even all of Dickens? Certainly science fiction often attempts to escape, escape from the pettiness of much of life.

I do not regret the *Sturm und Drang* of my own life. It is less to be feared than what H. G. Wells called Everydayness.

XXX

The Hill

work² **don't get worked up (about it)**, (ne) t'emballe pas/(ne) te
monte pas le bourrichon/t'excite pas. (*See* **lather¹**; **sweat¹**)
Harrap's Slang French-English Dictionary

Commentators like to tell us that the family is threatened, even
doomed, just as we hear that the novel is dead. Perhaps this
is not the case. When the family disappears, society falls apart. In
those stormy years of ours, I would often happily have lost my life;
I never wished to lose Margaret.

There was something in her quiet adherence to traditional values
– an adherence which went along with a rejection of religion –
which strengthened me. I, the arguer, found it inarguable. At the
beginning of our falling out, another woman, tempting me, said,
'You must fulfil yourself.' It was the voice of sixties philosophy
speaking. I immediatcly perceived its seductive error, a counsel
of imperfection that could lead to havoc – and I broke from her.
Margaret too eventually broke from a liaison she had maintained
for some years.

If marriage can be made to work, there lies fulfilment. It is a
greater thing than self-fulfilment. What a hard lesson to learn! The
protagonists of Ibsen's plays struggle with it.

There was that wonderful thing in Margaret: even if she shunned
me, she continued her reasonable life – her underplayed life, damn
it! She never quit.

I too had more than one good reason not to quit. Consideration
embraced more than just the pair of us. If we could provide an
example of stability and calm for the four children, then that would
be part of the healing process for Clive and Wendy. Like the rest of
us, they would need affection throughout life.

The thing was to soldier on. Even when we had nothing to say to each other, I saw Margaret's graceful walk through life, her non-materialist outlook, her calm, and felt that all who knew her must feel the better for it. She was sensible, she spoke ill of no one – and these were not minor virtues. We cared for our children. This was no minor virtue, either.

We continued to work to hold things together. Gradually, life's summer weather returned and the birds sang again. As they still do. The visitation by my anima left me with a peace of mind I had never previously known. This great benefit I could share.

The argument for marriage is this: that without that solemn agreement, that contract, we would most likely have broken apart; and then our personality problems would not have been resolved.

My surviving sister Betty had been rather a remote figure for several years. She enjoyed a varied career before working as costume designer for Alec Shanks, the costumier for many plays, West End and otherwise.

After several years with Shanks, she moved on to the BBC Costume Department. Here she had many assignments. You still see her name on repeats of episodes of the long-running television comedy, *Porridge*. She also dressed Regency plays and *The Goodies*. Her most successful long run was when she dressed the cast of *The Duchess of Duke Street*, starring Gemma Jones. Here Betty was working within her favourite period, the late Victorian age.

In 1981, shortly after Dot's death, Betty was married, rather to the family's surprise. Perhaps it was rather to Betty's surprise that all our children regarded this as a jolly family event; she had been too busy to pay them much attention. But we all celebrated this occasion, and enjoyed the reception held in Betty's charming house in Ealing.

Betty married an old friend of hers and Dot's, a journalist by name Antony King-Deacon. Antony had a ready laugh. He suffered from a slight family shortage and, in consequence, was the more ready to embrace the Aldiss tribe. Antony proved amusing and resourceful. Henceforth, he and Betty became much more a part of that tribe.

When Betty took early retirement from the BBC, she and Antony moved up to Norfolk to live.

Wendy married in 1984. In 1990, to our delight, she and her husband Mark came to live in Oxford, near us. We remain very close.

The marriage of our elder daughter was certainly an event. Like a suitor of old, Mark had come to my study and asked for the hand of Wendy in marriage. I consented. I then again had proof of that special love that exists between father and daughter, not least between *this* father and *this* daughter: for Wendy came to me afterwards and said that she would not have gone against my word had I said no to Mark. Well, I hope she would have done.

Wendy did not want an Isle of Wight wedding, which friends of hers might not be able to attend; she had visualised Orchard House as a good place for the reception. But our tax problems had caused us to sell up. We were too cramped in North Oxford for wedding receptions.

It happened that I was with our solicitor, Brian Heath, when one of his partners came along and said a client of his was trying to sell a house on Boars Hill. We bundled the children into the car on a Saturday morning, and drove to look at 'Woodlands'. At once all the family enjoyed the atmosphere of this beautiful Edwardian house, and by evening, I had agreed to buy.

Here Wendy and Mark could stage their wedding reception. They could be married at the bottom of the hill, in Sunningwell church. Mark's idea was that they should leave the reception by helicopter, which could land on one of our lawns. There proved to be not quite enough clearance over the trees – but it was a sparkling event, all the same. Clive flew over for the celebrations. Mark, as Antony had done, immediately became one of the family.

This reception was held only a fortnight after we moved into Woodlands.

With enterprise typical of them, the newly married couple plunged off to the Far East, to see something of China before entering Burma, where both of their fathers had spent a seminal part of their youth.

Our new home had been built in 1907. It was the house to which an admiral, Admiral Robey, retired. Perhaps for that reason, Margaret at first regarded it as a masculine house, whereas I tended to think of it as my version of H. H.'s Whitehall. Like the long vanished Whitehall, Woodlands had a tower as well as an air of seclusion. A sense of continuity had been reclaimed.

Woodlands stands on the brow of a slope that leads down into undeniable and untended woods. A meandering path tempts one into a copse, which fills with flowers early in the year. When the trees are bare, snowdrops, daffodils, bluebells, carpet the glade, each in their turn. Once we sighted a fugitive fritillary. The woods enfolded the house to such an extent that we did not see our distant neighbours to either side. A light showed through the trees only during winter months, when the leaves had fallen. We had a footpath through the woods to the nearest neighbour, our friends the Horwoods.

Our house had six or seven bedrooms. Most of its Edwardian features had been preserved intact. Far away, down at the bottom of the garden, hidden among bushes, was the septic tank, a marvel of Edwardian construction with a vaulted brick roof.

My study had one door into the house and one out to the conservatory. Our living room was thirty feet long, with a high clerestory ceiling – ideal for parties. Details of woodwork were exceptionally pleasing; it was a house designed for people to live in happily and rationally (which we did, as far as it was within our capacity).

I loved everything about the house, although it often was cold in winter, like something in an old Russian novel. Here I learned to be calm, as far as it was within my nature, taking a lesson in that respect from Margaret. Here I did not have to learn to be happy. Here we were stable and content, the centre of the family. Here we were domestic – although here too I was to engage in two long pieces of work that eventually led nowhere. Where once this might have left me in depression, I now sailed evenly along, chalking everything up to experience. Perception is all.

In Woodlands, it was a pleasure to come downstairs in the dark of night, to wander about, perhaps to brew up a mug of tea, putting on no lights, disturbing the minimum number of cats. Unlike the houses in which Margaret and I had grown up, houses nowadays have twinkling eyes everywhere, red, white, green, as security, computer, printer, smoke-detectors and various other LCDs shine from floors, desks or ceilings.

By moonlight, the garden too held grandeur. The shrubs were mature. On the top lawn stood a magnificent Portuguese laurel, forty feet high. It was in full flower on the day we saw the house, was one of the reasons prompting the purchase. When it flowered, its fragrance floated down over the whole garden.

Here we discovered the music of Abbess Hildegard of Bingen ('A Feather on the Breath of God') – long after everyone else, apparently. For a while we played Gorecki's Symphony No. 3 over and over, supplanting even Smetana's 'Ma Vlast', that joyous expression of a man's love for his country.

Since Tim and Charlotte were both at school, Margaret spent more time in the study. With her help, I managed without a typist for the first time in twenty years. After the visitation by my anima, life was transformed, and Margaret and I entered into our new and rewarding partnership.

I admired her patience and endurance. She enjoyed the garden, hoeing her flower beds while I was rushing about with a chain saw cutting down those prolific weeds, the sycamores, to let real trees live. She filled the conservatory until it overflowed with plants. One year, when Margaret had the garden in good order, we opened it to local residents. They turned up in great numbers and we held a tea party on the terrace.

Margaret undertook to water her plants by hose, about a mile's length of which was required. This I regarded as a boring occupation. When I said something to this effect, she replied, 'Watering gives you the opportunity really to enjoy the plants.'

From then on, I saw the garden with fresh eyes, and rejoiced in everything that grew – sycamores always excepted.

Indeed, the whole world presented itself afresh. A light-heartedness filled me as never before. There are parts of the globe, Scandinavia and the Gulf of Bothnia, for instance, where the land still rises, celebrating the end of the Ice Age, the retreat of the glaciers.

One effect of the miseries that had been was that I cared much less what people thought of me. Being less burdened by my self, I was less preoccupied with myself.

So I went on the stage.

In the long association with A. P. Watt, over a quarter of a century, I had only one falling-out with them. They appointed a new media agent with whom I could not get on on sensible terms. So the break came. I stayed with Watt, but went off to find my own media agent. Frank Hatherley came back into my life.

Frank had been a script editor for BBC television when Robin Chapman and I scripted *Hot Local and Galactic News* for a series of one-off plays for them entitled *The Eleventh Hour*. Our chief actor was one Patrick Stewart. The *Eleventh Hour* plays were made in Lime Grove studios in one week. We began work on a Monday, in the large sound stage, at a meeting where all involved presided, and put together everything, story, sets, casting, rehearsals, photography, during the week. The finished play went out live on Saturday evening. It was a daring and pulse-generating experiment for all concerned. Stewart was being rehearsed on Wednesday while Robin and I were still writing the last pages of the script.

It was Stewart's – or rather the character he played's – job to work a miracle and walk on water. The difficulties of producing the Sea of Galilee at short notice defeated the props department. In the event, come Saturday, Stewart stood on top of the water contained in a large bucket.

Thus I advanced the career of the man who was later to captain the starship *Enterprise* in *Star Trek*.

Later on, Frank organised the launch of *The Aldiss Connection*. We were to present four adaptations of SF novels with the same care and respect BBC 2 was then giving to *The Golden Bowl*, *Point Counterpoint* and similar classics. The four novels were Wilson Tucker's *Year of the Quiet Sun*, a fine time-travel piece, my *Non-Stop*, John Wyndham's *The Chrysalids*, and Philip K. Dick's *Martian Time-Slip*, for which we earmarked a disused airstrip. Using the new technique of Color Separation Overlay, we planned to make the airstrip resemble Mars.

Alas, at the last minute, the BBC did not get an expected increase in its licence fee and *The Aldiss Connection* became disconnected.

So did Frank. He left the BBC and became media teacher in Communications at what is now the University of Westminster.

Frank volunteered to be my media agent, and in no time was sprouting wild schemes. Fascinated by his energy, I went along with everything he suggested. With Margaret, and with our money, we founded a small media company – very eighties – which Frank decided should be called Avernus, after the observation satellite which orbits Helliconia.

One of Frank's best ideas was *Science Fiction Blues*. This was an evening review of sketches and poems which Frank selected and edited from my writings. One of the most successful pieces was 'Drinks with the Spider King', culled from one of my least successful novels, *The Eighty-Minute Hour*. Another favourite was 'Supertoys Last All Summer Long'.

There were three of us in the show: Ken Campbell, Petronilla Whitfield and I. Frank, with Margaret's assistance, did everything backstage and front. He was a master at creating from the least promising venues comfortable space in which we could work. We printed free programmes and an illustrated souvenir brochure which Margaret sometimes sold at the door.

Our idea was to take SF to the masses – which on some nights numbered twenty-four.

It was tremendous fun. On we marched, to the tune of Ray Charles' 'Hit the Road, Jack'. Ken and Pet were gallant troupers. Ken I had first met in Newcastle years earlier, when he was running the

Ken Campbell Road Show with Bob Hoskins and Chris Langham. He was full of energy, confidence and good humour. When Ken was on stage, everything was well.

Pet was equally amusing, and good at taking direction, never forgetting what she had been told. Her reading of 'Juniper' was the high point of the show.

Ken had been the prime mover behind the remarkable series of *Illuminatus* plays, at the Liverpool Theatre of Language, Music, Dream and Pun, in 1972. The *Guardian* allowed me a column in which to enthuse over the production. Ken's masterpiece was based on a trilogy of novels written by Robert Anton Wilson and Robert Shea. There were five plays, all involving feats of memory by the actors, which played consecutively from Monday to Friday. On Sunday, the entire five were performed with short breaks between, from eleven in the morning until eleven at night. Twenty-five actors played to a cramped audience of one hundred. It was extravagant and extraordinary.

My *Guardian* review was instrumental in bringing the production down to London, where it was the first play to open at the new Cottesloe Theatre on the South Bank. Clive and I went to see it. In London it had the additional advantage of Sir John Gielgud as the voice of the computer.

SF Blues played all round England, and in Germany and Holland. One of our best nights was in Birmingham, where the local SF group turned out in force. We experienced in miniature all the delights and sorrows of a touring company, the disappointments, the triumphs, the moods of the leading lady, the dark behind the stage, the binge after a performance, and the camaraderie.

We played once at the University of East Anglia, so that happily Betty and Antony were able to see a performance.

Although writers are tortured by self-doubt about their writing – is it good enough, is it the right subject, etc. – I never had a qualm about going on the stage, or wearing a false nose where necessary.

One of our packed houses was at the 48th World Science Fiction Convention in The Hague. It was almost the last time we performed *SF Blues*. Later, I ran another little show, *Monsters of Everyday*, with Maureen and Keith Pollock.

Further theatricals were the order of the day to honour Margaret's sixtieth birthday. The family surprised her with my playlet *The Mock-Tempest*, a variation on Shakespeare's last play, packed with family allusions. All the family available took part, together with

Charlotte's then boyfriend, Gerry Byrne. Wendy, as Ariel, was actually pregnant at the time, though the news was yet to be announced.

Mark, as Prospero, was fresh from his role in the film, *Shadowlands*, and played Prospero in white tie and tails.

We performed the playlet under the oak tree on the rear lawn, to an audience of one. Although Betty and Antony had planned to drive down from Norfolk to be with us, something detained them at the last minute, so Margaret sat in solitary grandeur in the stalls. Finally, a Caliban at heart, I could seize on my chance to play Prospero's downtrodden native!

At the end of the play, Ceres, played by one of Tim's girlfriends, Helen Parker, comes to spread her feast before the company. Whereupon the cast invite the audience to share a teatime spread, with birthday cake, *sur l'herbe*.

Some years after Phil Dick died in 1982, I wrote a playlet about Dick in the afterlife, entitled, *Kindred Blood in Kensington Gore* (Kindred being Dick's middle name). This was a two-hander in which I took the role of Dick. Petronilla took the opposing role in England and a young actress, Colleen Ferro, in the USA. My favourite line is when Dick's dead sister asks him, 'What great religion ever promised that life was going to be a picnic?'

For some years, Colleen and I have read or enacted stories and poems at the Conference of the Fantastic. She is a hard-working and popular lady.

When Roger Corman came along with an offer for the rights of *Frankenstein Unbound*, Frank and I got a good media lawyer to iron out the wrinkles of the contract. Roger is charm itself, enviably lean, enviably calm. He invited the whole family, and Frank, to Italy, to the shores of Lake Como, to watch some of the shooting. This was to be the first film Roger had directed for twenty years; he made it for the Mount Company.

When Father has another novel published, the family exhales a silent 'Ho hum'. Some may read it, some do not. It's a free country. But when Father has a film in production, the family starts to jump up and down, yo-yo fashion.

Among the celebrated actors in the Corman film were John Hurt, Raul Julia and Bridget Fonda. Fonda played Mary Shelley. As bait for the pop-lovers, Roger cast Michael Hutchence as Shelley, to Charlotte's delight. We stayed in the charming little town of

Bellagio, in a hotel overlooking the lake. Tim was then in a photography mode, at which he was expert; he took a series of memorable black-and-white photographs of a wild night we spent with John Hurt, in which grappa featured largely.

He has a shot of Margaret in John Hurt's fond embrace, and one of me staring lasciviously at Bridget Fonda in period costume, to which we gave a spoonerism title, 'A Wish Called Fonda'.

People often ask what I think of the film made from my book. Authors should keep mum on that score, and be grateful when anything is made from their work. The scenery in the movie is good. And the acting. But Mary Shelley was never Byron's whore.

Roger and his producer, the ebullient Kobi Jaeger, came to dine with us at Woodlands. I told Roger he should film the sequel to *Frankenstein Unbound* next.

'What sequel?'

'*Dracula Unbound*.'

'You write it, I'll film it.'

It happened that I was able to use some leverage to get Roger and his wife Julie invited as guests of honour to the Conference of the Fantastic the next year. They proved a very popular couple. Roger showed his *Little Shop of Horrors*, which has Jack Nicholson in an early role. By then I had submitted a screen treatment of *Dracula Unbound* to Roger.

All he said of it was, 'I can't afford to make it, Brian. I'm a cheap-o outfit.'

A very pleasant way of rejecting a script. But *Frankenstein Unbound* had not met with great success. It was released in 1990, a year in which it had to compete with such SF films as *Back to the Future III*, *The Handmaid's Tale*, *Predator II*, *Robocop II*, and *Total Recall*.

The money from the film was soon frittered away. Avernus published the *Science Fiction Blues* souvenir brochure and, more ambitiously, the book of the revue, illustrated, in 1988. I was keen to publish a series of novels, perhaps more surreal than science-fictional, in limited editions. However, Frank became excited about a sort of novel written by one of his students. It was called *Trip City* and concerned the kind of slummy activities one associates with drug-taking in a slummy part of London.

I had no enthusiasm for *Trip City*, but was somewhat willing to let Frank have his way. This proved to be a mistake. Instead of producing this minor book in a minor key, Frank went to some trendy designers dressed in black, the Gothic mode, who decided the text should be printed in green. Then, a new idea, attach a cassette of music by a new black singing rock 'n' roller to the book and you would double the potential audience for it. This was lost on me; from my bookselling experience, I knew that such mixed-media combinations rarely worked. But there was no stopping Frank. Next thing was, the book had an expensive launch at the Polish Club in Queens Gate. Loud music played, champagne was swigged by a rent-a-crowd who came galloping in.

Hating to be a wet blanket, I kept my misgivings to myself.

Trip City sold twenty copies.

Thus, it probably found its true audience.

Margaret and I lost about £15,000 on the venture.

My regret is that, if we were to publish a disaster, it was not a piece of writing I could look back on with pride: a small neglected masterpiece, to be rediscovered at a time where the phrase 'market forces' had been forgotten.

My instinct at Woodlands was to relax and enjoy the place. We liked Boars Hill more and more. If I went into Oxford, it was to park the car in the Broad and go into Blackwell's for a book.

But seeds of work, sown in the past, were sprouting. My academic side, if it is worthy of that name, was catching up with me. *Billion Year Spree* in 1973, and the related anthologies, had opened new prospects. Although these productions had apparently been coolly received in the United States, a growing audience had been listening – the scholars.

As I was frequently told, I had been one of the few authors who had actively embraced the movement towards a growing body of SF criticism and teaching. While many writers, famously including Asimov, were fearful of the new development, I regarded it less as an epiphyte on an old tree than a new individual growth enhancing the previous one. Every literature has an attendant critical literature. I wanted SF to be no different in that respect.

In 1978, I was invited to Iowa, to the annual meeting of the SFRA, the Science Fiction Research Association, established as a spin-off of the MLA. There I was presented with a Pilgrim Award for distinguished contributions to the study of science fiction. This was followed later by the first Distinguished Scholarship Award, bestowed by the IAFA, the International Association for the Fantastic in the Arts, in 1986; the J. Lloyd Eaton Memorial Award for Best Critical Work of the Year, in 1988; a Hugo Award for Best Non-Fiction in 1987; and a President's Award for Independence of Thought in the Field of Science Fiction. All these awards are American or American-dominated.

Most of the awards stemmed from *Billion Year Spree* or its successor, *Trillion Year Spree* (1986), in which David Wingrove built greatly on my original work.

This reputation as a scholar has led to work on television and radio. It led also to an involvement with Stanley Kubrick.

Kubrick phoned me one day in June 1976. He had picked up a copy of *Billion Year Spree* on a bookstall, and read there that he was to be considered one of the great science fiction writers of the century. From this sprang what you might call a kind of friendship. We met and had a long jovial lunch. Stanley was then at the height of his powers and his reputation. *Dr Strangelove* had appeared in 1963 and *2001: A Space Odyssey* in 1968. His reputation was that of a reclusive genius. He dressed and looked, with his curly beard, like Che Guevara.

After that, we remained in contact. I sent him Philip Dick's *Martian Time-Slip* suggesting it would make a good film.

Stanley became interested in a short story of mine entitled 'Super-Toys Last All Summer Long', which had appeared in *Harper's Bazaar* in 1969. Eventually he bought it.

As he had made a two-thousand-word story by Arthur Clarke, 'The Sentinel', into *2001: A Space Odyssey*, so he hoped to achieve something similar with my 'Super-Toys', another two-thousand-worder. At first, I was against the idea, preferring to keep my story as a vignette; but one fatal day, when Margaret and I were breakfasting in Woodlands, a sudden vision came to me of how it might be expanded. I rang Stanley. I went to work with him in his pad, which is approximately the size of Blenheim Palace. He did not accept my idea.

In 1982, I signed a contract with one of Stanley's companies. A limousine arrived in our drive every morning to collect me. I worked alone or with Stanley in his house, lunched with him, worked until the limousine took me home. There I worked again on what we had discussed, finally faxing the results to him at about midnight.

At first, I was dismayed to wander among the gloomy glories of Stanley's palace, those great rooms, one leading into another, airless and silent, filled with apparatus; for there too on some walls were hung oil paintings, large, bright canvases, spilling over with flowers and light, with a joyfulness which revealed a hidden side of Stanley. They were signed simply 'Kubrick'. I found later they were the work

of Mrs Kubrick, Christiane. Occasionally, Stanley and I would visit
her as she painted. She worked in a large barren room, the windows
of which looked out across their ample grounds.

While working with Stanley the first time, I was writing *Helliconia
Winter* and still suffering from the PVFS. What I really did not care
for was working with or for someone else. I had long grown out of
the habit. Moreover, few of my ideas suited Stanley. His idea of
inserting a Blue Fairy – for he had overdosed on *Pinocchio* – was
anathema to me.

'Be a genius, Brian,' he said. I could not help smiling. Stanley, I'm
from East Dereham . . .

He said it more than once, as we discarded scenario after scenario.
In that wish of his, I saw Stanley's wish for himself. Just as the child
is father to the man, according to the poet, so the wish is father to
the deed. He had wished himself into an extraordinary position, a
hermit who produced a film when he felt like it, financed by Warner
Brothers, in whom he rarely confided.

I still think of him, pacing his rooms when the rest of the world
is sleeping its sinful sleeps. He keeps the world at arm's length.
The films reflect that, their special quality is that they come from
an inner isolation. In a time of financial upheaval, perhaps when
Nigel Lawson was Chancellor of the Exchequer, Stanley was upset
and gave me some sound advice. 'Sell all your stocks and shares,
Brian, and buy gold bars.'

The words of a man none too well acquainted with the harsh
realities of life. Which is to say nothing of his artistry, much of
its timbre. Marcel Proust lived in a cork-lined room.

It is becoming the fashion to decry Kubrick. True, he is both
misanthropic and misogynous – so one deduces from his crushing
portraits of women in *The Shining*, *A Clockwork Orange* and elsewhere. However, another reading is possible. Since his portraits of
men are also often hostile, it may be that a sympathy for women
as victims is being shown, without sentimentality, without any
hope of some *deus ex machina* coming to save them. The idea of
torturers and victims comes easily to Stanley's mind.

We spent some while turning 'Supertoys' into a concentration
camp story. It seemed to me an *outré* path to take, even while
I recognised that *outré* paths were his strong point. One of his
weaknesses was that he would not allow argument. Everything was
yes or no. One morning, he abandoned that line of development, and
no more could be said.

'Be a genius . . .' One must forgive genius much. His two science
fiction films are works of genius, totally free of the mawkishness
one associates with *Star Trek* and *Star Wars*. And *2001* contains a
shot which so excellently catches a leap of imagination that it has
become one of the great moments in the history of movie-making.
This is the scene where our ape predecessor comes to appreciate
the power of the tool, the weapon. He wields an animal femur with
which he has vanquished the enemy, in jubilation flinging it into the
air. Cut to the spaceship as it heads towards the space station: mankind's new tool and weapon. If that's not genius, I'm a Dutchman.

Stanley and I parted company in the end and my old friend Bob
Shaw took over. No word of thanks from Stanley, no word of
farewell, only the next fag in mouth, the turned back. Although
I liked Stanley, I was not surprised.

Bob Shaw had to make difficult train journeys to see Stanley. He
would phone me and complain. I used covertly to feed him ideas,
but even via the genial Bob they proved unpalatable. Later, Arthur
Clarke wrote Kubrick a concluding episode to 'Supertoys', taking
the whole shebang into the galaxy and beyond. Even that seemed
to gain no approval.

There were elements of that period I enjoyed – the concentration,
the dissection of dialogue, Stanley's sharp perceptions, the different
experience. It was no worse than the army.

By the time I left Castle Kubrick, I had amassed 328 pages of notes,
research items and storylines which were never used. I was missing
two million dollars but I was a free man once more, vowing never
again to be otherwise.

Christmases at Woodlands were traditional. Tim and Charlotte
came with us to select a tree from the Sea Scouts off Donnington
Bridge. Our trees stood every year in an old yellow bucket, reserved
for the occasion, round which went a Swedish wrapper. The garden
yielded plenty of holly to stick behind pictures.

Greetings cards poured in – and out. Presents in glittering garb
were piled under the tree, and every year we were ashamed at how
many presents there were. Margaret cooked with great good will,
as the cats cadged scraps of turkey.

Clive was over from Greece to be with us, and with Wendy and
Mark. Sometimes, Betty and Antony arrived from Norfolk, adding
their own uproar to the proceedings.

Then the miracle of the turning year, the thin sun gaining substance through mist, green shoots appearing in the copse. And

more green shoots – happy thoughts always of leading a better life.

And there was that companion of the *Zeitgeist*, the *Grenzegeist*, the ancient frontier-ghost! English life, that plant for ever about to run to seed . . . Mrs Thatcher had fought her battle against the Argentinians in the Falklands, and won; she had fought her battle against Arthur Scargill in the coal mines, and won. Later, everything Scargill had warned against came true. Pit after pit closed. Those bygone Carboniferous horizons were sealed away in their tombs.

British social life was changing. Many saw it as crumbling. England, proclaimed the new orthodoxy, was supposed to live off its service – instead of its manufacturing – industries. 'There is no society, only individuals,' crowed Mrs Thatcher. Had what she said not been a lie, we would be experiencing anarchy now. We need, and hedge ourselves round with, many groups, societies, and other cohesive forces.

During the Falklands War in 1982, I wrote to *The Times*, agreeing with Tony Benn on the recklessness of sending ships along 5,000 miles of the not particularly friendly coastline of South America. In response, I had a phone call from an Oxford don, *an Oxford don*, who asked me how I would like it if he came round with a bunch of his students, as he intended to do, and camped out in my garden. I replied that I would not mind at all if my garden was 5,000 miles away. Nevertheless, if he and his rabble came round to my Oxford garden, I would repel them with every means in my power.

Later, I contributed to a book called *Dear Next Prime Minister*, edited by Neil Astley (1990); writers such as Margaret Drabble, Marina Warner, Ben Pimlott and Ted Hughes also had their say. A sad aspect of the whole Falklands affair had been to see how easily xenophobia and jingoism – sanctifying madness – awoke in the breasts of the English.

My letter to Mrs Thatcher reminded her that patriotism carries heavy cash and ecological penalties in the modern world.

Auberon Waugh told Mrs Thatcher that 'there are signs you are leading the country on the rocks of isolation . . . by your attitude to the proposed EC integration of 1992 . . . Please go away.'

In 1984, when Mrs Thatcher was in full flow, our gallant old Aunt Dorothy died, well into her nineties. That was the year we bought Woodlands. It was also the year when someone of greater importance than Mrs Thatcher came to prominence. Mikhail Gorbachev was appointed General Secretary of the Communist Party of the Soviet Union.

Here was the breath of the new, the unpredictable which makes the future so astonishing and impenetrable. The pressure-cooker threat of nuclear warfare went off the boil. 'Gorby' and his smart wife Raisa toured the world, smiling, shaking hands like there was a tomorrow. In 1989, journalists hailed him Man of the Decade.

And then the Berlin Wall broke down!

Among the scenarios Kubrick and I discussed in 1982 was one in which the West sent in robots and androids to help Russia when the Soviet system had collapsed. I wrote a page or two on it. We knew that the Soviet economy was in a poor state, but we could not think of a plausible way, to be shown in a film, by which Soviet rule might collapse. We quickly abandoned the idea and talked about something else.

Just supposing we had hit upon the startling events of 1989. Suppose by conjecture we had arrived at a scenario whereby gaps began to show in Eastern Europe: the Hungarians allowed East German refugees to pour into the West: a man called Egon Krenz with strange ivory teeth spoke to us kindly from the DDR; the Berlin Wall was breached, with happy crowds pouring into West Berlin, to be gladly welcomed; and the USSR just ceased to be, faded away like the frown of the Cheshire cat, with little bloodshed. Suppose we had struck the genuine vein of prophecy in such matters, and Stanley had filmed it . . . No one would have believed a word of it.

Besides, who would have played Egon Krenz?

Looking back down the long dismal perspectives of the century, we have to wonder if the human species should not put itself in the dock and convict itself of madness. The thought must have occurred to P. B. Shelley, himself part-mad, when he wrote *The Defence of Poetry*. He says, 'We have more moral, political, and historical wisdom than we know how to reduce into practice; we have more scientific and economic knowledge than can be accommodated to the just distribution of the produce which it multiplies.' Later in he same essay, he says, 'We want the generous impulse to act that which we imagine . . . we have eaten more than we can digest . . . The cultivation of those sciences which have enlarged the limits of the empire of man over the external world has, for want of the poetical faculty, proportionately circumscribed those of the internal world; and man, having enslaved the elements, remains himself a slave.'

If Shelley were alive today, he might be asking how it was that millions submitted themselves to the rule of tyrants such as Ceauşescu, Enver Hoxha, Hitler, Stalin, and the monsters in South

America: or, indeed, why it was that such as Ceauşescu, Hoxha, et al., wished to assume the role of tyrant. Is it not a miserable, isolating thing, a commitment to paranoia and tyranny?

The Kayapo people of Amazonia, we read, classify one hundred and fifty types of diarrhoea. If miseries were also classified, when the human brain is fully mapped, perhaps persons might be treated, as the Kayapo – whom one imagines living in somewhat fetid surroundings – treat their various types of malady, with biotic medicines.

Margaret's mother died in 1986. She had at least the opportunity to see us installed in Woodlands.

For Margaret and me, a new period of stability had begun. Woodlands was a congenial place for love and friendship, as it sprawled at ease on its low ridge.

At one time or another, all the members of the family sheltered under its roof. Charlotte, being the youngest, was the last to leave us. She found a flat in Oxford when she secured a job in the HMV record store. Tim left, to live in Oxford and work in Pizza Express; but he returned home with a girlfriend. They set up a flat at the north end of the house, and did a good job of redecoration. Clive came and lived with us for a while, during a teaching period in Oxford. Wendy and Mark, who had lived in Chiswick during their early married years, stayed with us for some months before finding a house near Cirencester; we converted a small upper room into a study for Mark. Very entertaining and welcome they all were.

Margaret looked after them all.

In my study, I wrote more concentratedly than ever. As ever, I filled notebooks and diaries. We walked in the Pilkington woods near by. I thought about my characters in *Forgotten Life*, which slowly accumulated, month by month. I hoped to capture something of present-day Europe.

Every family is happy in the same way. You scarcely notice the weeks passing. Particularly in a haven like Boars Hill.

Various holidays and visits had convinced us of the attractions of the North Norfolk coast. Margaret bought a property there which we could all enjoy, and furnished it with many of the Manson family things. From the front windows, we look over the creek and the marshes, which flood at extremely high tides, to the distant sand bars and seas.

Between other activities, we conspired to improve house and

garden. In the house, we renovated the kitchen and created a new bathroom. On the face of it, the fact that the house had only one bathroom was odd. But there were fireplaces in every bedroom. The original owners and their guests would have had hot water brought by maids to their bedrooms. An elaborate system of bells still functioned, to summon servants here, there and everywhere.

We remodelled the terrace at the rear of the house, installing steps down to the lawn. A local landscape artist designed and built a pond for us. What a success it was! Not merely for us but for all the toads, frogs, newts, ducks, dragonflies, kingfishers, herons and other birds which came swarming along to enjoy a new riviera.

Back in the seventies, I had succeeded in including *Martian Time-Slip* in Harry's and my SF Master Series' with New English Library. This marked its first appearance in hardcover. It had been published originally as a paperback, in both the US and the UK. I had recommended it to Kubrick as a filmable novel. Came the nineties, and Frank Hatherley and I became involved with turning the novel into a screenplay.

Almost before the Kubrickian dust had settled, we were negotiating with Paramount UK to transform Dick's novel into a film.

Now why should I have bothered? I admired the clever way in which Dick has one of his central characters, Arnie Kott, die in an hallucinatory delusion. But – I had my own novels I wished to write; indeed, by now I was sure I was improving and extending my art; the narrative with Mrs Green at psychotherapy and, even more, the address by my supposed anima, had given me confidence and buoyancy.

Above all, my contemporary novel *Forgotten Life*, published in 1988, had in it a vital spark. It was the second volume of my *Squire Quartet*; I knew that I could continue writing about the new shape of Europe, that I had hold of something vital.

Yet I wanted to update someone else's sixties SF novel and turn it into a screenplay. That endeavour was to occupy Frank and me for almost two years, and come to nothing in the end.

Our motives are often obscure to ourselves. Let's put it this way.

I once was witness to an historic sight, P. B. Shelley's poem, 'Onzymandias', made flesh, Gibbon's works made concrete.

This was during the tour of the Soviet Union with Jon Stallworthy, Elaine Feinstein, Charles Osborne and others. We flew over the Caucasus to Georgia where our Tbilisi hosts took us on a trip in a convoy of cars. The day was hot, and we sweated together on the shiny plastic in the back of their archaic transport.

We arrived at a dusty undistinguished town, and were led into a large field, which a banner proclaimed was The People's Park of Recreation and Procreation, or words of similar intent. At one end stood a vast brick building. Keble College Oxford had pupped.

This was the Stalin Museum. We were in Gori, birthplace of Stalin, so help us.

The year was 1977, during the 'Years of Stagnation' under Leonid Brezhnev.

Stalin had been denounced by Khrushchev. We were informed as we entered the portals of the building that this was the only Stalin Museum left in the Soviet Union. 'And in the rest of the world,' some of us muttered under our breath.

The tour of the museum proved lengthy. Every headline of *Pravda* was explained at length by our guides. To add to its deadness, the museum was deserted except for our party.

Growing bored, I asked one of our guides and keepers where the toilets were. When he offered to come with me, I said I could hold my own. He laughed and, rather surprisingly, allowed me to wander off alone.

The vast building was empty. I found my way down to a shadowy basement. There were no lights in the corridor, which ran the length of the building, finally to close in darkness and distance, like the last sentence of *Frankenstein*. One side was a blank wall. Such illumination as there was filtered through frosted glass panels set in a series of doors on the other side. As I walked down the corridor, I became curious about these doors.

I tried a handle of one, expecting it to be locked. It opened.

Here was an immense storeroom, stretching the length of the building. It contained but one object – or rather, umpteen varieties of the same object. That object was the bust of Joe Stalin.

In that storeroom stood or lay thousands of busts of Stalin. They came in many materials. Some were small enough to stand on your mantelpiece, if you had one. Some were big enough to stand in your town square, or cast gloom over your stadium. All had presumably been returned to Gori when the tyrant fell from grace – and would lie there, gathering heroic dust, until he returned to popularity . . .

Having witnessed the end of the British Empire, I was here, in this dusty cellar, witness to the end of a more dreadful epoch.

I stood there in the dreary light, staring at this awful accumulation until it occurred to me that perhaps I could be arrested for even setting eyes on it. Shutting the door, I returned upstairs to my friends.

Here was the eclipse of one of the most dreadful ogres of the century, a man who had held millions in fear and misery – and not only those within the frontiers of his own domains, vast though those domains were. What was an ephemeral paperback book, Dick's book, published in the sixties, by comparison?

The answer is a complex one, to do with loyalty to a dead friend, belief in science fiction, the wish to see quietist, psychological material filmed – in other words, once more to nudge SF in the way I believe it could most fruitfully go – and an affection for a story that bears within it in metaphorical form the ghastly distortions of life which Stalin enforced.

So Frank and I were walking down Wardour Street, one fine day in 1991. After much negotiation, and some down payment, we had secured screenplay rights in Dick's novel. After *Blade Runner* and *Total Recall*, hewn from Dick material, Dick was considered a hot property. And after more negotiation, we had gained an ally in Ileen Maisel, head of Paramount UK. This was the lady we were going to see on that fine day.

Ileen dressed in startling ways, often being clad in black plastic, and sat in a rocking chair when talking to clients, using the chair's mute eloquence to reinforce points: fast rocking, agreement; standstill, no way, baby! As a resourceful American lady, she knew delectable little restaurants in Holland Park the English had never happened on. She was likable and dynamic. She was going to sign the contract. We had reason to feel cheerful.

Half-way down Wardour Street, Frank popped into a news shop and bought a copy of *Variety*.

He scanned the headlines as we walked along.

'My God,' he said. 'Ileen's been sacked.'

We decided we would go into the Paramount offices saying nothing. It would be up to Ileen to break the bad news to us.

The Paramount offices were generally scenes of industry, with phones ringing and personable young ladies moving rapidly but personably from office to office. This morning – silence everywhere, from phones and humans. The young ladies sat personably at their desks, probably scanning the Appointments Vacant columns of their daily papers.

Ileen came in, looking much as usual, although eschewing the rocking chair. After a few minutes of desultory chat, she said, 'I'm sorry to disappoint you guys, but I'm all washed up here. I've just gotten the push. I had to read it in *Variety*. The bastards didn't even have the guts to call me.'

That was it. Ileen said she would be back, and would call us. I believed her. We are still awaiting her call.

More trotting about. More negotiations. Another stroke of luck. We secured the interest of Michael Wearing, in charge of Drama at the BBC. His approach to *Martian Time-Slip* was pragmatic. Was this all fantasy? I prepared a paper, setting out factually how a space vehicle could get to Mars, and how that planet might be terraformed so as to make it habitable to humanity – subjects which are matters of everyday conjecture. Wearing showed some enthusiasm.

Dick wrote his novel in 1962. It was at that date still possible to believe in an old autochthonous race of intelligent beings living on the Red Planet – or at least it was if one had acquired the discipline of pocketing disbelief for the sake of the ride, such as SF promotes. In the early nineties, we had to recognise scientific advances. Autochthonous was out for all but single-cell bacteria.

Margaret had made an expedition into Tibet some years earlier. That was in the summer of 1987, when Charlotte and I practically lived on a diet of strawberries, raspberries and double cream, while her mum was away. Afterwards, Margaret built up a small library of books on the subject of Tibet; we had both become intrigued by Buddhism, and at one time underwent a practical course in Zen Buddhism (silence, the lotus position, commands by a wooden tongue, downcast eyes, the breath feather-light). So I hit on the idea of substituting indentured Tibetans for Dick's autochthons. Tibetans were used to cold climates, frugality, rarefied air, and have lost freedom in their own country. In our version of Mars, the Tibetans are the early colonists of Mars. The West takes over later, oppressing the Tibetans, or 'bleekers', as they are known.

This scheme won enthusiastic support from the BBC people. On these grounds, Wearing was prepared to commission a screenplay.

Margaret wrote to the Tibet Society, asking them to translate six sentences into the Tibetan tongue. They demanded £200 for the task. We forgot about it and went ahead without them.

Then followed a period of lunches in expensive restaurants and West End hotels, after which Frank and I would retire to one of his classrooms in Riding House Street, behind Broadcasting House, to sort out scenes on a white board. Hours were spent, writing and rewriting, rejecting, adapting, adopting.

Always I could go back to Margaret and the family on Boars Hill at the end of the day; always Margaret was there, my friend, lover and confidante. She cultivated her garden and the quiet virtues. We were yin and yang, together making a whole. Frank had to go back uncomplainingly to a failing marriage.

Those sessions in the dusty classrooms were valuable. There is an addiction in paring everything down, arguing about character, dissecting every sentence. It is a writerly pleasure. There is also the pleasure of a partnership, two minds working to the same end, able to argue with good nature on both sides. We developed excellent ideas on the script. It is a story with tremendous impact, relying on strange areas of human character and flaws in time, rather than on the special effects that characterise most SF films.

While Frank and I beavered away in the Spartan classrooms of Riding House Street, the world was changing. By the early nineties, the tremors from the Soviet earthquake had reached Jugland. Jugoslavia was beginning to tear itself apart. It seemed incredible that the men who ruled that extraordinary country would allow it to happen. Slovenia escaped to independence: most of the rest of the country plunged down into civil war and genocide.

Many of the quiet places Margaret and I had known became headline news: Tuzla, Banja Luka, Mostar, Travnik, Sarajevo itself. It was said of Srebrnica that here the worst massacre on European soil since World War II took place. We noted that the commentators said 'European soil'. Only a few years previously it would have been 'Balkan soil'.

We sat on our terrace on the Hill and mourned. It seemed that President Tito had been a miracle-worker, holding the separate ethnic groups together in something like accord. We remembered the rumour we had heard down in Montenegro (Crna Gora) that in fact the real Tito had been killed in the Spanish Civil War, and a British agent resembling him had taken his place, remaining undetected until his death.

Absurd, of course. But much about that tragic country had been absurd. The city named after Tito had been absurd. We had stayed in Titograd in 1964. Kerbs and pavements of hypothetical streets had been laid out. Then the hypothesis had died in the heat. Apartment blocks had been built among fields, mysteriously never to be occupied. Cicadas chirruped, failure threatened.

Yet we had liked the hotel, with its large melancholy rippling Slav mirrors in the foyer, where one light bulb in seven worked.

Thunderstorms occurred punctually at three each afternoon. Afterwards, a sprightly band came into the garden to play old dance tunes, 'Aurora', 'Destiny', 'Tangerine'. Their signature tune was a little different – the military march, 'Colonel Bogey' – known throughout the British Army as 'Bollocks'. Directly it sounded, Margaret and I would rush from our room on to our balcony to take the salute. Perhaps there was something in the Tito rumour after all . . .

Whatever was happening elsewhere, Frank and I laboured on with *Martian Time-Slip*, turning it into a brilliant screenplay.

And in the end we got nowhere. A year's work was wasted, thrown away at the last moment. I learnt only indirectly that the BBC wanted something with more topical relevance. Which turned out to be yet another cop show.

Margaret said, 'Why not just write another novel?'

XXXI

The Years

We look before and after,
And pine for what is not:
Our sincerest laughter
With some pain is fraught;
Our sweetest songs are those that tell of saddest thought . . .

P. B. Shelley
'To a Skylark'

I wrote another novel. I could tell my writing was improving: my sales figures kept getting worse.

The third novel of what is now *The Squire Quartet* was *Remembrance Day*. Its canvas was broader than that of its predecessor, *Forgotten Life*. While the latter dug backwards into a lifetime, the former, centred in Norfolk, spanned much of Europe and beyond. Published first in 1993, *Remembrance Day* had its genesis in a real incident, when the IRA threatened to plant bombs in a number of English seaside resorts. Their plan did not work out. In the novel, a small bomb explodes in a small hotel in Great Yarmouth. Four people are killed.

That is not all the story. At the core of the novel is an account of the troubles of a humble Norfolk worker and his wife, when he falls into financial problems through generosity to a friend.

Among the diverse scenes, a thread of suspense is drawn. We do not know until the end who among the characters is going to die in the Hotel Dianoya. An American Professor Embry is studying the lives of the four who were killed, to strengthen his theory that some prior disaster in their personal histories may have compelled them to further disaster.

When published in the States by St Martin's Press, *Remembrance Day* received several long reviews. Most reviewers there saw that my game plan was based on a novel for which I once had great admiration, Thornton Wilder's *The Bridge of San Luis Rey*. In Britain, the novel received one small paragraph in the *Daily Express* and another in the *Daily Telegraph*; among the nationals, that was all.

Perhaps I had been spoilt in the past. I was accustomed to receiving generous review space for my books, science fiction and otherwise. Now something like a cold shoulder had greeted one of my most ambitious novels.

The quality of my inner life had much improved since the visitation by my anima. Even metaphorically speaking, I had been held out of the window but *not dropped*. My life was now in my own hands. While I had had good fortune in my writing life, I felt myself immeasurably fortunate in those blessings, a happy marriage and family. Even there, I had been given a second chance. We had all avoided being locked up or locked out.

It is true that the chill greeting of *Remembrance Day* cut deep, but I faced it more buoyantly than once would have been the case. My perception of the world had changed.

Most of my editors have been remarkably considerate, within their limits and sometimes beyond. Consideration! – One of the minor virtues. I have always been too considerate for my own good. It has entailed years of difficulty.

Some would say it was a rash move to turn from SF to contemporary novels. But rashness, as Mae West said of goodness, has nothing to do with it. The world changed dramatically in 1989, and I could not see myself doing anything else but chronicle some of those changes. The material often chooses the writer.

I was compounding my errors by having more poetry published. Energetic Tom Maschler had published my poem 'Pile', accompanied by Mike Wilkes's extraordinary architectural drawings, in 1979. Poems had appeared in *Barefoot* and *Brothers of the Head*. Not until 1992 did I have a separate volume of poems published, and that was *Home Life with Cats*, devoted solely to those eponymous little creatures. The event passed off without incident.

Meanwhile, my patient and erudite wife was producing her first book. *The Work of Brian W. Aldiss: An Annotated Bibliography & Guide*, by Margaret Aldiss, was edited by Boden Clarke and published in the United States by The Borgo Press, San Bernadino. It was never properly distributed in England. Not only prophets, their wives too are without honour in their own country.

Margaret's book contains 360 close-printed pages, itemising everything. No one else could have done it. Her work was enthusiastically received in America, although I do not remember a single English review.

'Whatever happened to England?' It was Kubrick's question. The Channel Tunnel was built at last – one of those dreams of the future that used to excite us. Surely it is a technological triumph. Do the British enjoy it? They complain – they even boast – that they are afraid to travel under the sea.

Was it that the carnage of the First World War drained the best genetic reserves of the country, as well as its financial resources? Living alone is reportedly fashionable. I'm proud of my family, of Wendy and Clive and Tim and Charlotte, and of Margaret who binds us together, and of those who love and live with our offspring. They still have warm blood, they're cheerful and humorous and loving. All support each other, and still run on high-octane principles.

It's almost with guilt, you have to say, that we survived the recession and unemployment of the eighties and early nineties, although it was painful to see the difficulties Clive earlier and Tim later underwent to find decent jobs. Mark also had a struggle, and was supported by Wendy. Yet our lives remained buoyant and crowded with incident.

In the year that Mrs Thatcher stood down as Prime Minister, we did a great deal of celebrating. Margaret, aided and abetted by Frank and Malcolm, sprang an extraordinary surprise for my sixty-fifth birthday. It is a proof of my innocence – or my blindness – that I never suspected anything.

Margaret and I drove up to London in July, as we often did. The occasion was supposedly a party thrown by the English SF magazine *Interzone*, edited by David Pringle. This was to be in the Groucho, the writers' club (as it was originally), of which I am one of the founder members.

I was led in like an ass to graze, only to find this was a real case for whoopee! The family had been busy, and had come up trumps. Wendy, Tim and Charlotte had been shepherding distinguished guests into a pub just along the way in Dean Street, ready to launch them when the time came.

Margaret and Frank made announcements, and in filed the guests to greet me. In came Harry and Joan Harrison, David Wingrove and Sue Oudot, Kingsley Amis, Doris Lessing, Kit and Joe Reed, the actress Sue Porrett, old school friend John Watts and his gorgeous Madelaine, Hilary and Helge Rubinstein, and many other celebrities – and *Clive*! Clive flew in specially from Greece for the occasion, the icing on the cake.

Among other amazements, my normally retiring wife spoke in public for the first time, giving an assured and amusing speech.

Capping the extraordinary event, Frank, Margaret and Malcolm had managed to squeeze, by methods unknown, tributes from the guests and others; the results were edited in a book (mainly Frank's work) entitled *A is for Brian*. It included kind words from American friends such as Fred Pohl, David Hartwell and Charlie N. Brown – both David and Charlie, Margaret and I had met on our first visit to the States in 1965. Other contributors included Jimmy Ballard, Christopher Priest, Colin Greenland, Mike Moorcock, Bob Silverberg, Tom Shippey, Anthony Storr and other well-known names.

After this extraordinary ceremony, a crowd of us swarmed up to one of the Groucho's private dining rooms for dinner. Sam Lundwall, with true gourmet instinct, arrived from Sweden just in time to join us for the meal. Only a week previously, we had been in Sweden with him and his wife, Ingrid.

Apart from a slender booklet, *A is for Brian* was the last Avernus publication, the end of a hobby. It was also the last time but one I spent any time with Kingsley Amis. He was becoming difficult. The humour of which he was once so full had turned sour.

I had escaped from Castle Kubrick, and had been elected a fellow of the Royal Society of Literature. It was a good year. Like ground elder in a garden, old associations kept springing up, most of them more welcome than ground elder. Singapore was one such.

Towards Singapore I have always had the most friendly feelings, not least when liberals condemn its Draconian laws. Those laws represent the formula for its success story. Singapore is about the size of the Isle of Wight. It has no natural resources beyond its brains and manpower, and the fact that it dominates the one viable western sea route to the Pacific Ocean and its nations.

Although the arts held a low priority on the island, in 1980, I was invited to open the First Asian Book Fair. Margaret Drabble followed me in 1990. Through my energetic friend, Kirpal Singh, I was able to sample modern Singaporean living, its pace, the heat, the delights of the local cuisine. Kirpal introduced me to another Sikh, a publisher. For him, I wrote a number of stories with an Eastern background. ('None of your science fiction, please, Brian – it does not go down extremely well.') These stories he published in hardcover and paperback editions, entitled *Foreign Bodies*. I was proud to write for and be published in – and incidentally exploited by – the Third World. I never allowed the book to be published elsewhere.

To the south of Singapore island is the small isle of Sentosa. It's a kind of play area, growing smarter and becoming more built-up every year. In the museum is a large upstairs hall which contains a full-size tableau, with wax figures, of the surrender of the Japanese to the British in 1945. Men in different uniforms confront each other across a long table. There sits a life-size Supreme Commander, Admiral Mountbatten in his white uniform, together with the good old Commander of the XIVth Army, Field-Marshal Bill Slim, and other commanders-in-chief. Opposite to them are smaller men in green uniforms, the defeated Japanese commanders. Field Marshal Itagaki of the Imperial Japanese Army is about to sign the surrender document.

It was early in the morning when I went to see this life-size still life. It happened there were no other visitors at that hour – fortunately, as it turned out. In the surrender hall, hidden music was playing 'Land of Hope and Glory'. I took a look at the tableau and suddenly found myself in tears.

I could not stop crying.

I stood there for five minutes, in a storm of sobbing. Some pent-up thing was released in me. Perhaps I was crying for youth long departed; perhaps I was crying for a time when Britain played a nobler role in the world; perhaps I cried for History itself, the grand abstraction which rules our lives. Perhaps it was all of those things.

In 1990, I paid two more visits to Singapore. Wendy came with me as photographer for an article I wrote for the *Daily Telegraph* covering the opening of a new history trail round the island.

Like an iceberg sailing northwards from the Ross Ice Shelf, the Soviet Union was by this time disappearing. The world felt good.

Wendy and I met up with Kirpal and other friends. We were able to mix with amiable people from various sectors of the population, Muslim and Indian as well as Chinese and British, and be welcomed into their homes.

One incident would have particular powers of instruction in racially troubled Britain. Wendy and I were eating in the evening at one of the outdoor pick-and-choose restaurants, where everyone hob-nobs while Tiger beer is drunk. Three coal-black young Tamil brothers joined us at our table. Their faces shone. When our conversation moved on from football, which in my case it tends to do fairly rapidly, they told us how happy they were to be in Singapore. No one discriminated against them.

'It is the finest place in the world,' they told us. 'Even in India we were not so free.'

Compared with such liberty, a law against chewing gum is nothing.

Margaret and I visited Singapore that same year, when we celebrated our silver wedding anniversary. This was Margaret's first visit to the East. We met Kirpal again, and Teck Meng and Rosie, and other friends. That proud boast often seen on posters in Changi airport, 'Never Under Thirty', served as a warning to her that she was going to find the heat hard to take. Since we did not like to leave Tim at home alone, he was with us some of the time, in Singapore and on Penang Island. The food everywhere was delectable, and the people humorous.

Unlike Singapore, Penang, situated on the west coast of Malaysia, still retains some kampongs. I have a photograph of a woman squatting on a rock in her sarong, gutting a fish she has recently caught in the river. She is framed in foliage. It conjures up a vision, illusory but nevertheless strong, of a paradise we have lost, or forsaken: the kind of place Paul Gauguin must have sought when he sailed away from Europe.

Tim and I got up early one morning, before dawn broke, and went on a jungle trek. Through nine kilometres of pretty dense jungle we moved as the sun rose, with birds and monkeys all about us, calling, calling. We emerged into the open by a series of waterfalls, where a hearty picnic breakfast was arranged by our hotel. We ate after we had soused ourselves in the waterfalls.

Less ambitiously, Margaret and I swam in the luxurious hotel pool, a pool dotted with tiny islands, carefully arranged to summon up visions of Dorothy Lamour. One day, the hotel was filled with male visitors; they were American troops, on their way to the Gulf War, to fight what Saddam Hussein had promised, in a memorable phrase, would be the Mother of all Battles. It turned out to be a turkey shoot. When they were gone, peace closed over our island, and I went paragliding over the ocean.

The ocean by the shore was a curious milky white. We swam in it – later to learn that Hindus cast the ashes of their departed dear ones into the waters, giving it that particular quality.

That autumn Margaret became involved in editing a third book. The Boars Hill crowd recognised their community as somewhat unique, and set about gathering material for an anthology. Margaret was soon elected to be editor – a post for which her capacity always to remain organised and even-tempered well qualified her. She had an enjoyable time collecting memoirs from hill-dwellers, several of them old and ailing.

There comes a time when you realise your years are passing. Once, at Heath House, friends came to visit; we had not seen them for some while. It was a shock to perceive that they had grown older; the facts were written on their faces. As on theirs, so on our own. And yet throughout the second half of the eighties and the first half of the nineties, our lives went on their own sweet way, much as before.

Wendy and Mark produced my first grandchild, Thomas, to the family's delight. Clive decided to marry Youla, again to the delight of the family. That ceremony took place on the Isle of Wight. Within a year, Clive and Wendy's mother, my first wife, died, and was buried close to the father she had loved, near Stow-on-the-Wold.

Young Thomas Lodge was born on Christmas Eve 1993. He is the brightest and liveliest child that ever lived, and fortunate in his devoted parents. Wendy is the best of mothers.

As for Youla Notia, the family was much pleased to have a Greek lady in our midst, for her own sweet sake, and to dilute the Englishness of things. We now had good reason to fly regularly to Greece and various Greek islands. This was particularly fortunate, since Jugoslavia was no longer a place for holiday-makers. We enjoy good relations, too, with Youla's parents. And already Thomas has a special relationship with Youla.

It must come hard for a child to realise he is not the centre of the universe. I never had that problem. The truth is, Thomas is the centre of his universe, at least for a short while. Many of his sentences begin, 'I want—'. But already he starts to go to playschool: a toe in the shallows of the real world. It's the route many of us have taken: the slow realisation that the world is not particularly made for us. Then parents are most necessary. Preferably two of them.

* * *

In May of 1993, Margaret and I flew out to Greece, hired a car, and visited a place Clive had particularly recommended. Monemvasia stands high on a knuckle of the easternmost finger of the Peloponnese. From this Greek Gibraltar one can gaze over sea and rugged coastline, the eye and imagination being led farther and farther south. The place has been a fortress since Byzantine days and earlier. Here, meditating high above the Aegean, we felt the ancient spirit of Greece enter into us. I hope it entered into the poem I wrote then.

After a while, we returned to Athens, where Clive and Youla looked after us in their flat in Prigipou. In Prigipou, you can pretend you're not really in Athens.

In 1995 we returned again to Greece, this time visiting the island of Santorini with Charlotte. Santorini, with its white walls, perches on the lip of a huge extinct volcano, into the crater of which blue sea has flowed. Here, as in Lake Toba in Sumatra, beauty has succeeded ancient violence.

From Santorini, we flew to the Cyclades, to meet up with the rest of the family on Paros. In the immaculate little town of Naoussa we celebrated Clive's fortieth birthday. Clive is now well ensconced in Greece and must have visited over a hundred islands. His photographic collection of those happy places has been built on a Practika he has owned for almost twenty years. We for our part are won over by the simple pleasures of Greek sun, sea and food. And Metaxa. And I have a friendly Greek publisher Makis Panorios. He published *Non-Stop* in 1996 – and painted the cover!

Our life continued as ever, each year punctuated by five or six trips abroad, generally to lecture, and often at the instigation of the British Council.

By 1995, all the family had left Woodlands. Charlotte had gone to work in Exeter, Tim in Brighton. Wendy and Mark and Thomas were settled not far away in North Oxford. Clive and Youla often came from Greece to stay with us. But, on the whole, Margaret and I were alone in our large Boars Hill house, still fighting a battle against the encroaching woods, where sycamores threatened to outnumber the native oaks.

Margaret said she did not wish to spend the rest of her years in a situation where decline would prove inevitable, for us and for the house. There was truth in what she said, although for my taste I could have stayed for ever, as long as stories continued to pour from me. I adored the ease of the house, the silence of the nights. It was almost as if we had been excused humanity! However, the logic of the situation was clear. We decided we needed a smaller place in town, and must move.

So ended eleven years in Woodlands. It was the longest I had lived in any house, a time of revelation and reconciliation and the happiest period of my life. I trust of our joint lives.

XXXII

The Black Desert

Many's the man who meets with some success,
While many more are starving, more or less.
The world echoes to all their loud distress.
My own lament was heard throughout an age.
                              Makhtumkull
                    'Making My Dear Life Lost'

This book has lifted a few roots of potatoes from the furrows of my life. One theme is my wonder that the fragile individual survives so much change, from the deaths of friends and publishers to the decline of entire nations and empires. Even a Gibbon would be taxed to encompass the vast spectacle of disarray which this century affords. As I write today, a million displaced people await death by starvation in East Zaïre.

The amazement is how many people everywhere persist in behaving reasonably, rearing families, weathering misfortune. This ill-educated son of the Enlightenment veers between laughter and sorrow at the spectacle, ultimately coming up with nothing more profound than the old Army shrug of resignation, *Well, what do you expect?*

It was to be expected that, much as sunshine follows rain, the world might be a better place after the tyrannies of the Soviet system passed away. The period of euphoria proved comparatively brief. Running sores on the body politic developed. The war in Jugoslavia, the slaughter in Chechnya, the civil slaughters in Africa – even, to some extent, the Chinese determination to extinguish an old culture in Tibet – were internal wars rather than invasions. The

United Nations and such agencies as the North Atlantic Treaty Organisation were unable to deal with such problems. We do need better organisations for peace.

World events at the time of the dissolution of the USSR were of obsessive interest. Mine took me to Turkmenistan, experiencing something of the new order, and the confusion following in the wake of the old.

In the summer of 1991, shortly before I had my double hernia operation and the Soviet Union dissolved itself – all things are equal in the sight of God – Margaret and I were holidaying in the slumbrous heart of France. Perigord Noir is one of the loveliest parts of that lovely country. We rented a restored farmhouse near the infinitesimal village of Lacombe. The countryside drowsed deep in grasses, walnut trees and Charolais cattle, while the pale cows drowsed up to their hocks in scarlet poppies. Never was a place better designed for relaxation.

Most evenings, we climbed the hill to the small *auberge* in Orliac, passing through a farm on our way. There the farmer doffed his hat sweepingly to Madame as if the *ancien régime* had never passed into history.

Yet even there, I felt compelled to write. I sat in our little court-yard with a bottle of red wine at my elbow, under the shade of a horse chestnut, and finished *Remembrance Day*. Only in the last three days of the holiday was I entirely free of it. Margaret did not complain, and we also explored the country round about, visiting Sarlat, where is held the biggest open-air market in Europe.

We recall the time as one of great happiness. Tim enjoyed driving us down there, and Charlotte came from Toulouse where she was spending a year studying French. Before we began the drive home over excellent French roads, I found a scheme for another novel springing up like a young tree, in a mind I wished would lie fallow for a while.

The problems my sons had suffered in finding appropriate jobs led me to think of a character, immediately named Burnell, who was forced to leave England to find work in Germany. My own earlier problems led me to the idea that Burnell had had all memory of the past ten years of his life stolen. This got Burnell into difficulties since, unbeknownst to him, he had during that period become married – and divorced.

Burnell's work in Germany was with a cultural institution with an international character to catalogue, and if possible preserve, items of threatened cultural heritage. Burnell is despatched to regions that reflect the contemporary state of a world from which Communism has just receded. His excursions covered in the book are to two very different countries, one provisionally Christian, one provisionally Muslim, Trans-Caucasian Georgia, and Turkmenistan.

Georgia I had visited. Turkmenistan I had only recently heard of.

Having been entangled in the messy collapse of two empires, the British and the Dutch in the East, I was interested to see what emerged after the demise of the Soviet Empire. One region of that vast land mass remained almost unknown, Central Asia. It was to human conjecture more remote than China.

When the Soviet Union dissolved itself, the retreat of the tide revealed, on the long beaches of Asia, high and very dry, five new republics. Previously, they had been little more than departments, ruled from Moscow, supervised locally by governors. One bright and sunny morning, these men awoke and found themselves presidents of extensive new nations or, rather, ghosts of unborn nations.

The new states were Kazakhstan, Uzbekistan, Tadzhikistan, Kirghizia and Turkmenistan. They stretch like a row of worn beads from the Caspian Sea to the frontiers with China, and are home to about fifty million people. Of these millions, only about four million live in Turkmenistan.

Turkmenistan is the most westerly of the five republics. Situated in the middle of a vast land mass, most of it is desert – the formidable Kara Kum, the Black Sands – in all about the size of France. Turkmenistan has the sort of climate one would expect: baking hot in summer, intolerably cold in winter. No wonder it is relatively free from crime; Ashkhabad, the capital, is either too hot or too cold for malefaction – except at government level. Rainfall is practically zero. Much of Ashkhabad's water supply comes via canal, a dismal open Styx which drains water from the dwindling Aral Sea.

There is a kind of creepy thrill in taking a shower in Ashkhabad, knowing you are thereby contributing to the world's biggest ecological disaster.

Until the nineties, we heard little of Central Asia, and still less about this poorest state of the USSR, one exception being the Baikonur spacedrome in Kazakhstan. The Central Asians, presumably, had heard little of us. Communistic paucity of *glasnost* had hidden them from the outside world.

After nineteenth- and early twentieth-century explorers and adventurers, and the players of the Great Game, have had their say, a silence falls over these territories. Ashkhabad suffered a severe earthquake in 1948. Much of the city was destroyed, together with its inhabitants. As with various Russian nuclear accidents, not a word of this disaster leaked to the outside world. All was always eternally well with *Homo Sovieticus* . . .

I read what I could find about Turkmenistan. It was real: it also seemed a country of the mind, absent from non-Commie consciousness for seventy years. The region makes an appearance in English literature, in Matthew Arnold's poem, 'Sohrab and Rustum', which, when we learnt it at West Buckland, was known as 'Sore Arse and Rusty Bum'.

Very little modern information was available. However, a researcher working for me turned up an article from the great Soviet Encyclopaedia, which proved useful.

Much of the sparse data on which I relied proved misleading. When the republics appeared from under the Communist floodwater, the USA decided that here was an opportunity to draw five more nations into the hospitable warmth of the UN, and to sell them Coca-Cola. US Secretary of State James Baker paid a lightning visit to Central Asia in 1991, doing the round of capitals. Media reports following the visit suggested the republics might do a Gadarene at any moment and turn to Islamic fundamentalism, following the Iranian pattern. In the case of Turkmenistan, this was incorrect. It ignores the fact that the Iranians are predominantly Shiite, while such religious feeling as exists in Turkmenistan is Sunni.

In their search for national identity, the republics sought out national figures round which people could rally. Genghis Khan would be an obvious choice, a case of Local Boy Making Good. Turkmenistan made a startling choice. They selected a poet.

Mentions of Makhtumkuli occurred, even in the great Soviet Encyclopaedia. Some of his poetry had been translated into Russian by the father of the film director, Andrei Tarkovsky. The image suggested a rather sad eighteenth-century man, a Sufi beset by doubts, camels and marauding Persians. A strange choice for national figure, rather as though on top of the monument in Trafalgar Square stood not Nelson but Wordsworth or Philip Larkin.

Beside this attraction lay a more nebulous one. When writing *Barefoot in the Head*, I had wanted a junkie messiah, and had lighted on P. D. Ouspensky. Ouspensky is a sort of sly guru and confidence trickster, from whose book *In Search of the Miraculous* I had borrowed some bizarre ideas.

Didn't Ouspensky, possibly with his even nuttier friend Gurdjieff, wander somewhere in the wilds of Central Asia and find wisdom there? The idea was intriguing, even if you believe that wisdom is generated from within, if at all.

During my researches for *Burnell's Travels*, the novel which eventually became *Somewhere East of Life*, I came across the title of a literary newspaper published in Ashkhabad, and wrote to the editor. I told him I was writing a novel, and asked him one question: what was the state of religion in Turkmenistan?

Answer came there none.

The novel, when finished, was accepted by my British and American publishers. While it was being typeset, a letter arrived at Woodlands with an Ashkhabad postmark. I called to Margaret, 'Hey, Turkmenistan really exists!'

The letter was a reply from the editor of the literary paper, a Mr Tirkish. I was not to know that mail to and from Ashkhabad still travelled via Moscow. And that that paragon of efficiency, the Moscow Post Office, had even less interest in speeding mail on to the provinces, now that those provinces were no longer possessions.

Mr Tirkish said that the question of religion was complex. A reasonable response. Had he asked me the state of religion in Britain, I would have been equally taxed to answer.

Continued Mr Tirkish, I should come to Ashkhabad, where I would be welcome to discuss anything I liked. Meanwhile, he gave me the name of a friend in Reading who might help. The friend was a Dr Azemoun, currently working on the poems of Makhtumkuli.

'Shall I get involved?' I asked Margaret.

'You are involved,' she said.

I rang the friend in Reading.

Since then, Youssef Azemoun has become a friend of ours, as has his Turkish wife, Guzin. Youssef is an intellectual – speaks German, plays a silver flute: prime qualifications for intellectuality – and has a mischievous sense of humour. Youssef immediately invited me to a festive evening. In Reading (of all places) I met a whole jolly gathering of people from all over Central Asia, all celebrating and drinking vodka like Russians. Delicious food was served, strongly built women danced, the platform shook, and poems of Makhtumkuli were read out in Turkic and rather flat English.

Carried away by it all, I became a Friend of Makhtumkuli on the spot. Exchanges of blood, oaths, debaggings, total immersion, a tenner, and I was in. And – to cut a curious story short – I received an invitation to be present at Ashkhabad's Festival of Makhtumkuli.

Of recent years, the British Council has played a benevolent role in my life. I have seen how much useful work it does abroad. It has found me happy to travel to places where other authors were not keen to go. So I have found myself lecturing in Kuchin, the capital of Sarawak, and – most memorably – in Israel at a time of crisis, and elsewhere. And in Ashkhabad . . .

But before I left England, along came proofs of *Somewhere East of Life* from HarperCollins. Nestling among its pages were four lines of Makhtumkuli's verse I had made up. Either guilt or circumspection caused me to remove them, substituting four genuine lines. This may be the first appearance of Makhtumkuli's verse in an English book. I took the long flight eastwards with a clear conscience.

So in May 1994, I found myself in the city where Burnell had already travelled. Throughout my time there, I was haunted by the ghost of Roy Burnell.

Ashkhabad. No report speaks very kindly of Ashkhabad, although the Lonely Planet guide to Central Asia is indulgent. 'Ashghabat [alternative spelling] is not the end of the world, but you feel that it surely can't be more than a short bus ride away.'

True, nothing much happens in Ashkhabad. Still, its mere existence is a kind of miracle, a Declaration of Human Rights over Desiccation.

Following the 1948 earthquake, the city was rebuilt on a relaxed grid pattern. Every avenue is tree-lined, and supplied with channels of running water against the fearsome heat of mid-summer. Birdsong is the only form of pollution. No smog, no guns, no beggars. A peaceful city in a peaceful country.

Main streets are wide and well paved. Only pampered Europeans complain about the odd pothole. Among the Ladas trundling about, Volvo 850s could be seen, brilliant in metallic cerise. This was in the year when Margaret and I decided we could not afford that new model. No camels. They're outside the city, where the desert begins. Burnell did not know that.

So Ashkhabad represents a human victory over desiccation. The price is high; the success remains. The inhospitable dunes of the Kara Kum are held at bay, just beyond city limits. If anyone could make Mars habitable, the Turkmen could.

Indeed, driving beyond the city, one enters a super-heated Mars.

There's nothing for miles except various unpleasant types of un-
created land, baffling landscapes, and the worn-out Plasticine of the
Kopet Dagh Mountains. In one's ears, the phantom whisper of camel
bells from Borodin's tone poem, 'In the Steppes of Central Asia'.

It was the Volvo 850s which bothered me most. When interview-
ing the pleasant Minister of Culture (some months later removed
from his post for being too pleasant), I asked him about the shiny new
vehicles. Why were there so many on the streets of Ashkhabad?

He replied casually. 'We did a deal with the Uzbeks.'

It was impolitic to ask further. Clearly, there were secrets in Central Asian economics with which Europeans should not meddle.

The question remains, What deal had the Swedes done with the
Uzbeks? How many oranges equal one engine?

Turkmenistan had something to celebrate. Not merely the Festival of Makhtumkuli, but three years of independence as a nation,
nominally free of the system that had veiled the country from the
gaze of the outside world. The streets of Ashkhabad were gay with
bunting and coloured lights. People were chatting and strolling in
their best clothes, under a blue Central Asian sky. The young ladies
of the capital wear a fetching black number, ankle length, which
shows off their trim figures. Many wear gold-painted sandals. They
look tremendously elegant as they trip towards the barren shelves
of their supermarkets.

Far gloomier are the statues of Makhtumkuli going up everywhere, all carved from a dense grey pumice. Wearing his huge hat,
the poet sits moodily in the posture of Rodin's famous *Thinker*,
clenched fist under chin, desperately trying to think up a rhyme
for 'Ashkhabad'.

President Saparmurat Niyazov puts in an appearance in the central
park. A band strikes up. School children chant his name. Niyazov is
the centre of a cult of personality.

He was in power in Soviet days, and remains still firmly in control.
Nor have the KGB exactly hung up their electric prods and taken to
the old rocking chair. Those who were in power retain power.

The regime in Turkmenistan is a dismal one, with a dismal
record, although the President appears to be popular. Strolling in
the sunshine of the park, Niyazov looked good-humoured in a heavy
way. Later, he sat two rows behind us at an entertainment, laughing
unselfconsciously at a comedian's jokes. He is a chubby, stocky
man. Some of his greying hair is dyed yellow, Georgian-style.

Younger and more colourful portraits of the chubby face look
down from most public buildings.

Just the thing to make democratic Americans unhappy! Just the thing to get a bad press in the capitals of Europe! I thought differently as I photographed Niyazov from a distance of six feet. He had arrived in a big car, without any convoys of tanks or motorcyclists. No kalashnikov-cluttered guards patrolled the roofs of nearby buildings. A few soldiers stood about, licking ice cream. Not a gun in sight. Niyazov shook a few hands and disappeared into a ceremonial yurt, to coin one of the more surreal sentences in this book. Everyone else got on with a pleasant afternoon. The chubby face, the velvet glove . . .

The population, and especially the President, with his obsession with building himself new palaces instead of improving the country's ailing infrastructure, uses up water as if they were all sitting by the Niagara Falls. There is no talk of revolution – but then, how low must be the expectations of the populace!

Burnell, creepily enough, had also attended a celebration similar to the one I attended, with large portraits of both President and Poet in evidence in the square. Chapter Fifteen is entitled 'Makhtumkuli Day'. I found myself a slave to my own printed page.

Geological surveys suggest that much of Central Asia, including Turkmenistan, floats on enormous reserves of oil. Some oil still gets piped northwards to Russia. Talk of a pipeline to the West (with its promise of hard currency) remains literally a pipe dream.

As long as the world depends on exhaustible fossil fuel, these countries are in with a chance. Turkmenistan grows little food, imports most of it, together with everything else. It can pay with oil. Once ways are found of getting this oil in abundance to the West, it might be that the Middle East would lose its present strategic importance.

That could be a valuable contribution to world peace.

Burnell is obliged to lecture at short notice at Ashkhabad University. While writing the book, I wondered if there was such an institution. I put it in. I was guessing.

Then I was called on to lecture at short notice at Ashkhabad University. There it was in reality, nature imitating art! I was the first British writer ever to enter those portals which, did my hosts but know it, had already entered English literature . . .

Only there, before a pre-graduate audience, did I need no interpreter. The young take English as a third language, after native Turkic and Russian. I spoke in many places, including giving an impromptu speech at a huge wedding festival.

Burnell got into trouble at the university. Perhaps for that reason he failed to mention the stench from its toilets. Why do those delicate young ladies and men endure such humiliation? Does no one ever clean the place? In the minds of that handsome generation, the humanities will be forever associated with the stink of piss.

There are other symptoms of unease. Much of the housing stock of the city is in sad disrepair. Decent hospitals have not been built. The whole infrastructure needs energetic overhaul. Instead, the old Communists, now the Democratic Party, build themselves grand villas, while gaudy hotels go up to attract over-rich Arab visitors: ten-suite hotels with no TVs or telephones in the bedrooms and a daily charge of $250 US. Twelve similar hotels in a row . . . Burnell was too innocent to imagine such things.

Unlike Burnell, I had company on the trip, a viola-player, Richard Crabtree, and a lady from the BBC World Service, Susan Waldram. Sue's wry humour and mine helped form a mutual support group.

Like Burnell, I hunted the city for a postcard to send home. Like Burnell, I went to the railway station. The first moment we had a break from the constant round of talks and meetings, I dragged my friends there, where Burnell has an enjoyable if strange time.

There the station was, whitewashed by sunshine, in all its rather militaristic Russian glory! The lines run from Krasnovosk, now re-christened Turkmenbashi, on the Caspian, to Tashkent and beyond. Yes, this is the Golden Railroad to Samarkand! Thronging with life in the novel, it was strangely deserted when we visited. On the platform – evidence that Secretary of State James Baker's visit had not been in vain – stood a Pepsi Cola stand. *Geschlossen*. And the restaurant, crowded, oozing with pilaffs and kebabs in Burnell's day, was almost medicinally empty. Two soldiers, possibly Russian, sat in a corner of the room, disconsolate or drunk.

So much for reality. Nevertheless, on that station, stuck forgotten in a kiosk window, lodged the one and only postcard in all Ashkhabad! Faded, buckled, forlorn, it was printed with a four kopeck stamp – a symbol of the *Ancien régime*, for Turkmenistan had just introduced its own currency, the *manat*. I posted the card to Clive and Youla in Athens, and it reached them. The best four kopecks I ever spent!

We met the artist who designed the *manat* notes. Not a burdensome job, you might think, since all denominations bear portraits of a certain chubby face . . .

Ashkhabad station features on the English jacket of *Somewhere*

East of Life. The artist had never been there, any more than I had, at the time.

Traces of Muslim faith remain, much like traces of Christianity in Western countries. For weddings and funerals, people turn to God or Allah. But from what I saw, Western clothes, television, and drink – not to mention the hope of an oil pipeline to the West – are powerful incentives to keep the mullahs at bay.

With my two English companions, I travelled out to Anau to visit a Harvard University archaeological team. Anau lies in pleasant country, among plantations of vines and mulberry trees. You might be in Israel. Cuckoos call with an English accent, poignant enough to penetrate the sad heart of Ruth, standing amid the alien corn. The Americans are uncovering remains of the twelfth-century Parthian Empire. In more distant Merv, muds that speak of Zarathustra and Scheherazade are being dug. Lost empires lie everywhere, older even than the tsars.

My novel paints – how could it be otherwise? – a picture of a new place, a semi-imaginary Ashkhabad. Some guesses are accurate. Like Burnell, I found in Turkmenistan a world part rejoicing in, part regretting their freedom from an order that crumbled away recently, into the sands of history.

Somewhere East of Life was published three months after my return to England. I had circumvented the conventional method of writing, which is to give an account of a distant country after you have visited it, rather than before.

Time pours more slowly through the hourglasses of Central Asia than of those in the West. Hanging About is a mainline hobby. While waiting for a car to drive us to another banquet, Youssef gave me a prose translation into English of one of Makhtumkuli's poems. I turned it into verse.

As for those banquets, they came rather too often for my taste, and lacked the conviviality and variety of the Georgian ones. We asked each other how frequently the general public ate, for the markets were poorly provided, and we were told that food was expensive. Every banquet starred chicken drumsticks. The puzzle of the drumsticks nagged us. We never saw the unique Turkmen Bodiless Red in local hencoops. Finally we asked.

'Chicken breasts are allocated to Kirghistan,' we were told. 'Drumsticks are allocated here.'

At least there was a refreshing chilled orange juice to drink, Tropicana by name. Nosing round after one banquet, I came across some empty cartons of the juice. It originated in Florida. The Sell By date had passed some eighteen months earlier.

Turkmenistan was living on UN handouts. Those handouts were going down the throats of the bosses of the old regime.

I asked for another poem. I versified that. It was an exercise, as one does a crossword, to see if one can. But the idea took hold. Back in England, Youssef fed me poem after poem. Poems were still being discovered; Makhtumkuli's poems had had to be hidden during Stalin's and Brezhnev's reign. Some people hid them in wells, some under floorboards – those fortunate enough to have floorboards.

So I found myself with a full-time job. Well, not entirely full time. I was also amassing stories for my most ambitious collection of short stories, entitled *Common Clay* in the States and *The Secret of This Book* in Britain. Eventually, I would illustrate the paperback edition myself.

Sometimes I read out my Makhtumkuli translations at the parties Youssef and Guzin liked to throw, where the orange juice was fresh and whole chickens were devoured. I eventually turned into English verse all the poems of this eighteenth-century Sufi poet. It was not hard to empathise with poems about fears of Judgement Day and eternal damnation. I had heard all about that from Edna V. Rowlingson, back in the Cowper Memorial Church in Dereham. My boyhood had paid off at last.

This collaboration with Youssef Azemoun, *Songs from the Steppes of Central Asia: The Collected Poems of Makhtumkuli*, was published in 1995.

There is a postscript to this story which tells us something about dictators. Youssef phoned early in 1996 to tell me that my name had been submitted for the annual Makhtumkuli Award. I asked him what my chances were.

'A pretty good one. Yours is the only name on the list.'

He rang again a few weeks later.

'Unfortunately, they say you are disqualified this year because we did not get your name in by January the first. They are not usually so punctual.'

Later we learned the truth. President Niyazov had decided to award the medal to himself. For the second year running . . .

Central Asia can be recommended. Despite the Volvos, it is about the most ancient place you can find within six hours' flying time.

'Time sadly overcometh all things, and is now dominant, and

sitteth upon a Sphinx, and looketh unto Memphis and old Thebes, while his sister Oblivion reclineth semisomnous on a pyramid, gloriously triumphing, making puzzles of Titanian erections, and turning old glories into dreams.' So said Sir Thomas Browne (or James Crossley), in a *'Fragment on Mummies'*.

Of course, in Browne's day the future had not been invented. In these happier days, we can turn dreams into new glories.

And hope that all will turn out for the best, after all.

Envoi

The Path

O Lord, I reach the gateway of old age,
    Look upon me.
As I stand now in your draughty forecourt
    Look upon me
In my bewilderment. Preserve in me
A late ambition to be wise. Forgive
My sins, my cowardice, my blindness. Save
Me from a righteous rage to denigrate
Those follies which I once myself enjoyed.
Lend me support to aid me on my way
To that more dreadful gate I have to go
Through, unafraid, whenever you decide.

O Lord, in whom I've sought to disbelieve,
    Look upon me.
Fortify an atheist's lack of faith.
    Look upon me,
Greyer, older, that as faculties
Decay and fade I shed my self-regard.
Lord take this burden of my character
Away I've shouldered all my years. At last
I near the final step. Then may I make
No special claims, that all those whom I love
May not by fears be shamed – remembering
They too must travel down the path I tread.

INDEX

The author gratefully acknowledges permission to quote from the following:

'Fauna of Mirrors' and 'The Garden of Forking Paths' by Jorge Luis Borges, are extracts from *Fictions*. Copyright © 1974 Jorge Luis Borges. Reprinted by permission of The Calder Educational Trust.

One Fat Englishman by Kingsley Amis. Copyright © 1963 Kingsley Amis. Reprinted by permission of Victor Gollancz Ltd.

The Sirens of Titan by Kurt Vonnegut. Copyright © 1962 Kurt Vonnegut. Reprinted by permission of Curtis Brown Ltd, London.

Imagination and Time by Mary Warnock. Copyright © 1994 Mary Warnock. Reprinted by permission of Blackwell Publishers.

'The Landscape of His Dreams' from *An Anthropologist on Mars* by Oliver Sacks. Copyright © 1995 Oliver Sacks. Reprinted by permission of The Wylie Agency Ltd.

Rites of Passage by William Golding. Copyright © 1980 William Golding. Reprinted by permission of Faber and Faber.

Every effort has been made to trace the copyright holders and to clear reprint permissions for the following:

The Teachings of Don Juan: A Yagui Way of Knowledge by Carlos Castaneda.

The Lost Steps by Alejo Carpentier.

Ethics in Andalusia by Aldous Huxley.

Knots by R. D. Laing.

Harrap's Slang French-English Dictionary.

If notified, the publishers will be pleased to rectify any omission in future editions.